Frederick Wiseman

EDITOR

THOMAS R. ATKINS, General Editor of the Monarch Film Studies Series, is an Associate Professor at Hollins College, and Chairman of the Theatre Arts Department. Founder and Editor of *The Film Journal*, he has contributed articles to *Kenyon Review*, *Contemporary Literary Scene*, *Sight and Sound*, and many other publications. His books include *Sexuality in the Movies* for Indiana University Press and *The Fire Came By* for Doubleday.

Copyright © 1976 by
SIMON & SCHUSTER, Inc.

Standard Book Number: 671-08101-2

Library of Congress Catalog Card Number: 75-23547

Designed by Denise Biller

Published by
MONARCH PRESS
a division of Simon & Schuster, Inc.
1 West 39th Street
New York, N.Y. 10018

CONTENTS

ACKNOWLEDGMENTS

The editor wishes to thank Fred Wiseman and Jennifer Tarlin for their generous help and advice on this book. All photographs are courtesy of Zipporah Films, Inc.

The introductory essay appeared originally in slightly different form in *Sight and Sound*, Vol. 43, No. 4 (Autumn 1974).

Grateful acknowledgment is also made to the following authors and publications for permission to reprint:

John Graham's interview is from *The Film Journal*, Vol. I, No. 1 (Spring 1971) and *Contempora*, Vol. I, No. 4 (October/November 1970).

Alan Westin's interview first appeared in *The Civil Liberties Review*, Vol. I, No. 2 (Winter/Spring 1974), pp. 56-67. Copyright © 1974 by the American Civil Liberties Union. Reprinted by permission of the copyright holder and the publisher, John Wiley & Sons, Inc.

Richard Schickel's review is from *Life* (December 1, 1967). Reprinted by permission of the author.

Pauline Kael's review of *High School* from *Deeper into Movies* is reprinted by permission of Little, Brown and Co. in association with The Atlantic Monthly Press. Copyright © 1969 by Pauline Kael.

Richard Fuller's review is from *The Film Journal*, Vol. I, No. 3-4 (Fall-Winter 1972).

Patrick J. Sullivan's review of *Essene* is Copyright © 1973 by The Regents of the University of California. Reprinted from *Film Quarterly*, Vol. 27, No. 1, pp. 55-57, by permission of The Regents.

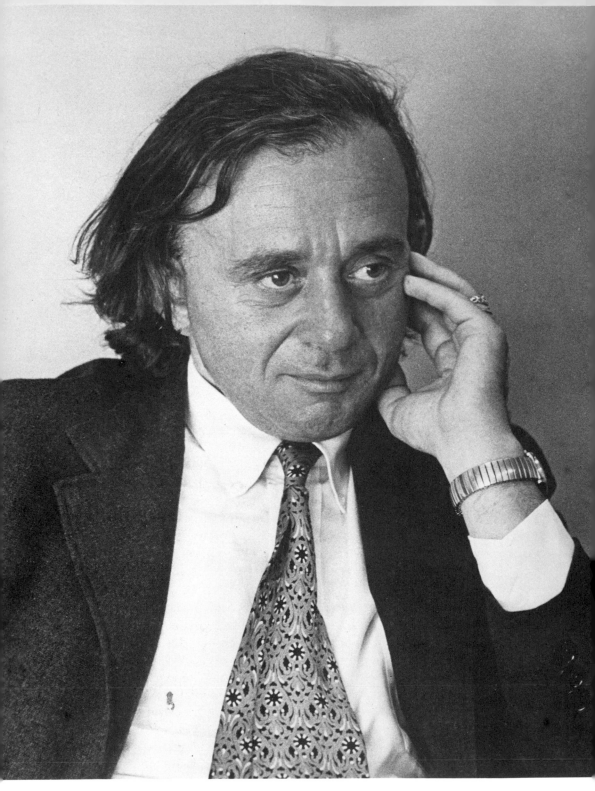

Frederick Wiseman

PREFACE

> You want something about my politics? Well, they're kind of anarchic. As the saying goes, the Marx is more Groucho than Karl.
>
> — Wiseman in *The Civil Liberties Review*

This volume is designed to illuminate and celebrate the cinema of Frederick Wiseman. A Boston lawyer and teacher of criminal law who in 1967 turned to filmmaking, Wiseman has made a series of powerful and controversial documentaries dealing with American institutions. These films or "reality fictions," as he prefers to call them, are remarkable not only because of his unusually spare method — all of his films are shot with lightweight, hand-held 16mm equipment on black-and-white film which he edits himself — but also because of the films' extraordinary impact upon viewers and their lasting value both as artistic and social documents.

His first film, *Titicut Follies*, brought him immediate recognition as an important talent and became the only documentary ever to be banned by a U.S. Supreme Court. In 1969 after the release of his second feature, *High School*, critic Pauline Kael described Wiseman as "probably the most sophisticated intelligence to enter the documentary field in recent years." Most of his films have premiered on the Public Broadcasting Service, and he has won three Emmys as well as numerous awards from U.S. and foreign film festivals. The fall 1975 premiere of his ninth film, *Welfare,* was greeted with similar critical acclaim and added to his already well-established reputation as one of the major artists of contemporary cinema.

With the exception of the introductory essay and the closing samples of critical reaction, this book is largely a collection of interviews. Since he allows his subjects to address their audience directly in his films, it is appropriate that Wiseman speak for himself in this volume, without too much editorial intrusion. Although modest about the usefulness of his statements, preferring instead to let viewers interpret his films according to their values, Wiseman is an extremely lucid, articulate individual with strong opinions about his work. Like his films, these interviews are a form of documentary revealing, as novelist George Garrett has observed, "a gentle man, but starched and ironed with rigorous honesty; a man of feeling, his feelings controlled by the calm and inexorable logic of a good lawyer; a humble man with an easy, open pride in his mastery of the craft of filmmaking."

Following a showing of *Primate,* Wiseman was urged by an audience member to "expose himself" by revealing what had personally motivated him to abandon law practice and become a documentary filmmaker. He replied, "My mother was a documentary filmmaker." Wiseman's exceptionally sharp sense of humor subtly enriches his work but is seldom noted by critics. *High School* and *Basic Training,* with their lengthy funny episodes, contain the most obvious examples of his humor; yet *Titicut Follies* and *Primate,* despite their depressing subjects, are essentially black comedies akin to the plays of Samuel Beckett or the novels of Kurt Vonnegut, Jr. The humor is earthy, unsettling, and somewhat subversive; he is suspicious of pretentious rhetoric and inflated sentiments. Yet at the same time Wiseman's vision is always compassionate — sympathetic to the ordinary person's daily struggle to retain some dignity against overwhelming odds.

Welfare

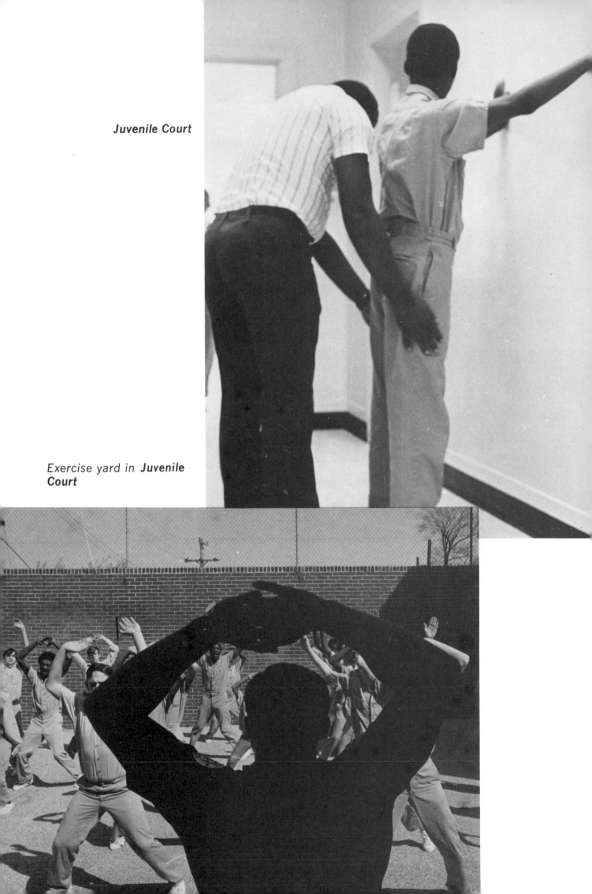

Juvenile Court

Exercise yard in **Juvenile Court**

WISEMAN'S AMERICA:
TITICUT FOLLIES TO
PRIMATE

Thomas R. Atkins

The first image is a far shot of the downtown district of a large American city. Then we see a three-story building with a sign reading "Juvenile Court 616." A squad car turns into the parking lot and as it stops we see on the door "Police City of Memphis." Inside the court building handcuffs are unlocked from a young boy's wrists. Another boy says on the telephone, "If you love me, you want to come up here and get me out cause I ain't done nothing." As a policeman leads him to a chair in a waiting area, a small kid pleads, "I don't want to go, I don't want to go." An officer inspects a lethal-looking blade taken from a youth. A girl arrested for shoplifting listens impassively while a Lieutenant explains her legal rights. A seemingly endless stream of young people, black and white, of all sizes and ages, with parents and alone, are waiting to be processed — frisked, photographed, interrogated, psychologically tested, and eventually brought to trial. During the holding period before trial they pass the time by watching television and exercising in a yard. Their record cards are placed in long revolving trays containing thousands of court files on young lawbreakers.

1 /

This is the opening of *Juvenile Court*, the seventh film produced, directed, and edited by Frederick Wiseman for his American institution series, an experiment unique in motion picture history. All of his films start in a similar fashion — with a rapid flow of brief images and sequences, almost a montage effect, that immediately immerses the viewer, without comment or explanation, into the complex, troublesome reality of various contemporary institutions in a supposedly democratic society. In eight films he has taken us inside a prison for the criminally insane, a middle-class high school, a metropolitan police department and a hospital, an Army training center, a religious monastery, a juvenile

Juvenile Court

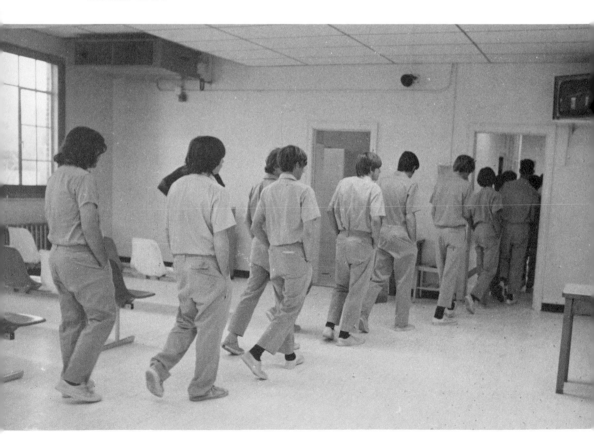

court, and a center for primate research. Aside from getting permission to film, Wiseman usually does little advance research beyond making sure that his subject is "a reasonably good or even superior institution of its kind and not a sitting duck." Because his audience is largely unfamiliar with the daily workings of the institution and because he is often surprised by what he and his cameraman William Brayne find with their 16mm camera and sound recorder, Wiseman has called the making of his films "a voyage of discovery."

For *Juvenile Court* Wiseman and Brayne spent over a month in Memphis, Tennessee, where they shot more than sixty hours or about 125,000 feet of black-and-white film. Then in his headquarters in a warehouse building overlooking Boston harbor, Wiseman edited the footage to 144 minutes. In the cutting he is careful not to simplify the material or to distort it to fit an abstract ideological "truth"; instead he works to create a film reflecting the complicated and ambiguous actuality that he encountered during the filming in order to make it a true "discovery" experience for the audience. The editing, he has said, is not so much a totally rational procedure as "a process of dreaming," involving a long period of responding intuitively and imaginatively to the vast amount of footage until the relationships between the disparate events and persons emerge into a unified, coherent but still unresolved form.

In contrast to documentaries like *Salesman* or *An American Family*, Wiseman's films do not concentrate on a few individuals or stories; they have no leading characters or dramatic narrative in the conventional sense. What Wiseman gives us in *Juvenile Court* and his other films is an enormous cast, a teeming variety of different people of all ages, shapes and colors, some appearing only once, others recurring many times, all playing their parts in a brilliantly selected mosaic of separate activities and episodes, relationships and conflicts, that gradually reveals an overall pattern of behavior illuminating both the morality of the institution and of the society that created it.

Unlike most other documentary directors, Wiseman does not tell his viewer how to interpret the pattern. Although his films are obviously the products of a strong viewpoint, he makes no editorial statement either directly through narration or indirectly through the interview technique, nor does he use music to manipulate the spectator's feelings. This absence of explanatory devices, plus his avoidance of more popular (and profitable) subjects, may help account for the fact that some of his films have a reputation for being difficult to understand. Actually his purpose, as he has explained, is to deepen the spectator's involvement in the material by making his films so "there's no separation between the audience watching the film and the events in the film. It's like the business of getting rid of the proscenium arch in the theatre, and, by analogy, narration is the proscenium arch because it immediately separates you from the experience of what you're going to see and hear, by telling you that it has nothing to do with you or by telling you what to think about it." The viewer, in short, is asked to be far more than a passive witness; he must become an active participant, working out his own meaning and deciding for himself how to relate to the events occurring on the screen.

A major difference between Wiseman and nearly every other American filmmaker today is that he is an artist capable of exercising a multiple consciousness — of seeing life from his own personal perspective while at the same time being objective enough to allow, even to encourage, other opposing perspectives. This quality is apparent not only in the great variety of situations and characters he uses but in his ability to get inside numerous different roles simultaneously — particularly in a film like *Juvenile Court* where, for instance, he shows us the problems of the court system from the vantage of the judge, the lawyers, the social workers, the parents, as well as the accused.

In one of the film's most disturbing cases we watch a psychologist question a thoughtful 15-year-old boy accused of sexually molesting a small girl while babysitting. The boy calls the charges "all a lot of bunk." In the juvenile court judge's chamber we meet the girl's mother, an extremely nervous, sexually obsessed individual, who describes how her two children told her about the boy's behavior. When the judge talks to the defendant, reminding him of the seriousness of the allegations, the boy agrees to take a lie detector test. The attorneys and various counsellors speculate with the judge about the possibility that the mother, who had warned the boy in advance about her distrust of male babysitters, might have had a similar event in her own childhood and consequently may be exaggerating or even imagining the charges. We do not hear the results of the lie detector test, which would not have been conclusive anyway. The characters have spoken for themselves, and each viewer can have his own reaction, make his own judgment according to his particular prejudices and values. The implications of the legal issues and human attitudes revealed by the case extend far beyond the innocence or guilt of this specific defendant, raising tough questions about the system of juvenile justice as well as the condition of society in general.

TITICUT FOLLIES

This multiple view, the painstakingly balanced portrait of numerous sides of a situation, is typical of all of Wiseman's work, even his first film *Titicut Follies*, made in 1967, which contains one of the strongest condemnations of an institution and its governing officials. The condemnation, of course, is implicit in the existing material and not the result of any editorializing or manipulation by the director. Wiseman got the idea for the film while taking his law classes on visits to the Bridgewater, Massachusetts, State Hospital for the Criminally Insane. The film, which takes its title from an annual review staged by the hospital staff and "patients," is the most controversial documentary ever made by an American director and the only such film to be officially barred from general public showings by order of a United States court. Although *Titicut Follies* was made with their permission, the officials of Bridgewater and the state attorney general changed their minds when it received negative reactions from some state legislators and in the press. The attorney general decided to take legal action against the film, and in the subsequent trial *Titicut Follies* was banned from public screenings in the state on the

Titicut Follies

grounds that it represented a breach of contract and that it had violated an inmate's privacy.

Wiseman has commented, "There was no evidence introduced at the trial that the film was not an honest portrayal of the conditions. There is some question about whether the inmates had any privacy to begin with. If (then state attorney general Elliot) Richardson and the other politicians in Massachusetts were genuinely concerned about the privacy and dignity of the inmates of Bridgewater, they would not have allowed the conditions that are shown in the film to exist. They were more concerned about the film and its effect on their reputations than they were about Bridgewater." Later when the case was appealed, the Massachusetts Civil Liberties Union opposed the film. Recently CLUM has reversed its original position, but *Titicut Follies* remains under court restriction in the state.

It is ironic that Wiseman should be accused of ignoring the privacy of his subjects, for it would be difficult to find another contemporary director more aware of the legal issues involved in the matter of the individual's right to privacy and the public's right to be informed about tax-supported institutions, or one who has paid such close attention to the plights of forgotten people — criminals, mental patients, the poor — often buried in state institutions. A dominant concern throughout his series is the individual's attempt to preserve his humanity while struggling against laws and systems that often seem to have a dehumanizing effect. Sometimes the degrading process is obvious, as when the Bridgewater inmate in *Titicut Follies* complains to the staff that the place is driving him mad; but usually, as in Wiseman's next film *High School*, the process is more subtle and nearly invisible to the participants.

Although some critics have felt that *Titicut Follies* and *High School* are more straightforward indictments or simple exposés of the institutions than the later films, Wiseman believes that his approach has been basically the same in all of his films. *Titicut Follies* may appear one-sided at first largely because most viewers are almost totally unfamiliar with the subject, but Wiseman has carefully presented differing arguments about Bridgewater and a wide spectrum of individuals working in the system. The guards, for example, are often revealed as decent people with a real sense of failure and genuine feelings for their prisoners. *High School* is also a more complex presentation than it may seem on first viewing. The film's point of view is enlarged by showing — through the parents — that the school's repressive ideology is actually an expression of the goals of the surrounding community. Neither film merely indicts or judges one institution but uses them to isolate and exemplify broader issues. *Titicut Follies* has implications for the entire medical profession, while *High School* reflects upon public values about education and parental authority.

HIGH SCHOOL

In a key sequence in *High School*, which was shot in 1968 at a large, chiefly white and middle-class school in Philadelphia, Pennsylvania, the dean of discipline says to a student, "We are out to establish that you can be a man and that you can take orders." This message — learn to take orders and respect your elders — is reiterated in nearly every student-faculty encounter shown in the film and reinforced by every conference between school admin-

Student in corridor between classes in **High School**

istrators and parents. Self-effacement and blind obedience emerge finally as the practical values, as opposed to the professed ideals, of the American secondary educational system and of the parents whose children are caught in the system.

One of the funniest scenes in *High School* shows a group of girls performing exercises to the tune of "Simon Says." Beneath the humor, of course, is the suggestion that the school, while ostensibly aiming to develop the individual's potential, is actually encouraging its students to be Simple Simons, putting their hands on their heads and clapping their hands in the air in unquestioning acceptance of their teachers' authority. The result, as Wiseman shows us repeatedly in the film, is apathy, depression and waste — the sad waste of human potential in even the best schools.

An obstacle in making an engaging film about high school is that to most Americans the subject is excruciatingly familiar. Wiseman solves this difficulty by concentrating only on certain aspects of the high school experience — primarily on relationships between students and teachers — and by making the familiar seem unfamiliar again, or rather by reminding us of the essential strangeness of the whole experience. One of his chief methods is to point out and underscore the comic qualities of high school, to make us laugh at the ludicrous rigidity and inflexibility of the system and of the people who run the system. Administrators and instructors

Dean of Discipline reprimanding
student in **High School**

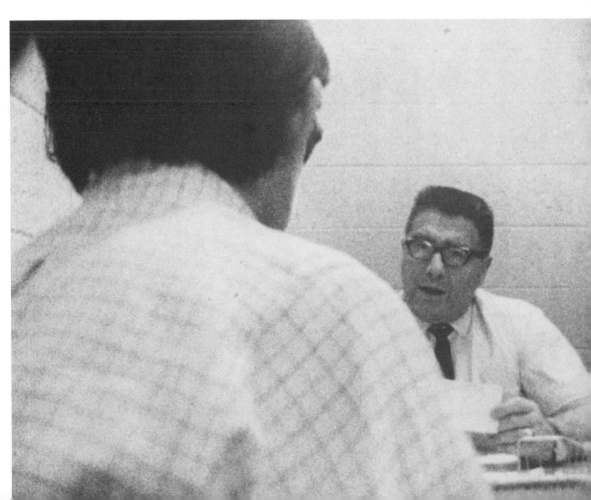

become comic figures as they attempt to force their values —
about everything ranging from family life and sexuality to dress
habits — upon the students with no consideration for the students'
actual needs. The main motif of the film, as in traditional comedy,
is the effort of the older generation to suppress or restrict the life
and spontaneity of the younger generation.

Wiseman's camera is continually focusing on the many different costumes that students must wear in high school. In scene
after scene we watch young people playing various roles in special
outfits — almost as if they were actors in a play. They wear aprons
and play at being cooks; they wear homemade dresses and play
at fashion shows; they wear spacesuits and play at being astronauts;
and they discuss the importance of wearing tuxedoes and formal

*Student astronauts after completing simulated space
flight in **High School***

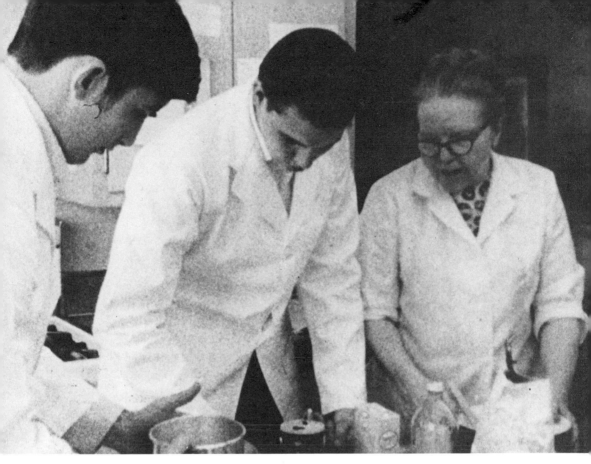

Cooking classes for boys in **High School**

gowns to dances just like real adults. The girls dress up as drum majorettes and play with rifles, while the football team dresses up as cheerleaders and plays at being girls. None of these costumes or roles is necessarily harmful, of course, but what is damaging is the attitude toward the different roles fostered by the educators and the resulting detachment or boredom on the part of the young participants. The educators do not encourage involvement and self-realization, and consequently the roles seem more like disguises masking the students' actual identities than fulfilling activities offering possibilities of self-discovery.

The goals of the extracurricular games they are all playing are self-effacement and obedience once again, and it goes on in the classroom discussion as well. In the film we watch teachers playing with knowledge, and students talking about unions and employees,

11   /

poverty in America, and Martin Luther King's assassination with the same detachment that they memorize musical notes on the blackboard. Connections are seldom made between the ideas and events discussed in the classroom and the realities of the world outside in which the students live — chiefly because no connections are intended by most of the educators. Making such connections in the classroom — say, the relationship between the problems of union members and students — might be threatening to the security of the educational system.

Early in *High School* we hear a teacher discussing cause and effect with his students. The end of the film shows the ultimate effect of the system, its methods and values. In a faculty meeting the principal reads a letter from a former student who writes that he is about to be dropped behind the DMZ in Vietnam and wishes to leave his G.I. insurance to the school in the event of his death. The principal praises the letter as an example of the success of the school. Indeed it is, for the attitude expressed in the letter is totally submissive. Here is one version of the final role and costume that students — the males at least — are expected to wear and a perfect version of complete self-effacement: meek acceptance of death behind enemy lines. In the letter the young man aptly describes himself as "only a body doing a job."

BASIC TRAINING

Basic Training, which Wiseman filmed in 1971 at a U.S. Army training center in Fort Knox, Kentucky, provides an excellent followup to *High School*, for both are about the suppression of the individual and the nurturing of a mentality that accepts regimentation and conformity as normal. In each film we see young people being trained to become obedient bodies in service of society. Even the methods of training in the films are basically the same — fear and humiliation. The rebels and misfits are punished or discarded; the ones who "go along with it" are praised and rewarded at graduation.

Drill sergeants in **Basic Training**

One of the misfits in *Basic Training* is a skinny young man named Hickman who is almost comic in his inability to keep in step during drill practice. "You're going to have to think about what you're doing, Hickman," says the drill officer, "or you're not going to make it." We have seen the stock figure of the awk-

13   /

*Trainees in **Basic Training***

ward private in countless movies about Army life, but Wiseman does not allow him to remain a stereotype. The next time we see Hickman we learn that he has taken an overdose of sleeping pills. The First Sergeant discusses his case on the phone with the Chaplain describing him as having "suicidal tendencies . . . Seems like he wants to knock hisself off."

Hickman is then sent to the Chaplain, a black man with a perpetually cheerful face and a ready answer for every difficulty. When Hickman tells him that the other soldiers are harrassing him and that he feels "a little depressed today," the Chaplain responds, "That doesn't sound like a man who is really trying to get to the top." Although the Chaplain invites Hickman to drop in his office whenever he feels depressed, it is obvious that he does not wish to deal with Hickman as an individual nor try to understand the personal problems that drove him to near suicide. "I don't care how good a person is," says the Chaplain, "he has those days when he is not as good as he wants to be . . . Stay in the ring and keep struggling . . . fighting." The Chaplain has managed to say all the wrong things, and by the end of the session Hickman looks completely lost. He winds up serving as guinea pig in a demonstration of how to take a prisoner from behind and kill by strangling him with his helmet strap and finishing him with a heel stomp. Throughout the demonstration Hickman smiles in embarrassment.

At the opposite extreme from the insecure and sick private is the example of the company commander who has long ago successfully fallen into step and decided to make a career of the Army. His wife and family are present to witness a ceremony in

Basic Training

which he is promoted from First Lieutenant to Captain for "100% efficiency increase" in his work. As he beams with childlike pleasure before his family and superior officers, his mother observes, "I think he's found his niche in the world."

In between these two extremes of success and failure are the rest of the young men who either accept or quietly resist the military environment with its lack of women and atmosphere of hostility. Somehow they manage to get through all the discipline and marching, physical hygiene training, weapons and bayonet practices, simulated war games, without attracting too much attention. Their responses range from the private who proudly displays his M-16-A1 rifle to his visiting relatives, boasting that he can fire 900 rounds in less than a minute, to the black man who

Graduation drill in **Basic Training**

defends his behavior in refusing fire guard by stating simply that he doesn't want any medals: "I want my life . . . that's my medal."

Throughout *Basic Training* we see trainees marching together, gradually forming tighter lines, boots stomping more evenly on the pavement, until finally at the commencement exercise that concludes the film the company passes by the grandstand in perfect order. As the band plays patriotic tunes, many of the officers and families in the grandstand are extremely moved by the spectacle. Because of the way Wiseman has structured his film, our reactions to this "graduation" are likely to be mixed. He has encouraged us to ask disturbing questions about the notions of orderliness and manliness that are fundamental both to the tradition of basic training and to the American way of life.

While listening to the recipient of the American Spirit of Honor Medal tell his fellows that they must "take up the banner," we may be reminded of such examples as Hickman who could not cope with the training or the black man who scoffed at heroics because he felt that "this isn't my country." Wiseman never allows us to forget the reality behind the regimentation and parading — that these one-time civilians are training for actual combat where they may have to kill somebody with that "black licking stick" — as one officer calls the M-16-A1 — and where many of these young men may lose their own lives.

LAW AND ORDER

In no other film is Wiseman's concern for presenting a multiple point of view more evident and effective than in *Law and Order*, shot in Kansas City in 1969. The specific subject is the daily routine of the police force, chiefly in the black district with one of the city's highest crime rates; the implied and broader subject is the dilemma of law enforcement in the United States. In a time of simplistic and hysterical slogans for and against the police, Wiseman has created a provocative work that challenges superficial notions of law and order in society by encouraging us to view the issue from numerous perspectives.

Roll call at police station in **Law and Order**

Although *Law and Order* contains examples of police insensitivity and brutality, Wiseman has no special axe to grind against the police themselves. He does not see police behavior as the root of the difficulty but as an important symptom, a manifestation of a far deeper and more malignant sickness in society in general. The community that pays the police and prescribes the laws that the police must enforce is infected with racism and blighted with poverty. At his best the policeman can temporarily ease the problems; at his worst he contributes to the problems. Yet as nearly every scene in *Law and Order* demonstrates, the police alone cannot cure the fundamental social ills.

The most explosive episode is a night raid in which a member of the vice squad kicks in a tenement basement door and nearly strangles a young black prostitute. "Don't choke me no more," she pleads. Another policeman responds, "He wasn't chok-

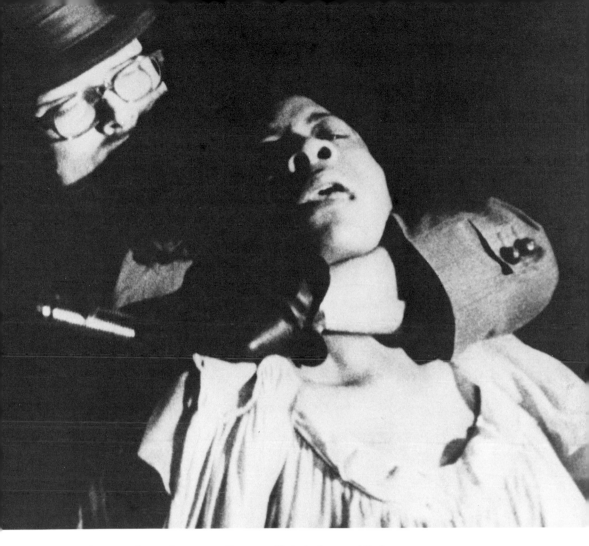

*Vice squad member strangling prostitute in **Law and Order***

ing you. You're imagining." It is too simple-minded an interpretation to blame the excessive cruelty of this event exclusively on the police department. Wiseman does not set up the vice squad member as representative of all policemen, anyway, but as an individual with his own peculiar neurosis who unfortunately happens to be a policeman. Stripped of externals, the scene shows a white male attacking a black female. The man obviously feels hatred for all women, especially those who are black and conse-

quently, in his mind, morally inferior. Society condones his behavior while leaving the woman defenseless. The fact that the man
is a policeman simply permits him to act out, ostensibly in the
line of duty, emotions that other citizens must keep hidden or
express only indirectly.

Much of the film is occupied with following the police through
a series of actions that are, for the police, ordinary and routine:
locating a stolen purse, caring for a lost child, settling a dispute
over a taxi fare. There are humorous moments — or moments in
which humor and sadness are mixed, such as a policeman's attempt to remove an old lady's real teeth before taking her to the
hospital. What makes most of these scenes so effective is the
filmmaker's careful attention to small details, sudden intimate
gestures that may reveal more than larger, more dramatic actions.

Officer arresting attempted hold-up suspect in **Law and Order**

Officer mediates fight between husband, wife, and landlady in
Law and Order

Wiseman has said that an important part of *Law and Order* is concerned with "how the police have to cope with what people do to each other, as opposed to what the police do to people." Consequently we often see the police caught in the emotional crossfire of a neighborhood or family quarrel, and we experience the frustration not only of the police but of all the people involved in the crisis as well. In one of the film's most moving scenes, the police attempt to settle an argument between a young couple who are separated. The wife has taken up with another man, and the husband desperately wants to get his child away from her. The situation, however, cannot be resolved by the police who can simply make suggestions and try to keep the peace. "If you want your child," the policeman says to the hus-

21 /

band, "you go down and get a lawyer and file for divorce against your wife." The husband asks, "What's he doing with my wife?" The policeman can only reply, "I don't know, and I don't care." The husband has no job, cannot afford a lawyer and says that he doesn't know what he is going to do now. "It's ridiculous, sure," says the policeman, "but there's nothing we can do about it."

The final effect of Wiseman's film is not to persuade us either to look down upon the police as oppressors or to overly sympathize with them as victims. By showing us the policeman's daily job from multiple perspectives, he encourages us to look beyond surface behavior to causes — such factors as the pervasive tension and hostility of the community in which the police must work, and the policeman's natural human response toward being constantly confronted with this hostility. As Wiseman has said, "The police are no different from the rest of us . . . Police brutality is shown as part of a more generally shared violence and not something isolated or unique."

HOSPITAL

Hospital, which won two Emmys for Best News Documentary of 1970, begins in an operating room in New York City's Metropolitan Hospital where an incision is about to be made on a patient. Another filmmaker might have panned or cut away at the moment of incision, but Wiseman shows the surgeon's scalpel opening the abdomen. Stylistically and metaphorically this scene sets the tone for the entire film; the view of human suffering and of an institution's attempts to ease that suffering is steady and unflinching. The unsentimental, matter-of-fact quality that is maintained throughout *Hospital*, even in the most painful scenes, helps to create a special involvement and intensity for the spectator.

Our values about social problems and our sensitivity to the human misery surrounding us are constantly called into question by the film. The emergency ward and out-patient clinics are the main settings, for it is here that the hospital staff works under the greatest pressures and encounters its severest tests. The results of

Patient talking to psychiatrist in **Hospital**

our worst urban ills flow through the emergency doors: victims of stabbings and drug overdoses, abused children, forgotten old people, and the mentally disturbed. The stream of afflicted individuals seems endless, and all demand immediate treatment from a staff that is, like the police, frustrated and overworked. Yet despite the pressures, most of the hospital staff respond with sympathy and understanding.

Many of us are acquainted in a general way with the welfare problem, but Wiseman brings home the inadequacies of the system in a personal and direct manner by showing a physician on the phone trying unsuccessfully to obtain aid from a welfare center

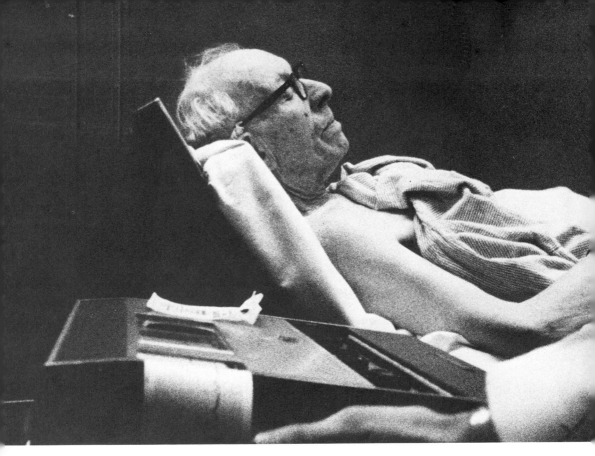

*Patient having electrocardiogram in **Hospital***

for a young man whom he wishes to keep out of the hospital. "This is an emergency situation," he explains. "The man is suffering from schizophrenia . . . I'm asking for the assistance of welfare." The welfare official, aptly named Mrs. Hightower, stalls the physician with a barrage of bureaucratic red tape and then finally hangs up on him.

It is one thing to intellectually consider the problem of drug abuse in our society, but quite a different matter to witness a powerful demonstration of its effect. In one sequence, for instance, we see a young man in physical and emotional agony from an overdose of mescaline. Attempting to reassure him, the doctor says, "You're not going to die . . . You're going to be okay." Later while waiting to see the hospital psychiatrist, the young man suddenly throws up and slips down on the floor. Helplessly he says, "I'm so sorry, I'm so sorry . . . Can you play music or some-thing?"

Like all of Wiseman's films, *Hospital* is much more than simply a study of a single institution or a challenge to improve specific problems. Before the film is over, the crowded waiting room in Metropolitan Hospital has become an image, a graphic metaphor for the condition of society and for our present ability to cope with that condition. Our ability to cope and find solutions, Wiseman's film suggests, depends not so much upon the institutions themselves but upon the values that create and govern the institutions. The final shot in the film is a long shot of the exterior of the building and the nearby freeway crowded with traffic rushing past the hospital.

PRIMATE

Nearly all of the motifs and images of Wiseman's earlier works recur and are carefully re-examined in his eighth film *Primate*, which places the viewer inside a federally-funded scientific institution, the Yerkes Primate Research Center in Atlanta, Georgia. The film opens, like *Law and Order*, with a series of mug shots — portraits of Pavlov, Darwin, and other famous behaviorists. As in *Titicut Follies*, the institution is a maximum security prison, although the inmates are not humans but apes caged for experimentation and dissection. The officials at the center, like the authorities in *High School*, *Basic Training*, and *Juvenile Court*, are concerned with means of conditioning and determining behavior, particularly sexual and aggressive behavior, supposedly for the benefit of mankind.

Wiseman has called the film a "science fiction documentary," for it is about man's use of sophisticated technology to attempt to manipulate the present and project himself into the future. The trial and error program of experimentation conducted at the center is placed within the broader context of evolution by a scientist doing electromyographic studies of an orangutan's muscular movements. In explaining his research the scientist speculates that *probably somewhere between fifteen million years ago and ten million years ago the ancestors of man and the ancestors of the great apes — chimpanzee and gorilla in particular — diverged. I believe this divergence was initiated in the trees — that is, the African apes' ancestor was doing something rather different from man's ancestor in the trees. This moved the center of gravity down into the pelvis, so that when the two lineages, the members of the two lineages, began to experiment with terrestrial locomotion and habitation, the ape tipped over and became a knuckle-walker, whereas man was predisposed to walk bipedally on his hind feet. By walking bipedally on his hind feet his hands were free to carry objects and, of course, to carry tools once he had learned to make them. And subsequent to that then man ventured out into the open savannah and became a hunting animal, which again is a rather unique attribute of Pleistocene man.*

Thus, in this institution, what we are seeing is the hunting animal — the tool-carrying killer primate — experimenting on his relative, the knuckle-walking primate, in order to understand and control his own evolution. This is the exact reversal of the situation depicted in the movie *Planet of the Apes*, and its implications are far more bizarre and chilling.

In one sequence, a male rhesus monkey with electrodes implanted in his brain is put in a cage with two females. When the scientists stimulate certain portions of his brain with current, the rhesus mounts a female and begins to copulate. When the current is turned off, he stops and waits passively. In other experiments aggressive behavior can be stimulated in a similar manner. Although the scientists never raise the issue in the group discussion sessions shown in the film — indeed they seldom discuss anything beyond data, methodology, or fund-raising — the obvious implication is that someday the same experiments may be performed on people: human sexual and aggressive activity may eventually be regulated by the same methods.

Scientist conducts electromyographic studies on monkey in Primate

Primate ends with an image that is real, yet pure science fiction in its associations. As part of a flight experiment, a rhesus with a brain implant is strapped inside an enclosed box and placed on board a huge U. S. Air Force transport jet. Inside the jet we watch the men floating in the air as the plane dives to simulate weightlessness. One man snaps pictures with a camera. As its reactions are monitored, we see the small monkey in the box; its face is impassive. Finally, on a monitor of a tracking camera, we watch the jet with its unusual cargo of higher and lower primates soar upwards into the sky — and possibly into our own future.

A CUMULATIVE NATURAL HISTORY

Wiseman regards his films as closely interrelated works, each serving as a separate part of a larger work-in-progress. Just as *Basic Training* develops the concerns of *High School*, the conflicts in *Law and Order* are examined from a different vantage in *Juvenile Court*. *Hospital* shows another kind of professional staff attempting to deal with our metropolitan ills, while *Essene* explores the difficulties of "law and order" in a voluntary monastic community. In *Primate* a community of scientists searches for technological solutions to some of the problems of modern society. Taken together, Wiseman's films provide an unparalleled cumulative "natural history" of certain basic facets of American experience in the late sixties and early seventies. While other directors have focused on rock festivals and film stars, Wiseman has chosen

Celebrating Mass in **Essene**

to study man's complicated relationship with some of the institutions that reflect his values and determine his life.

The overall impact of Wiseman's film history of America is not particularly comforting, but it is all the more valuable and useful because he has firmly refused to take sides, cast blame, or offer solutions. Over the years he has become increasingly skeptical about any broad legislation or sweeping reform programs that might quickly solve the problems affecting the institutions. His approach in his films is not to propose or to protest but, in the deepest sense, to inform — to enable the participating viewer to see the problems more clearly.

INTERVIEWS

*Drunken man strapped in wheelchair in **Hospital***

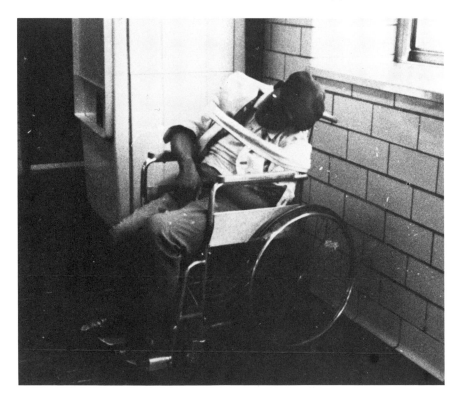

"THERE ARE NO SIMPLE SOLUTIONS"
WISEMAN ON FILM MAKING AND VIEWING

An Interview by John Graham

John Graham, Professor of English at the University of Virginia at Charlottesville, conducted this interview in June 1970 at the Hollins College Conference on Creative Writing and Cinema. Wiseman was a guest speaker at the conference, where screenings were held of his first four films: Titicut Follies, High School, Law and Order, *and* Hospital.

GRAHAM: I dont want to split any kind of hairs, Fred, but do you see yourself as a reporter or an historian, or an editorial writer, or maybe all of these?

WISEMAN: Well, at the risk of possibly evading the question, I see myself as a filmmaker, and in the same way that . . . Well, I was going to say, in that same way that a novelist reports on events, even the documentary filmmaker reports on events. But you have to make a film that works in film terms, the same way a writer has to create a structure of a book that works in literary terms, in verbal terms. If the films are anything they're really a kind of natural history. It would be rather interesting, for example, if we had films of hospitals and prisons and police departments at the time of the Civil War, for comparison purposes.

33 /

GRAHAM: Twain used to get so angry at painters who would paint portraits of "minor" people instead of painting pictures of historical events occurring at the time so that the future would have a record.

WISEMAN: Right — and the technology has advanced to the point now where we really can have a record. It's a very filtered record, it's a record of the way the filmmaker sees the material, and it's interpretive and subjective. But a film has to work in film terms. All I mean by that is it has to satisfy the guy that makes the film.

GRAHAM: I've been talking with a great many novelists and poets over the past two weeks here at the Hollins Conference, and one of the things that they all seem to want to wind up talking about is this sense of discovery they go through when they're writing, and I get the same reaction with you. I don't think you were being facetious in your answer when some student asked you today, "What was your objective when you started filming *Hospital* and *Law and Order?*" Your answer was "I don't know — to make a film really, I didn't have a theme yet."

WISEMAN: I've been trying to make a series of films on contemporary American institutions, but each time I go out, it's a kind of voyage of discovery. I think if you knew what the film was going to look like before you started, then you'd simply be imposing a stereotype on a situation, and you wouldn't be learning anything or thinking about what you'd experienced.

GRAHAM: There'd be the problem of sterility, the kind of mechanically made film, or the committee-made film — which would be worse in a way.

WISEMAN: Get you closer to Hollywood, maybe.

GRAHAM: You are able, through these comparatively inexpensive documentaries, you are able to transcend that awful trap of the committee-made film. You are the filmmaker in the total sense, are you not? This equipment has changed things, hasn't it? You were talking about shooting with no light all the time.

WISEMAN: Yes, well, it's always just available light and black and white film; it's fast film, and really the technical developments that have made such things possible are only maybe eight to ten years old at most — where you can run a camera and a tape recorder synchronously, with no wires between them, the equipment is all hand-held, and you have total mobility, so you can run around and make a synchronous sound movie of any subject whatsoever. As a consequence, what's an acceptable subject for a movie, or what's not even an acceptable subject, but what's a *movie* subject, can now encompass anything.

GRAHAM: I want to hang in on this idea of your report of your experience. This is your independence, really, because one of the "things" you pointed out today. You shoot forty hours for an hour's worth of film. Now, the process in filmmaking that is teasing me is this business of editing, and in talking about your next film you thought it would be a "fiction film," as I think you put it. The thing that interests me, Fred, is that in shooting the film, in fact you are substituting for the memory that the novelist would have; and then when you go to edit, in effect, you're remembering, and just as the novelist remembers and then imagines some too of course — I don't want to lock him in on reporting simply — but it seems to me that I'm having a great deal of trouble seeing the difference between a documentary film and a fictional film. In a sense a documentary or fictional film is involved with memory and imagination, because your imagination is functioning, when you put side by side, or in a certain sequence, certain frames . . .

WISEMAN: Sure, your imagination is working in the way you see the thematic relationships between the various disparate events being photographed, and cutting a documentary is like putting together a "reality dream," because the events in it are all true, except really they have no meaning except insofar as you impose a form on them, and that form is imposed in large measure, of course, in the editing. I mean, the limits of the form you can impose are the limits of the raw material you have in your eighty thousand feet or forty hours of film. You finish shooting, but in that framework, you can make a variety of movies, and it's the way you think through your own relationship to the material that produces the final form of the film.

GRAHAM: This must be a tremendously exciting stage, is it not?

WISEMAN: It is. It's a combination of being terribly boring and terribly exciting.

GRAHAM: You must make noises to yourself as you're looking at these things — shouts, maybe, of glee, or groans . . .

WISEMAN: There's a lot of very mechanical work in it, too, because you have an idea and you've got to cut. It takes a while to cut the film and make sure you haven't lost the synch and all that, and then you want to test it out in relation to other things, and so it may take a couple of days to see if your idea works or not. But it's very exciting as you begin to shape the material from the forty hours, and then you finally get a four or five hour version of the film, and then it goes so rapidly.

GRAHAM: You have to boil it down and boil it down . . .

WISEMAN: A constant process of compression, and when you get it to two and a half hours, and it's still not a movie yet, it's just a vast — well, a somewhat reduced lump — but then you can make the connections much faster; and at that stage, where it's teetering on the edge of being a film, it really is very exciting. And then you make some changes, and in three or four months it finally is there, you look at it one day and it's a movie.

GRAHAM: In a lot of ways, again, talking with these novelists and poets, here at the Conference, this is so much the process they use. So often they will write the 200 page novel originally as an 800 page novel, and then they have to cut.

WISEMAN: The editing process is very similar, in the sense that you have this gross material and you put it all down, and shooting is the equivalent of putting it all down.

GRAHAM: Do you have to fight, given these examinations of institutions, do you have to fight against — or would you just as soon give into — a temptation to direct society? I should imagine you have to be very careful not to be heavy-handed lest you become a simple propagandist.

WISEMAN: That's the danger. I personally have a horror of producing propaganda to fit any kind of ideology, other than my own view of what this material should be, and I don't like even to be propagandistic or didactic. I like the material to speak for itself. I think the films that I've done, documentaries, all have — to me, at least — a very clear point of view, but it's a point of view that the audience has to work with the events of the film in order to . . . in a sense they have to fight the film, they have to say, "What the hell's he trying to say with this?" — if indeed I'm saying anything. And they have to think through their own relationship to what they're seeing. I don't think it's necessarily a rigid point of view that somebody has to come to a conclusion about, because you're dealing with reality. The material is complex and ambiguous, and very often the way somebody will respond to the film will depend on the values they bring to the events that they're assessing.

GRAHAM: Actually, in a lot of ways, one thing you're saying is you'd just as soon each individual had a multiple response to it.

WISEMAN: Exactly! Because the material's not simple-minded. To reduce it to "high schools are bad," or "police are all terrible," or "big city hospitals have difficulty coping with the problems," is to reduce it to a vast kind of commercial cliché, which doesn't in any way accurately reflect the experience of the material, or is fair to the kinds of issues that you're dealing with.

GRAHAM: With the whole business of the documentary film, and now you are kind of teasing yourself into seriously thinking about fiction film, what changes in you are going to take place, as a film-maker. Have you crossed any funny little bridges?

WISEMAN: I'm not giving up doing documentaries. I always want to continue to do them, but I'd like to see if I can produce a fiction film with the same look as a documentary, and that's really the problem that interests me. But really, the issue is to find out how far you can go, and so I don't know what the answer is to that. One of the reasons I want to do a fiction film is to see what I can do with it.

GRAHAM: Do you see any inherent limits in the documentary? It would seem to me you could go into a kind of fantasy in parts of it. It could be manipulated a great deal, couldn't it? Or am I trying to warp a form?

WISEMAN: You know, I don't know. Certainly there's always the possibility it can be manipulated, but I think the test again is the *subject*. You have to be fair to the experience and the material as you understand it. There's always the danger that you don't understand the material and your viewing experience will be totally different than anybody's and other people who know something about the subject will say "You missed it." That's always a risk, but if you miss it fairly, O.K. Then that's the risk you're taking. You don't want to miss it by starting out with the idea of doing somebody in, or taking advantage of physical characteristics in a way that would distort the meaning, just making fun of people. I don't think that's fair.

GRAHAM: One point you make is that we ought to go to films, in a sense, passively but receptively, rather than analytically.

WISEMAN: I think you have to be open to the experience that the film presents. Often in a documentary film, the subject will be something about which the audience knows relatively little. In some cases they'll think they know a lot, but frequently, at least in some of my documentaries such as the one on Metropolitan Hospital or on the Kansas City Police Department, the audience really knows very little. We think we know something about the police: if we're middle-class types, we know the police from traffic tickets or accidents. Yet we don't have any intimate experience with the day-to-day operations of the police, although we all have our stereotyped view of how the police operate.

Ideally the film will present a series of fresh experiences, and I can't prescribe how the audience should react, but I hope the audience would say, "Well, this is different than I thought it was

*Police try to quiet a dispute in **Law and Order***

going to be!" And they would place themselves in the middle of the event. For example, there's one sequence in my *Law and Order* — a sequence at the end of the film, where police are called because a husband and wife are separated, the husband's found out the wife is living with another man, she's got the kid. The husband starts a fight with the wife on the street, and the police are called. The police are asked by the husband to give him his kid back. Then the guy asks the police to help him get a lawyer, and he says he doesn't have a job. Then he starts to get in a verbal fight with a friend of the wife, and he tries to grab the kid away. It's that kind of situation. What are the police supposed to do? They can't be his lawyer, they can't be marriage counselors, they can't provide him with a job. On the other hand, the poor man's terribly frustrated and he says, "I've never committed a crime before but I don't know what I'm going to do now," and he runs off down the street. Well, watching that sequence, the audience can at various times identify with the rejected husband, with the kid, with the wife, or with the police.

GRAHAM: With the police — wondering what on earth can be done for the man.

WISEMAN: There's a multiple point of view present, and if the film works, people will realize the complexity of the problems, the multiple roles involved, and that there are no simple solutions. Your "solution" to the event depends not so much on what's going on in the movie but on the values you have about the events you see in the movie. So it may nudge your values a little bit, and you may say, "You know, these police have a tough job here, handling all this" or "I wonder what services the community could provide that would get this guy a lawyer, help him get a job?"

GRAHAM: One thing that occurred to me as you were summarizing this very real possibility, that we might leap inside any one of these four or five characters immediately before us: this is something the novel can do much more efficiently, really, by showing us a scene of all of these people together . . .

WISEMAN: The novel can *or* the film . . . The novelist's got to set you up, and it may take eight pages — the film can do it in twenty seconds . . .

GRAHAM: And a popular technique in many novels is to tell a story or incident in three parts from three points of view. Two men and one woman looking at a relationship, for instance, but that takes a lot of time; while the filmmaker can convey in twenty seconds the complexities, the real complexities of life . . .

WISEMAN: Yes, but you see, you've got a different problem. The novelist can deal with ideas simply by stating them. He can take you inside the character's head or he can give you the omniscient narrator.

GRAHAM: He can provide a history, where this woman came from and so forth.

WISEMAN: The novelist can really say anything he wants, and he can state things with a degree of abstraction. One problem that

Exterior of school in **High School**

really interests me about filmmaking is how you express ideas in film terms. That's very much related to the editing of the film — the way you structure the events, the timing of the various events, and the connections between them. Not only the connections, say, between scene one and scene two, but the connection between scene one and scene thirty-five, which is your last scene. For example, *High School* starts off with a shot of the back of a row of houses, and then you see a whole bunch of little cleaning establishments and five-and-ten stores as you're driving into this school. The first shot of the school is from the back, and you don't know it's a school — it could be a General Motors assembly plant. Then, in the last sequence the principal of the school reads a letter from a soldier in Vietnam who is writing to say that if he gets killed he wants to give his G.I. insurance to the school because the school was so nice to him, and he describes his feelings about being a soldier. He says he's only a body doing a job. Well, *he* is the Chevrolet that is produced by this particular factory . . .

GRAHAM: So the depersonalized shot at the beginning sets us up for this dehumanized product . . .

WISEMAN: Thematically, there is a relationship, which doesn't necessarily have to strike the viewer in the sense that he says, "Well, the school is a factory and, therefore, it produces a Class A model doomed to conform." Hopefully the audience will ask, "What is the relationship between the opening shot of the school and the end sequence of the soldier in Vietnam." Also, "What is the general point of view of the film, the over-all structure of the film, and the relationship of the structure of the film with the things that concern people in the larger society."

GRAHAM: A handy term for this was fed to me by critic Albert Guerard. It is the opening shot of the impersonal school that strikes "on the rim of consciousness." You don't need to think at that moment "why?" "how impersonal," but you will, in fact, take in this impression visually, a piece here, a piece there, and suddenly — you've got an attitude.

WISEMAN: That's it, and you don't have to formalize it as a series of rational statements. It's more important that there be some kind of fusion between feeling it and thinking it, than to be able to state it. That's what the editing process is about, too. On the one hand, it's highly rational, and you try to think through all these connections; on the other hand, the process that leads you to the connections in the first place is a non-rational one. When I'm editing I try to work out a very elaborate theory which I set down as I talk to myself: for example, "Well, this fits this way" and "that fits that way," but in the way I finally get to it I can see that the rationalization frequently comes after the connection exists.

GRAHAM: Yes, often I'll write an outline after I've finished a paper but the paper comes first — the psychic energy.

WISEMAN: It's like that bromide about waking up in the morning and suddenly seeing that the relationship between something you shot on the first day and something you shot on the thirty-first day is true. That's not a process of deduction, that's a process of dreaming.

GRAHAM: I'm interested in the amount of anticipation that the filmmaker, especially the creative filmmaker, goes through. Have you looked back at that possible outline and at your final product, and seen vast differences?

WISEMAN: No. Before I start shooting one of these films I prepare an outline, which I present to the people I'm asking to let me film. What the outline says is, I want to make a film about a hospital and why I want to make a film about a hospital, and these are the kind of events that I expect to get. For example, waiting around in the Emergency Ward, medical services in the clinic, police bringing in somebody from the street, a drug addict being brought in, X-ray, and so on — but the events are still sufficiently general . . .

GRAHAM: They give you room to move . . .

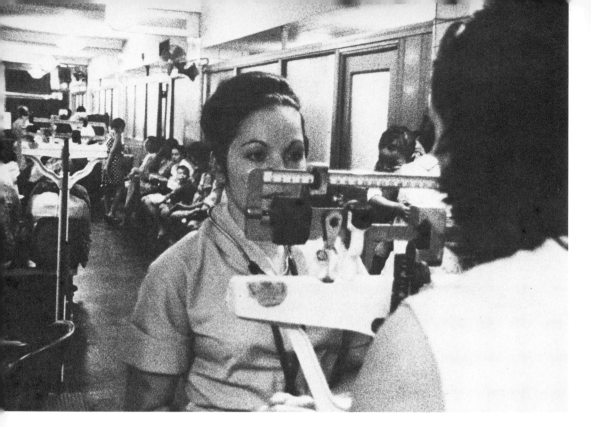

*A patient is weighed at clinic in **Hospital***

WISEMAN: They give you plenty of room, but I never say, this is going to be it. I say, illustratively, here are fifteen or twenty classes of events that I think I'll get, but I'm in no way limited to those events. My description of those events in the outline is vague by necessity, because I don't know what people are going to say to each other. For example there is a scene in *Hospital* where a kid has taken an overdose of mescaline. I had noted in my outline the problem of drugs, but I had no idea that this kid was going to be brought in and go through the experience shown in the film.

GRAHAM: To go back to a problem you mentioned before: the problem of the narrator —

WISEMAN: The way I try to make a documentary is that there's no separation between the audience watching the film and the events in the film. It's like the business of getting rid of the proscenium arch in the theater, and, by analogy at least, narration is the proscenium arch because it immediately separates you from the experience of what you're going to see and hear, by telling you that it has nothing to do with you, or by telling you what to think about it. If you hear a narrator say, "You're about to go behind the bars of a maximum security prison and that man's a psychotic and that man's a rapist and that man is a traffic violator who is being sent up as an example to other people who don't pay their traffic tickets," well, that immediately — whether you accept it or not, and many people do — gives you an attitude toward the people you see . . .

GRAHAM: Almost a false sense of security . . .

WISEMAN: It's like having a butterfly collection with everything labelled. Whereas if you see somebody and you don't know whether he's an alcoholic or whether he's a rapist or whether he's a murderer or whether he's a psychopath — whatever those terms may mean, if in fact they have any meaning at all — *you* have to decide how you feel about the guy.

Law and Order

Woman with empty purse retrieved by policeman
in **Law and Order**

"YOU START OFF WITH A BROMIDE"

WISEMAN ON FILM AND CIVIL LIBERTIES

An Interview by Alan Westin

Alan Westin, Editor of The Civil Liberties Review, *recorded this conversation in the fall of 1973 at Wiseman's studio on Lewis Wharf in Boston.*

CLR: How do you decide which particular school, hospital, police force, or other institutions to go to?

WISEMAN: The standards I use in selection are first, that I can get permission to film, and second, that it's a place that is considered a reasonably good or even superior institution of its kind and is not a sitting-duck institution. There must be some sense that people are making a genuine effort, however short of some ideal standard that may fall. I have no way of determining what's typical, normal, average, standard, or whatever. I don't pretend to be an expert in any of these fields.

CLR: Do you do much research before you film?

WISEMAN: I don't believe in doing very much research before going in to shoot. The shooting of the film is the research. The

47 /

editing is like writing the book. The research instead of being on 3-by-5 cards is on film. The final film is the product of studying and thinking about how you are going to structure, order, and find a form for the chaotic raw material of the research. In this process 100,000 feet of film are reduced to 3,000 feet, and the film emerges.

In *High School* I went to what was regarded as a fine middle-class school, and I didn't know what to anticipate. Then after a short time the boredom of the school began to get to me. The school grounds looked like a General Motors assembly plant, the playground like a huge parking lot. The last day of shooting I got a sequence that put together some of the feelings I'd had after being in the school for a month. At a faculty meeting the principal read a letter from a recent graduate, a boy on an aircraft carrier off Vietnam. The boy said he was making the school the beneficiary of his GI insurance in case he got killed. He wrote, "I have been trying to become a Big Brother in Vietnam, but it is very hard to do. . . . Am I wrong? . . . If I do my best and believe that what I do is right — that is all I can do . . . I am only a body doing a job." The principal thought he was an excellent product. After reading the letter she said, "Now when you get a letter like this, to me it means that we are very successful at Northeast High School." This boy wanted to show his appreciation to the school for all it had done to teach him about duty, authority, and self. His uncritical, unthinking acceptance made him just like a Chevrolet rolling off the GM line.

CLR: Does this mean that you sometimes don't know how you are going to portray an institution until you get there?

WISEMAN: That's right, and that's one of the things that interests me about making a film. You start off with a little bromide or stereotype about how prison guards are supposed to behave or what cops are really like. You find that they don't match up to that image, that they're a lot more complicated. And the point of each film is to make that discovery. Before the film the tendency is to simplify. The discovery is that the actuality is much more complicated and interesting. The effort in editing is to have the completed film reflect that discovery.

CLR: Is there a film in which that discovery was particularly surprising to you?

WISEMAN: It's been true in all of them. *Law and Order* is a good example, however. I went to shoot *Law and Order* right after the police rioted at the 1968 Democratic Convention in Chicago. It seemed to me a golden opportunity to "get" the cops by showing how they behaved like "pigs." But after I rode around in police cars for a few days (and eventually for more than 400 hours), I realized what a simpleminded, naive view that was. The police are no different from the rest of us. The film dealt more with what people do to each other, the behavior that makes police necessary. Police brutality is shown as part of a more generally shared violence and not something isolated or unique.

Something of the same thing happened when I went to film at Metropolitan Hospital. I expected to find a lot of bureaucratic callousness and a hardened staff, indifferent to the problems of the poor. What I generally found, though, were a lot of doctors, nurses, and hospital personnel who really cared, trying to deal with the medical consequences of bad housing, illiteracy, no jobs, malnutrition, and so on.

CLR: Does this explain the ambiguity that many reviewers have noticed about your films, that one person can see a Wiseman film and come away appalled at what that institution is doing, and another person will conclude that the officials are doing a relatively good job under trying conditions?

WISEMAN: I think all the films have a well-defined point of view. My point of view toward the material is reflected in the structure of the film — the relationship of the sequences to each other and the themes that are developed by this particular order. However, a person's reaction to the film in part depends on his values and experience. Since the reality is complex, contradictory, and ambiguous, people with different values or experience respond differently. I think that there should be enough room in the film for other people to find support for their views while understanding what mine are. Otherwise I'd be in the propaganda business.

CLR: Let's talk about what your films reveal of civil liberties issues, particularly the question of how the rights of individuals are — or should be — treated in public institutions. As you probably know, the American Civil Liberties Union has recently sponsored a series of handbooks on the rights of various groups in American society — teachers, students, mental patients, prisoners, women, etc. The main premise of many of these books is that it would be better for American society if the rights of individuals caught up in its institutions, many of them involuntarily, could be more fully defined and protected. In general, do you share that view?

WISEMAN: Of course. But, in a way, saying that is like coming out in favor of motherhood when that was popular. What intrigues me is the discrepancy between ideological statements like that and what actually goes on.

CLR: Let's apply what you just said to *Law and Order*. You have some striking sequences that show the use of excessive police force. For example, there's the black youth who's being arrested for stealing a car. The way he's thrown down on the automobile hood by the policeman, although he's manacled and poses no physical threat, is quite shocking. He was cursing the police, of course, but didn't pose any physical threat to the 2 officers there.

WISEMAN: Right. There was certainly no reason to beat that kid's head against the car, and I'm sure the policemen knew it. But a situation in which somebody's calling you a motherfucker and saying "I'm gonna get you," is intense. It's not surprising that in those situations police like the rest of us sometimes lose control. How do you train a cop or anybody else *not* to react harshly to that kind of provocation?

CLR: But the policeman is an officer of the law, invested with a gun, and we do expect him to control the way he responds. Not to do so degrades the system of law the police are sworn to uphold.

WISEMAN: Yes; of course; we expect him to be that way. That's the ideology. But we've also got to recognize that we're asking him to exercise more restraint and control than most of us are capable of. Which is not in any way to excuse or forgive police brutality, but it suggests that the cop is not alone in having those kinds of aggressive or wild responses.

Police arrest car theft suspect in **Law and Order**

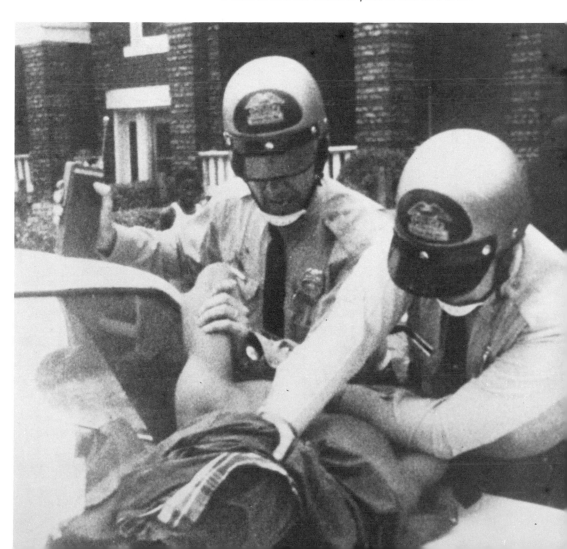

CLR: That brings us back to the question of whether more defined rights for people would improve the situation. I gather that you have some doubts about that.

WISEMAN: Take the situation in *High School*. Even if the law were to declare that students had more defined rights, I wonder whether it would make a great difference. I saw lots of passive, indifferent students at Northeast High. The only activists at the school that I met, really, were some kids in a human-relations discussion group shown in a sequence toward the end of the film, and everyone in that group was on the verge of flunking out for one reason or another.

Furthermore, it's a question of what values the kids are being taught at home, and whether they would want to challenge parental authority. Several of the sequences in the film showed the parents expressing the same kinds of values the school officials were enforcing. In one sequence a mother is talking to the guidance counselor about an incident in which her daughter has been accused of a disrespectful act toward her teacher. And the mother says to the guidance counselor, "The main thing in our home has always been respect for an adult. I was brought up that way; my husband was. And we have been trying to teach our children the same thing. To me, I think, one of the worst offenses is being disrespectful to an older person. Irregardless of what the condition may be." That's almost word for word what the dean of discipline tells the kid in an earlier sequence, to take his punishment and obey orders without dispute. What comes through is that this school is a perfect expression of the values of the people in this community. They wouldn't think in terms of rights and authoritarianism. It would be a matter of learning to do the right thing — regardless of what the condition may be. There are discipline sequences in *Basic Training* that are almost word for word from *High School*.

CLR: Didn't you find any form of student protest in Northeast High?

WISEMAN: No. A few days after Martin Luther King, Jr. was killed, there was a 2-hour meeting of the student council. And a very serious debate about whether to send fruit or flowers to Mrs. King. The decision was made in favor of fruit.

CLR: Where does that leave you in terms of deciding whether the expansion of student rights would make schools like Northeast more democratic?

WISEMAN: Well, it makes me somewhat pessimistic about how much difference it would make. It would make *some,* and therefore expanding student rights is worth the effort. But a theme in almost all the films is that there is already a gap between the formal ideology and actual practice, between the rules and the way they are applied. In almost all these institutions, the officials talk as though they believed people have some rights. In practice, they

Dean of Discipline's office in **High School**

do whatever they think is necessary to carry out their jobs, acting all the time out of a belief, often quite sincere, that this is the best way to help those they are teaching and guiding.

In *High School* the ideology of the school is revealed in the daily bulletin, the signs on the walls. There's one that says: "The mind is like a parachute, it functions best when open." The announced values are democracy, trust, sensitivity, understanding, openness, innovation — all the wonderful words we all subscribe to. But the practice is rigidity, authoritarianism, obedience, do as you're told, don't challenge.

CLR: And from the standpoint of what you thought would be fair and democratic, how did you react to the way the dean of discipline conducted himself?

WISEMAN: In one sense I was appalled; in another I thought I was watching a television situation comedy. But most situations aren't that clear-cut. Their strength as film sequences lies in their ambiguity and the expression of conflicting values. A rigid ideological approach to some of these questions can diminish the film by making it one-dimensional. For example, in *Titicut Follies* the young patient-inmate, Vladimir, is shown making a perfectly accurate critique of Bridgewater — that he isn't getting any real treatment, that his psychiatric sessions are a farce, and that he wants to go back to a regular prison where he can get better treatment. You see him appearing before a review board consisting of a psychiatrist, a psychologist, and several social workers who hear out his complaints, mumble a lot of parody psychiatry, and conclude that Vladimir can't be transferred, but rather his drug dosage should be increased. No one responds to Vladimir's needs. Vladimir really *is* sick; he keeps saying that he thinks his thorax has been poisoned by the food. The situation is complex because Vladimir's critique is accurate and he is also quite sick. Once the label paranoid schizophrenic is attached to him the staff is satisfied. The fact that he has problems or has been convicted of a crime doesn't mean that he should be subjected to the kind of "treatment" he's getting. The film doesn't say what the alternative should be, but I believe it says clearly that alternatives are needed.

CLR: Did you find that problem with formal rights in other institutions? How about *Juvenile Court*?

WISEMAN: People's reaction to *Juvenile Court* and their assessment of the court depends on how much they know about the law and how much they believe formal rights must be observed. The more they know about the law, the more critical they are of some of the procedures shown in the film. The less they know about the law, the more impressed they are with the humanitarianism and the practical solutions to difficult problems that are arrived at. *Juvenile Court* shows people of good will trying hard to deal decently with very complex problems, many of which are totally insoluble by any known or existing therapies. The question is whether more rigid application of due process standards would result in any better dispositions of the cases.

CLR: It's interesting that what you stress in your answer is "better dispositions," because that's different from the average civil libertarian's key question: Are people's rights violated? Am I characterizing fairly what you said?

WISEMAN: I'm sure that's a fair comment on what I've said. I guess, in part, I'm a little leery of a kind of professional civil libertarian view that can be just as pompous and as rigid as some of the ideologies that are being mocked in *High School*.

CLR: Is it rigid to believe that we should extend more legally-enforceable rights — of privacy, due process, and free expression — to people who are subject today to almost unchecked authority in so many of these institutions?

WISEMAN: I don't have any difficulty agreeing with your rhetoric. It's that I have doubts about the capacity to have such rights administered on a large scale in these types of institutions. I don't see the signs that people want such rights granted and then would be willing to support their enforcement in practice. Consider the massive effort that it took to make the American people think about the Vietnam War, or about integration, or any other major social problem. I come away with doubts about the capacity to motivate people to what is usually called large-scale social change.

CLR: Did you start off in 1967 with such pessimism?

WISEMAN: No, it's developed as I've made more films. I no longer have the view that I had in the beginning that there might be some direct relationship between what I was able to show in these films and the achievement of social change. Nor have I observed any particularly successful strategies of change, as they're called.

CLR: But millions of people are seeing your films; don't you expect or at least hope that they will be spurred to seek changes in public schools, prisons, hospitals, the army?

WISEMAN: Of course, but it's not for me to say what the change should be. What the films do is give people some information. Hopefully on the basis of this and other information people will be able to make more informed decisions about what, if any, change they would like to have take place. It's not my wish to impose solutions; that would be presumptuous.

CLR: In what sense? You're a trained lawyer, you're sensitive to issues of social justice, you've gotten inside half a dozen institutions as a filmmaker; why aren't you entitled to draw up some prescriptions?

WISEMAN: I'm not a pharmacist. I've had an opportunity to observe how middle-class reformers play the social change game. I guess I've gone very far away from the liberal clichés and bromides that I started with, especially the simpleminded social-work view of help and intervention.

I was once involved with what was called a social science consulting firm in Cambridge, and it was a grand boondoggle. And this was only an aspect of the larger consulting game, which was in turn made available through a variety of federal programs where millions of dollars at the federal level got pissed away on nothing. It went to middle-class professionals who were just sitting around in rooms, speculating about experiences they knew nothing about.

Then I go out to work on a film and see all this misery and there just doesn't seem any relationship between the talk and what you observe in people's lives. I suppose it's one of the sad conclusions of the experience of making the films that a lot of the solutions seem grandiose and the change agents, as they call themselves, full of pious goodwill.

Juvenile Court

CLR: Is that what you concluded in your latest film?

WISEMAN: *Juvenile Court* is concerned with the limits of intervention. The court has to deal with problems of incest, murder, rape, child abuse, and parental neglect, to name only some. The judge and his staff work hard and ably to cope with the suffering they have to deal with on a daily basis. Competent people from medicine, social science, and social work are available to the court. There is no way of knowing whether the interventions are useful, preventative, therapeutic, inconsequential, or harmful.

CLR: There's one thing that troubles me a bit, in terms of my experiences with some of these institutions. In all your films, we see confrontations and encounters between individuals and authorities. But there are no professionals there directly representing the individuals, such as lawyers in the Kansas City police stations, or any organized groups pressing the claims of their members, such as

Judge in **Juvenile Court**

student groups, racial groups, welfare-rights groups, patient-rights groups. Why are these groups absent from your films?

WISEMAN: In the 6 weeks in Kansas City I rarely saw a lawyer either at the precinct or headquarters. It wasn't that those sequences were cut out; they just didn't exist. I had the same experience with the other films. At Northeast High there was no student protest or activist organization. At Fort Knox most of the trainees seemed to enjoy basic training. There had been a coffeehouse which was a center of anti-war activity, but the local authorities had closed it down some months before the film was shot. In the month in Memphis I was in the courtroom every day and no representatives of the sorts of organizations you have in mind were present. In 1967 there were no prisoners' rights groups that came to the defense of *Titicut Follies*, nor were they active inside Bridgewater.

CLR: Yet the very clear message of your films is that the individual has no intermediate institutions between himself and the authorities in these public organizations — no groups to protect his interests and assert his rights. And that contradicts what we know is happening in many institutions of the type you have filmed.

WISEMAN: At the times and places the films were made, these intermediate institutions weren't there. Their absence makes me wonder whether such civil liberties and civil rights groups are covering their turf as well as they should.

CLR: You're quoted in many interviews as saying it's still remarkable to you how much people are willing to reveal about themselves while you're filming them. Have you given any more thought to why that's so? Why do people talk about the most private kinds of things — sex, drugs, alcohol use, personal relationships — right in front of you and for the public to see later?

WISEMAN: A combination of reasons: pleased that they're in a film, passivity, a sense that it's important that others know about their work, and indifference.

CLR: As you know, your work has raised questions about invasion of privacy. Anyone watching your films is impressed almost immediately by the realization that these are not actors but real people — being stripped nude and inspected at Bridgewater, discussing their sexual misconduct with a psychiatrist, admitting to all kinds of anti-social behavior before probation officers in juvenile court, and so on. We see parents talking intimately to their children, ministers counseling kids, doctors talking to patients and about patients. This raises some issues about the boundary lines between publicity and privacy that you've been involved with since your first film. What are your thoughts on the ethical and legal aspects of this?

WISEMAN: These are films about public institutions, supported by public money, taxpayers' money, and the public has a right to know what goes on in them.

CLR: But the privacy issue involves the individual people who are caught up in such public institutions, not the privacy of the state.

WISEMAN: That's right. Film technology now allows us to look at the relationship between the individual and the state in these publicly-supported institutions in a way that wasn't possible 20 years ago. Each sequence describes a relationship between private citizens not on the public payroll and other people who are state employees: doctors, policemen, nurses, school teachers, drill sergeants, judges, social workers, etc. One way of asking the question is: What are the limits to be placed on the technology that makes the documentary film form possible and, by setting those limits, what kinds of information unique to the documentary form do you prevent the public from having? I think it comes down to a pragmatic consideration: At what point does the individual's right of privacy bend to a more general need to share that information with other people? Documentary films are just as valid news as newspaper stories about the same events.

CLR: How do you deal with the individual's own right to decide what he reveals about himself, which is the conventional definition of the right to privacy?

WISEMAN: I don't get written releases, but I do get consents. Either before the sequence is shot or just after, I explain to the participants that I'm making a film that's going to be shown on television and generally to the public both nationally and in the community where the film is made. I ask whether they object to my using the sequence in the film. And I tape record the question and the answer. Also before the shooting begins there are announcements on bulletin boards, and stories in local newspapers, and institutional newsletters explaining the film and its uses.

CLR: Do they ever object?

WISEMAN: Very rarely. And if they do object, I don't use the sequence. But the objection has to be registered at that time. In other words, I don't go back and look for people a year after the film is edited and ask permission then.

CLR: I know that there have been threats of invasion-of-privacy suits, and trouble over showings in some communities with several of your films, but none has produced the epic battle that *Titicut Follies* stirred. Could we go into this?

WISEMAN: Ever since I began to take law classes to Bridgewater I'd wanted to do a film there. The superintendent at Bridgewater approved the idea, but permission had been denied by the state commissioner of corrections. Then a friend of mine who was a state legislator arranged for me to see Elliot Richardson, who was then lieutenant governor and had health, education, welfare, and correctional institutions under his jurisdiction. I saw Richardson, explained what I wanted to do, and he called the commissioner of corrections in my presence, endorsing the idea. A few weeks later the commissioner of corrections wrote that I could go ahead if I got the permission of the state attorney general, then Edward Brooke. Brooke's office issued an advisory opinion saying a film could be made in Bridgewater if I had the permission of the super-intendent, and pictures were taken of "consenting" inmates.

Since I had the permission of the superintendent, I went ahead and made the film. Richardson was one of the first persons I showed the completed film to, in a screening room along with the superintendent of Bridgewater and Richardson's driver. Richard-son thought the film was great. He understood it, understood what I was trying to do with it, and congratulated me warmly. The superintendent asked him whether I should show it to anybody else in state government, and Richardson said no, not even the governor, who was then John Volpe. The conversation took place in a sound studio. Unfortunately, it wasn't recorded.

That was in June of 1967. In the fall of '67 the film was about to be shown publicly, and it had begun to be reviewed. A former social worker wrote to the governor saying how dreadful it was that a film showing naked men could be shown publicly. Then some state legislators decided to hold public hearings, not about the dreadful conditions at Bridgewater that the film showed, but rather about how I had gotten permission to film there. I was at-tacked viciously in the press, the *Boston Herald*, for example, for exploiting the poor inmates at Bridgewater and trying to make money off their misery.

Richardson — who had then shifted from lieutenant governor to state attorney general — was in trouble because he had not told his advisors that he had been instrumental in getting me permis-sion to make the film. When he told them, I think he was advised that he had better move actively against the film to protect him-self. So he got a temporary restraining order from a superior court judge against showing the film in Massachusetts. That's what started the proceedings.

CLR: Did you ever have any contact with him about his change in position?

WISEMAN: We had a meeting in his office before he got the re-straining order. Richardson said he always had liked the film, but he now expressed concern, for the first time, about the privacy of the inmates. Then, in his capacity as attorney general, claiming to be the legal guardian of incompetent persons in state institutions, he hired 2 special assistant attorney generals from his former law firm to pursue the film in court. Their tactical position was that the film was an obscene document.

CLR: What was the trial based on?

WISEMAN: Actually, there were 3 allegations made by the state. One was that I had breached an oral contract giving the attorney general, the commissioner of corrections, and the superintendent at Bridgewater the right to exercise final censorship over the film. Secondly, they charged the film was an invasion of the privacy of one of the inmates. This man is taken naked from his cell, is slapped by the guards, shaved by them while they banter about his past as a school teacher, taunted about why he doesn't keep his cell clean, and then returned naked to his cell. The third claim was that all receipts from the film should be held in trust for the inmates.

At the trial, the Judge found that I had breached an oral contract and had violated the inmate's privacy, but he rejected the trust requirement. He ruled that the film could not be shown to the general public in Massachusetts, and that all prints and negatives should be destroyed. He said that there were no First Amendment issues, and that the film was "a nightmare of ghoulish obscenities."

CLR: Richardson wrote a letter to *The New Republic* defending his action against the film, stating:

> It would seem that a decent regard for the dignity and privacy of those who happen to be patients at Bridgewater State Hospital could easily have been reconciled with the announced intention of the film and the conditions at the institution honestly depicted without violating the rights of individuals.

How do you react to that?

WISEMAN: It's a high-winded pomposity. There was no way of making a real film about Bridgewater without shooting people's faces and becoming involved in the intimate aspects of the daily routine there. Richardson certainly knew that, and certainly approved of the film as it was made. There was no evidence introduced at the trial that the film was not an honest portrayal of the conditions. There is some question about whether the inmates had any privacy to begin with. If Richardson and the other politicians in Massachusetts were genuinely concerned about the privacy and dignity of the inmates of Bridgewater, they would not have allowed the conditions that are shown in the film to exist. They were more concerned about the film and its effect on their reputations than they were about Bridgewater. The superintendent of Bridgewater certainly originally wanted the film made because he was fed up. He couldn't get any support from the legislature or the politicians to bring about any changes there. At that time there was neither a statutory nor a common law right of privacy in Massachusetts. If the public in Massachusetts had seen the film, some voters might wonder about their elected officials. Instead, the state acted as a censor and prevented people from learning about Bridgewater. So that I think that Richardson's concern about privacy, while sounding very good, was essentially a fake issue in terms of the realities of Bridgewater.

CLR: The Civil Liberties Union of Massachusetts was involved in the case, wasn't it?

WISEMAN: My experience with the civil liberties union illustrates the discrepancy between ideology and practice I've been discussing. My first lawyer in the case was then the chairman of the CLUM. One day, a cartoon appeared in the *Boston Herald* showing 2 white horses going in opposite directions, one labeled "Titicut Follies" and the other "Massachusetts Civil Liberties Union," and my lawyer, Gerald Berlin, was shown astride them. That same day he told me that he could no longer represent me because the CLUM would lose contributions if he did so, and besides he now thought that I didn't have a good case and suggested that I give

Patient in **Hospital**

Hospital

it up. I left the office furious because his primary obligation was to me, his client, and not to CLUM. I then retained other lawyers who were not professional civil libertarians.

Despite Berlin's prior involvement, CLUM took a position in the case against the film. On appeal to the Massachusetts Supreme Court they filed an amicus brief written by 5 people who, to my knowledge, had never seen the film or read the trial transcript. They came up with the Solomon-like solution that I should cut out the faces of the inmates, and that the film should only be seen by audiences made up of limited groups, such as social workers and medical professionals. The latter was essentially what the Massachusetts Supreme Judicial Court decided, and remains the rule for showings in that state. The conditions under which I can show the *Follies* are so restrictive that I have not shown the film rather than comply with the terms of the restraining order. The moral insensitivity and cowardice of CLUM and its chairman were for me the worst part of the *Follies* case. The response of Richardson and most members of the Massachusetts legislature was at least consistent with their general public political behavior.

The national ACLU stayed out of the case. All I could get at the New York office were a few stale ironies from the staff general counsel. Fortunately, other organizations did not react with the same muted interest. The American Sociological Association and the American Orthopsychiatric Association filed amicus briefs in support of the film, arguing strongly that it was fully protected by the First Amendment. At the present time the *Follies* is the only film in American constitutional history (other than those dealing in obscenity) that has court-approved restrictions on its use.

CLR: Do you have any parting thoughts on any aspect of your film work and civil liberties?

WISEMAN: I hope that if I were to do a film on the Civil Liberties Union I would be as surprised as I was with the police.

ELLIOT RICHARDSON ON TITICUT FOLLIES

Wiseman's comments about the legal troubles of Titicut Follies *in the preceding interview prompted this letter which appeared in the Summer 1974 issue of* The Civil Liberties Review. *It is followed by Wiseman's reply.*

Most of Frederick Wiseman's statements about my relationship to *Titicut Follies* are inconsistent both with the documentary record and findings by the Massachusetts courts in proceedings brought by the Commonwealth and supported by the Civil Liberties Union of Massachusetts.

Our proceedings against the film were not motivated by any desire to cover up conditions in Bridgewater. On the contrary, I initially endorsed Wiseman's project of filming at Bridgewater State Prison (I was lieutenant governor at the time) because I believed that a thoughtful, sensitive, and fair presentation of conditions at Bridgewater would be helpful in getting support to improve those conditions, and because I did not then have any reason to doubt that Wiseman would observe the rights of the inmates and patients.

The state officials in charge were, from the onset, quite rightly concerned about the privacy of the inmates. Virtually all of them had been committed to Bridgewater involuntarily because of acute mental disease. They were wards of the state, and the state had a responsibility to protect them.

Most of the conditions to Wiseman's permission to photograph patients were spelled out in letters from Superintendent Gaughan and Attorney General Brooke, to which Wiseman expressly agreed. It was specified in these letters, prior to the filming, that (a) "the rights of the inmates and patients at Bridgewater should be fully protected" (b) Wiseman "would only use the photographs of inmates and patients who are legally competent to sign releases" and (c) Wiseman "will obtain a written release from each patient whose photograph is used in the film." Wiseman also agreed that the completed film would not be shown or released without having first been reviewed and approved by the commissioner of corrections and the superintendent of Bridgewater — a condition imposed for the purpose of assuring that the rights of the inmates would be observed.

As the court found, Wiseman violated all of these conditions in the course of his filming at Bridgewater and commercial exhibition of *Titicut Follies.*

When I first saw the film, I raised at once the problems of the rights of the individuals shown. I asked Wiseman whether he had obtained releases from all these people, and he replied that he had. I reminded him the film would have to be shown to the commissioner of corrections, and Wiseman promised not to release it pending this review.

While we were exploring possible compromises, such as the obscuring of identities and the adding of subtitles to explain various scenes, Wiseman, unknown to me, was negotiating with Grove Press for public commercial exhibition of the film. At about the same time he told the Lincoln Center Film Festival, in connection with its exhibition of the film, that "I have secured releases from those people who are in the film or from their authorized representatives." In fact, as was shown at the trial, he had not obtained releases from any of these patients.

The efforts of the state to prevent the showing of the film

were not motivated by a fear of an adverse effect on the reputation of state officials. As the complaint in the case shows, and as all the evidence bore out, the state's concern was for the privacy of the inmates. This was also the concern which led the Civil Liberties Union of Massachusetts to file its amicus brief supporting the state. The case was fully litigated through the Massachusetts courts, and these agreed that the film constituted a massive invasion of privacy and a breach by Wiseman of all the conditions to which he had assented.

ELLIOT L. RICHARDSON
Washington, D.C.

Frederick Wiseman replies: Elliot Richardson is a moral and virtuous man. If there is any doubt about the morality and virtue of his position in the *Titicut Follies* case, he immediately informs us that his view is supported by the Civil Liberties Union of Massachusetts. Indeed, a more virtuous combination could not be found.

In order that the "documentary record" be clearer: The Massachusetts Civil Liberties Union never supported the proceedings brought by the Commonwealth of Massachusetts. As I pointed out in the interview in *The Civil Liberties Review*, CLUM submitted an amicus brief to the Massachusetts Supreme Court which dealt with the abstract issues in the case. The writers of the brief had neither seen the film nor read the trial transcript. Mr. Richardson's position was that the film should be banned. CLUM's abstract position was that the film should be seen by professionals able to cope with the content of the film. CLUM's position was compromised by the fact that my first attorney in the case, who was the then chairman of CLUM, had said he felt CLUM would lose contributions if he continued to represent me.

On May 8, 1974, the board of CLUM voted unanimously to support an action to be brought in the state and federal courts to have the film shown without restriction to the general public. I hope that Mr. Richardson will support this CLUM position so that they can continue to have a comity of interests.

Mr. Richardson seems to have a very selective concern for

the welfare of the inmates at Bridgewater. At no time does he show any sensitivity to the rights of the public to know about the conditions at a maximum security prison at which the Massachusetts Supreme Judicial Court found that the medical and psychiatric facilities were inadequate, and an investigating committee of the Massachusetts bar and medical association determined that there were as many as 300 men who had been detained illegally, some for as many as 30 to 40 years, without a trial.

Mr. Richardson expresses his profound concern for the privacy of the inmates. He does not mention that throughout his term as lieutenant governor there were 8,000 to 10,000 visitors a year at Bridgewater. These visitors saw the same things that viewers of the film saw. I have, in the out-takes of the film, a tour of a group of students being taken through Bridgewater by their high school coach to expose them to the folly of a life of crime. Also in the outs is a picnic on the Bridgewater grounds for a group of students from St. Coletta's School for Exceptional Children. The fact is that for good or bad reasons, up until the time of the film, Bridgewater was run as an open institution because the superintendent wanted the public to be informed about the institution. He initially supported the film as an extension of this policy.

Titicut Follies could not have been made without the cooperation of the state officials. Bridgewater is a maximum security prison. The attorney general of Massachusetts had written an advisory opinion that photographs could be taken of consenting inmates. I undertook to make a documentary film at Bridgewater and to photograph only those individuals who consented to be photographed and were represented as competent to consent. The decision as to the competency of the inmates was left solely to the superintendent and his staff, one or another of whom were present at all times during the filming. No person was photographed who objected or if objection was made by the superintendent or a member of his staff. No hidden cameras or microphones were used.

The theory of censorship by the superintendent, the commissioner of corrections, and the attorney general was cooked up as a way of trying to ban the film. There was no "documentary evidence" at all to support their view introduced at any of the trials.

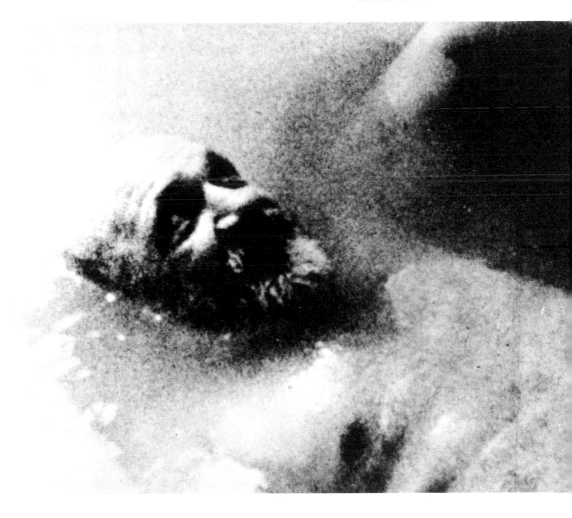

Inmate in **Titicut Follies**

The issue was my word against that of three state officials, and the judge chose to believe them. I know of no documentary filmmaker who would agree to work under such intolerable conditions, and I certainly did not.

The question that Mr. Richardson never faces is whether the inmates had any privacy in an institution that kept men naked in isolation cells as a form of punishment, offered no competent medical or psychiatric treatment, and tolerated physical abuse of the inmates by the guards. The comments of Dr. Leon Shapiro, the former Chief of the Division of Legal Medicine of Massachusetts, are relevant in this respect. He wrote:

> Even though I was an experienced psychiatrist and had already worked on violent disturbed mental hospital wards and maximum security prisons, Bridgewater was the first institution where I felt personally in danger. My reaction to the inmates and the institution during the years of my visits would border on despair each time I went. When I would leave I would quickly put the place out of mind and get busy with other things. In spite of the fact that my job was to help set up new services there, I found myself putting Bridgewater business at the bottom of my list. After I left the Division of Legal Medicine I would think about the place only when it made the headlines in relation to some new sordid business. I give you this brief personal reminiscence because the film in an enormously effective and painful way revived the old feelings of depression and with it the anger at myself for continuing to ignore the problem. . . . I think in a small way my reactions are a clue to why institutions like this continue to exist. There are some things we prefer not to know about — I am afraid not too unlike the Germans who lived near Dachau. Seeing your film should be a mandatory (and repetitive) part of the training of every physician and lawyer and would be a remarkable antidote to public complacency about our "collective crime." I am sure you will get lots of static about "privacy," etc. but the real resistance (like mine) will be the wish not to know.

In the course of three hearings in New York, two trials in Massachusetts and two weeks of legislative hearings, the state did not produce even one witness representing the interests of an inmate or inmate's family who complained about the film. I received letters and calls from many inmates and their families expressing their support of it. Mr. Richardson is a man of intelligence and sensitivity caught in the conflict between his political career and his private reactions. Both he and I know what his reaction to the film was. It is too bad he doesn't have the courage to say in public what he said in private.

"REALITY FICTIONS"
WISEMAN ON
PRIMATE

An Interview by Thomas R. Atkins

Primate was first shown publicly at the Riverside Church in New York City on November 22, 1974, and this interview took place later that evening. The national premiere of the film followed on the Public Broadcasting Service on December 5.

ATKINS: How did you find out about the Yerkes Primate Research Center and decide to make a film about it?

WISEMAN: Well, I've wanted for a long time to make a film on some aspect of scientific research. A friend of mine had visited Yerkes and told me that she thought I should consider it. So I called the officials and arranged to go down to Atlanta for a visit. And indeed I was immediately struck by the film possibilities. I formally asked for permission. Within a relatively short time after it was given, I started shooting.

ATKINS: When did you begin shooting *Primate*?

75 /

Primate

WISEMAN: We started in the end of January and continued through February of 1973.

ATKINS: When did you finish the editing?

WISEMAN: I finished editing the film in May of 1974.

ATKINS: *Primate* seems to be a culmination of many motifs that recur in your films — the mug shots at the beginning, the maximum security environment, the institution trying to regulate sexual and aggressive behavior. Despite its surface differences, *Primate* is closely related to your other work, isn't it?

WISEMAN: Yes, exactly.

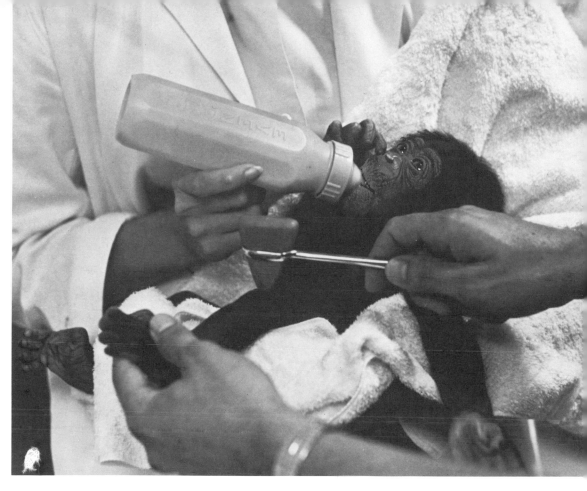

Primate

ATKINS: The tone of *Primate* is slightly more comic — I don't mean in terms of humorous or laughable material as in *High School* — but its coolness and distance towards the subject. It has the detachment of comedy.

WISEMAN: That's a fair statement.

ATKINS: Of course, it's a harrowing type of comedy. For me a key scene in the film is the one in which the scientist explains his theory about the divergence of the ancestors of man and the African apes — the higher primate's center of gravity moved into

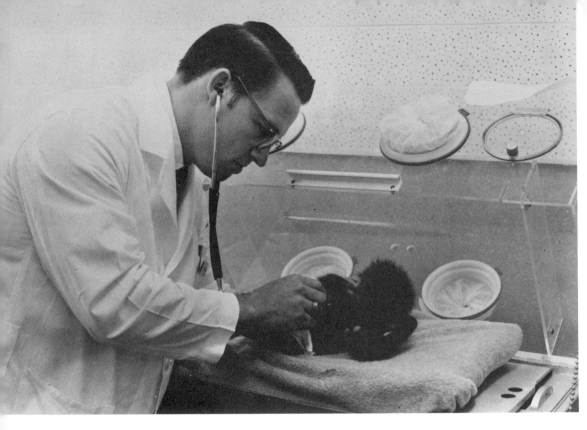

Primate

his pelvis and consequently he could walk upright and use tools, while the lower primate's center of gravity moved into his chest, causing him to become a knuckle-walker.

WISEMAN: That's right.

ATKINS: So the film shows the present relationship between the two animals. The tool-carrying primate is now experimenting on the lower primate to forward his own evolution.

WISEMAN: (Laughing) I think that's a very fair interpretation.

ATKINS: A lot of the audience tonight, at least many of the ones who commented afterwards, missed the broader aspect of the film. They wanted it to be a documentary either justifying or criticizing the various experiments at the institution, but you've never made this kind of simplistic informational or protest film. *Primate* goes far beyond these approaches.

WISEMAN: I'm delighted to hear you say these things because it's nice to know that what you're doing in a film gets across.

ATKINS: Many viewers tonight were apparently expecting the film to contain some kind of direct message or summary.

WISEMAN: They're looking for the literal — something ideologically trendy and socially conscious in a simplified form. And that doesn't interest me. My politics are my politics. I don't say my films aren't influenced by them, but to boil down the reality and

Primate

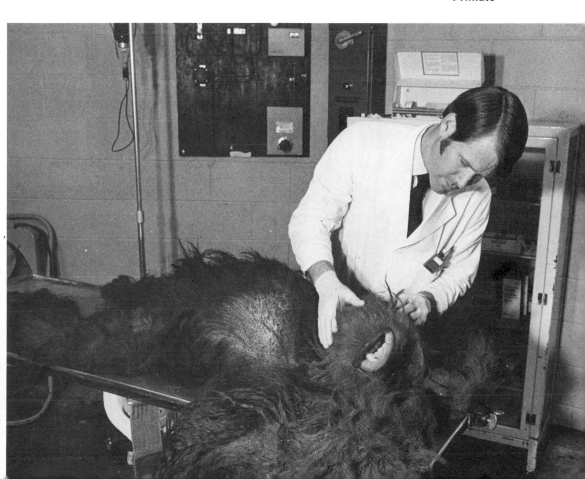

make it one-dimensional in order to make the film meet some fleeting ideological assumption is unfair — it's unfair to yourself, unfair to your audience, and unfair to the people who let you make the film about them. Most of all, it's unfair to reality.

ATKINS: The reality captured in *Primate* is quite complicated and strange. After the mug shots, one of the center officials explains that they don't want the animals "doing things sexually," as he puts it, unless they're watching. He shows a photo of gorillas copulating and talks about their position. While these scientists are busily recording and photographing the primate behavior, their own behavior is being studied as well — by your camera.

Primate

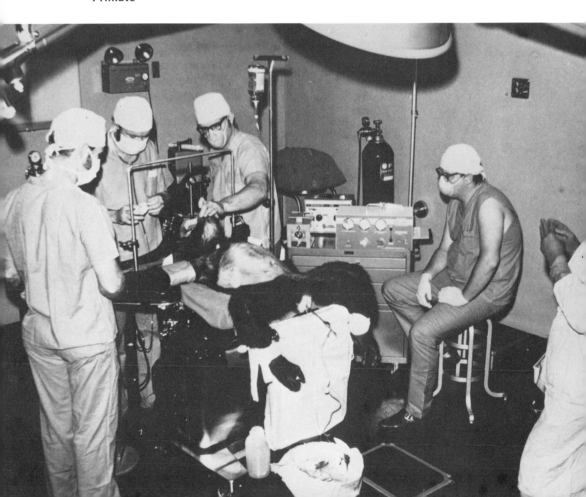

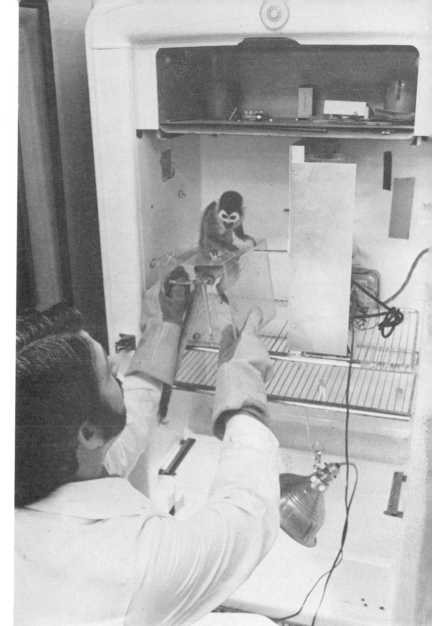

Primate

WISEMAN: Yes. The use of one observation technique to observe another observation technique.

ATKINS: And the behavior observed is often very unusual or funny. There is the fellow who sits in the corridor with his check sheet and timer, for instance, and does nothing but watch and record the activities of the monkeys. One of the funniest sequences involves the monkey whose head is wired up for electrical control. A man and woman are working on him, and as they stimulate him sexually with the current, the woman watches the monkey and says, "Very nice erection." Now, in the usual social context, this comment might be considered very bizarre.

WISEMAN: Yes, it would.

ATKINS: But in that context it's just passed off as . . .

WISEMAN: As science.

ATKINS: You've called *Primate* a "science-fiction documentary." I assume this means in part that while its subject is real, the structure is artificial. Its structure is related to fiction, and it has the scope and impact of fiction.

WISEMAN: I think the phrase "reality fictions" is a better description of what I'm doing than documentary. For *Primate* I filmed events that existed in so-called real life, but structured them in a way that has no relationship to the order or time in which they actually occurred — and created a form that is totally fictional. So from a structural point of view, my films are more related to fictional technique than to documentary technique. The whole issue of documentary and "truth" is frequently oversimplified because a film is always an interpretation of reality — a selection from a vast amount of footage. Even if it's a three-hundred-and-sixty hour film, it's still a selection. And the methods used in structuring the material are very similar to writing a novel or to journalism.

ATKINS: So like a novelist, you have your own response to a real experience, and then you edit or reshape the raw material so that the audience has another experience from the reality of the film.

WISEMAN: Yes, but the final experience is very much dependent not only on the sequences themselves but on the whole pacing of the sequences and their relationship to each other. What's involved in the editing process is thinking your way through the material, and thinking not simply in a deductive way but in an associational way. And trusting those little thoughts that pop up at the edge of your head about the possible connections between sequences. And then finally seeing whether it works. It's an interesting combination of the highly rational — or what you think is rational — and the highly non-rational in the sense of associative. You have to discover whether what you think you can do is in any way matched with what you can actually do when you splice the sequences together.

ATKINS: Do you find that you have a different reaction to an event when you're filming it than later when you look at the event on your film viewer?

WISEMAN: Yes, sure you do. Because when you're there, things are happening too fast. You know, you might be working twelve to fourteen hours a day, and you might shoot eight or ten rolls of film a day. Then at night you look at rushes of material shot three days earlier. And all you can really remember in specific detail are some of the high scenes — the sequences you know you're going to use, like the kid who has an overdose of mescaline in *Hospital* or the cop strangling the girl in *Law and Order*. You remember the dramatic scenes. But the common garden variety type of scenes, the everyday sequences that make up the bulk of the films — you can't keep all those in mind while you're shooting. There's no real need to keep them in mind — except for a sense of when you have enough and the shooting should be over. It's only when you get back, sync up the rushes and study what you have that the intriguing part of the process begins. Then you begin to figure out what each event means to you and develop, deductively or associationally, some kind of theory of the structure. You work out a theory as to why this shot goes with that — or why *Primate* should start with shots of famous old scientists. In order to make this choice, you have to have some kind of recognition of what each sequence means to you and what it means in relation

83 /

to the other sequences. Once you've arrived at this recognition, you rationalize it by saying, "I think this represents A through B or A through E or whatever, and it's connected to the next sequence for the following reasons." And you say, "If I put these two sequences together, I make these points." But then after you've put the two sequences together, you may find that there's no visual connection at all. So you have to ask, "What kind of corridor sequences do I have? Can I end this sequence at a different point to make a smoother cut to the next one? And will the cut work both pictorially and thematically?" Of course, you don't have a checklist to make sure you consider all of these things, but that's what you go through in shaping the film. These are some of the things that go through your head in discovering the form.

ATKINS: What is your working day like when you're shooting?

WISEMAN: Well, I usually get up around six-thirty, have breakfast, and arrive at the place at seven or seven-fifteen. And then go from ten to twelve hours, sometimes longer. A work day is frequently ten to twelve hours.

ATKINS: At the Yerkes Research Center did you know in advance what might happen on a particular day? Was there a schedule of experiments or did you just happen to catch certain events?

WISEMAN: The first thing you do is cruise around the corridors to see what's happening. There's a certain amount of casing that has to go on every day. When I was filming *Juvenile Court*, for example, the docket would be on the judge's desk in the courtroom at nine o'clock every morning. Although court didn't start until nine-thirty, the clerk would be there and I'd ask him about the cases. Or I'd ask one of the social workers, "Who are you interviewing today?" Or sometimes I'd just walk up and down the corridors, and something would start happening and I'd begin shooting. That's the way it happens. You hang around and trust your judgment. It's a combination of luck and judgment. You follow your intuition about where you should be; sometimes you guess right, other times you're wrong. The events are uncontrolled. In *Hospital*, for example, the emergency doors would pop open and things would start happening. Other times you have to case it out. You may find that there's going to be a staff meeting at three o'clock on Friday afternoon, so you go to this meeting. Sometimes nobody bothers to tell you about the meeting because they don't know whether you're interested. So you go to all the secretaries and ask, "What's going on today?" When you arrive in the morning, you make a quick cruise of the building and ask, "Are there any meetings? Are there any tours coming? Any visitors?" Frequently you get to know the people at the place very well; they become your informants, in the best sense of the word. They'll say, "I'm going to do an experiment this afternoon" or "I've got the family of this kid coming in to see me this afternoon" or "I'm teaching some medical students at ten-thirty — in case you'd like to come." I got the "Casey at the Bat" sequence in *High School* because this kid came up to me and said, "You ought to come see my English teacher."

ATKINS: There seems to be a lot of give and take between you and the people you're filming.

WISEMAN: You very quickly establish a relationship with the people, and they have to have a sufficient amount of confidence in you. At the same time you're making instant decisions about whether a sequence is worth shooting. And, of course, the people who see you regularly, the staff, are making their own judgments — they're deciding whether you're okay or whatever being okay may mean in their terms. They make a judgment about whether they can trust you sufficiently so that you can record what they're doing.

ATKINS: Obviously they must feel that your attitude toward them is non-judgmental, that you're going to let the events occur and allow them to speak for themselves. Otherwise they might not relax in the presence of your camera.

WISEMAN: Yes, I think that's right. It's not the total explanation. It's true of the staff, but it doesn't cover the situation where only the staff knows in advance and people come in from the outside. For instance, that explanation takes care of *High School, Basic Training,* or *Essene,* where the entire community knows that a film is being made. But it doesn't cover *Hospital* where half of the participants are just coming in the doors. They don't know in advance that a film is being made, and it's hard to say exactly why they aren't bothered by the camera. One other explanation, although I think it's an incomplete one, is that they're in a crisis situation and consequently more interested in getting whatever service they hope to get from the place. This is more important to them than worrying why a film is being made. But again, that's not an adequate reason because you also get a situation like the one in *Essene* where we followed a monk into a hardware store. The people in the store didn't ask anything about what we were doing there, why their pictures were being taken or their voices recorded. And yet there was no crisis. The monk was just buying a potato peeler.

ATKINS: What about the outsider in *Primate* — the woman who asks questions about the experiment with the monkey?

WISEMAN: She was the sister of the guy in charge of the experiment.

ATKINS: As an outsider, she had more conventional reactions. She was worried about the monkey.

WISEMAN: That's right. You know, I think part of the reason that the outsiders don't question the filming is that cameras are so commonplace in America. People watch television so much that it's not such a big event to see somebody making a film. Or they might just be flattered that you're taking their picture. Another possibility is that it has to do with passivity.

ATKINS: Just non-reaction.

WISEMAN: Yes, non-reaction. People simply don't respond. Even though you may explain what you're doing and you know it's understood, it's still a matter of indifference, really, whether you take their picture or not. They're indifferent to it. I don't understand the total explanation.

ATKINS: It's more like an aspect of the unpredictable behavior that you're observing.

WISEMAN: Yes, that's right. Perhaps it's good that there is no adequate explanation to the way people may react to the camera. If there was an explanation, you'd be able to predict it and it's just as well you can't.

ATKINS: What will you do next? Another film using the documentary form?

WISEMAN: Well, there are still a lot of things I want to do using this technique. I'm very interested in seeing how far you can push this approach.

ATKINS: In a sense all of your films are like a single film, aren't they?

WISEMAN: Yes, that's my view of it.

ATKINS: And you keep adding pieces to the total work.

WISEMAN: That's right. And they relate to each other. There are connections between some of the later films and the early films or between the early films and the most recent ones.

ATKINS: No matter how many films you make, it will still be a work in progress.

WISEMAN: Yes, it'll be a matter of seeing what you find out about yourself and about the possibilities of this kind of filmmaking.

CRITICS RESPOND
TO WISEMAN'S FILMS

Titicut Follies

TITICUT FOLLIES

Richard Schickel

Titicut Follies is a documentary film that tells you more than you could possibly want to know — but no more than you should know — about life behind the walls of one of those institutions where we file and forget the criminal insane. In this instance it is the state prison hospital maintained at Bridgewater in Massachusetts. The movie avoids nothing as it relentlessly pursues the horrible truth of a horrible situation and, in the process, reveals once again the seemingly infinite capacity of man to visit inhumanity on his fellow men.

It has been regarded as an exposé by critics, the public and the commonwealth of Massachusetts, which after letting Producer-Director Frederick Wiseman in with his camera, has been seeking in sundry ways to prevent him from showing what he shot. And an exposé it surely is. Wiseman assures us that the issues it raises extend beyond the boundaries of the Bay State, that indeed Bridgewater is a rather decent place, compared to similar snake pits elsewhere.

If so, we can be glad he limited himself to this one. The Bridgewater atmosphere is one of aimless hopelessness punctuated by outbursts of unthinking, almost ritualized violence. A psychiatrist turns an interview with an inmate into a sadistic baiting, or, with malicious cheerfulness, force-feeds a dying old man, while we wonder whether the ash from the doctor's carelessly dangling cigarette is really going to fall into the glop being funneled into the convulsively shuddering throat.

A society's treatment of the least of its citizens — and surely these are the least of ours — is perhaps the best measure of its civilization. The repulsive reality revealed in *Titicut Follies* forces us to contemplate our capacity for callousness. No one seeing this film can but believe that reform of the conditions it reports is urgent business, both as a matter of simple decency and as a symbolic act of concern for all who are desperately downtrodden.

Yet there is an esthetic dimension to the film that transcends the reformist. Because it was shot with hand-held cameras, and edited with deliberate lack of slickness, because it eschews even a voice-over narration to tie things together, this dimension has been overlooked by its critics. But it is present. Cutting back and forth from a variety show put on by the inmates — the *Titicut Follies* of the title — and the daily life of the place, Mr. Wiseman provides an adequate structure. But the esthetic dimension gains far more from sequences quite casually thrown at us within the larger scheme.

Examples: An inmate delivering an interminable, rational-sounding theory of history and politics which is, of course, totally mad; another inmate tonelessly singing to no one *The Ballad of the Green Berets*, the lengthy lyrics of which he has for some reason perfectly memorized; a paranoid making perfect sense as he argues for his release until, made desperate by his listeners' incomprehension, he presses too hard and reveals the depth of his illness.

The result in these instances is a shock of partial recognition, a sudden realization that these people are uncomfortably like us, their behavior only an exaggeration of that state we are pleased to call normal.

A similar identification is felt with the good folks of prison society — the rough-hewn but kindly head guard, the volunteer worker who somehow manages to organize a game of pin the tail on the donkey without being patronizing, the simple-hearted nurse who finds her reward in a thank-you letter from a released inmate. The ordinary human decency of these people is extraordinarily touching in this context. It is what we like to think we would offer if we were the sorts who lit candles instead of occasionally cursing the darkness, and it is both poignant and maddening to realize that such goodness is not enough, that this dismal atmosphere created by the state must inevitably snuff out the little lights they — or we in their situation — manage to fan into flame.

For all the fuss that was made over *Marat-Sade*, the self-consciousness of that representation of life in a 19th century French madhouse diminished its force. It was always careful at dangerous moments to remind us of its artificiality, of the fact that these were just actors miming craziness and not to worry about them.

There are no such easy outs for us in *Titicut Follies*. We cannot forget that its "actors" are there to stay, trapped in their own desperate inventions. When a work achieves that kind of power, it must be regarded as art, however artlessly, or even crudely, it generates it.

Boys dressed as cheerleaders in **High School**

HIGH SCHOOL

Pauline Kael

Movies sometimes connect with our memories in surprising ways. My vocabulary loosened up during my freshman year at Berkeley, and I was quite pleased when my mother remarked that the more educated I got the more I sounded like a truck driver. When I was a sophomore, a group of us went on a trip to Los Angeles, and our car broke down in Oxnard; we were huddled there in the garage at night when two garage mechanics got into an argument and started swearing at each other. As the rhythm of their fury and venom built up, those words that I had been so free with sounded hideous. I hadn't understood their function as swearwords — hadn't understood that they were meant to *insult* the person receiving them, that they were a way of *degrading* another person. That night at Oxnard came back when I saw Frederick Wiseman's *Law and Order* on N.E.T.: the police were cursed constantly by thieves and drunks. I had assumed that the police, coming from stricter and more religious backgrounds, didn't understand that college kids use the words in that liberated way that empties them of degradation or any real power; I hadn't considered that they hear that kind of talk so much they probably just can't stand it anymore. They're drowning in obscenity. College students are sometimes contemptuous of the cops for fearing *words,* but in the film those words really *are* weapons — often the *only* weapons of angry, frustrated people — and they're directed against the police all the time. *Law and Order* was the most powerful hour and a half of television that I've seen all year, and, since it won an Emmy, one might suppose that it would stir up interest in Wiseman's other films, but the New York Film Festival, which featured so many mindless forms of "artistic" moviemaking in the main auditorium, tossed some of the best new American pictures into the two-hundred-seat hall, and among them was Wiseman's *High School,* in its first New York showing.

There's a good deal to be said for finding your way to movie-making — as most of the early directors did — after living for some years in the world and gaining some knowledge of life outside show business. We are beginning to spawn teen-age filmmakers who at twenty-five may have a brilliant technique but are as empty-headed as a Hollywood hack, and they will become the next generation of hacks, because they don't know anything except moviemaking. Wiseman is a law professor and urban planner turned filmmaker, a muckraking investigative journalist who looks into American institutions with a camera and a tape recorder, and because he doesn't go in with naïve and *limiting* concepts, what he finds ties in with one's own experience.

Many of us grow to hate documentaries in school, because the use of movies to teach us something seems a cheat — a pill disguised as candy — and documentaries always seem to be about something we're not interested in. But Wiseman's documentaries show what is left out of both fictional movies and standard documentaries that simplify for a purpose, and his films deal with the primary institutions of our lives: *Titicut Follies* (Bridgewater, an institution in which we lock away the criminally insane), *High School* (a high school in a large Eastern city), and *Law and Order* (the Kansas City police force). Television has been accustoming us to a horrible false kind of "involvement"; sometimes it seems that the only thing the news shows can think of is to get close to emotion. They shove a camera and a microphone in front of people in moments of stress and disaster and grief, and ram their equipment into any pores and cavities they can reach. Wiseman made comparable mistakes in *Titicut Follies,* but he learned better *fast.*

High School is so familiar and so extraordinarily evocative that a feeling of empathy with the students floods over us. How did we live through it? How did we keep any spirit? When you see a kid trying to make a phone call and being interrupted with "Do you have a pass to use the phone?" it all floods back — the low ceilings and pale-green walls of the basement where the lockers were, the constant defensiveness, that sense of always being in danger of breaking some pointless, petty rule. When since that time has one ever needed a pass to make a phone call? This movie takes one back to where, one discovers, time has stood still. Here is the girl humiliated for having worn a short dress to the Senior Prom, being told it was "offensive" to the whole class. Here it is all over again — the insistence that you be "respectful," and the teachers' incredible instinct for "disrespect," their antennae always extended for that little bit of reservation or irony in your tone, the tiny spark that you desperately need to preserve your *self-respect.* One can barely hear it in the way a boy says "Yes, sir" to the dean, but the dean, ever on the alert, snaps, "Don't give me that 'Yes, sir' business! . . . There's no sincereness behind it." Here, all over again, is the dullness of high-school education:

> *Teacher: What on the horizon or what existed that forced labor to turn to collective bargaining? What was there a lack of?*
>
> *Girl: Communications?*
>
> *Teacher: Security, yes, communications, lack of security, concern for the job. The important thing is this, let's get to the beginning. First of all, there was the lack of security; second of all, there was a lack of communication. . . .*

The same old pseudo-knowledge is used to support what the schools think is moral. The visiting gynecologist in a sex-education class lectures the boys:

> *The more a fellow gets into bed with more different girls,*

97 /

the more insecure he is, and this shows up actually later in all the divorce statistics in America. . . . You can graph right on a graph, the more girls fellows got into bed with or vice-versa the higher the divorce rate, the greater the sexual inadequacy. . . .

And there's the beautiful military doubletalk when it's a question of a teacher's incompetence or unfairness. A boy protests a disciplinary action against him by a teacher, and after he has explained his innocence, the dean talks him into accepting the punishment "to establish that you can be a man and that you can take orders." The teachers are masters here; they're in a superior position for the only time in their lives, probably, and most of the petty tyrannies — like laying on the homework — aren't fully conscious. They justify each other's actions as a matter of course, and put the students in the wrong in the same indifferent way. They put a student down with "It's nice to be individualistic, but there are certain places to be individualistic," yet they never tell you where. How can one stand up against such bland authoritarianism? The teachers, crushing and processing, are the most insidious kind of enemy, the enemy with corrupt values who means well. The counsellor advising on college plans who says "You can have all your dream schools, but at the bottom you ought to have some college of last resort where you could be sure that you would go, if none of your dreams came through" certainly means to be realistic and helpful. But one can imagine what it must feel like to be a kid trudging off to that bottom college of last resort. There's a jolly good Joe of a teacher staging a fashion show who tells the girls, "Your legs are all too heavy. . . . Don't wear it too short; it looks miserable." And she's not wrong. But, given the beauty norms set up in this society, what are they to do? Cut off their legs? Emigrate? They're defeated from the legs up. Mediocrity and defeat sit in the offices and classrooms, and in those oppressive monitored halls.

We went through it all in order to graduate and be rid of passes forever, and once it was over we put it out of our minds, and here are the students still serving time until graduation, still sitting in class staring out the windows or watching the crawling hands of those ugly school clocks. So much of this education is part of an obsolete system of authority that broke down long ago, yet the teachers and administrators are still out there, persevering, "building character." *High School* seems an obvious kind of film to make, but as far as I know no one before has gone into an ordinary, middle-class, "good" (most of the students go to college) high school with a camera and looked around to see what it's like. The students are even more apathetic than we were. Probably the conflicts over the restrictions come earlier now—in junior high — and by high school the kids either are trying to cool it and get through to college or are just beaten down and sitting it out. We may have had a few teachers who really got us interested in something — it was one of the disappointments of the movie *Up the Down Staircase* that, treating this theme, it failed to be convincing — and, remembering our good luck, we could always say that even if a school was rotten, there were bound to be a few great teachers in it. This movie shows competent teachers and teachers who are trying their best but not one teacher who really makes contact in the way that means a difference in your life. The students are as apathetic toward the young English teacher playing and analyzing a Simon & Garfunkel record as toward the English teacher reciting "Casey at the Bat," and, even granted that as poetry there might not be much to choose between them — and perhaps Casey has the edge — still, one might think the students would, just as a *courtesy*, respond to the young teacher's attempt, the way one always gave the ingénue in the stock company a special round of applause. But it's very likely that high schools no longer *are* saved by live teachers, if hostility and cynicism and apathy set in right after children learn their basic skills. The students here sit on their hands even when a teacher tries. That's the only visible difference between this school and mine. I think we would have responded appreciatively to obvious effort, even if we thought the teacher was a jerk; these kids are beyond that. So the teachers are trapped, too. The teachers come off much worse than the police do in *Law and Order*. *High School* is a revelation because now that we see school from the outside, the teachers seem to give themselves away every time they open their mouths — and to be *unaware* of it.

At the end, the principal — a fine-looking woman — holds up a letter from a former student, on stationery marked "U.S.S. Okinawa," and reads it to the faculty:

> *I have only a few hours before I go. Today I will take a plane trip from this ship. I pray that I'll make it back but it's all in God's hands now. You see, I am going with three other men. We are going to be dropped behind the D.M.Z. (the Demilitarized Zone). The reason for telling you this is that all my insurance money will be given for the scholarship I once started but never finished, if I don't make it back. I am only insured for $10,000. Maybe it could help someone. I have been trying to become a Big Brother in Vietnam, but it is very hard to do. I have to write back and forth to San Diego, California, and that takes time. I only hope that I am good enough to become one. God only knows. My personal family usually doesn't understand me. . . . They say: "Don't you value life? Are you crazy?" My answer is: "Yes. But I value all the lives of South Vietnam and the free world so that they and all of us can live in peace." Am I wrong? If I do my best and believe in what I do, believe that what I do is right — that is all I can do. . . . Please don't say anything to Mrs. C. She would only worry over me. I am not worth it. I am only a body doing a job. In closing I thank everyone for what they all have done for me.*

And the principal comments, "Now when you get a letter like this, to me it means that we are very successful at [this] high school. I think you will agree with me."

It's a great scene — a consummation of the educational process we've been watching: They are successful at turning out bodies to do a job. Yet it's also painfully clear that the school must have given this soldier more kindness and affection than he'd ever had before. There must be other students who respond to the genuine benevolence behind the cant and who are grateful to those who labor to turn them into men. For those students, this schooling in conformity is successful.

Wiseman extends our understanding of our common life the way novelists used to — a way largely abandoned by the modern novel and left to the journalists but not often picked up by them. What he's doing is so simple and so basic that it's like a rediscovery of what we knew, or should know. We often want more information about the people and their predicaments than he gives, but this is perhaps less a criticism of Wiseman's method than it is a testimonial to his success in making us care about his subjects. With fictional movies using so little of our shared experience, and with the big TV news "specials" increasingly using that idiot "McLuhanite" fragmentation technique that scrambles all experience — as if the deliberate purpose were to make us indifferent to the life around us — it's a good sign when a movie sends us out wanting to know more and feeling that there is more to know. Wiseman is probably the most sophisticated intelligence to enter the documentary field in recent years.

Basic Training

BASIC TRAINING

——

Richard Fuller

You have to worry about civilization — American civilization, anyway — after seeing *Basic Training*. It is a sequel to *High School*. Two scenes from the earlier film are relevant here. An advisor chews out a student for not taking a detention — unfairly, the student insists, acting as his own lawyer. But justice is not the issue. "We want to prove to you," the advisor says, "that you're a man, that you can take orders." What young boy can resist proving "that you're a man"? Consider the alternative, in spite of Women's Lib. The other scene: the school principal, who happens to be a woman, reads a letter from a former Northeast student. He is in Vietnam. He does not know whether he will survive. If not, he wants his $10,000 insurance to be used as a scholarship. He has survived high school. He would sustain the system. He is the perfect student. He is a man. He takes orders.

The best way to go through basic training is do what you're told as you're told and they'll be no problems.

They climb down off a bus, these survivors of high school, and troop into a building for processing. Their bodies are measured, their heads shaved, their fingers printed. A strip of ID cards slides out of a machine. The image is a preview. There are interviews. A boy is asked if he is a conscientious objector. He replies no. They are lined up and injected. Another preview. The injections are shot into their arms as if from a pistol.

> *When you start trying to fight the system, that's when you get in trouble. So if you go along with the system, that's fine.*

Orientation. The recruits are standing. The camera is on the band leader. The field artillery march marches as an officer strides up the aisle. The camera pans with him as he climbs to the stage, then swings back to the director, who glances over his shoulder at the man of the hour and winds up the music. Another hint. Music will be an important theme in this post-high school world.

"Good morning, gentlemen," the CO says with assuring ease, and his last word lingers ironically in your memory, considering the ultimate aim of these "gentlemen." He welcomes them to Fort Knox "because your country needs your services. But I also extend to you a personal welcome on a person-to-person basis, so to speak." Then, as if reading Wiseman's mind, the CO says that the training is "essentially the same training that is given to other soldiers in basic training centers throughout the army." The part that stands for the whole process.

> *You just do what you're told as you're told and don't cause trouble, you'll have no problems.*

Basic training is not without humor and ironic wit. A recruit is instructed, with sober efficiency, in how to clean urinals. Serious. You've got to get down there to clean them because "the people try to shoot from way back." (Note the military language, even with regard to urinating: "shoot from way back.") Wiseman cuts from the urinal cleaning to a kid brushing his teeth to a film on the proper method of brushing teeth, complete with bouncing music. He conveys the effectiveness of that music by having his cameraman pan down to a kid's tapping foot. That music. It works.

Basic Training

The army is not just one man. It's millions of people. You come into a system, so to speak. You can't be the individual, as such, that you'd like to be.

They march toward and past the camera. The image is like a musical refrain that will recur throughout the film. Rhythm. Music.

They get their rifles. Ah, their rifles. A poem to their rifles: "This is an M-16 A One weapon. Not to be confused with the M-16. Now study it very carefully nut for nut, screw for screw, rivet for rivet and you will find very shortly that it is *exactly* — *exactly*, my friends — the same as the one I have in my hands. Millimeter for millimeter, square inch for square inch, the weapon you have in your hand is exactly the same as the weapon I have in my hand."

Why would you ever again need a woman? Consider the rifle range. A soldier demonstrates the weapon, not gun. ("A gun is a high trajectory weapon.") The soldier holds the weapon against his shoulder and fires. Then against his chin and fires. Against his thigh. His crotch. ("He's a married man." Laughter.) The link is perfect. The weapon is a phallus. It is virile. It kills. ("Prove that you're a man.")

What I say is when you get out in the jungle in Vietnam I don't believe the thought of killing a man will enter your mind if you get hit from three sides. Automatically, the only thing that's going to go into your mind is self-preservation. You probably won't have anything in your mind except survive, survive, survive.

This business of self-survival, during the education called basic training, takes different forms with different recruits. One youth, visited by his family, shows them his weapon, saying proudly, "Six pounds. $165. Semi-automatic. 20 rounds in three seconds." Dad advises, "The only thing is, you do what you're supposed to at all times." While Mom adds, "If you don't come out of here and become a true man, you'll never be a man. A true American soldier."

Another recruit, who happens to be black, discusses surviving and court martials with a white sergeant. "The army way," says the sergeant, "is you do what you're told and then you find out after." The black soldier drinks from his canteen and says, "Some things, you can do what you're told you might not live to come back and tell it." The sergeant suggests he might come back from combat with a medal. "I don't want no medals," says the black soldier. "I want my *life*. That's my medal."

There are ways of dealing with troublemakers. You can lose a month's pay, which goes to the old soldier's home, and you can serve seven days in correctional custody. But perhaps the most effective way is the combination of overt and subtle force used on troubled young Hickman. We first see him being marched back and forth separately from his platoon. He does not march well. "You're going to have to think about what you're doing, Hickman, or you'll never make it."

He obviously thinks too much about trying to "make it" because he attempts to kill himself. An officer calls the chaplain to discuss the problem: "He's got suicidal tendencies and, uh — suicidal tendencies. In other words, it seems like he wants to knock hisself off." The scene that follows, between Hickman and the chaplain, is one of those privileged sequences that are rare

Basic Training

enough in fiction films. They happen, miraculously, all the time in Wiseman's films. The camera holds on Hickman's young, still unformed face while the chaplain inquires why he tried to kill himself. It seems his fellow recruits do not like him because he fouls up. They think he is helpless. They have threatened him with a blanket party.

"You felt," says the chaplain, "that to, a, solve your problem you'd just put yourself to sleep, huh?"

"Yes."

"That the way you usually solve your problems?"

"No."

"I would much rather you come in here and tell me, 'Chaplain, I'm a little depressed today. Chaplain, I'm running into some difficulties.' Than to, you know, to just swallow a bunch of pills and say, 'Well, I'll just forget the whole thing.' That doesn't sound like somebody who's really trying to, a, really trying to get to the top. Does it?"

"No."

"All of life is really a lot of ups and downs, isn't it? And the difference, the difference between us is not so much whether we lose today or whether we win today but, you know, what we do as a result of having won or having lost. If we go around feeling sorry for ourselves, then there's no *hope* for us."

"Yes."

"The doctor can help you, the mental hygienist can help you, and I can help you. But you have to be willing to help yourself, too. If you fall down in the mud, you have to be willing to get up."

Hickman is thus helped up out of the mud. The chaplain walks him to the door, promising that he will be available for further conversation. After Hickman leaves, in another of those revealing touches that mark a Wiseman film, the chaplain glances at his watch. Time, and basic training, marches on.

As does Hickman. Later in the film, he is used by an instructor to demonstrate how to kill a man with a blackjack. Irony. Hickman is a good, obedient "victim." He gets a hand from the recruits in the bleachers.

If life is "really a lot of ups and downs," the army is in another category according to this pep talk laid on the recruits: "If you'll think about some of the teams in sports, which I know you follow either amateur or professional, all the great champions that you've ever thought of never went undefeated the whole time. The United States Army has never lost a war. It is undefeated. Think about that. That's quite a record. And you're part of this army at this time. And it's up to you to carry on this tradition." Pride. It could almost qualify as hubris.

> We all hope to get some of this war squared away by the time you young men get over there. But if we don't, it's going to be your job to carry on the tradition like myself, your forefathers, and theirs before them. They fought to keep this country free. They got your independence. It all started back, way back there about the Boston Tea Party. And it kept working up.

The film ends with an echo of the ending of *High School*. Graduation exercises. A young soldier, whose face could be used on recruiting posters and probably will be, gives an acceptance speech. He is receiving the American Spirit of Honor Award. He calls up that Spirit from Valley Forge, from Gettysburg and San Juan Hill. He remembers the doughboys of World War I in the trenches of France and Belgium. "When Fascism reared its ugly head, the American Spirit came forth and slew the dragon." (But it did not slay those time-honored clichés which, unlike old soldiers, do not fade away.) "And now Southeast Asia. Laying aside the political controversies surrounding this conflict, we see once again displayed that American Spirit of Honor. Fighting men dying for their nation and democracy. It's up to us to continue to fi--." A significant choking pause. "Fight. To pick up the banner." He concludes saying, "Lord, give us the strength to meet the challenge. I thank you."

He means it. He really means it. He is the perfect A-student graduate of basic training. And the officers mean it too. They believe with a messianic singlemindedness that is frightening. And the music comes up and the troops march by and the credits appear for this brilliant film.

Basic Training

It will not be possible — for me, anyway — to see war films in quite the same way after experiencing *Basic Training*. While watching Hickman try to endure the system, I thought of Private Robert E. Lee Prewitt in Fred Zinneman's *From Here to Eternity*. Considering that he is a thirty-year army man, Prew's definition of manhood is curious: "If a man don't go his own way, he's nothin'." Sergeant Warden, older and wiser in the army way, answers Prew: "Maybe a man *could* go his own way in the days of the pioneer. But today you gotta play ball." Time and Wiseman have proved Warden right. Prew ended up dead. Hickman ends up a willing "victim," eager to please. He plays ball.

I also thought of David Lean's *The Bridge on the River Kwai*, which ends with a reprise of the Colonel Bogey March. That music is moving and stirring near the beginning of the film when Colonel Nicholson leads his men into the prison camp. After the slaughter at the end, the music is ironic and the doctor's repeated cry of "Madness" hovers over the carnage. The music at the end of *Basic Training* works in a similarly ironic way. It is counterpoint to a system that seems, in the doctor's word, like "madness." *Basic Training* explains how a Colonel Nicholson gets created: you do what you're told. Period.

Frederick Wiseman, on sound, and William Brayne, on camera, work together like two hands on the same body, directed by the same alert, sensitive intelligence. If camera position is meaning — and it should be — Brayne's camera is invariably in the right place. The scene, for instance, when the CO arrives for orientation. The

Basic Training

camera is on the band leader because music is a large part of what basic training is about. There are ten brief sequences throughout the film of the platoon's marching and sometimes singing: they serve as a kind of musical refrain, they give the film pace, and they are exposition. Repetition is what the process is all about. And for once, long-lens shots have point and meaning beyond a striking pictorial touch: as the platoon marches away from the camera, individual bodies are flattened by the lens into a moving mass.

Wiseman invites our participating intelligence while watching his films. We begin to see echoes in his films: basic training is an extension of high school. And contrasts: compare the scene of Hickman and the chaplain with the scene in *Hospital* when a psychiatrist telephones a welfare worker to get help for a disturbed youth. The gulf between the chaplain's apparent concern and the psychiatrist's real concern is Grand Canyon wide. You might expect otherwise in a big city hospital. The problem with these institutions is that you cannot generalize, not with Wiseman around.

ESSENE

Patrick J. Sullivan

Viewers of Wiseman's documentaries may be quietly astonished at the nature and the impact of *Essene*, which does not take place in the gritty, ominous corridors of a prison or in an oppressive high school, nor in the congested interiors of an urban hospital, nor in the all too representative streets of a large American city. The film pays its attention to an Anglican religious community which on the surface has little or no connection to the urgent social and economic problems of the previous films. A monastery in a rural setting — what could constitute a more radical departure from the concerns of those earlier visions of institutional inhumanity? In *Essene* we watch instead the rituals, routines, exchanges among a group of men committed to a life which secludes them from the deterioration of cities, the profanities of schooling, the anxieties and paralysis of so many institutional roles. Instead of routine cruelty to a prisoner or student we have a benevolent laying on of hands in a monastery's Pentacostal prayer service; instead of tough white talk to a tough black juvenile we have a soft-toned discourse from the abbot regarding pharisaical and Christian definitions of law; instead of tears of shame, rage, and frustration in the other films we have the fears of a long-

A monk in **Essene**

haired postulant as he bemoans his difficulty in becoming a part of the community.

With *Essene* Wiseman focuses our attention on the quite specific collisions between a quite limited number of individuals. The examination of social issues in this film is not accumulated through quick-cut series of collage sequences of particulars so much as it is achieved through the close-quartered, representative drama of reconciling self-discovery and contentment with social responsibility and cooperativeness. The film as a whole is paced with several short scenes conveying the daily realities and routines of life in a monastery: farming, meals, drives to town; but Wiseman creates this film's special energy, complexity, and dramatic unity through five or six fairly lengthy sequences (*Essene* has fewer sequences than any of the other films). As *Essene* disengages us from the visual immediacy of a more familiar world, we come into the presence of a more freshly dramatic situation than any of the other films provided.

The film opens with shots of individual monks sitting in a group — strong but tight faces, unimpressive and familiar in a tense sort of dignity. It is a prayer meeting of sorts, each person calling the rest to join him in remembering a worthy person or occasion. There is a sustained evocation of a woman in New York whose group therapy became "an experience in community" and whose memory seems to judge in some way the present group. There is mention of Buber, and Hiroshima. There is strong emotion, but muted and ritualized by both the place and the persons. The group is a collection, the film makes us feel, of individuals struggling quietly to create community. The spoken word appears an awkward and weak vehicle.

Cut to a conversation between the abbot and a stern, disagreeable monk who disapproves of being called by his first name and who eyes the abbot throughout the exchange with crochety suspicion and fear. The abbot seems to be appealing for means of drawing this man into the fold, of discovering some basis in mutually shared values to overcome the other's resistance, his rigidity. But when the abbot invokes the shared belief in Christ as a means of community, his opponent declines the offer of such kinship. Though these men live together, they are temperamentally and spiritually worlds apart.

This mean yet comic antagonist to the abbot's soft-spoken and benign hopefulness we see later as he drives into town for a potato peeler and other odds and ends. In the hardware store he repeatedly fails to flinch at being called by a wrong first name, and his smile and easy manner are in remarkable contrast to what he "gave" the abbot. He partly enjoys the stereotypes of the monastery the store worker promotes. This monk, we realize, is reaching for nothing beyond his own self-protection and secure status as an individual in an atomized, not communal, society. His stubborn, undramatic resistance to the community's growing emphasis on the shared life represents one decided strain on the monastery's attempts to manage the message of its faith.

115 /

The viewer can locate the many problems of this world through this man. The ritual of the Mass service is now group-oriented and in English, and the monastery holds prayer vigils heavily emotionalized. Clearly this monk stands opposed to these tides of change. He may be only one, but he continually captures the attention of the community in its analysis of its faulty movement and recurring disabilities. The world of the town and the monastery may be bridged by this man, but only here does he act as any sort of connection or mediator. No bridge over troubled water is he meant or likely to be. Loneliness masked as self-righteous isolation and fear hiding behind sterile personal dogmatism: as others reach out for joy and sing "Heal him, sweet Jesus," the implacable loner heads for town.

If this monastery is in actuality anything but ideal, here is clearly one reason. In a setting where everyone counts, those who discount others take a stiff toll on the group. In a setting where each is living a life *immediately* symbolic, revelatory of one's ultimate values, the reactionary is influential, seen, pronounced in his individual authority (this monk plays the anti-abbot, in fact). By his presence he then strains community for others by denying it for himself, diminishes a sense of collective authority and leadership by refusing to recognize as valid the private level of need, trust, and hope which motivate such values in the first place.

Such a refusal, symptomatic of bigotry and paranoia themselves symptomatic of a stunted emotional growth, is not the only sort of behavior which threatens this small group of men. More visible and volatile, the catalyst for *Essene's* evolving drama, is the presence of a highly emotional and assertive postulant who incarnates not rigid retreat but anarchic reformation. His arch-opponent is law made legalistic and petty by a small mind and a man fearful of compassion. But the hungry postulant's other enemy is — in an important way — community itself, an entity whose sustenance demands either a merging of individual selves or a transcendence of those selves as merely individual. This postulant, however, is seeking a salvation in and through this community, and he wants that community "now!" He might pronounce sentimentally the platitude that "people understand in the long

Essene

run," but his full self is cinematically captured as he sits expansively alone at a piano moaning a song of self ("Deep River") which drifts in currents of personal preoccupation all but impossible to deliver over to the shared experiences of a community.

Two sorts of individualism threatening a never yet and always to be realized community: *Essene* gradually focuses on this basic drama, and more intently on the principal arbiter and cypher for the entire group, the abbot himself. He must attempt to mute or erode the mean-minded reactionary spirit of the one monk while at the same time giving some direction and criticism to the wild

117 /

Celebration of Mass in **Essene**

intensity and desperate theatricality of the other. Through the centuries-old monastic theology he must attempt to articulate a therapy for the lives of men often dangerously far from "authentic contemplative peace," the ideal of a monastery according to one scholarly treatment. So the abbot speaks in this film always in a context of disputes and personal animosities. Visually he remains benign and sympathetic, his voice calm and cautious, a blend of quiet judgment and pious hopefulness. He speaks of the necessity of the "Spirit infusing the letter of the law," and how in Biblical times the Pharisees irresponsibly tamed the dialectic by siding with law over against Spirit. That spirit infusing law the abbot is clearly reaching for in his community, one which he notes is filled with tension because it rejects the pharisaical approach to life.

That rejection involves in this case a perplexing and perplexed affirmation from this monastic group of the "Pentacostal movement" in the Anglican Church: a new emotionalism and group-consciousness in liturgy and prayer. Such a movement feeds the troubled spirit of the postulant toward angry and chaotic outbursts of passion as it feeds the no-first-namer with greater disgust for change and accommodation to such trends in the brotherhood. *Essene* then portrays a small society at work redefining itself both in the light of its particular members but also in light of larger cultural forces it both moves toward and with. The abbot is trying to steer a middle course between firm rejection and over-eager acceptance of the new spirit (he is clearly troubled by many of its psychological and social consequences).

Looked at as a whole, the film sympathetically directs our attention first to the absence of shared experiences and directions in the community and then gives us several opportunities to witness modes of defining and arbitrating the conflicts. As the film builds to its complex conclusion, the question of leadership burns incandescently. The abbot has led in the past through a mild but skilled consensus-building, carefully avoiding outright exclusions of anyone and therefore vulnerable to the consequences of an uneasy truce. As the film develops, that uneasy truce shows clear signs of no longer serving its limited purpose. One monk, the senior mentor figure, and others at one point insist that the dissidents must stop fighting and "start loving the brothers." The abbot alone is faced with the task of finding a politics fitted to that simple commandment. He comes to examine the style of his own leadership near the end, and appears to emerge renewed for the possibly larger confrontations to come as the "center" ceases to hold and the community's very survival is at stake.

He works for rapprochement, renconciliation, the fusion of opposites: Martha — Mary, law — spirit, passion — discipline, his own hortatory teaching and the "laying on of hands" group spirituality. His leadership is actually and potentially only so effective, however, as the larger questions and authority become apparent. Can the group generate a collective strength insuring cooperativeness and tolerance? Can the past traditions accommodate

119 /

Essene

themselves to a consciousness so group-oriented that the contemplative ideals are not hopelessly compromised? Can an ages-
old theological symbol-system fulfill the demands for personal
therapy placed on it by these new group dynamics?

Such questions emerge organically from *Essene,* and they are
scarcely so private to the world of an Anglican monastery somewhere in the midwest that they don't deserve our secular and
even "anti-denominational" attention. Wiseman has shown in his
accustomed documentary style — heavy on representative situations
and encounters, a patient watching and listening for accumulated
meanings — that any group which has accepted the necessity of
reconstitution in today's culture is battling with basic problems
of social philosophy and practice. The abbot remains affirmative
that Martha and Mary can occupy the same household and serve
the same master. Others may wonder if they are even any longer
sisters in anything but name. *Essene* is a film with a special
resonance which may make it Wiseman's most important to date.

EXCERPTS FROM REVIEWS

Wiseman doesn't "get" the cops, and he doesn't glorify them. What he does get is a vivid impression of their working lives and through this a complex sense of what it means to be in their position in a large American city. It's not an enviable position: much of the work is banal and repetitive and inconclusive, but there is the implicit threat of violence in any radio call. Moreover, the cops are expected to dispose of countless routine problems — drunks, accidents, family quarrels — that can't be "solved" to anyone's satisfaction and that most "decent" or privileged middle-class people don't want to touch.

> — **Gary Arnold**
> *The Washington Post*
> (March 7, 1970)

In some ways, *Basic Training* is the most demanding of Wiseman's films. In *High School,* there was the limitation of graduation. Bad as high schools may be, they don't kill many people, and the odds are pretty good that one may live through the experience. In *Titicut Follies* and in *Hospital* the affliction was mostly external and given. Madness and illness happen in the world, and while our institutions ought to respond better, we have learned to accept certain kinds of tough realities. (It was precisely in those scenes in *Titicut Follies* where the psychiatrists were clearly driving the patients crazy, those scenes in *Hospital* where the doctors were dealing with demented social workers who were causing the suffering, that one writhed most energetically.) Here, the whole thing is man-made. There is nobody to turn to, nothing to blame but ourselves. And, just as in *Law and Order,* the very virtues of the institution and its men (the police there, the instructors and officers here), turn the rage back where it belongs — upon us, members of the intelligent, concerned responsible public.

— **David R. Slavitt**
Contempora
(September-February 1972)

The outstanding and inexplicable quality of Wiseman's cinema is his ability to be ever present, to capture with his camera and recorder a half-spoken word or the shadow of a lie, without ever seeming to intrude or to condition the way his subjects behave in the presence of the film crew. Beyond this is the power to organize the material (the editing is a mammoth task of sifting through many more miles of film than ever appear on the screen) so as never to compromise the truth of the record, but to convey at once the chaos of human activity in a society where the social machines are perilously overloaded, and the makeshift sort of order that can sometimes be imposed by sheer force of good will.

— **David Robinson**
The (London) Times
(November 30, 1973)

Essene is one of the best religious films ever made. This, despite the fact that it lacks a temple rape, chariot race, trace of brimstone, or even a soundtrack of God shouting through echo chambers. It is also talky, intellectual, and has no stars.

But brace yourself for the intensity in *Essene* and fasten your safety belt. Before the film has ended, a viewer has been plummeted into an ecclesiastical *Who's Afraid of Virginia Woolf?* with emotions rawly exposed. Fred Wiseman's cinema vérité look at life inside a monastery also studies the essential meanings inherent in any institutional framework. . . . It is a fluid, extraordinarily honest .and non-theatrical experience that stands in stark contrast to the extravagant, banal, vulgarly celebrity-studded revivalist hours purchased in prime-time TV or the million-dollar treacly spiritual thuds coming out of a Hollywood factory.

> — **Malcolm Boyd**
> *The New York Times*
> (November 12, 1972)

A subtle novel often develops an explicit point of view, and so does *Primate* . . . most firmly, yet most poetically, in a decapitation sequence near the film's end. The victim, a winsome little squirrel monkey, is shown swinging happily in his cage. Then, step by horrifying step, he becomes less and less a sensate creature and more a specimen. . . . The "de-animalization" of the monkey becomes a metaphor for the subtler kind of de-humanization afflicting our social institutions generally — emergency room, classroom, monastery, barracks. And, as *Primate* so vividly demonstrates, it permeates even the realm of "pure" science, with animals the inanimate means to dubious ends.

It is easy to forget these institutional abuses until a Frederick Wiseman points his camera and reminds us with merciless clarity that when society's institutions are as insensitive as this, many of society's members are as exploited as those monkeys on a cold steel table.

> — **Chuck Kraemer**
> *The New York Times*
> (December 1, 1974)

123 /

BIOGRAPHY

Born in 1930, Frederick Wiseman lives in Cambridge, Massachusetts, with his wife and two children. He is a member of the
Massachusetts Bar Association. His films are distributed through
his own company, Zipporah Films in Boston.

1951	B.A., Williams College
1954	L.L.B., Yale Law School
1955-56	U. S. Army
1956-57	Student Law Faculty, University of Paris
1958-60	Instructor in Legal Medicine, Boston University Law-Medicine Institute
1959-61	Lecturer-in-Law, Boston University Law School
1961-62	Russell Sage Foundation Fellow, Graduate School of Arts and Sciences, Harvard University
1963-71	Research Associate, Department of Sociology, Brandeis University

1963	Producer, Shirley Clarke's *The Cool World*
1966-70	Treasurer, OSTI, Inc. (Organization for Social and Technical Innovation, Inc.), a consulting company
1967	Directed, produced, and edited his first film, *Titicut Follies*
1970-present	Founded Zipporah Films, Inc.
1972	Recipient, U. S. State Department Grant to attend Belgrade International Film Festival U.S.I.A. sponsored Film Festival Tour of Yugoslavia and Poland Public Media Panel, National Endowment for the Arts
1973	Received Honorary Doctorate of Humane Letters, University of Cincinnati

Visiting Lecturer:
   Yale Law School; Harvard College; University of Iowa; University of Pittsburgh; Portland State College; Nebraska Wesleyan; Hollins College; Salisbury State College; SUNY at Buffalo, New York; Earlham College; Baldwin-Wallace College; Case Western Reserve University

Publications:
   "Psychiatry and Law: Use and Abuse of Psychiatry in a Murder Case," *American Journal of Psychiatry*, October 1961.
   Co-author, "Implementation," section of *Report of The President's Commission on Law Enforcement and Administration of Justice*, Government Printing Office, Washington, D. C.
   "Law and Order," a comment on the making of the film, *Police Chief*, September 1969.

FILMOGRAPHY

TITICUT FOLLIES (1967)

Director, Producer, and Editor: Frederick Wiseman.
Photography: John Marshall.
Running time: 87 minutes. Black & white.
Filmed at the State Prison for the Criminally Insane at Bridgewater, Massachusetts.
Best Film, Mannheim International Filmweek, 1967.
Best Film Dealing with the Human Condition, Festival Dei Popoli, 1967.
Exhibited at: New York Film Festival, 1967; Edinburgh Film Festival, 1968.

HIGH SCHOOL (1968)

Director, Producer, and Editor: Frederick Wiseman.
Photography: Richard Leiterman.
Running time: 75 minutes. Black & white.
Filmed at Northeast High School in Philadelphia, Pennsylvania.
Exhibited at: Festival Dei Popoli, the Spoleto Film Festival, Edinburgh Film Festival, 1969; San Francisco International Film Festival, 1969; and the New York Film Festival, 1970.

LAW AND ORDER (1969)

Director, Producer, and Editor: Frederick Wiseman.
Photography: William Brayne.
Running time: 81 minutes. Black & white.
Filmed in Kansas City, Missouri, and at the Kansas City Police Department.
Emmy Award, Best News Documentary, 1969.
Exhibited at: Spoleto, 1969; Venice Film Festival, 1969; Edinburgh Film Festival, 1969; Festival Dei Popoli, 1970.

HOSPITAL (1970)

Director, Producer, and Editor: Frederick Wiseman.
Photography: William Brayne.
Running time: 84 minutes. Black & white.
Filmed at Metropolitan Hospital in New York City.
Emmy Award, Best News Documentary and Best Director, 1970.
Catholic Filmmaker's Award, Mannheim, 1970.
Dupont Award, Columbia School of Journalism Award for Best Documentary, 1970.
Exhibited at: Edinburgh Film Festival, 1970; Festival Dei Popoli, 1970; National Education Film Festival, San Francisco, 1969.

Welfare

BASIC TRAINING (1971)

Director, Producer, and Editor: Frederick Wiseman.
Photography: William Brayne.
Running time: 89 minutes. Black & white.
Filmed at Fort Knox, Kentucky.
Exhibited at: Edinburgh Film Festival, 1971; London Film Festival, 1972.

ESSENE (1972)

Director, Producer, and Editor: Frederick Wiseman.
Photography: William Brayne.
Running time: 86 minutes. Black & white.
Filmed at a Benedictine Monastery in Michigan.
Gabriel Award, 1972, Catholic Broadcasters Association.
Exhibited at: Edinburgh Film Festival, 1972; Festival Dei Popoli, 1972.

JUVENILE COURT (1973)

Director, Producer, and Editor: Frederick Wiseman.
Photography: William Brayne.
Running time: 144 minutes. Black & white.
Filmed at the Juvenile Court of Memphis and Shelby County, Tennessee.
Silver Phoenix Award, Atlanta International Film Festival, 1974.
Emmy Nomination, Best News Documentary, 1974.
Cine Gold Eagle Award, Council of International Nontheatrical Events, Washington, D. C., 1974.
Exhibited at: London Film Festival, Festival Dei Popoli, 1973.

/   130

PRIMATE (1974)

Director, Producer, and Editor: Frederick Wiseman.
Photography: William Brayne.
Running time: 105 minutes. Black & white.
Filmed at the Yerkes Regional Primate Research Center in Atlanta,
Georgia.

WELFARE (1975)

Producer, Director, and Editor: Frederick Wiseman.
Photography: William Brayne.
Running time: 167 minutes. Black & white.
Filmed at two welfare centers in New York City. National television
premiere on September 24, 1975.

In addition to his own films, Wiseman also produced *The Cool
World* (1963), directed by Shirley Clarke and based on the novel
by Warren Miller.

RETROSPECTIVE SCREENINGS

8th Annual Chicago International Film Festival, 1972, Gold Hugo
    Award, presented in conjunction with a retrospective of all of
    Wiseman's films from *Titicut Follies* to *Essene*.
American Film Festival, Educational Film Library Association, 1974,
    Red Ribbon Awards for *High School, Hospital, Essene*, and
    Juvenile Court.
London Film Festival, National Film Theatre, 1972, showings of
    High School, Law and Order, Hospital, Essene, and *Basic
    Training*. British premiere of *Juvenile Court*, 1973, and *Primate*,
    1974.

TELEVISION SHOWINGS

Law and Order, Hospital, Basic Training, Essene, Juvenile Court, Primate, and *Welfare* have been broadcast nationally by the Public Broadcasting Service.

RENTAL SOURCES

Except for *Titicut Follies*, Frederick Wiseman's films are available for rental in 16mm from: Zipporah Films, Inc., 54 Lewis Wharf, Boston, Massachusetts 02110; telephone (617) 742-6680.
Titicut Follies is available for rental in 16mm from Grove Press Film Division, 53 East 11th Street, New York, N. Y. 10003.

Welfare

SELECTIVE BIBLIOGRAPHY

Arnold, Gary. *"Law and Order,"* *The Washington Post* (March 7, 1970).

Barsam, Richard Meran. *Nonfiction Film: A Critical History.* New York: Dutton, 1973. Portion of a chapter devoted to Wiseman.

Berg, Beatrice. "I Was Fed Up With Hollywood Fantasies," *The New York Times* (February 1, 1970). Interview.

Boyd, Malcolm. *"Essene,"* *The New York Times* (November 12, 1973).

Boyum, Joy Gould. "Watching Real Life Problems," *The Wall Street Journal* (October 1, 1973). Review of *Juvenile Court*.

Cass, James. *"High School,"* *Saturday Review*, 52 (April 19, 1969).

Coles, Robert. "Stripped Bare at the Follies," *The New Republic*, 158 (January 20, 1968). Essay on *Titicut Follies*.

Crain, Jane Larkin. "TV Vérité," *Commentary* (December 1973).

Denby, David. "Documenting America," *The Atlantic*, 225, 3 (March 1970).

Desilets, Michael E. "Fred Wiseman: *Titicut* Revisited," *Film Library Quarterly*, IV, 2 (Spring 1971).

Featherstone, Joseph. *"High School,"* *The New Republic*, 160 (June 21, 1969).

Film Facts, X, 21 (December 1, 1967). Summary of reviews of *Titicut Follies*.

Friedenberg, Edgar Z. "Ship of Fools: The Films of Frederick Wiseman," *The New York Review of Books*, XVII, 6 (October 21, 1971).

Halberstadt, Ira. "An Interview with Fred Wiseman," *Filmmakers Newsletter*, VII, 4 (February 1974).

Kael, Pauline. "*High School*," *The New Yorker*, 45 (October 18, 1969).

Kraemer, Chuck. "Fred Wiseman's *Primate* Makes Monkeys of Scientists," *The New York Times* (December 1, 1974).

McClean, Deckle. "The Man Who Made *Titicut Follies*," *Boston Sunday Globe Magazine* (July 27, 1969).

McWilliams, Donald E. "Frederick Wiseman," *Film Quarterly*, XXIV, 1 (Fall 1970). Interview.

Mamber, Stephen. "The New Documentaries of Frederick Wiseman," *Cinema*, VI, 1. Article and interview.

_____. *Cinema Vérité in America: Studies in Uncontrolled Documentary*. Cambridge: MIT Press, 1973. Chapter on Wiseman.

Morgenstern, Joseph. "It Don't Make Sense," *Newsweek*, 75 (February 9, 1970). Review of *Hospital*.

Newsweek. "Tempest in a Snakepit." 70 (December 4, 1967). Review of *Titicut Follies*.

Schickel, Richard. "Where Misery Must Be Confronted: Frederick Wiseman's *Hospital*," *Life*, 68 (February 6, 1970).

Sidel, Victor W. "*Hospital* on View," *The New England Journal of Medicine*, 282, 5 (January 29, 1970).

Slavitt, David R. "*Basic Training*," *Contempora*, II, 1 (September-February 1972).

Sterritt, David. "*Juvenile Court*," *Christian Science Monitor* (October 1, 1973).

Sullivan, Patrick J. "What's All the Cryin' About? The Films of Frederick Wiseman," *The Massachusetts Review* (Summer 1972).

DATE DUE

Contents

The preceding chapters illustrate a relatively new direction for reading research. To be successful this line of research requires an overarching framework—a model of the reading system within which to make sense of findings on particular skills and individual differences. One way to construct such a model is component skills analysis.

Much progress has been made in conducting good basic research on reading. Some progress has been made in establishing productive interactions between basic research and applied research. However, very little progress has been made in using the results of this research in formulating classroom practice. What can be done?

Several journals that publish high quality research on reading and a number of books that provide systematic introductions to the area are available.

Editor's Notes

This volume presents five chapters and two commentaries concerned with how children become readers of a language that previously they only spoke. Though the chapters address a wide range of topics, they share an underlying theoretical theme: Reading is a complex, skilled performance whose mastery depends on establishing an information-processing system that is partly new and partly old. The old part consists of the integrative cognitive processes by which the information content of spoken language is comprehended, remembered, and used to answer questions, draw inferences, solve problems, and carry out other acts of thought. The new part consists of the perceptual processes by which information is obtained from the printed page and fed into the integrative processes, plus additions or modifications to the integrative processes needed to accommodate differences in form and function between written and spoken language. The new perceptual processes include mechanisms by which printed words can be recognized. They may also include mechanisms by which expectations about upcoming words can be formed and used to aid the mechanisms of word recognition, though this is a hotly debated issue (compare, for example, Becker, 1982; McConkie and Zola, 1981; Seidenberg, 1983; Stanovich, 1980). The modifications or additions to the integrative processes include the knowledge and skills for handling types of information, syntactic constructions, rhetorical devices, and discourse-organizing techniques that are found much more often in written language than in spoken language.

According to this skill theory of reading development, both the new perceptual processes and the modified integrative processes must eventually be acquired. However, a working assumption is made that, early in reading experience, integrative processes are much the same whether one is listening or reading, whereas the perceptual processes are highly specialized to deal with the particular input medium that is involved. Though only a first approximation to the truth, as Bock and Brewer show in Chapter Four, this assumption generates a hypothesis from which follow skill theory's two major predictions about beginning reading. The hypothesis is that the initial transition from reasonably successful listener to equally successful reader requires new perceptual processes to be established and coordinated with already existing integrative processes of comprehension, memory, and thought. The first of the consequent predictions is that the primary task among the many obstacles facing the beginning reader is to learn to recognize words in print rather than in speech. Effective word recognition is held to be a setting condition for the successful operation of the integrative processes, both old and new. Therefore, if word recognition is not mastered, little progress toward skilled reading is likely to be

1

made. Second, the nature of the information-processing system, and especially how well its old parts and new parts work together, is as important to reading progress as the individual strength or weakness of any particular process that contributes to the system. A reader with poorly integrated skills is potentially just as handicapped, though in a different way, as the reader with an actual skill deficit.

Neither of these points is new as a claim about reading development, but their emergence together as the joint prediction of a potentially systematic and coherent cognitive theory is relatively new. No single researcher has created skill theory. It is arising from the collective efforts of a large number of cognitive, developmental, and educational psychologists. Whereas all information-processing approaches emphasize the characteristics of particular component processes, the skill-theoretic view differs from many others in the extent of its emphasis on systemic factors in reading success. One can see the roots of this aspect of the approach in the work of the group led by Eleanor Gibson and Harry Levin at Cornell University (see Levin and Williams, 1970, and especially Biemiller, 1970, as well as the classic text of Gibson and Levin, 1975) and in the more recent efforts of Guthrie (1973) and Rumelhart (1977). In line with this emphasis, the first commentary, Chapter Six, is built on the claim that recent reading research has focused too much on studies of single processes that contribute to reading and too little on studies of the system into which these processes are organized. Similarly, recent research has focused too much on studies of single factors that are correlated with individual differences in the success of reading development and too little on studies of the overall pattern of individual differences to which the factors contribute. The goal of Chapter Six is to describe a particular method of research and theory construction intended to overcome these deficiencies.

Despite its concern with the concept of a reading system, however, skill theory also differs from the so-called psycholinguistic approach (for example, Goodman, 1967, 1981; Smith, 1978, 1979) by emphasizing, within the systemic framework, the central importance of the perceptual processes, especially for beginning readers (see Carr, 1981; Carr and Evans, 1981; Lesgold and Perfetti, 1981; Singer, 1982; Stanovich, 1980) and by stressing the need to take account of the differences as well as the similarities between written and spoken language (see Rubin, 1980; Tannen, 1982). The emphasis on perceptual processes is implicit in the choice of topics covered in the chapters as a group and quite explicit in the arguments made by Brown and Haynes in Chapter Two and by Evans in Chapter Five. The stress on differences between written and spoken language is admirably represented by Bock and Brewer in Chapter Four.

The purpose of this volume, then, is to illustrate the skill-theoretic approach by example. The particular examples included were chosen for two reasons: They touch systematically on the range of levels of processing from visual encoding to comprehension and memory, and they provide an indication

of both the theoretical and the practical implications of the approach. Thus, the chapters start with the relation between orthographic knowledge and phonological knowledge as factors in the development of word recognition and spelling and proceed through several levels to the role of knowledge of the conventions of spoken discourse organization in comprehension and memory of written text. In all the chapters, the primary concern is with interactions or interdependencies between two or more levels of processing or the associated bodies of knowledge that support the processing. Chapters One, Four, and Five pay special attention to the relationships between the old part of the information-processing system (the part that deals with spoken language) and the new part being established to deal with written language. In Chapter Two, Brown and Haynes are concerned with the interaction between reading-specific skills already established for one language and new reading-specific skills needed for a second language. In Chapter Three, Omanson investigates the interaction between the meanings of words and the meaning of the text comprised by the words, given that the words have been encoded. These chapters are followed by the two commentaries. Chapter Six addresses the other chapters from a theoretical perspective, attempting to explicate the systems-oriented, skill-theoretic approach that aspires to unite them, whereas Chapter Seven addresses the issues raised in the preceding chapters from a practical perspective, attempting to evaluate their potential to influence classroom teaching.

Thomas H. Carr
Editor

References

Becker, C. A. "The Development of Semantic Context Effects: Two Processes or Two Strategies?" *Reading Research Quarterly*, 1982, *17*, 482–502.

Biemiller, A. J. "The Development of the Use of Graphic and Contextual Information as Children Learn to Read." *Reading Research Quarterly*, 1970, *6*, 75–96.

Carr, T. H. "Building Theories of Reading Ability: On the Relation Between Individual Differences in Cognitive Skills and Reading Comprehension." *Cognition*, 1981, *9*, 73–114.

Carr, T. H., and Evans, M. A. "Classroom Organization and Reading Ability: Are Motivation and Skill Antagonistic Goals?" In J. R. Edwards (Ed.), *The Social Psychology of Reading*. Silver Spring, Md.: Institute for Modern Language, 1981.

Gibson, E. J., and Levin, H. *The Psychology of Reading*. Cambridge, Mass.: M.I.T. Press, 1975.

Goodman, K. S. "Reading: A Psycholinguistic Guessing Game." *Journal of the Reading Specialist*, 1967, *4*, 126–135.

Goodman, K. S. "Letter to the Editor (Reply to Stanovich)." *Reading Research Quarterly*, 1981, *16*, 477–478.

Guthrie, J. T. "Models of Reading and Reading Disability." *Journal of Educational Psychology*, 1973, *65*, 9–18.

Lesgold, A., and Perfetti, C. A. *Interactive Processes in Reading*. Hillsdale, N.J.: Erlbaum, 1981.

4

Levin, H., and Williams, J. P. *Basic Studies on Reading.* New York: Basic Books, 1970.

McConkie, G. W., and Zola, D. "Language Constraints and the Functional Stimulus in Reading." In A. M. Lesgold and C. A. Perfetti (Eds.), *Interactive Processes in Reading.* Hillsdale, N.J.: Erlbaum, 1981.

Rubin, A. "A Theoretical Taxonomy of the Differences between Oral and Written Language." In R. J. Spiro, B. C. Bruce, and W. F. Brewer (Eds.), *Theoretical Issues in Reading Comprehension.* Hillsdale, N.J.: Erlbaum, 1980.

Rumelhart, D. E. "Toward an Interactive Model of Reading." In S. Dornic and P. M. A. Rabbitt (Eds.), *Attention and Performance VI.* Hillsdale, N.J.: Erlbaum, 1977.

Seidenberg, M. "Two Kinds of Lexical Priming." Paper presented at the annual meeting of the Psychonomic Society, San Diego, Calif., November 1983.

Singer, M. H. (Ed.). *Competent Reader, Disabled Reader: Research and Application.* Hillsdale, N.J.: Erlbaum, 1982.

Smith, F. *Understanding Reading.* New York: Holt, Rinehart and Winston, 1978.

Smith, F. *Reading Without Nonsense.* New York: Teachers College Press, 1979.

Stanovich, K. E. "Toward an Interactive-Compensatory Model of Individual Differences in Reading Fluency." *Reading Research Quarterly,* 1980, *16,* 32–71.

Tannen, D. (Ed.). *Spoken and Written Language.* Norwood, N.J.: Ablex, 1982.

Thomas H. Carr is associate professor of cognitive and developmental psychology at Michigan State University.

Theories of syllable structure, such as the notion that initial consonant clusters are cohesive units, can help us to understand the development of reading-related skills.

Phonemic Analysis, Spelling, and Reading

Rebecca Treiman

To understand how children learn to read and spell and the kinds of difficulties that they face, we need to know more about their conceptions of spoken language. Such knowledge is important because written English is primarily an alphabetic system—to a first approximation, it represents the sounds of the spoken language. Although exceptions occur, each letter (or pair of letters) generally corresponds to a unit of sound called a *phoneme* (Venezky, 1970). Because of the alphabetic nature of English writing, many investigators have suggested that the ability to conceive of spoken words as sequences of phonemes is important in learning to read and write (Gleitman and Rozin, 1977; Gough and Hillinger, 1980; Liberman, 1982; Mattingly, 1972; Routh and Fox, 1984; Rozin and Gleitman, 1977; Stanovich, 1982; Tunmer and Bowey, 1984). For example, unless a child is aware that the words *bat* and *bread* begin with the same phoneme, the child will not understand why both words' spellings begin with the same letter, *b*. Unless a child is aware that *motorcycle* contains more phonemes (nine) than *mow* (two), he or she will not understand why the

The author gratefully acknowledges the assistance of Peggy Ericson, Shellie Haut-Rogers, and Brett Kessler with the research described here. The research reported here and the preparation of this chapter were supported by grants from NSF, NICHHD, and the Spencer Foundation.

T. H. Carr (Ed.). *The Development of Reading Skills.* New Directions for Child Development, no. 27. San Francisco: Jossey-Bass, March 1985.

former has more letters in its spelling than the latter (Rozin and others, 1974). Although adults who are literate in an alphabetic writing system can easily analyze spoken syllables, such as *bat* and *mow,* into phonemes, such analysis is difficult for many prereaders and beginning readers. For example, young children often have difficulty counting the number of phonemes in a syllable (Liberman and others, 1974; Treiman and Baron, 1981) or determining whether a syllable contains a certain phoneme (Marsh and Mineo, 1977; McNeil and Stone, 1965). The substitution of a specified phoneme or group of phonemes with other phonemes is difficult even for older children (see Golinkoff, 1978). Furthermore, phonemic analysis skill correlates with and predicts success in learning to read and spell (Baron and Treiman, 1980; Bradley and Bryant, 1978, 1983; Calfee and others, 1972; Jusczyk, 1977; Liberman and Shankweiler, 1979; Perfetti and others, 1981; Routh and Fox, 1984; Treiman and Baron, 1981). Training children in phonemic analysis appears to increase their ability to learn spelling-sound correspondence rules (Bradley and Bryant, 1983; Rosner, 1971; Treiman and Baron, 1983; Vellutino and Scanlon, 1979), and indeed such training is part of several successful reading programs (Wallach and Wallach, 1976; Williams, 1980).

To show how phonemic analysis skills can be studied, this chapter considers one particular aspect of consonant clusters that occur at the beginnings of spoken syllables. I present evidence that syllable-initial consonant clusters behave as cohesive units in several kinds of phonemic analysis tasks. I argue further that children's difficulty in decomposing clusters into phonemes affects their ability to read and to spell those clusters. The link between phonemic analysis and reading and spelling skill proposed here fits well with the notion that phonemic analysis relates closely to the acquisition of an alphabetic writing system. My research also indicates a specific area in which children's conceptions of spoken language may influence their ability to read and spell.

Before considering the effects of syllable-initial consonant clusters on children's performance in tasks related to phonemic analysis and to reading, I must discuss the linguistic status of these clusters. The hypothesis that children have difficulty analyzing initial consonant clusters into phonemes is based on theories of the structure of spoken syllables. These theories, along with the linguistic and psycholinguistic evidence supporting them, provide the background for all that follows.

Initial Consonant Clusters in Theories of Syllable Structure

Several psychologists and linguists (Fudge, 1969; Halle and Vergnaud, 1980; Hockett, 1967; MacKay, 1970, 1972; Vergnaud and Halle, 1979) have proposed that the spoken syllable is not simply a string of phonemes. Rather, the phonemes in a syllable are grouped into two major constituents—an optional onset, which consists of a consonant or consonant cluster, and an obligatory rime, which consists of a vowel and any following consonants. In

English, the onset may contain one, two, or three consonants, (as in *ray, tray,* and *stray,* respectively). The rime may be a lone vowel (which is the minimal syllable, as in *eye*) or a vowel followed by one, two, three, or four consonants (as in *limb, limp, glimpse,* and *glimpsed,* respectively). Although some of the theories just listed differ in technical details, all agree that onset and rime are the primary constituents of the English syllable.

Linguistic evidence for the distinction between onset and rime is of two main varieties. One type of evidence is distributional; that is, it concerns the constraints on the locations of consonant and vowel phonemes within the syllable. According to Fudge (1969), any initial consonant or consonant cluster can occur with any vowel, and there are only minor restrictions between initial and final consonant clusters. For example, a syllable with *n* as the second phoneme of the onset cannot also have *n* as the first phoneme of the final consonant cluster. For the most part, however, onsets and rimes can be selected independently of one another without violating the phonological structure of English. In contrast, there are severe restrictions on the co-occurrence of vowels and final consonant clusters (Fudge, 1969; Vergnaud and Halle, 1979). For example, *lp* can occur after short vowels, such as *e,* but not after long vowels, such as *ee*. Three-consonant clusters, such as *lfth,* can also occur after short vowels (as in *twelfth*) but not after long vowels. The many restrictions between vowels and final consonant clusters motivate their treatment as part of one larger unit, the rime. A second type of linguistic evidence for the distinction between onset and rime is that only the rime plays a role in the assignment of stress in English (Chomsky and Halle, 1968). The nature of the onset is not relevant for stress rules, providing a further motivation to distinguish onset from rime.

Psycholinguistic Evidence from Adults

The linguistic evidence that onset and rime are in some respects independent is supported by behavioral evidence from adult subjects. The results of these psycholinguistic studies provide converging evidence for the validity of the distinction between onset and rime. They also indicate that this distinction plays a role in linguistic performance.

In one set of experiments (Treiman, 1983b), college students were exposed to novel word games that divided syllables in various ways. The syllables were presented only in spoken form, and all were phonologically legal in English. I expected that word games that divided syllables at the boundary between onset and rime would be preferred to and easier to learn than word games that divided syllables within the onset or within the rime. Traditional word games, such as pig latin, do involve an onset-rime division, as when *tree* becomes *ee-tray* rather than *ree-tay*. Of interest was whether such a rule would prove easier to master than other potential rules for a word game to which subjects had not been exposed.

Subjects in one of the experiments were taught two different word games in separate sessions. In one game, consonant-consonant-vowel-consonant (CCVC) syllables were transformed into two new syllables by placing *az* after the first two consonents of the stimulus and *p* before the vowel. For example, *slosh* became *slaz–posh*. This game should be relatively easy to learn, as it requires one to divide the stimulus CCVC between the initial CC or onset and the final VC or rime. The game was taught by giving subjects two examples and then asking them to use the same procedure to transform new syllables. The second game used the same teaching method and the same stimulus syllables but transformed the syllables differently. Here, *az* was added after the initial C and *p* before the CVC. Thus, *slosh* became *saz–plosh*. I expected that this game would be more difficult to learn than the first one, since it requires subjects to divide the onset of the stimulus syllable. In fact, subjects made more than twice as many errors in learning the second game (6.6 errors of thirteen possible) than they did in learning the first (2.7 errors of thirteen), although they eventually did master both games. Thus, although adults *can* learn a word game that divides the onset, such a game is more difficult to learn than one that does not require such division.

In another study (Treiman, 1983b; see also Treiman, 1984), subjects heard two stimulus syllables and were asked to blend them together to form one new syllable. The stimulus syllables were CCVCCs, such as *smulch* and *twikt*. Four different blending rules were considered. One, the CC/VCC rule, combined the whole onset of the first syllable with the rime of the second (giving *smikt*). This rule should be easy to learn, since it involves the postulated natural constituents of the syllable. The other three rules (C/CVCC, CCV/CC, and CCVC/C) all forced either the onsets or the rimes of the syllables to be broken apart, and for this reason they should be more difficult to learn. To compare subjects' ability to learn the rules, each subject received all four rules in a random order. Each rule was taught in a separate session by a procedure similar to that of the study just discussed. As predicted, the CC/VCC rule led to fewest errors — an average of .6 of thirteen, as compared to 1.8 for C/CVCC, 6.2 for CCV/CC, and 4.2 for CCVC/C. The relative ease of the CC/VCC rule supports the view that onset and rime are the major constituents of the syllable.

Further evidence that initial consonant clusters function as units comes from studies using a phoneme monitoring task (Treiman and others, 1982). In this task, subjects hear a syllable and then judge as quickly as possible whether the syllable begins with a previously specified target phoneme. In our experiments, subjects made their judgments by pressing a button marked *yes* or a button marked *no*. The experimental procedure was under computer control, with the computer presenting digitized natural-speech stimuli and recording subjects' responses and response times. Of primary interest were subjects' response times to three types of syllables that began with the target — CV syllables (for example, *sa*), CVC syllables (for example, *san*), and CCV syllables

(for example, *sna*). If the initial consonant cluster behaves as a unit, and if subjects require additional time to analyze this unit into its constituent phonemes, response latencies to CCV syllables should exceed those to CVC and CV syllables. The lengthened response times should occur because *s,* for example, is only part of the onset in *sna* but the entire onset in *san* or *sa.* The predicted pattern of latencies was in fact found in one experiment involving the target phonemes *s* and *f* and in another involving the target phonemes *p, t, k, b, d,* and *g.*

Studies by other investigators show that onsets also behave as units in speech production. MacKay (1970, 1972) studied two types of speech errors: spoonerisms and blends of words with similar meanings. Spoonerisms are reversals in the serial order of speech, as when the Reverend Spooner reportedly said, "You've hissed my mystery lectures" instead of "You've missed my history lectures". MacKay (1970) pointed out that reversals often exchange consonant clusters or consonant clusters and single consonants. Examples (from Fromkin, 1971) are *sweater drying* pronounced as *dreater swying* and *throat cutting* said as *coat thrutting.* Spoonerisms in which initial consonant clusters are broken up (as in Fromkin's 1971 example in which *brake fluid* was produced as *blake fruid*) are uncommon, although they do occur. The relative frequencies of these two types of spoonerisms make it appear that initial consonant clusters are strongly (but not completely) integrated. Blends of words with similar meanings tend to follow the same pattern, as when *flavor* and *taste* join to produce *flaste* rather than *faste.* (See Shattuck-Hufnagel, 1982, and Stemberger, 1983, for further discussion of speech errors.)

Taken together, the studies just discussed suggest that onsets behave as units in speech production, speech perception, and games requiring the conscious analysis of speech. These results support the view that units intermediate between the syllable and the phoneme play a role in linguistic performance, at least for adults. One of these constituents — the one of particular interest here — is the syllable onset. Adults can and sometimes do divide onsets into phonemes, but they usually prefer to treat them as units.

Effects of Initial Consonant Clusters on Children's Phonemic Analysis Performance

Given children's difficulty in analyzing speech into phonemes, and given that onsets appear to be cohesive even for adults, one might expect that children would have particular difficulty analyzing onsets into their components. This expectation is confirmed by the results of studies that employed a variety of different tasks.

One such study (Treiman, in press) involved a phoneme substitution task. The subjects, who averaged eight years of age, were shown a game in which each stimulus syllable was transformed into a new syllable by changing some of its sounds. The children were given a series of stimuli, and the experimenter provided the correct response for each stimulus if the child did not know it. In the condition of particular interest here, the stimuli were CCV syl-

lables, such as *froo* and *gway*. One rule replaced the first and second phonemes of each syllable with two constant phonemes, in this example *sl*. Thus, *froo* became *sloo*, and *gway* became *slay*. Another rule replaced the second and third phonemes of each stimulus with *lee*. *Froo* therefore became *flee* and *gway* became *glee*. The two rules were taught to children in separate sessions, with the order of the rules being balanced across subjects. The first rule, which replaced the onset as a unit, proved easier to learn than the second. Children made fewer total errors on this game, had longer runs of successive correct responses, and achieved their first correct response more quickly. That this result did not arise simply because children could deal more easily with the first two phonemes of a syllable than with the last two phonemes was shown by the results of a second condition. This condition used CVC stimuli. Here, the rule that replaced the second and third phonemes of each stimulus (for these syllables, the rime) was easier to learn than the rule that replaced the first and second phonemes. The second result provides evidence that the vowel is linked with the final consonant rather than with the initial one. Thus, the results of this study converge on the distinction between onset and rime as units of the syllable and show that children as well as adults are sensitive to the distinction.

An easier type of phonemic analysis task — a recognition task — was used to probe further the cohesiveness of the onset among children. In one experiment (Treiman, in press), five-and-one-half-year-olds were asked whether spoken syllables began with a specified target. Two targets, *s* and *f*, were used. The syllables that began with the target were the same CVs, CVCs, and CCVs used in the phoneme-monitoring study with adult subjects discussed earlier (Treiman and others, 1982). The pattern of children's error rates on the three types of positive stimuli mirrored the pattern of response times found for adults. Children missed the target in CCV syllables relatively often — 28 percent of the time. Error rates to CV and CVC syllables were significantly lower (12 percent and 14 percent, respectively) and did not differ reliably from one another. Thus, children were more likely to deny that *sna* began with *s* than that *sa* or *san* began with *s*. Another experiment (Treiman, in press) used pictures rather than spoken syllables as stimuli and the printed letters *S, F, P,* and *B* as targets. In that experiment, children were asked whether the name of each picture began with the target letter. Preschoolers (mean age four years eight months) and kindergarteners (mean age five years six months) made significantly more errors on cluster items (for example, a picture of a snake) than on singleton items (for example, a picture of a sink). For preschoolers, the error rates were 33 percent and 28 percent on clusters and singletons, respectively. For kindergarteners, the error rates were 12 percent and eight percent. Supplementing these results on initial phonemes, I recently found that five-year-olds have more difficulty recognizing the second phoneme of a cluster than the same phoneme in syllable-initial position. For example, it is harder for them to detect the *l* in *blee* than in *a — lee*. These findings all reinforce the view that children have more difficulty analyzing syllable-initial consonant clusters into phonemes.

The results of my studies are supported by results reported by Barton and others (1980). Working with four- to five-year-old children, these authors found evidence from several different kinds of tasks that children treat initial consonant clusters as units before they segment them into phonemes. In one task, children were asked for the first sound of words like *swing*. Many said *sw* rather than *s*. However, when the same children were given words beginning with singletons, they could segment just the initial consonant. These results suggest that many children treated the instruction to give the first sound in the word as an instruction to give the onset. The onset appears to be a more natural unit for a child than does an initial phoneme.

Previous studies (Liberman and others, 1974; Treiman and Baron, 1981) found that the ability to analyze speech into syllables developmentally precedes the ability to analyze speech into phonemes. For example, children can indicate the number of syllables in a word before they can indicate the number of phonemes in a syllable. The phoneme substitution and phoneme recognition studies discussed here, together with the results of Barton and others (1980), suggest that phonemic analysis tasks that require the division of syllables into onsets and rimes may be easier than and developmentally prior to tasks that require the division of onsets into phonemes. Onsets and rimes—units smaller than syllables but larger than phonemes—may play an important role in the development of phonemic analysis skills. Indeed, training in the analysis of syllables into onsets and rimes may be a helpful intermediate step in phonemic analysis instruction.

Children's Reading of Initial Consonant Clusters

If phonemic analysis is important for mastering the rules by which speech corresponds to print, children's difficulty in analyzing onsets of spoken syllables might be expected to influence their ability to read and to spell. In particular, children might have difficulty dealing with initial consonant clusters in printed words, just as they do in spoken words. As a first study of this possibility, I compared the ability of first graders (mean age six years ten months) and second graders (mean age seven years eleven months) to decode nonsense words with and without initial clusters (Treiman, in press). Children were presented with twenty printed stimuli, half pronounced as CVCs and half pronounced as CCVs. The items in a pair used the same letters but in a different order. Examples include *SAN* and *SNA, KEER* and *KREE, SOOM* and *SMOO*. Particularly at the first-grade level, children had more difficulty with CCVs than with CVCs. Using a strict criterion, under which all phonemes had to be pronounced in a phonetically correct manner, first graders erred on 74 percent of the CCVs and on 61 percent of the CVCs. Using a more lenient scoring system, under which the vowel did not have to be produced correctly, the error rates were 60 percent and 36 percent, respectively. For second graders, the difficulty on CCVs relative to CVCs appeared to be less pronounced. According to the strict scoring system, second graders erred on 29 percent of

the CCVs and on 23 percent of the CVCs. The error rates for the lenient scoring system were 17 percent and 11 percent, respectively.

First graders' difficulty in decoding initial consonant clusters was reflected in the types of errors that they made. They tended to misread CCVs as beginning with singleton, not cluster, onsets. In contrast, they did not generally transform singletons into clusters. For example, first graders sometimes read the second and third phonemes of a CCV in the wrong order, producing *san* for *SNA*. The comparable error on a CVC (for example, *SAN* read as *sna*) was significantly less frequent. Children were also more likely to give two-syllable pronunciations for CCVs than CVCs. Most errors of this type retained both consonants of the stimulus and inserted a vowel between them, as when *SMOO* was pronounced *so-mo*. The insertion served to produce two syllables with singleton onsets instead of one syllable with a complex onset.

The results of this study add to our knowledge of the factors that influence misreading. Previous investigators (for example, Shankweiler and Liberman, 1972; Fowler and others, 1977) have shown that vowels are misread more often than consonants and that final consonants are misread more often than initial consonants. The final consonant–initial consonant difference was interpreted by these investigators as reflecting the differential difficulty that children experience in segmenting sounds in spoken words: Final phonemes may be harder to segment than initial ones. The present results suggest a further parallel between phonemic analysis and reading: Initial consonant clusters are difficult to analyze in spoken syllables and are also difficult to decode. If the thesis of this chapter is correct—that phonemic analysis is intimately involved in learning an alphabetic system—many such parallels between phonemic analysis and reading should exist.

Children's Spelling of Initial Consonant Clusters

Children's spelling, perhaps even more than their reading, can provide a window onto the way in which they conceptualize the sounds of speech. For example, Read (1975) noted that some children spelled *tr* with *CH,* producing spellings like *CHRIE* for *try.* Although that spelling may at first appear bizarre, it reflects the children's categorization of *t* before *r* as phonetically similar to *ch*. Such a categorization is most likely to appear in children's spelling if children are encouraged to spell words as they hear them. Indeed, the children studied by Read (1975) were preschoolers who began to write without formal instruction, sometimes as young as age three. Their spellings showed a number of nonstandard features, many of which have been reported by other investigators (Bissex, 1980; Ehri, 1984; Henderson and Beers, 1980; Treiman, 1983a).

To study further children's conceptions of sounds and how they are reflected in spelling, I am currently analyzing a large set of first graders' spellings. Their teacher used, to the extent that the school system permitted, a "language experience" or "whole language" approach to the teaching of reading and

writing (see Chapter Five in this volume). As that approach advocates, the children were given time each morning to write creatively. For example, the teacher might read from a story, and the class would discuss ways of ending it. Each child would then depict his or her version in drawing and print. Early in the school year, the print tended to be minimal. Children often drew a picture accompanied with only their name or an unrecognizable string of letters. As time progressed, the children began to write longer stories with recognizable words. The teacher or teacher's aide wrote the word that the child said he or she had intended over each word in the child's story but did not explicitly point out or correct the nonstandard spellings. At other times during the school day, the children read from basal readers and from other books. School policy dictated that they memorize ten spelling words a week, beginning in January, but the teacher did not place great emphasis on that task. In any case, most of the children had already begun to spell the assigned words correctly. My data base contains 5,617 spellings produced by forty-three first graders who attended that classroom over a two-year period. Data from one child with severe articulation problems and several children who spoke black dialect are not being analyzed at this time. For most of the children, the spellings span the period from the end of August until April. Both standard and nonstandard spellings are included in the data base, and roughly half the spellings are nonstandard.

There are many interesting phenomena in the children's spellings (see Treiman, 1983a, for some examples), but the focus here is on children's representations of syllable-initial consonant clusters. If children tend to consider initial clusters as units, and if they have trouble breaking these units into components, they might spell clusters with one letter only. In fact, many such spellings occur. For two-phoneme initial clusters, examples include *BO* for *blow, HASAK* for *haystack, SEERT* for *secret,* and *TEE* for tree. Three-phoneme clusters were also simplified, as in *SET* and *SRET* for *street* and *STEETS* for *streets.* As these examples show, and as the analyses reported later in this section confirm, the second phoneme of a cluster (the third phoneme in the case of a three-phoneme cluster) was more likely to be deleted than the first phoneme.

The omission rate for the first phoneme of a syllable-initial consonant cluster was 2 percent, while the omission rate for the same phonemes as syllable-initial singletons was .9 percent. This difference was statistically significant but small in magnitude. In contrast, the omission rate for the second phoneme of a syllable-initial cluster was 23.3 percent. This greatly exceeded the rate of omission for the same phonemes in syllable-initial position (1 percent). Thus, *l* was much more likely to be deleted in a word like *blow* than in a word like *live.* This phenomenon was particularly strong during the first half of the school year, but it continued into the second half of the year as well. That the omission of the second phonemes of onsets did not reflect a general failure to represent the second phonemes of words is suggested by the finding that children were more likely to omit a phoneme when it was both the second phoneme of a word and the second element of a cluster (23.3 percent omissions) than when it

was the second phoneme of a word and syllable-initial (2.7 percent omissions). For example, children more often omitted *l* from a word like *blow* than from a word like *along*. Similar phenomena occurred with the third phonemes of onsets. The omission rate for the third phoneme of an initial consonant cluster (which in the data base was always *r*) was 22.7 percent, exceeding the rate for syllable-initial *r* (3.8 percent).

The phonemes *p, t,* and *k* are particularly interesting in the context of onsets, since they can occur either as the first element (for example, *pr, kl*) or the second element (for example, *sp, sk*). As the preceding discussion suggests, the omission rate for *p, t,* and *k* was much higher when they were the second phoneme of a cluster (36.1 percent) than it was when they were the first phoneme (1.3 percent). I should also mention that the phonemes that appeared in syllable-initial clusters sometimes also occurred across syllable boundaries. For example, in *bedroom, d* and *r* are in different syllables. In cases of this kind, both phonemes were usually represented (twenty-three of twenty-five cases). Thus, the omission of the second consonant from a sequence of consonants appears to characterize consonants at the beginning of a single syllable.

The view of syllable structure presented here may help to explain why children simplify syllable-initial consonant clusters in their spelling. They may do so because they tend to consider onsets of spoken words as units. Children have difficulty analyzing these units and representing each element separately. Instead, they sometimes represent only one phoneme of the cluster. That children more often omit the second phoneme of the cluster than the first suggests that, even though they consider a cluster like *sn* as a unit, they more readily categorize that unit as similar to *s* than as similar to *n* when they are forced to represent it in print.

The spelling analyses described so far concern initial consonant clusters or onsets. These analyses support one aspect of the syllable structure theory presented here—that onsets are treated as units. They do not speak to other implications of the theory. However, preliminary results suggest that other phenomena in the children's spellings can be understood in terms of syllable structure and its effects on children's ability to analyze words into phonemes. For example, children omitted syllable-final single consonants (7.2 percent) more often than they omitted syllable-initial single consonants (1.1 percent). This result fits the notion that a syllable-final consonant is part of a larger unit (the rime), whereas a syllable-initial singleton is an independent unit (the onset). The deletion of syllable-final singletons appeared to be most prevalent for the liquid phonemes l and *r*. Vowel-liquid sequences may be most likely to be spelled with just a vowel (as in *TAYE* for *tail* and *CA* for *care*) because they form the most cohesive units (Treiman, 1984).

Conclusions

In the past, linguistic concepts of syllable structure, such as onset and rime, have not been applied to studies of phonemic analysis, reading, and spelling. However, cross-area contact of this kind has several benefits. Linguistics

benefits because psycholinguistic research provides additional support for theories of syllable structure. For example, the distinction between onset and rime in linguistics is largely motivated by distributional evidence. A vowel is considered to be part of the same syllable constituent as the final consonant or consonants because the restrictions on vowels and final consonants are closely related. The finding in the CVC condition of the phoneme substitution task described earlier — that the VC is more easily treated as a unit than the CV — provides a new kind of evidence that vowels are more closely tied to final consonants than to initial consonants. Similarly, the finding that children (and even adults, in some circumstances) have difficulty analyzing onsets into phonemes supports the view that onsets are true constituents of the syllable. In some cases, psycholinguistic research may even support one theory of syllable structure over another.

Just as psycholinguistic studies can be of interest to linguists, linguistic concepts can be helpful to psychologists and educators. For example, a notion like onset can help us to understand phonemic analysis, reading, and spelling. Phonemic analysis tasks that require children to subdivide onsets (as in the questions, Does *sna* begin with *s?* and Does *blee* contain *l?*) tend to be more difficult than tasks that allow them to deal with the onset as a unit (Does *san* begin with *s?* Does *a–lee* contain *l?*). The spelling of initial consonant clusters also causes difficulty, consistent with the view that children's conceptions of speech sounds are reflected in their spellings. First graders often fail to represent both phonemes of a cluster like *dr* even though they can pronounce the cluster, even though they can spell both *d* and *r* individually, and even though they can spell a *dr* sequence that crosses a syllable boundary. Finally, children seem to have difficulty decoding initial consonant clusters in print. All these phenomena, disparate though they may at first appear to be, make sense when considered in light of linguistic theories about onset.

The research discussed in this chapter begins to show how specific aspects of the way in which children conceptualize speech — here, their tendency to treat onset as a unit — influence their learning of written language. As such, this research supports the view that spoken language and written language are intimately related at early stages in the acquisition of reading and writing skill. Difficulties in the analysis of spoken language can lead to difficulties with written language. Thus, linguistically based studies of children's conceptions of spoken language can help us to understand how children learn an alphabetic system.

References

Baron, J., and Treiman, R. "Use of Orthography in Reading and Learning to Read." In J. F. Kavanagh and R. L. Venezky (Eds.), *Orthography, Reading, and Dyslexia.* Baltimore, Md.: University Park Press, 1980.

Barton, D., Miller, R., and Macken, M. A. "Do Children Treat Clusters as One Unit or Two?" *Papers and Reports on Child Language Development,* 1980, *18,* 93–137.

Bissex, G. L. *Gnys at Wrk: A Child Learns to Write and Read.* Cambridge, Mass.: Harvard University Press, 1980.

Bradley, L., and Bryant, P. E. "Difficulties in Auditory Organization as a Possible Cause of Reading Backwardness." *Nature,* 1978, *271,* 746–747.

Bradley, L., and Bryant, P. E. "Categorizing Sounds and Learning to Read: A Causal Connection." *Nature,* 1983, *301,* 419–421.

Calfee, R. C., Chapman, R. S., and Venezky, R. "How a Child Needs to Think to Learn to Read." In L. S. Gregg (Ed.), *Cognition in Learning and Memory.* New York: Wiley, 1972.

Chomsky, N., and Halle, M. *The Sound Pattern of English.* New York: Harper & Row, 1968.

Ehri, L. C. "How Orthography Alters Spoken Language Competencies in Children Learning to Read and Spell." In J. Downing and R. Valtin (Eds.), *Language Awareness and Learning to Read.* New York: Springer-Verlag, 1984.

Fowler, C. A., Liberman, I. Y., and Shankweiler, D. "On Interpreting the Error Pattern in Beginning Reading." *Language and Speech,* 1977, *20,* 162–173.

Fromkin, V. A. "The Nonanomalous Nature of Anomalous Utterances." *Language,* 1971, *47,* 27–52.

Fudge, E. C. "Syllables." *Journal of Linguistics,* 1969, *5,* 253–286.

Gleitman, L. R., and Rozin, P. "The Structure and Acquisition of Reading I: Relations Between Orthographies and the Structure of Language." In A. S. Reber and D. L. Scarborough (Eds.), *Toward a Psychology of Reading: The Proceedings of the CUNY Conference.* Hillsdale, N.J.: Erlbaum, 1977.

Golinkoff, R. M. "Phonemic Awareness Skills and Reading Achievement." In F. Murphy and J. Pikulski (Eds.), *The Acquisition of Reading.* Baltimore, Mass.: University Park Press, 1978.

Gough, P. B., and Hillinger, M. L. "Learning to Read: An Unnatural Act." *Bulletin of the Orton Society,* 1980, *30,* 179–196.

Halle, M., and Vergnaud, J.-R. "Three-Dimensional Phonology." *Journal of Linguistic Research,* 1980, *1,* 83–105.

Henderson, E. H., and Beers, J. W. *Developmental and Cognitive Aspects of Learning to Spell: A Reflection of Word Knowledge.* Newark, Del.: International Reading Association, 1980.

Hockett, C. F. "Where the Tongue Slips, There Slip I." In *To Honor Roman Jakobson.* Vol. 2. The Hague: Mouton, 1967.

Jusczyk, P. W. "Rhymes and Reasons: Some Aspects of the Child's Appreciation of Poetic Form." *Developmental Psychology,* 1977, *13,* 599–607.

Liberman, I. Y. "A Language-Oriented View of Reading and Its Disabilities." In H. Myklebust (Ed.), *Progress in Learning Disabilities.* Vol. 5. New York: Grune & Stratton, 1982.

Liberman, I. Y., and Shankweiler, D. "Speech, the Alphabet, and Teaching to Read." In L. B. Resnick and P. A. Weaver (Eds.), *Theory and Practice of Early Reading.* Vol. 2. Hillsdale, N.J.: Erlbaum, 1979.

Liberman, I. Y., Shankweiler, D., Fischer, F. W., and Carter, B. "Explicit Syllable and Phoneme Segmentation in the Young Child." *Journal of Experimental Child Psychology,* 1974, *18,* 202–212.

MacKay, D. G. "The Structure of Errors in the Serial Order of Speech." *Neuropsychologia,* 1970, *8,* 323–350.

MacKay, D. G. "The Structure of Words and Syllables: Evidence from Errors in Speech." *Cognitive Psychology,* 1972, *3,* 220–227.

MacNeil, J. D., and Stone, J. "Note on Teaching Children to Hear Separate Sounds in Spoken Words." *Journal of Educational Psychology,* 1965, *56,* 13–15.

Marsh, G., and Mineo, R. J. "Training Preschool Children to Recognize Phonemes in Words." *Journal of Educational Psychology,* 1977, *69,* 748–753.

Mattingly, I. G. "Reading, the Linguistic Process, and Linguistic Awareness." In J. F.

Kavanagh and I. G. Mattingly (Eds.), *Language by Ear and by Eye: The Relationships Between Speech and Reading.* Cambridge, Mass.: M.I.T. Press, 1972.

Perfetti, C. A., Beck, I. L., and Hughes, C. "Phonemic Knowledge and Learning to Read." Paper presented at the meeting of the Society for Research in Child Development, Boston, April 1981.

Read, C. *Children's Categorization of Speech Sounds in English.* National Council of Teachers of English, Research Report No. 17. Urbana, Ill.: National Council of Teachers of English, 1975.

Rosner, J. *Phonic Analysis Training and Beginning Reading Skills.* Publication 1971/19. Pittsburgh: Learning Research and Development Center, University of Pittsburgh, 1971.

Routh, D. K., and Fox, B. "Mm... Is a Little Bit of May: Phonemes, Reading, and Spelling." In K. D. Gadow and I. Bialer (Eds.), *Advances in Learning and Behavioral Disabilities.* Vol. 3. Greenwich, Conn.: JAI Press, 1984.

Rozin, P., Bressman, B., and Taft, M. "Do Children Understand the Basic Relationship Between Speech and Writing? The Mow-Motorcycle Test." *Journal of Reading Behavior,* 1974, *6,* 327–334.

Rozin, P., and Gleitman, L. R. "The Structure and Acquisition of Reading II: The Reading Process and the Acquisition of the Alphabetic Principle." In A. S. Reber and D. L. Scarborough (Eds.), *Toward a Psychology of Reading: The Proceedings of the CUNY Conference.* Hillsdale, N.J.: Erlbaum, 1977.

Shankweiler, D., and Liberman, I. Y. "Misreading: A Search for Causes." In J. F. Kavanagh and I. G. Mattingly (Eds.), *Language by Ear and by Eye: The Relationships Between Speech and Reading.* Cambridge, Mass.: M.I.T. Press, 1974.

Shattuch-Hufnagel, S. "Sublexical Units and Suprasegmental Structure in Speech Production Planning." In P. F. MacNeilage (Ed.), *The Production of Speech.* New York: Springer-Verlag, 1982.

Stanovich, K. E. "Word Recognition Skill and Reading Ability." In M. Singer (Ed.), *Competent Reader, Disabled Reader: Reserach and Application.* Hillsdale, N.J.: Erlbaum, 1982.

Stemberger, J. P. *Speech Errors and Theoretical Phonology: A Review.* Bloomington: Indiana University Linguistics Club, 1983.

Treiman, R. "Phonetic Aspects of First Graders' Creative Spellings of Consonants." Paper presented at the Boston University Conference on Language Development, Boston, October 1983a.

Treiman, R. "The Structure of Spoken Syllables: Evidence from Novel Word Games." *Cognition,* 1983b, *15,* 49–74.

Treiman, R. "On the Status of Final Consonant Clusters in English Syllables." *Journal of Verbal Learning and Verbal Behavior,* 1984, *23,* 343–356.

Treiman, R. "Onsets and Rimes as Units of Spoken Syllables: Evidence from Children." *Journal of Experimental Child Psychology,* in press.

Treiman, R., and Baron, J. "Segmental Analysis Ability: Development and Relation to Reading Ability." In G. E. MacKinnon and T. G. Waller (Eds.), *Reading Research: Advances in Theory and Practice.* Vol. 3. New York: Academic Press, 1981.

Treiman, R., and Baron, J. "Phonemic Analysis Training Helps Children Benefit from Spelling-Sound Rules." *Memory and Cognition,* 1983, *11,* 382–389.

Treiman, R., Salasoo, A., Slowiaczek, L. M., and Pisoni, D. B. *Effects of Syllable Structure on Adults' Phoneme-Monitoring Performance.* Research on Speech Perception Progress Report No. 8. Bloomington, Ind.: Speech Research Laboratory, 1982.

Tunmer, W. E., and Bowey, J. A. "Metalinguistic Awareness and Reading Acquisition." In W. E. Tunmer, C. Pratt, and M. L. Herriman (Eds.), *Metalinguistic Awareness in Children: Theory, Research, Implications.* New York: Springer-Verlag, 1984.

Vellutino, F. R., and Scanlon, D. M. "The Effect of Phonemic Segmentation Training and Response Acquisition on Coding Ability in Poor and Normal Readers." Paper presented at the meeting of the American Educational Research Association, San Francisco, April 1979.

Venezky, R. L. *The Structure of English Orthography.* The Hague: Mouton, 1970.

Vergnaud, J.-R., and Halle, M. *Metrical Phonology.* Unpublished manuscript, Department of Linguistics, M.I.T., 1979.

Wallach, M. A., and Wallach, L. *Teaching All Children to Read.* Chicago: University of Chicago Press, 1976.

Williams, J. P. "Teaching Decoding with an Emphasis on Phoneme Analysis and Phoneme Blinding." *Journal of Educational Psychology,* 1980, *72,* 1–15.

Rebecca Treiman is associate professor of psychology at Wayne State University in Detroit, Michigan.

Whether or not reading a first language facilitates reading a second language may depend on the degree to which the two writing systems share certain features.

Literacy Background and Reading Development in a Second Language

Tracy L. Brown
Margot Haynes

There are several reasons for including the topic of second-language (L2) reading acquisition in a volume on reading development. One is the practical reality of nonnative speakers of English in public schools and universities. A better understanding of the challenges that these learners face in becoming proficient users of written English can help in preparing L2 students to profit fully from our educational system. There are also questions of theoretical interest. Can models of reading development in a first language (L1) be fruitfully applied to L2 reading? If not, what are the differences between L1 and L2 reading, and what might they imply about the acquisition of reading skill in general? What is the impact of literacy background—including prior instructional methods, the social context of literacy, and the writing system itself—on the development of L2 reading skill?

To answer these questions, we may begin by distinguishing universal principles of reading development from those tied to specific learning contexts and writing systems, thus placing the findings of reading research into a more comprehensive framework. Moreover, by examining the patterns of transfer from one language to another, we may uncover aspects of reading develop-

T. H. Carr (Ed.). *The Development of Reading Skills.* New Directions for Child Development, no. 27. San Francisco: Jossey-Bass, March 1985.

ment that are difficult to detect and describe when studied in the context of a single language.

In addressing this area, one needs first to identify the basic differences between the contexts of L1 and L2 reading acquisition. For example, L2 learners, especially at the college level, are likely to be competent readers in their first language, possessing highly developed skills in extracting meaning from print via the mapping system used in their L1 script. The preexistence of well-developed reading skills may influence L2 reading development in a variety of ways. At a general level, L2 students' first-language experience may influence their overall conceptualization of what reading is like, not only of its social and cultural functions but also of how the reading process actually works and of what strategies should be applied in mastering it. Besides this general effect, the skills of L1 reading may interact with the acquisition of L2 reading skills, with the possibility that transfer or interference may occur as a function of the pattern of similarities and differences between the two languages.

A second and less obvious difference between L1 and L2 reading acquisition contexts is that formal L1 reading instruction typically begins well after a basic speaking competence has been achieved, while L2 reading instruction is more likely to be concurrent with the emergence of speaking and listening skills. The acquisition of reading skill in the absence of a well-developed oral-aural competence is apt to be very different from the typical L1 reading context, in which knowledge of phonology, vocabulary, and syntax is generally much better developed (see Chapters One, Three, and Four in this volume).

Despite its potential, research on the differences between L1 and L2 reading has tended to be limited in its scope and generality. Most studies have focused on specific contrasts between L1 and L2 readers. For example, it has been found that L2 readers tend to be more attentive to visual details in text than L1 readers are (Hatch and others, 1974; Cziko, 1980); to spend more time, on the average, for each eye fixation (Oller and Tullius, 1973); and to have difficulty profiting from semantic and discourse constraints within a text (Chihara and others, 1977; Cziko, 1978) and in applying background knowledge to support comprehension (Carrell, 1983).

While these findings document specific differences between L1 and L2 reading, they fail to provide a coherent framework for conceptualizing the reading process and for establishing systematic contrasts between the two. An attempt to do this has been made in miscue analysis studies (for example, Riggs, 1977; Devine, 1980), which focus on errors made in reading aloud (see Goodman, 1967; Clarke and Silberstein, 1977). Unfortunately, miscue analysis has been weakened by its failure to confront a central methodological difficulty. In miscue analysis, oral reading errors are not automatically counted but are first evaluated in terms of their acceptability within the reader's spoken dialect (Goodman and Burke, 1972). While a researcher may make certain assumptions about an L1 reader's dialect, the linguistic knowledge or interlanguage (Selinker, 1972) of an L2 reader is a developing and variable system (Tarone, 1982) characterized by change and unpredictability (Bley-Vroman,

1983). Without a defined spoken dialect as a reference point, miscue analysis researchers can only guess at the acceptability of an L2 reader's miscues. As a result, the procedure of miscue analysis is somewhat compromised in its applicability to the study of L2 reading.

In addition to problems of methodology and scope, research in this area has tended to ignore potentially important subject variables. All too frequently, analogies are drawn between child and adult L2 readers without regard to differences in cognitive development and literacy background. Furthermore, no systematic comparison of language learners from different L1 backgrounds has been undertaken. Many studies have sampled from a theoretical population of all L2 learners, mixing language and writing system backgrounds together in a single group assumed to be homogeneous. Other studies have sampled readers from a single language and script background, generalizing their results to all L2 readers. Clearly, a more systematic approach is needed to address the effects of prior literacy experience.

One might begin with the consequences of literacy in general, that is, with how reading acquisition may be influenced by knowledge and skills basic to reading in any language. Studies comparing L2 reading acquisition in children who are or are not readers in their native language have shown large benefits for children with native language reading experience (Rosier and Holm, 1980; Modiano, 1966; Kreusler, 1961). These studies and others (for example, Haddad, 1981) suggest that prior literacy experience of any sort may influence reading development in a second language.

In addition to the potential differences between literacy and nonliteracy, another class of potential effects stems from the contrast between different types of literacy experience. These can include, for example, the variations between languages in the mapping relation between writing and speech and in the methods of instruction and the types of practice encouraged in L1 education, as well as a host of general cultural variables ranging from the functions of writing in L1 to the social valuation of literacy skills in general (see Scribner and Cole, 1981).

In summary, contemporary L2 reading research has two shortcomings: It lacks a methodologically sound and coherent conceptual framework, and it fails to distinguish between important literacy background variables. In the remainder of this chapter, we will describe our own efforts to address these problems: first, to formulate a general theoretical framework and second, to show how the quality of prior literacy experience may influence L2 reading development.

Component Skills in Reading

Component skills analysis models the reading process as a complex and dynamic system characterized by the interaction and cooperation of theoretically isolable component skills (Carr, 1981; Frederiksen, 1978, 1981; LaBerge and Samuels, 1974; Singer, 1982). In this view, reading ability can be analyzed

in terms of the development and integration of the skill components that comprise it. By emphasizing the identity, development, and interrelations among component skills, this approach gains three appealing features. First, it places the development of reading skill into the context of skill acquisition in general (see MacKay, 1982), allowing the dynamics of reading development to be addressed with reference to what is known about skill acquisition (Anderson, 1982; MacKay, 1982; Fitts and Posner, 1967; Bryan and Hartner, 1899). Second, it provides a powerful medium for the modeling of individual differences (Frederiksen, 1981) by establishing a multidimensional framework in which readers may differ not only with respect to overall reading skill but also with regard to the pattern of strengths and weaknesses that they show across component skills. Third, by modeling reading as an interactive system of subskills—each of which can be weak or strong and well or poorly integrated with other subskills—the component skills view provides a more comprehensive alternative to single-factor theories of reading ability and disability (Carr, 1981).

In empirical applications of the component skills approach, researchers must consider carefully how to select, conceptualize, and assess the component skills of interest. While there is no firmly established set of required subskills for reading, various lines of evidence have indicated that six skill components can be addressed usefully: first, the use of graphotactic regularities (systematic variations in the patterning of letters) in the visual perception of graphemic features (Carr and others, 1979; Barron and Henderson, 1977; Baron, 1975; Mason, 1975); second, the ability to apply orthographic rules in spelling-to-sound translation (phonological recoding) (Frederiksen, 1978; Mason, 1978; Perfetti and Hogaboam, 1975; Chapter One in this volume); third, vocabulary knowledge (Anderson and Freebody, 1981; Chapter Three in this volume); fourth, the use of semantic and syntactic context (Stanovich and West, 1981; Perfetti and others, 1979; West and Stanovich, 1978, 1982); fifth, the ability to encode and maintain information in short-term or working memory (Levy, 1975; Baddeley and Hitch, 1974); sixth, the coordination of general word knowledge with textual information to sharpen and elaborate what is comprehended (Chapter Four in this volume; Graesser and others, 1980).

In addition, some overall measure of reading competence is needed, that is, some indication of the operational efficiency of the reading system as a whole. By comparing the relationships between the subskills and overall reading competence, we can begin to distinguish those skills that contribute most to fluent reading and to determine whether different groups or individuals, such as good and poor readers, show different patterns of reliance across subskills (Vavrus and others, 1983). Computing the matrix of correlation coefficients between all variables creates a data set that is suitable for sophisticated and powerful multivariate designs, such as multiple regression (Singer and Crouse, 1981; Graesser and others, 1980), factor analysis (Frederiksen, 1981), and cluster analysis of individuals or variables (Vavrus and others, 1983).

Attention and Automaticity in Reading

The component skills model applied in our L2 research has been supplemented by an emphasis on the concepts of attention and automaticity, particularly as they pertain to the acquisition and transfer of skill (Anderson, 1982; MacKay, 1982; Norman, 1981; Reason, 1977, 1979). The work in this area has two relevant implications: First, people have a limited capacity for attending to the performance of a task (Broadbent, 1958; Kahneman, 1973; Posner, 1982); performance may break down if the attentional demands of the task exceed the performer's capacity (Anderson, 1982). Second, as practice increases, performance may become "automatic," requiring less attentional capacity (Logan, 1979; Shiffrin and Schneider, 1977) and becoming more resistant to inhibition, strategic modification, and conscious introspection (Hasher and Zacks, 1979; LaBerge, 1981; LaBerge and Samuels, 1974; Posner and Snyder, 1975).

For reading, these findings suggest that there may be a change in the focus of attention as reading skill is acquired, shifting from lower-level skills involving visual perception and spelling-to-sound translation to higher-level skills involving meaning and inference (LaBerge and Samuels, 1974; Perfetti and Lesgold, 1978). The implication is that the more fundamental skills of visual and phonological processing become automatic with practice and consequently less in need of conscious control and less prone to inhibition and strategic modification.

In the study of L2 reading acquisition, the potential interaction of subskills with attention and flexibility takes on added interest when one considers the potential for transfer or interference between L1 and L2 subskills. At one level, there is the possibility that the basic skills of L1, especially if they are well established and automated, are so specific to L1 that they are of little or no use in L2 reading, with the result that the fundamental skills of visual and orthographic processing must be learned from scratch. This could produce the L2 version of the situation that some have proposed to be problematic for beginning L1 readers, where the attentional demands of lower-level processes detract from the ability to form and remember the higher-level meaning-based representations necessary to comprehension (LaBerge and Samuels, 1974; Perfetti and Lesgold, 1978; Singer, 1982). At another level, there is also the possibility that automated low-level L1 processes, which vary with different writing systems (Hung and Tzeng, 1981; Chen and Juola, 1982; Treiman and others, 1981), may actually interfere with the acquisition or operation of emerging L2 skills when the two languages employ different scripts. Because such skills may be resistant to strategic modification and suppression, fundamental and hard to accomplish changes in the operation and coordination of subskills may be required, possibly resulting in slower development of L2 reading competence. Alternatively, automated L1 skills may facilitate the development of corresponding L2 skills when L1 and L2 scripts are the same

or quite similar in their visual or orthographic features. Component skills analysis is well suited to detect these kinds of effects, because it allows us to assess the degree to which component skills are developed and the manner in which they interrelate and interact in the service of comprehension.

Expectations and Surprises

Our research on literacy experience variables has focused on differences in visual and orthographic processing between students from Japanese, Arabic, and Spanish language backgrounds. Our attention to these groups was motivated primarily by the differences between the script systems used in these students' L1 and by the ways in which contrasts between these scripts might reveal patterns of interference or transfer between L1 and L2 orthographies. For example, Spanish and English share a common alphabet and similar orthographic systems — a situation that might facilitate the transfer of visual and orthographic skills to the reading of English. While the Arabic writing system also shares the abstract characteristic of being basically alphabetic (Barr, 1976), it uses a different set of graphemes, usually omits short vowels, and is read from right to left. In contrast, Japanese is represented by a combination of syllabic and logographic symbols and so differs from English not only in the characters used but also in the type of mapping relation between writing and speech (see Martin, 1972; Hadamitzky and Spahn, 1981). In general, our objective was to determine whether differences between these groups — particularly in regard to visual and orthographic processing — were consistent with the varying natures of the groups' L1 writing systems. (See Henderson, 1984; for analogous comparisons between Arabic and Spanish-speaking students.)

The data we collected were in two sets. First, we gathered a fairly broad spectrum of component skill measures on a relatively large sample ($N = 62$) of adult L2 learners in the English language program at our university. The principal measures of this battery of tests are detailed in Table 1. The results of the first investigation prompted a second project focused on visual processing differences between the language groups; the second project used a more complicated version of the same-different matching test from the component skills battery (see Table 2).

As one might guess from the choice of tasks for the second project, we were surprised by the direction of language group differences that the first project found in same-different matching. We expected the Spanish-speaking students to be fastest on this task, since their L1 script uses the same alphabet as English. Thus, Spanish-speaking students should have had much more practice in perceiving and discriminating letters of the Roman alphabet. Although the Spanish-speaking students were faster and less error prone than the Arabic students, the Japanese students were the fastest performers in this task and also the most accurate.

Table 1. Component Skills and Assessment Procedures in Experiment 1

Skill Assessed	Measurement Instrument	Comments
Overall reading proficiency	Standardized cloze test[a] Cloze test developed by authors Multiple-choice comprehension test developed by authors	Composite reading score based on average of tests, equally weighted
Visual discrimination efficiency of Roman alphabetic letter patterns	Same-different matching of high-frequency words, regularly spelled nonwords, and irregularly spelled nonwords, all of which were four letters long	Efficiency scores computed by dividing accuracy by time for for completion
Visual discrimination of nonalphabetic shapes	Matching-to-sample of complex figures developed by authors	Efficiency scores computed by dividing accuracy by time for completion
Translation from spelling to sound	Adapted version of Slosson Oral Reading Test (SORT)	Timed pronunciation of words and regularly spelled nonwords[b]
Vocabulary knowledge	Standardized vocabulary test[a]	
Grammar knowledge	Standardized grammar test[a]	
Listening comprehension	Standardized listening test[a]	
Progress measures	Difference scores on standardized tests	Term final minus term initial scores on standardized tests

[a] Tests developed, maintained, and administered by staff at Michigan State University's English language program

[b] Accuracy estimated through recorded protocols

When we examined the groups' performance on a second visual task — this time involving visual discrimination of abstract figures rather than words and letter strings — we found that Japanese students maintained their large advantage in time and errors but that the performance of the Spanish-speaking students was essentially equal to that of the Arabic students. The change in relative performance levels between Arabic and Spanish-speaking students would be expected: When the advantage of letter familiarity was removed, the Spanish-speaking students should perform more like the Arabic students. However, the continuing overall advantage of Japanese students in both visual

Table 2. Variables and Effects in Same-Different Matching
of Letter Strings

Variable of Effect	Levels or Contrasts	Comments or Examples
Language background	Japanese, Arabic, or Spanish	Between-groups comparison
Stimulus type	Words, regularly spelled nonwords (pseudowords), or irregularly spelled nonwords (nonsense) strings)	Words: *pressing, dressing* Pseudowords: *prossing, drossing* Nonwords: *prngcsis, drngcsis*
Stimulus length	Four letters or seven to ten letters	will vs. devised well revised
Response type	Same or different	will vs. will well well
Position of difference	1st, 2nd, 3rd, or 4th quarter	1: pressing 2: promises dressing premiscs 3: irrigate 4: paradise irritate paradigm
Familiarity effect	Difference in reaction times between words and pseudowords	Can indicate contribution of visual familiarity or lexicality
Orthography effect	Difference in reaction times between pseudowords and nonsense strings	Can indicate contribution of spelling regularity while controlling for visual familiarity and lexicality

tasks suggests that their efficiency in visual processing is not specific to the graphemically based materials of the same-different matching task.

This interpretation of group differences in the visual discrimination tasks was qualified by the findings of a third task, a modified version of the Slosson Oral Reading Test (SORT), in which students were asked to pronounce as quickly and accurately as possible a list of twenty orthographically regular letter strings. Four lists were used, two consisting of words and two consisting of regularly spelled nonwords (called *pseudowords*) that students had not seen before. One list of each type consisted of short strings (three or four letters), and the other consisted of long strings (eight to twelve letters). The size of the difference in reading time between the word lists and the pseudoword lists (called the *familiarity effect*) can indicate the fluency of spelling-to-sound translation ability and the relative contribution of sight-word knowledge to performance. For example, if performance on pseudowords is substantially slower than performance on words, we can infer that spelling-to-sound translation skill is not very fluent and that sight-word knowledge may contribute heavily to performance on the word lists. In scoring SORT performance, we

measured the elapsed time for each list to be read and also estimated pronunciation accuracy through independent judges' scoring of the recorded protocols.

Analysis of variance on the speed scores, which were broken down by language group, stimulus length, and stimulus type (word or pseudoword), revealed no differences between language groups on short words and pseudowords. On the long letter strings, however, Japanese students were considerably slower than the other two groups, and they were affected more adversely by the shift from words to pseudowords. However, the overall disadvantage of speed for Japanese students was offset somewhat by a small (nonsignificant) trend toward greater accuracy. These findings suggest that the Japanese students' superiority in the visual discrimination and matching tasks did not carry over to spelling-to-sound translation. Japanese students' large advantage in both speed and errors in the tests of visual discrimination was not present in their performance on the SORT task.

Another aspect of the SORT data points to differences among groups in the nature of their pronunciation skills that complement the differences in visual discrimination. This aspect involves the interaction between language group, stimulus length, and stimulus type. The Japanese students tended to show a larger familiarity effect, which suggests that they relied relatively more on sight-word knowledge and relatively less on rule-governed spelling-to-sound translation than the Arabic and Spanish-speaking students did. The familiarity effect was smallest for the Spanish-speaking students, which might reflect some degree of transfer between their L1 and L2 orthographies. In addition, the greater decrement shown by Japanese students in the change from short to long stimuli suggests that some correlate of length (for example, increased visual or phonological complexity) is critical to their SORT performance. We will return to this question in connection with the second data set, where this possibility was addressed specifically.

So far, we have focused on simple group differences within and between the tasks, which can be viewed as reflecting differential degrees of development of component skills. There is still the question of how the component skills interrelate across and within the language groups. We do not have the space to deal with the correlational findings in detail here, so we will focus on some of the more informative results, extracting some general conclusions about literacy background variables and noting further support of our interpretation concerning visual and phonological processing.

One important relationship to assess is the degree of linkage between the comprehension of spoken language and the comprehension of written language (see, for example, Vavrus and others, 1983). Overall, the correlation between the listening test (see Table 1) and reading comprehension was + .55 ($p < .01$). While listening and reading correlated fairly strongly for Arabic and Spanish-speaking students (+ .57 and + .56, respectively), this correlation was negligible for Japanese students (+ .12, nonsignificant). For Japanese students, listening and reading may represent independent skill domains, where

skill in one area does not necessarily imply skill in the other. One reason for the absence of association may lie in the nature of English language instruction in Japanese high schools and universities, which emphasizes literacy skills over conversational skills (Ishii and Klopf, 1980; Kitao, 1980). Our own research supports this line of reasoning, because it shows that Japanese students tend to be better readers but poorer speakers and listeners — relative to Arabic and Spanish-speaking students — when they enter the English language program at our university. Viewed in this light, the low correlation between listening and reading comprehension seems quite plausible: If reading development outpaces the emergence of oral language skills, it makes sense that the association between the two is relatively weak. The same difference might also be implicated in the SORT findings, which showed that Japanese students tended to rely more on sight-word knowledge and which suggested that they may be less proficient at spelling-to-sound translation than Arabic and Spanish-speaking students are. To the extent that visually based skills outpace oral language skills, trying to recognize words through pronunciation may not pay off for these students. Moreover, the lagging development of oral language skills may make it more difficult for Japanese students to apply orthographic rules in determining the pronunciation of words. Finally, it should be noted that many of the Japanese logographic characters (Kanji) are pronounced differently in different contexts (Hadamitzky and Spahn, 1981). This situation may also encourage visual over phonological encoding.

These speculations about the special role of visual processing among Japanese L2 students led us to conduct the second project (see Table 2), which was designed to focus specifically on visual processing differences between the language groups. Our motivation for the second effort came from the intriguing possibility that the Japanese students were treating the letter strings of the matching task more like the abstract figures of the visual discrimination tasks. Thus, the Japanese students may have been working in a different mode of perceptual processing—one more in line with the logographic features of the script of their native language than with the basically alphabetic nature of English. However, since the same-different matching stimuli of the first project were short and uniform (all had four letters), it is possible that the length of the letter strings interacts with language background such that the advantage of Japanese students on short letter strings becomes negligible — or a disadvantage — on long letter strings. For example, if the shortness of letter strings in the matching task encouraged Japanese students to process them in a nonlinguistic and holistic way, then one might expect the change to long letter strings to be detrimental, as the added visual complexity of long stimuli may exceed the range over which holistic strategies can operate. That is what one might expect from the SORT findings, which showed that the performance of Japanese students on short stimuli was equal in speed to and slightly better in accuracy than the performance of Arabic and Spanish-speaking students, whereas the performance of Japanese students on long stimuli was considerably slower and no different in accuracy.

To investigate these possibilities, we ran a second, considerably expanded version of the same-different matching task with a number of improvements in experimental and statistical control (see design summary in Table 2). The main effect of language background tallied well with our initial findings: Japanese students showed a large advantage in speed and a smaller advantage in error rates over Spanish-speaking and Arabic students. However, the interaction between language group and stimulus length was not significant. Japanese students did not show a greater decrement for long stimuli than the other groups did. In fact, their reaction times increased 15 percent less in going from short to long strings than the reaction times of Arabic and Spanish-speaking students did. Therefore, whatever mode of perceptual processing the Japanese students used in the matching task was not disrupted by added stimulus complexity.

A particularly interesting finding was that the effects of stimulus type (word, pseudoword, or nonsense string) varied across the language groups (see Figure 1). Japanese students showed smaller differences between words and pseudowords and between pseudowords and nonsense strings than the other groups did. Thus, familiarity and orthographic regularity seem to have been less important determinants of matching performance for Japanese students than they were for the other students.

In a related analysis, each language group was divided into high and low L2 proficiency subgroups, based on standing in the English language program. This analysis produced an interaction between stimulus type and L2 proficiency level which showed that the more advanced readers, regardless of language group, were faster overall but that they were also affected more adversely by the loss of orthographic regularity when matching nonsense strings. This finding corresponds well with studies of L1 reading, in which increased sensitivity to spelling regularity is associated with better reading (Mason, 1975; Singer, 1982). The Japanese students exhibited the same pattern, with more advanced Japanese students showing larger orthography effects than beginning Japanese readers. So, while Japanese students may show smaller effects of orthographic regularity overall, their progress in reading English is nevertheless associated with increasing sensitivity to orthographic regularity — just as it is for the other L2 groups and for beginning L1 readers.

Conclusions

Taken together, these results suggest that there may be important differences among Japanese, Arabic, and Spanish-speaking students — particularly concerning visual and orthographic processing — as they acquire skill in reading English. Moreover, the nature of the differences appears to be largely consistent with the varying educational and literacy backgrounds of the groups that we studied. However, it is apparent that our research has posed far more questions than it has answered. In part, that was our intention: to take the

Figure 1. Reaction Times and Error Rates in Same-different Matching
as a Function of Language Background (Panel A), and Broken Down
by Stimulus Type (Panel B).

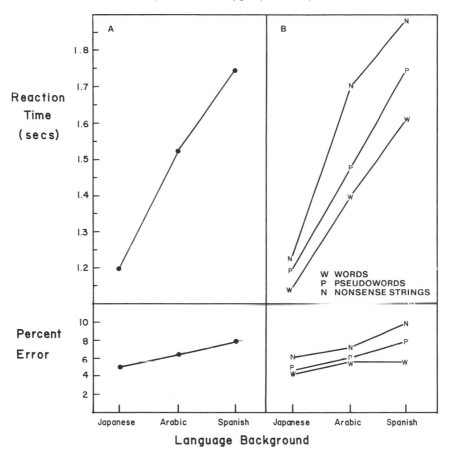

initial steps toward unpacking a class of potential literacy experience variables
and investigating their implications for the acquisition of reading skill. In the
process, we have sought to determine some of the ways in which students of
English from varying first-language backgrounds may differ — information
that can be of benefit to L2 educators in the United States. In regard to contemporary research on L2 reading, it seems clear that assumptions of homoge-
neity among L2 readers must be made with caution and that generalizations
across language backgrounds may frequently be unwarranted. Finally, we
have found at least one parallel between L1 and L2 reading development —
involving the association between language proficiency and orthographic
regularity in same-different matching — that reinforces and generalizes the
understanding of reading development in general. In turn, the ability of the

techniques that we used to produce these findings reinforces the utility of the component skills approach and suggests that continued application of that method may prove fruitful.

References

Anderson, J. R. "Acquisition of Cognitive Skill." *Psychological Review,* 1982, *89* (4), 369–406.

Anderson, R. C., and Freebody, P. "Vocabulary Knowledge." In J. T. Guthrie (Ed.), *Comprehension and Teaching.* Newark, Del.: International Reading Association, 1981.

Baddeley, A. D., and Hitch, G. "Working Memory." In G. Bower (Ed.), *The Psychology of Learning and Motivation.* Vol. 8. New York: Academic Press, 1974.

Baron, J. "Successive Stages in Word Recognition." In P. M. A. Rabbitt and S. Dornic (Eds), *Attention and Performance V.* London: Academic Press, 1975.

Barr, J. "Reading a Script Without Vowels." In W. Haas (Ed.), *Writing Without Letters.* Totowa, N.J.: Rowman and Littlefield, 1976.

Barron, R. W., and Henderson, L. "The Effects of Lexical and Semantic Information on Same-Different Visual Comparison of Words." *Memory and Cognition,* 1977, *5* (5), 566–579.

Bley-Vroman, R. "The Comparative Fallacy in Interlanguage Studies: The Case of Systematicity." *Language Learning,* 1983, *33* (1), 1–18.

Broadbent, D. E. *Perception and Communication.* Elmsford, N. Y.: Pergamon Press, 1958.

Bryan, W. L., and Harter, N. "Studies on the Telegraphic Language." *Psychological Review,* 1899, *6* (4), 344–375.

Carr, T. H. "Building Theories of Reading Ability: On the Relation Between Individual Differences in Cognitive Skills and Reading Comprehension." *Cognition,* 1981, *9,* 73–114.

Carr, T. H., Posner, M. I., Pollatsek, A., and Snyder, C. R. R. "Orthography and Familiarity Effects in Word Processing." *Journal of Experimental Psychology: General,* 1979, *108* (4), 389–414.

Carrell, P. L. "Three Components of Background Knowledge in Reading Comprehension." *Language Learning,* 1983, *33* (2), 183–207.

Chen, H., and Juola, J. F. "Dimensions of Lexical Coding in Chinese and English." *Memory and Cognition,* 1982, *10* (3), 216–224.

Chihara, T., Oller, J., Weaver, K., and Chavez-Oller, M. "Are Cloze Items Sensitive to Constraints Across Sentences?" *Language Learning,* 1977, *27* (1), 63–69.

Clarke, M. A., and Silberstein, S. "Toward a Realization of Psycholinguistic Principles in the ESL Reading Class." *Language Learning,* 1977, *27* (1), 135–154.

Cziko, G. "Differences in First- and Second-Language Reading: The Use of Syntactic, Semantic, and Discourse Constraints." *Canadian Modern Language Review,* 1978, *34* (3), 473–489.

Cziko, G. "Language Competence and Reading Strategies: A Comparison of First-and Second-Language Oral Reading Errors." *Language Learning,* 1980, *30* (1), 101–116.

Devine, J. "Developmental Patterns in Native and Nonnative Reading Acquisition." In S. Hudelson (Ed.), *Papers in Applied Linguistics: Linguistics and Literacy, Series 1: Learning to Read in Different Languages.* Washington, D.C.: Center for Applied Linguistics, 1980.

Fitts, P. M., and Posner, M. I. *Human Performance.* Monterey, Calif.: Brooks/Cole, 1967.

Frederiksen, J. R. *Assessment of Perceptual, Decoding, and Lexical Skills and Their Relation to Reading Proficiency.* Technical Report No. 1. Boston: Bolt Beranek and Newman, 1978.

Frederiksen, J. R. "Sources of Process Interactions in Reading." In A. M. Lesgold and C. A. Perfetti (Eds.), *Interactive Processes in Reading.* Hillsdale, N.J.: Erlbaum, 1981.

Goodman, K. "Reading: A Psycholinguistic Guessing Game." *Journal of the Reading Specialist,* 1967, *4* (1), 126–135.

Goodman, Y. K., and Burke, C. L. *Reading Miscue Inventory: Manual Procedure for Diagnosis and Evaluation.* New York: Macmillan, 1972.

Graesser, A. C., Hoffman, N., and Clark, L. F. "Structural Components of Reading Time." *Journal of Verbal Learning and Verbal Behavior,* 1980, *19* (2), 135–151.

Hadamitzky, W., and Spahn, M. *Kanji and Kana.* Tokyo: Charles E. Tuttle, 1981.

Haddad, F. T. "First-Language Illiteracy — Second-Language Reading: A Case Study." In S. Hudelson (Ed.), *Papers in Applied Linguistics: Linguistics and Literacy, Series 1: Learning to Read in Different Languages.* Washington, D. C.: Center for Applied Linguistics, 1981.

Hasher, L., and Zacks, R. T. "Automatic and Effortful Processes in Memory." *Journal of Experimental Psychology: General,* 1979, *108* (3), 356–388.

Hatch, E., Polin, P., and Part, S. "Acoustic Scanning and Syntactic Processing: Three Reading Experiments — First- and Second-Language Learners." *Journal of Reading Behavior,* 1974, *6* (3), 275–285.

Henderson, R. T. "An Analysis of the Role of Basic Perceptual and Cognitive Processes in the Reading Ability of Arabic-Speaking ESL Students." Paper presented at the annual conference of the Teachers of English to Speakers of Other Languages, Houston, March 1984.

Hung, D. L., and Tzeng, O. J. L. "Orthographic Variations and Visual Information Processing." *Psychological Bulletin,* 1981, *90* (3), 377–414.

Ishii, S., and Klopf, D. "Increasing Instructional Effectiveness: Reducing Classroom Apprehension." Paper presented at the international conference of the Japanese Association of Language Teachers on Language Teaching and Learning, Nagoya, Japan, 1980.

Kahneman, D. *Attention and Effort.* Englewood Cliffs, N.J.: Prentice-Hall, 1973.

Kitao, K. "Japanese Exchange Students' Evaluation of English Teaching in Japan." *Doshisha Daikagu Eigo Eibungako Kenkyu,* 1980, *25,* 121–141.

Kreusler, A. "Bilingualism in the Soviet Non-Russian Schools." *Elementary School Journal,* 1961, 62 (1), 94–99.

LaBerge, D. "Automatic Information Processing: A Review." In J. Long and A. Baddeley (Eds.), *Attention and Performance IX.* Hillsdale, N.J.: Erlbaum, 1981.

LaBerge, D., and Samuels, S. J. "Toward a Theory of Automatic Information Processing in Reading." *Cognitive Psychology,* 1974, *6* (2), 293–323.

Levy, B. A. "Vocalization and Suppression Effects in Sentence Memory." *Journal of Verbal Learning and Verbal Behavior,* 1975, *14* (3), 304–316.

Logan, G. "On the Use of a Concurrent Memory Load to Measure Attention and Automaticity." *Journal of Experimental Psychology: Human Perception and Performance,* 1979, *5* (2), 189–207.

MacKay, D. G. "The Problems of Flexibility, Fluency, and Speed-Accuracy Trade-off in Skilled Behavior." *Psychological Review,* 1982, *89* (5), 483–506.

Martin, S. E. "Nonalphabetic Writing Systems: Some Observations." In J. F. Kavanagh and I. G. Mattingly (Eds.), *Language by Ear and by Eye.* Cambridge, Mass.: M.I.T. Press, 1972.

Mason, M. "Reading Ability and Letter Search Time: Effects of Orthographic Structure Defined by Single-Letter Positional Frequency." *Journal of Experimental Psychology: General,* 1975, *104* (2), 146–166.

Mason, M. "From Print to Sound in Mature Readers as a Function of Reader Ability and Two Forms of Orthographic Regularity." *Memory and Cognition,* 1978, *6* (5), 568–581.

Modiano, N. "Reading Comprehension in the National Language: A Comparative Study of Bilingual and All-Spanish Approaches to Reading Instruction in Selected Indian Schools of the Highlands of Chiapas, Mexico." Unpublished doctoral dissertation, New York University, 1966.

Norman, D. A. "Categorization of Action Slips." *Psychological Review,* 1981, *88*(1), 1-15.

Oller, J. W., and Tullius, J. R. "Reading Skills of Nonnative Speakers of English." *International Review of Applied Linguistics in Language Teaching,* 1973, *11* (1), 69-79.

Perfetti, C. A., Goldman, S., and Hogaboam, T. "Reading Skill and the Identification of Words in Discourse Context." *Memory and Cognition,* 1979, *7* (4), 273-282.

Perfetti, C. A., and Hogaboam, T. "Relationship Between Single-Word Decoding and Reading Comprehension Skill." *Journal of Educational Psychology,* 1975, *67* (4), 461-469.

Perfetti, C. A., and Lesgold, A. "Discourse Comprehension and Sources of Individual Differences." In M. Just and P. Carpenter (Eds.), *Cognitive Processes in Comprehension.* Hillsdale, N.J.: Erlbaum, 1978.

Posner, M. I. "Cumulative Development of Attentional Theory." *American Psychologist,* 1982, *37* (2), 168-179.

Posner, M. I., and Snyder, C. R. R. "Attention and Cognitive Control." In R. L. Solso (Ed.), *Information Processing and Cognition.* Hillsdale, N.J.: Erlbaum, 1975.

Reason, J. "Skill and Error in Everyday Life." In M. Howe (Ed.), *Adult Learning.* London: Wiley, 1977.

Reason, J. "Actions Not Planned: The Price of Automatization." In G. Underwood and R. Stevens (Eds.), *Aspects of Consciousness.* London: Academic Press, 1979.

Riggs, P. "The Miscue-ESL Project." In H. D. Brown, C. A. Yorio, and R. H. Crymes (Eds.), *On TESOL '77: Teaching and Learning English as a Second Language: Trends in Research and Practice.* Washington, D.C.: Teachers of English to Speakers of Other Languages, 1977.

Rosier, P., and Holm, W. "The Rock Point Experience: A Longitudinal Study of a Navajo School Program." *Bilingual Education Series 8: Papers in Applied Linguistics.* Washington, D.C.: Center for Applied Linguistics, 1980.

Scribner, S., and Cole, M. *The Psychology of Literacy.* Cambridge, Mass.: Harvard University Press, 1981.

Selinker, L. "Interlanguage." *International Review of Applied Linguistics in Language Teaching,* 1972, *10* (3), 209-231.

Shiffrin, R. M., and Schneider, W. "Controlled and Automatic Human Information Processing II: Perceptual Learning, Automatic Attending, and a General Theory." *Psychological Review,* 1977, *84* (2), 127-190.

Singer, M. H. *Competent Reader, Disabled Reader: Research and Application.* Hillsdale, N.J.: Erlbaum, 1982.

Singer, M. H., and Crouse, J. "The Relationship of Context-Use Skills to Reading: A Case for an Alternative Experimental Logic." *Child Development,* 1981, *52,* 1326-1329.

Stanovich, K. E., and West, R. F. "The Effect of Sentence Context on Ongoing Word Recognition: Tests of a Two-Process Theory." *Journal of Experimental Psychology: Human Perception and Performance,* 1981, *7* (3), 658-672.

Tarone, E. F. "Systematicity and Attention in Interlanguage." *Language Learning,* 1982, *32* (1), 69-83.

Treiman, R., Baron, J., and Luk, K. "Type of Orthography Affects Use of Sound in Silent Reading." *Journal of Chinese Linguistics,* 1981, *9,* 116-125.

Vavrus, L., Brown, T., and Carr, T. H. "Component Skill Profiles of Reading Ability: Variations, Trade-offs, and Compensation." Paper presented at the meeting of the Psychonomic Society, San Diego, Calif., November 1983.

West, R. F., and Stanovich, K. E. "Automatic Contextual Facilitation in Readers of Three Ages." *Child Development*, 1978, *49* (3), 717-727.

West, R. F., and Stanovich, K. E. "Source of Inhibition in Experiments on the Effect of Sentence Context on Word Recognition." *Journal of Experimental Psychology: Learning, Memory, and Cognition*, 1982, *8* (5), 385-399.

Tracy L. Brown is completing postgraduate work in cognitive psychology at Michigan State University. His principal research interests include individual differences in reading ability and the roles of attention and automaticity in human performance.

Margot Haynes is an interdisciplinary doctoral student at Michigan State University, where she approaches comparative reading through the departments of Linguistics, English, and Psychology. She is currently working as reading coordinator at the International English Institute in Nashville, Tennessee.

It is not only whether a child knows the words in a text, but also how well the words are known that affects comprehension.

Knowing Words and Understanding Texts

Richard C. Omanson

Ideally, a school's reading program should be able to provide reading experiences that result in proficient reading skill for all children, including those who find reading difficult. In practice, schools fall short of this ideal. One reason is that children often have trouble comprehending stories that are part of their reading lessons. If reading an assigned story is so difficult for children that they understand and retain little from the experience, then it is likely that some of the processes involved in proficient comprehension are not sufficiently well practiced to enable the reading process to proceed smoothly and efficiently. Reading under such circumstances is not likely to foster either the motivation to read or the kind of improvement in reading that will change the circumstances.

One factor that has a big influence is the extent to which children are familiar with individual words. Most of the words encountered in basal reading selections are common and familiar. However, some unfamiliar words are included to give children practice in figuring out the meaning of words from context. Basal readers also contain words that have very recently been taught to the children. Current theories of reading suggest that such variation in word knowledge affects comprehension (for example, Rumelhart, 1977). According to these theories, variation in word knowledge is thought to affect not only the processing of individual words but also the processing of clauses

T. H. Carr (Ed.). *The Development of Reading Skills.* New Directions for Child Development, no. 27. San Francisco: Jossey-Bass, March 1985.

and sentences that takes place during comprehension. However, these theories have not spelled out exactly how comprehension processes change as a result of variation in word knowledge. Therefore, this chapter explores some different ways in which children's comprehension processes may be affected by variation in word knowledge. It also examines whether the effects of word knowledge on comprehension are similiar for skilled and less-skilled readers.

Effects of Word Knowledge on Recall

The first question to address is whether comprehension differs for texts that contain unfamiliar words and texts that contain recently instructed words. Comprehension refers to a person's understanding of what is stated in and implied by a text. There are a number of ways in which a person's understanding of a text can be assessed. Common procedures include answering questions, composing summaries, and recalling the text from memory. The method used to assess comprehension that will be considered here is recall. The rationale for using recall to assess comprehension is that recall reflects a person's representation of the text in memory that in turn is a result of the reader's particular understanding of the text (Kintsch and van Dijk, 1978). Moreover, since the goal of reading is to gain information that can be used at a later time, and since recall is a conservative measure of the information that has been gained from a text, the use of recall as a measure of comprehension is particularly appropriate.

I will begin by describing a study reported by McKeown and others (1983) and its subsequent reanalysis by Omanson and others (1983). McKeown and colleagues taught inner-city fourth-grade children approximately 100 words through an unusually rich and intensive vocabulary program that extended over a five-month period. At the end of that instruction, the children were given two texts to read and recall from memory. One text, called the instructed-words story, was 270 words long and contained thirty instructed words. The other text, called the uninstructed-words story, was of similar length and structure and contained thirty unfamiliar words. By comparing the children's recall of the two stories, the effects of recently instructed and unfamiliar words on comprehension could be compared. To ensure that any observed differences in the recall of the two stories were due primarily to the differences in vocabulary rather than to content or structural differences, the two stories were given to a second group of fourth-graders who had not been taught any of the words. If the recall of both stories by the control classroom was similar to the recall of the uninstructed-words story by the experimental classroom, it could be inferred that the recall differences were due primarily to vocabulary differences. Thus, there was one situation in which children recalled a story containing instructed words (experimental children's recall of the instructed-words story) and three situations in which children recalled stories

containing unfamiliar words (experimental children's recall of the uninstructed-words story and the control children's recall of both stories).

In order to score the recalls of the stories, each story was divided into units of meaning called *propositions* (Kintsch and van Dijk, 1978), which will be described in more detail later. Each child's recall was then scored according to whether the gist of each story proposition appeared in the recall. In this way, the percentage of the propositions recalled by each child could be computed. The performance of each group was the average percentage of propositions recalled by children in the group.

The results of the scoring indicated that recall was highest for the story containing words that had been taught to the children. The children recalled about 20 percent of the story containing recently taught words but only about 11 percent of the stories that contained unfamiliar words. Moreover, when the recalls of the children who were skilled in reading were examined separately from those of children who were less skilled in reading, the same pattern of results was obtained. Both skilled and less-skilled readers recalled about twice as much from the story containing recently taught words as from the stories containing unfamiliar words.

The variation in word knowledge not only affected how much was recalled, but it also affected which parts of the story were likely to be recalled. Among the propositions that were recalled, a characteristic pattern was observed. Propositions containing recently taught words were more likley to be recalled than propositions containing only familiar words, and propositions containing unfamiliar words were less likely to be recalled than propositions containing only familiar words. In other words, the children were biased toward remembering the parts of the story containing the recently taught words and against remembering the parts of the story containing unfamiliar words.

In order to get a better sense of the qualitative differences between the recall of the story containing recently taught words and of the stories containing unfamiliar words, prototypical recalls were constructed to approximate the recall of the instructed-words story by the experimental group (who had been taught the instructed words) and by the control group (who were not familiar with the instructed words). The prototypical recalls were constructed by, first, rank ordering the propositions of the story according to the number of children in each condition who recalled them. Next, the mean recall for each group was rounded off to the nearest whole number of propositions; then, that number of propositions was taken from the top of each group's rank ordering to create the prototypical recalls. The recalls generated in this way are presented in Table 1.

The plot of the instructed-words story centers on an ambitious violin novice, Sam, who gives a concert. A large woman interrupts Sam by talking to an acquaintance and by eating food from a table being set for a party after the

Table 1. Prototypical Recalls of the Instructed-Words Story for the Experimental and Control Groups

Experimental	*Control*
There was a man named Sam. Sam was a NOVICE at playing the violin. Sam gave a concert. There was a woman in the audience. The OBESE woman said something to an ACQUAINTANCE. There was something EDIBLE. The woman began to DEVOUR everything. Sam asked if the woman couldn't FAST. Sam THRUST his violin on the stage and began to TRUDGE away. There was an ALLY. He SEIZED Sam and suggested that they all play music. Some people began to play instruments. Everyone felt PLACID.	There was a man named Sam. Sam played the violin. He rented a hall, invited some people, and gave a concert. He began to play some notes. There was a woman in the audience. Some people began to play instruments. Everyone went home feeling PLACID.

Note: Instructed words are capitalized.
Source: McKeown and others, 1983.

concert. Soon, everyone begins to talk with each other, and Sam walks off stage. Fortunately, a friend runs up to Sam and suggests that the audience play music with him. Instruments are found for the audience. Everyone plays and leaves feeling content.

As Table 1 shows, there are large differences between the prototypical recalls of this story by the experimental and control groups. The experimental group's prototypical recall of the instructed-words story contains twenty propositions, thirteen of which contained instructed words. It provides a reasonable summary of the story, in that it includes the initial setting — Sam, a novice at playing the violin, gave a concert; the conflict — he was repeatedly interrupted by a woman, which caused him to walk away; and the resolution offered by Sam's ally — the audience joint him in playing music, which caused them to be content (see Chapter Four in this volume). In contrast, the control group's prototypical recall of the instructed-words story contains twelve propositions, only one of which contains an instructed word. It does not provide as good a summary, in that it omits from the setting the fact that Sam was a novice, it omits the conflict created by the interruptions while Sam was playing, and consequently it does not depict the audience's also playing instruments as a resolution to a conflict.

Thus, it is clear that vocabulary instruction can affect text comprehension. At this point we may ask whether the nature of the vocabulary instruction itself is important. That is, some types of vocabulary instruction may be much more successful than others in facilitating the comprehension of texts containing the instructed words. The few studies addressing the effects of vocabulary instruction on comprehension report conflicting findings. Some

report improved comprehension (for example, Beck and others, 1982; Draper and Moeller, 1971; Kameenui and others, 1982), while others report no difference (Jenkins and others, 1978; Tuinman and Brady, 1974).

If the instruction used in these different studies is compared, it appears that focusing on multiple aspects of vocabulary knowledge may be an important factor in the effect of vocabulary instruction on comprehension. For example, in the study by McKeown and others (1983), the words were taught in sets of eight to ten. Initially, the children received instruction on each set of words for five days. On the first day, definitions were established, and one or two activities were presented that involved the children with the words. On the second day, the children wrote sentences for each word and engaged in some additional activity that provided fairly easy practice with word meanings. On the third day, the children were given activities in which they generated contexts containing new words. The purpose of these activities was to broaden the students' understanding of the words by promoting the establishment of relations between new words and known words. The fourth day included an exercise that encouraged the children to think about the words in new ways and an activity in which the children repeatedly matched words and definitions while being timed. The second activity was designed to increase fluent access to word meanings. On the fifth day, students took a multiple-choice test on the words studied. In addition, there were review sessions in which the words received practice activities. Thus, for a typical set of words, students received about forty encounters with each word in a highly varied instructional environment.

This type of instruction stands in sharp contrast to that found in basal reading programs. The best situation in those programs occurs when a new vocabulary word is introduced in a sentence that elucidates its meaning; encountered in the reading selection, which prompts the child to look up its definition in the glossary; and appears in an activity completed independently after reading (Beck and others, 1983). Thus, in this best situation, the children only receive four, very limited encounters with each new word.

Effects of Word Knowledge on Comprehension Processes

Since the recall data reported by McKeown and others (1983) demonstrated that stories with unfamiliar words are comprehended differently from stories with recently taught words, we can now address how the comprehension processes are affected. Describing comprehension processes is difficult. One can observe and describe differences in an outcome of comprehension, such as recall. However, one cannot observe the comprehension processes directly to determine their nature or how they differ in different situations. What can be done is to construct different models of what the processing might entail and then to examine which model best predicts the observed pattern of recall. This was the approach adopted by Omanson and others (1983). The

models that were constructed by Omanson and colleagues were based on a model of comprehension processing presented by Kintsch and van Dijk (1978).

Kintsch and Van Dijk's Model. Kintsch and van Dijk's model of comprehension is concerned with the comprehension processes that operate on the meaning of clauses and sentences. According to their view, comprehension begins by deriving a conceptual, or propositional, representation of each sentence in the text. A proposition consists of a predicate, or relation, and one or more arguments. Arguments can be either concepts within propositions or other propositions. For example, the phrase *A fat dog bit John* can be represented by two propositions: BITE, DOG, JOHN and QUALITY OF, DOG, FAT, where BITE, DOG, JOHN, QUALITY OF, and FAT are concepts derived from the words in *A fat dog bit John.* In the first proposition, BITE is the predicate, while DOG and JOHN are arguments that stand in a particular relation to BITE. Specifically, DOG is the entity that BITES, and JOHN is the entity that gets BITTEN. Similarly, in the second proposition, QUALITY OF is the predicate, while DOG and FAT are arguments. Here, DOG is the entity that has the QUALITY, and FAT is the QUALITY.

While propositional notation may appear cumbersome, the rationale behind it is simple: It attempts to represent the meaning of sentences in a formal and unequivocal way that allows research on sentence meaning to be done systematically. The meaning of sentences involves concepts that are distinct from the surface form of the text. For example, the phrase *John was bitten by a dog who was fat* has a very different surface form than *A fat dog bit John* but approximately the same meaning. Within Kintsch and van Dijk's theory, to say that two sentences have the same meaning is to say that they have the same conceptual representation. Propositional notation is thus intended to be an approximation of this conceptual representation of sentences, which is derived from but not identical with their surface form.

As the propositions from each sentence are encoded, they are represented in memory as a coherent structure called a *text base.* The coherence that Kintsch and van Dijk consider is the extent to which concepts (that is, arguments) in a text are repeated. If two propositions have the same argument, like DOG in BITE, DOG, JOHN and QUALITY OF, DOG, FAT, the propositions can be connected by using that argument. Thus, to say that a reader constructs a coherent text base is to say that the propositions extracted from the text are connected to each other in memory on the basis of argument repetition (cf. Chapter Four in this volume).

Kintsch and van Dijk's model of how a text base is constructed begins with the assumption that a reader is limited in how much can be kept in mind, or in short-term memory, at any given time; as a result, a reader cannot comprehend a text all at once. Instead, the reader goes through the text in a series of processing cycles. For most texts, the processing cycle corresponds to single sentences. Upon reading a sentence, the reader extracts the propositions that constitute the sentence's meaning and connects the propositions of the sen-

tence to each other on the basis of argument repetition. The processing of the propositions of a single sentence is known as a *processing cycle*. The propositions that are processed are said to be *in the cycle*.

In order to illustrate cycling, let us consider the processing cycles for the propositions extracted from the first three sentences of the instructed-words story depicted in Figure 1. The cycles of the Kintsch and van Dijk model appear as the normal model in the left-most column. The propositions referred to in Figure 1 are presented in Table 2. (Ignore for the moment that some propositions are designated as instructed propositions.) In the first cycle, proposition 2, ISA, SAM, NOVICE, is selected as the lead proposition on an intuitive basis, because it best captures the gist of the sentence. The other propositions, propositions 1 and 3, are connected to the lead proposition on the basis of argument overlap. To depict this connection, lines are drawn from proposition 2 to propositions 1 and 3. Since propositions 1 and 3 are connected to proposition 2, they are subordinate to it. This subordination is depicted in Figure 1 by the fact that propositions 1 and 3 form a column to the right of proposition 2.

In addition to being connected to themselves, the propositions of the newly encoded sentence are also connected to a proposition derived from a prior sentence that was held in memory (carried over) from the previous pro-

Table 2. Propositions Contained in the First Three Cycles of the Instructed-Words Story

Propositions	*Text*
Cycle 1	
1. EXIST, SAM	Sam was a NOVICE at playing the
2. ISA, SAM, NOVICE	violin.
3. QUALIFY, 2, AT VIOLIN	
Cycle 2	
4. GIVE, VIRTUOSO, CONCERTS	He knew that usually a VIRTUOSO
5. QUALIFY, 4, USUALLY,	gave concerts, but he was AMBITIOUS.
6. KNOW, SAM, 4	
7. QUALITY OF, SAM AMBITIOUS	
8. CONTRAST, 4, 7	
Cycle 3	
9. RENT, SAM, HALL	So, one day Sam rented a music hall
10. QUALIFY, HALL, MUSIC	and invited some people to hear him
11. TIME, 9, ONE DAY	play.
12. CAUSE, 9, 7	
13. INVITE, SAM, PEOPLE	
14. PLAY, SAM	
15. HEAR, PEOPLE, 14	
16. PURPOSE, 13, 14, 15	

Note: Words in the text that were either unfamiliar or instructed are capitalized.
Source: McKeown and others, 1983.

Figure 1. First Three Cycles of the Normal, Substitution, Suppression and Remind Models for the Instructed-Words Story

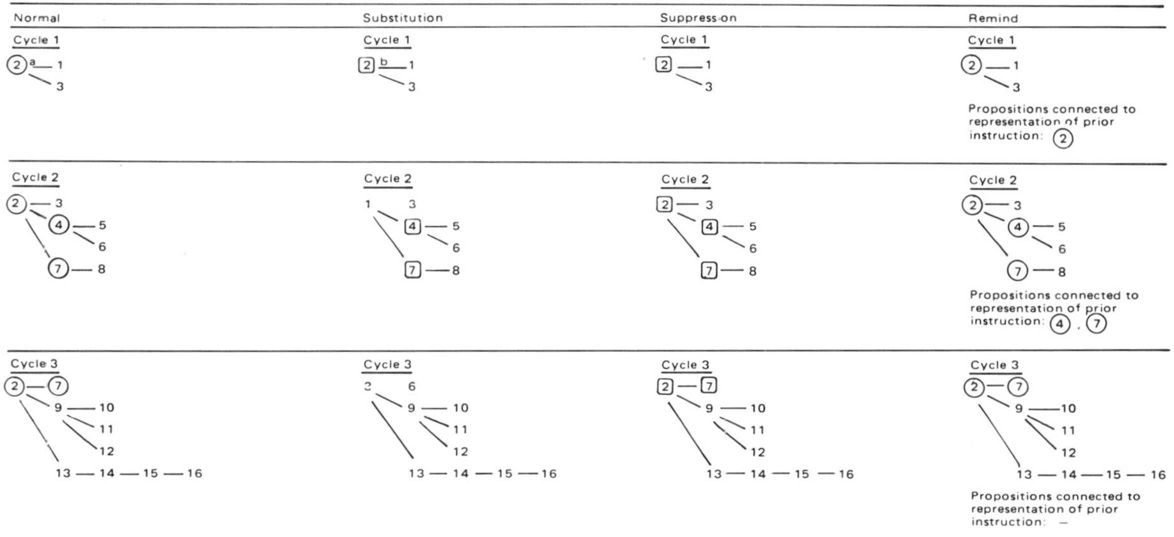

Credited Cycles of Selected Propositions

Normal: Proposition	Cycles	Substitution: Proposition	Cycles	Suppression: Proposition	Cycles	Remind: Proposition	Cycles
(2)	3	[2]	1	[2]	1	(2)	4
(4)	1	[4]	1	[4]	1	(4)	2
(7)	2	[7]	1	[7]	1	(7)	3
1	1	1	2	1	1	1	1
3	2	3	3	3	2	3	2
6	1	6	2	6	1	6	1

[a] Propositions assumed by model to be instructed are circled.

[b] Propositions assumed by model to be unfamiliar and incompletely represented are boxed.

cessing cycle. Because of the limitations of how much can be held in short-term memory, only a small number of propositions can be carried over from a previous cycle. Kintsch and van Dijk suggest that a leading edge strategy is used to determine which propositions are carried over. The leading edge strategy favors both important propositions (that is, propositions that are superordinate) and recent propositions (that is, propositions that were the last to be extracted and connected to the other propositions in the sentence). The leading edge strategy selects the most superordinate or lead proposition and the most recent propositions connected to the lead proposition. The text base is constructed by connecting the propositions of a sentence to each other and to propositions from previous sentences.

It sometimes happens that there is no argument overlap between the propositions carried over and the newly encoded propositions. In this case, a proposition from an earlier cycle that share an argument with one of the newly encoded propositions is retrieved from long-term memory. Retrieving propositions of a previous cycle from long-term memory is referred to as *reinstating* them. Once a proposition is reinstated, a connection is made between the reinstated proposition and one of the newly encoded propositions.

In summary, the text base of a text is constructed by organizing the propositions of each sentence into a coherence graph and by connecting these propositions to previously encoded propositions that are either carried over or reinstated from previous cycles. On the basis of these processing assumptions, Kintsch and van Dijk's model predicts that the probability with which a proposition will be recalled increases as the number of cycles in which it appears increases. The specific relationship is mathematically described as $1 - (1 - p)^n$, where p equals the probability of a reader's recalling a proposition that has appeared in a single cycle, and n equals the number of cycles in which the proposition has appeared. Using this mathematical expression for each proposition, the fit of the model can be tested against actual recall by calculating an optimal value for p and by computing the difference between the predicted and actual recall for all the propositions.

Texts with Unfamiliar Words. Within the framework of Kintsch and van Dijk's theory, we will consider models of two ways in which texts containing unfamiliar words may be comprehended. Both models share the same assumption about how propositions containing unfamiliar words are encoded. According to Kintsch and van Dijk, comprehension involves connecting in memory newly encoded propositions (hereafter called *new propositions*) to previously encoded propositions (hereafter called *old propositions*). Encountering a proposition containing an unfamiliar word (hereafter called an *unfamiliar proposition*) could conceivably affect both its encoding and its connection to new propositions. Since the Kintsch and van Dijk model describes comprehension after propositional encoding has taken place, it does not help to describe how the process of encoding itself might be affected. However, one can postulate that the product of the encoding process will be different for familiar and unfa-

miliar propositions. One possibility in this regard is that only a vague sense of the unfamiliar word's meaning will be encoded, resulting in an incomplete representation of the proposition. For example, if a reader is unfamiliar with the word *novice,* his or her representation of the proposition *The novice played the violin* may be akin to *Someone played the violin,* rather than to *The beginner played the violin.*

If unfamiliar propositions are incompletely represented, comprehension could be affected in several ways. One possibility is that a different text base might be constructed. This could happen if cycling followed a substitution principle, in which new propositions were connected only to familiar, not to unfamiliar, propositions. The motivation for such a principle is that readers may attempt to process unfamiliar propositions as little as possible, and as a result, they connect new information only to the parts of the text that they have successfully understood. (Anderson and Freebody, in press, propose a similar notion, which they call the *minimum effort principle.*)

Using Kintsch and van Dijk's model as a framework, we can represent the substitution principle by a substitution model, in which familiar propositions are substituted for unfamiliar propositions during cycling. The propositional structure created by this model differs from the propositional structure created by the Kintsch and van Dijk model. Unfamiliar propositions are connected to fewer propositions, and familiar propositions that otherwise would have been connected to few propositions are connected to more propositions, because they replace the unfamiliar propositions.

In order to illustrate the difference between the substitution model and the Kintsch and van Dijk model (hereafter called the *normal model*), we can consider the processing cycles presented in Figure 1. In the first cycle of the normal model, proposition 2, ISA, SAM, NOVICE, is selected as the lead proposition. This proposition, along with proposition 3, QUALIFY, 2, AT VIOLIN, is carried over into cycle 2. In the study by McKeown and others (1983), the word *novice* was unfamiliar to the children in the control group. Therefore, in the substitution model, even though porposition 2, ISA, SAM, NOVICE, is in the lead position, it is not carried over, and the familiar proposition 1, EXIST, SAM, is carried over instead.

At the bottom of Figure 1 is a summary of the number of cycles in which selected propositions appeared for the normal and substitution models. As this summary shows, unfamiliar propositions enter fewer cycles in the substitution model, and the familiar propositions that replace them enter more cycles than they do in the normal model.

Another possibility for the way in which unfamiliar words affect comprehension is that the structure of the text base is not altered but that the accessibility of unfamiliar propositions is reduced. This would occur if cycling followed a suppression principle, in which new propositions were allowed to be connected to either familiar or unfamiliar propositions. However, since we have assumed that unfamiliar propositions are represented incompletely and therefore rather vaguely, the probability of their recall is suppressed. This

is because only the incomplete representation of the unfamiliar proposition is processed each time it is connected to a new proposition. The suppression principle assumes that repeated processing of an incomplete representation of the unfamiliar proposition will not enhance the probability with which the unfamiliar proposition appears in recall as much as repeated processing of a complete representation will; indeed, at the extreme, recall of incomplete propositions may not be enhanced at all by repeated processing. In its extreme form, then, the suppression principle predicts that, regardless of how many times the incomplete representation of an unfamiliar proposition is processed, the probability with which the entire proposition will be recalled is the same as if it had been processed only once.

Using Kintsch and van Dijk's model as a framework, we can represent the suppression principle by a model in which unfamiliar propositions are connected to new propositions during processing, but they are given credit for appearing in only a single cycle. To illustrate the difference between the suppression model and the normal model, the third column of Figure 1 presents the processing cycles of the suppression model for the first three sentences of the instructed-words story. As Figure 1 shows, the processing cycles of the normal and suppression models are virtually identical. The difference between the models lies in the fact that incomplete representations of unfamiliar propositions 2, 4, and 7 are processed in the suppression model. As a result, the two models differ in the number of cycles for which these unfamiliar propositions receive credit, as the bottom of the figure shows. In the normal model, these propositions receive credit for all the cycles in which they appear. In contrast, in the suppression model, the same propositions receive credit for appearing in only a single cycle, and as a result they are predicted to be recalled less well.

Figure 1 also shows the difference between the suppression and substitution models. As the bottom of Figure 1 shows, in the substitution and suppression models, unfamiliar propositions receive credit for being in only a single cycle. The two models differ in that familiar propositions 1, 3, and 6 appear in more cycles in the substitution model than they do in the suppression model. In the substitution model, unfamiliar propositions appear in only a single cycle, because they are not used in processing subsequent to encoding, and selected familiar propositions appear in additional cycles, because they replace unfamiliar propositions during carryovers. In the suppression model, unfamiliar propositions appear in only a single cycle, because an incomplete representation, which does not benefit recall of an unfamiliar proposition, is carried over during cycling. However, because the incomplete representations are used, there is no substitution, and as a result the processing of familiar propositions is not affected.

Texts with Recently Taught Words. Kintsch and van Dijk's model can also be used as a framework to describe comprehension of texts containing words recently taught. We will consider here two ways in which such texts may be comprehended.

When a reader encounters a proposition containing a word about

which he or she has recently received instruction (hereafter called an *instructed proposition*), processing may be affected in one or another of several ways. One possibility is that processing follows a normal processing principle, in which instructed propositions are treated in the same way as familiar propositions are. Such a principle is assumed by most studies examining the effects of vocabulary instruction on comprehension (for example, Beck and others, 1982; Kameenui and others, 1982; McKeown and others, 1983). Using Kintsch and van Dijk's model as a framework, we can represent the normal processing principle by a model in which instructed and familiar propositions are processed in the same way. Such a model is the original version of Kintsch and van Dijk's (1978) model of comprehension, which makes no distinction between instructed and uninstructed propositions.

A second possibility of how instructed words affect processing is that processing follows a remind principle, in which encountering an instructed word reminds the reader that the word was the object of prior instruction. A number of researchers (for example, Jacoby and Craik, 1979) have demonstrated that remembering the context in which a fact was learned can enhance one's memory of the learned fact. Within this same vein, the remind principle assumes that recognizing a word as an instructed word involves making a connection between the instructed proposition and the reader's representation of his or her instructional experience. Thus, instructed propositions are initially processed twice: once during encoding and again when a connection is made between the instructed proposition and the reader's representation of the prior instructional experience. The remind principle can be represented by a model in which instructed propositions appear in their initial cycle twice. The first appearance is due to the proposition's being encoded into the coherence graph. The second is due to a connection made between the proposition and the reader's representation of the prior instructional experience. This remind connection does not become part of the coherence graph of the text or affect it in any way. Instead, it is processing during which the reader recalls from memory the learning context of the word. Even though being reminded of a word's learning context is not part of the comprehension process per se, it is additional processing, and as a result it might be expected to augment the probability of recall much in the same way as a text reinstatement would. Thus, the remind model expands the Kintsch and van Dijk model to account for not only the effects of text processing but also the effects of connections made to episodic memory parallel to text processing.

In order to illustrate the difference between the remind and normal models, the fourth column of Figure 1 presents the processing cycles of the remind model for the first three sentences of the instructed-words story. As Figure 1 shows, the coherence graphs constructed for the cycles of the normal and the remind models are identical. The two models differ in that instructed proposition 2, ISA, SAM, NOVICE, appears twice in cycle 1 of the remind model, once due to its initial encoding into the coherence graph and once due

to its connection to the reader's representation of the prior instructional experience. In contrast, instructed proposition 2 appears only once in cycle 1 of the normal model, due to its being encoded into the coherence graph. Similarly, instructed proposition 4, GIVE, VIRTUOSO, CONCERTS, and instructed proposition 7, QUALITY OF, SAM, AMBITIOUS, appear twice in cycle 2 of the remind model. The bottom of Figure 1 shows that the instructed propositions receive credit for being in one more cycle in the remind model than in the normal model.

Results. In order to assess how well the different models predicted recall, a computer program was used that calculated a value for p that minimized the difference between predicted and actual recall (Chandler, 1965). The fit of each model was obtained by summing the differences between the predicted and actual recall scores for each proposition; this sum was then standardized by taking the square root of its square divided by the number of propositions. This fit score is referred to as the *root-mean-square-deviation* (RMSD) score. Since RMSD scores reflect deviation from prediction, lower scores indicate better fit. RMSD scores for the four models are presented in Figure 2.

The suppression model best predicted the pattern of recall of the three situations in which children were not familiar with some of the words. This was true for both skilled and less-skilled readers. These results suggest that, when both skilled and less-skilled readers encounter unfamiliar propositions, they attempt to treat them as they do familiar propositions; they do not skip over them. Thus, it is likely that the adverse effects of unfamiliar propositions on text recall are due only to their making some parts of the text base inaccessible, as the suppression model suggests, not to the construction of a different text base, as the substitution model suggests.

Figure 2 shows further that the remind model best predicted the pattern of recall observed in the situation in which children had been taught some of the words; again, this is true for both skilled and less-skilled readers. These results suggest that, when the children encountered propositions containing instructed words, the fact that the target words had been the object of previous classroom instruction was called to mind, which entailed the additional processing that enhanced recall.

Implications

Implications for Theories of Processing. The fact that the suppression model, rather than the substitution model, best predicts the pattern of recall of texts containing unfamiliar words suggests that readers may attempt to minimize the effect that difficulties encountered during the processing of words have on comprehension. Thus, even though propositions containing unfamiliar words are likely to be represented incompletely, these results suggest that readers attempt to construct the same text base that they would construct if the unfamiliar propositions were familiar. This pattern creates a problem, in that

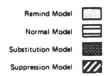

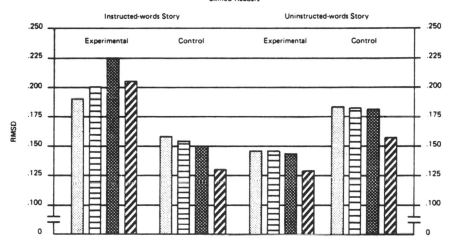

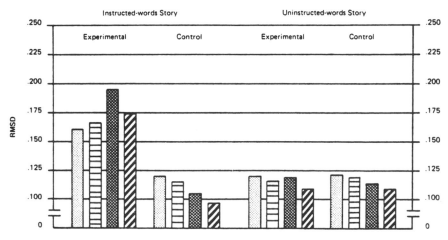

the unfamiliar propositions in the text base are relatively inaccessible during recall because they are incomplete.

The fact that the remind model best predicts the pattern of recall suggests that children can be familiar with words in differing ways, which can have various effects on comprehension. The instruction that children receive may make the context in which the word was learned so salient that it is called to mind whenever the instructed word is encountered. The result is that words learned through instruction may be treated differently than common words that children already know. It is quite possible that the salience of the learning context may diminish in a few weeks, especially as subsequent instruction on new words is encountered. However, without additional data, one can only speculate about how long-lasting or transitory the biasing effect of learning context may be.

The fact that the same pattern of results was obtained for skilled and less-skilled readers suggests that skilled and less-skilled readers adopt similar strategies when adapting to variation in word knowledge. There are many well-documented differences between skilled and less-skilled readers. Less-skilled readers read words more slowly (Perfetti and Hogaboam, 1975), with less semantic activation (Jackson and McClelland, 1979) and less verbatim memory (Goldman and others, 1980) than skilled readers do. However, they do not seem to differ in the nature of their susceptibility to the effects of variation in word knowledge. Of course, less-skilled readers may be more affected by this susceptibility in absolute terms than skilled readers are, simply because less-skilled readers know fewer words on the average than skilled readers do (Davis, 1944).

Implications for Education. The work just described has implications for both contextual and direct instructional techniques of teaching vocabulary. Many commercial basal reading programs assume that children can derive the meanings of new words encountered in a story from context (Beck and others, 1979). The fact that the suppression model best predicted recall is consistent with the assumption of contextual methods that readers attempt to use what meaning they glean from context during processing, rather than simply ignore the unfamiliar word. However, the fact that comprehension and recall were impaired by the presence of unfamiliar words cautions against overreliance on contextual methods. It seems wise to make sure that the contexts in which new words appear are pedagogical, in the sense that they are created with the intent of leading the reader to a specific, correct meaning of the word. At present, story contexts in basal readers are not so constructed (Beck and others, 1983). In contrast, intensive direct instruction appears to make the instructed words particularly salient and influential during reading. If we are to succeed in understanding and controlling the difficulty that children have with reading, we will need to understand not only how comprehension is affected by word unfamiliarity but also how it is affected by different types of vocabulary instruction through which children learn new words (see Chapter 5 in this volume).

Implications for Modeling. The focus of the work reported in this chapter has been on the construction and evaluation of models of text comprehension. Given the time and effort involved in modeling, it is appropriate to examine its strengths and limitations. The strength of modeling is that it expresses global principles about processing in an explicit form that can be evaluated. For example, a general notion—for example, unfamiliar propositions are avoided during processing—can be translated into a specific model—in this case the substitution model—from which recall predictions can be derived for each proposition. As long as principles are described only globally, it is difficult to assess the relative merit of competing principles. Committing the principles to explicit models provides the type of detail needed to evaluate which principle best accounts for observed performance.

Another benefit of committing general principles to explicit models is that models often allow us to discover unexpected effects. For example, when the substitution model was first constructed from the substitution principle, it was unexpected that the text base would be disrupted to the extent that it was. This realization suggested that an alternative principle would be one that did not alter the text base, and the alternative—the suppression model—turned out to be a good one.

One limitation of modeling is that the only theoretical explanations that can be considered are those employed by the particular model chosen. In the present study, the decision to base the models on Kintsch and van Dijk's (1978) theory of text comprehension limits the nature of the accounts given in several ways. First, it necessitates the use of propositions, not words, as the unit of analysis; this may cause the effect of unfamiliar and instructed words to be overestimated. It may be that encountering an unfamiliar word impairs the recall of only that word, not of the entire proposition. Within Kintsch and van Dijk's theory, the recall of individual words cannot be represented independently of propositions; thus, this alternative cannot be tested.

A somewhat more serious limitation involves alternative explanations for the bias observed in recall of instructed propositions. The explanation used in the remind model is that instructed propositions receive additional processing as a result of their being connected to representations of the instructional contexts. A number of competing explanations do not fit easily into the Kintsch and van Dijk framework. One alternative account is that, during encoding, the fact that the instructed propositions contain recently learned words may make them distinctive from the rest of the propositions; as a result, they would be more salient in the representation of the text, and consequently they would be more likely to be recalled (for example, Eysenck, 1979). This account could not be represented within the Kintsch and van Dijk framework without changing the basic assumption that the probability with which a proposition is recalled is due to the number of times that it enters a processing cycle, not to how it is encoded. (It appears, however, that the bias to recall instructed propositions is probably not due to their distinctiveness in comparison to uninstructed propositions. That is because the notion of distinctiveness is unable to

account for why unfamiliar propositions, which are also distinctive in comparison to familiar propositions, are less likely to be recalled.)

Another alternative that does not fit easily into the Kintsch and van Dijk framework is that readers may generate more elaborations for instructed propositions than they do for uninstructed propositions. For example, on reading *Sam was a novice at playing the violin,* readers may generate a number of specific details that are consistent with, but not necessarily implied by, the text. For instance, they might infer that Sam was just beginning to take violin lessons, that violin squeaked when he played it, or that Sam's violin was new and shiny (see Chapter 4 in this volume). Since the Kintsch and van Dijk model deals only with that part of a text representation that is directly derived from the text, there is no simple way in which reader-generated elaborations can be predicted or even represented. (Again, it appears that this alternative explanation is unlikely. A critical assumption to elaboration theories, such as that of Anderson and Reder, 1979, is that it is easier to generate elaborations about familiar material than it is about unfamiliar material. There were many familiar words in the uninstructed propositions that the children probably knew a great deal more about than they did about the recently instructed words. Therefore, according to most elaboration theories, propositions containing only familiar propositions should have been recalled better than propositions containing recently instructed propositions.)

Yet another limitation of modeling is that the number of models that could be considered is often unlimited in principle. For example, in the present study, a model of the comprehension of texts with instructed propositions could have been constructed from a biasing principle, under which instructed propositions are always carried over into the next cycle, whether they are part of the leading edge or not. A model based on this principle would have been interesting to consider, because it postulates that the improvement in recall for instructed propositions actually alters the text base that is constructed. The fact that the number of models that can be constructed for a given phenomenon is indefinite underscores the fact that modeling is only as useful as the questions that the models are designed to answer. Modeling is a powerful tool if we wish to decide between two competing accounts of processing. However, it does not guarantee that the accounts that we are evaluating are of theoretical or practical interest. Computer scientists have a saying: Garbage In, Garbage Out. The point is that there is nothing magic about using a computer to solve a problem. The solution one gets is only as good as the way one formulates the problem and the data one gives the computer to process. This same thing is true of modeling: It is only as good as the theories being modeled.

References

Anderson, J. R., and Reder, L. M. "An Elaborative Processing Explanation of Depth of Processing." In L. S. Cermak and F. I. M. Craik (Eds.), *Levels of Processing and Human Memory.* Hillsdale, N.J.: Erlbaum, 1979.

52

Anderson, R. C., and Freebody, P. "Reading Comprehension and the Assessment and Acquisition of Word Knowledge." In B. Hutson (Ed.), *Advances in Reading/Language Research: A Research Annual.* Greenwich, Conn.: JAI Press, in press.

Beck, I. L., McKeown, M. G., and McCaslin, E. S. "Vocabulary Development: All Contexts Are Not Created Equal." *Elementary School Journal,* 1983, *83* (3), 177–181.

Beck, I. L., McKeown, M. G., McCaslin, E. S., and Burkes, A. M. *Instructional Dimensions That May Affect Reading Comprehension: Examples from Two Commercial Reading Programs.* Technical Report No. 1979/20. Pittsburgh: Learning Research and Development Center, University of Pittsburgh, 1979.

Beck, I. L., Perfetti, C. A., and McKeown, M. G. "The Effects of Long-Term Vocabulary Instruction on Lexical Access and Reading Comprehension." *Journal of Educational Psychology,* 1982, *74* (4), 506–521.

Chandler, P. J. *Subroutine STEPIT: An Algorithm That Finds the Values of the Parameters Which Minimize a Given Continuous Function.* Bloomington: Indiana University, 1965.

Davis, F. B. "Fundamental Factors of Comprehension in Reading." *Psychometrika,* 1944, *9* (2), 185–197.

Draper, A. G., and Moeller, G. H. "We Think with Words (Therefore, to Improve Thinking, Teach Vocabulary)." *Phi Delta Kappan,* 1971, *52* (4), 482–484.

Eysenck, M. W. "Depth, Elaboration, and Distinctiveness." In L. S. Cermak and F. I. M. Craik (Eds.), *Levels of Processing and Human Memory.* Hillsdale, N.J.: Erlbaum, 1979.

Goldman, S. R., Hogaboam, T. W., Bell, L. C., and Perfetti, C. A. "Short-Term Retention of Discourse During Reading." *Journal of Educational Pscyhology,* 1980, *72* (5), 647–655.

Jackson, M. D., and McClelland, J. L. "Processing Determinants of Reading Speed." *Journal of Experimental Psychology: General,* 1979, *108* (2), 151–181.

Jacoby, L. L., and Craik, F. I. M. "Effects of Elaboration of Processing at Encoding and Retrieval: Trace Distinctiveness and Recovery of Initial Context." In L. S. Cermak and F. I. M. Craik (Eds.), *Levels of Processing and Human Memory.* Hillsdale, N.J.: Erlbaum, 1979.

Jenkins, J. R., Pany, D., and Schreck, J. *Vocabulary and Reading Comprehension: Instructional Effects.* Technical Report No. 100. Champaign: Center for the Study of Reading, University of Illinois, 1978.

Kameenui, E. J., Carnine, D. W., and Freschi, R. "Effects of Text Construction and Instructional Procedures for Teaching Word Meanings on Comprehension and Recall." *Reading Research Quarterly,* 1982, *17* (3), 367–388.

Kintsch, W., and van Dijk, T. A. "Toward a Model of Text Comprehension and Production." *Psychological Review,* 1978, *85* (5), 363–394.

McKeown, M. G., Beck, I. L., Omanson, R. C., and Perfetti, C. A. "The Effects of Long-Term Vocabulary Instruction on Reading Comprehension: A Replication." *Journal of Reading Behavior,* 1983, *15* (1), 3–18.

Omanson, R. C., Beck, I. L., McKeown, M. G., and Perfetti, C. A. *Comprehension of Texts with Unfamiliar Versus Recently Taught Words: An Assessment of Alternative Models.* Pittsburgh: Learning Research and Development Center, University of Pittsburgh, 1983.

Perfetti, C. A., and Hogaboam, T. W. "The Relationship Between Single-Word Decoding and Reading Comprehension Skill." *Journal of Educational Psychology,* 1975, *67* (4), 461–469.

Rumelhart, D. "Toward an Interactive Model of Reading." In S. Dornic and P. M. A. Rabbitt (Eds.), *Attention and Performance VI.* Hillsdale, N.J.: Erlbaum, 1977.

Tuinman, J. J., and Brady, M. E. "How Does Vocabulary Account for Variance on Reading Comprehension Tests? A Preliminary Instructional Analysis." In P. Nacke (Ed.), *Twenty-Third National Reading Conference Yearbook.* Clemson: National Reading Conference, 1974.

Richard C. Omanson is a postdoctoral fellow at the Learning Research and Development Center, University of Pittsburgh. He received his Ph.D. in child psychology from the University of Minnesota.

What children know about discourse and its conventions before
they start to read may influence their acquisition of reading skill.

Discourse
Structure and
Mental Models

J. Kathryn Bock
William F. Brewer

This chapter focuses on the discourse features of text and their influence on comprehension and learning to read. Our point of view is that discourse comprehension involves the construction by readers or listeners of mental models synthesized from the information in the text and their general knowledge. Within this framework, we examine five aspects of discourse comprehension, first in the context of young children's ability to understand spoken discourse, and then from the perspective of differences between speech and writing. These five aspects include the use of knowledge, the kinds of mental models that underlie different types of discourse, the global organization of texts, the use of discourse cues in the construction of mental models, and the integration of information into a mental model. We conclude by exploring some potential implications of this approach for the development of reading skill.

Preparation of this chapter was supported in part by National Institute of Education Contract No. HEW–NIE–C–400–76–0116. The authors thank Harry Blanchard, Anne Hay, and Stella Vosniadou for their comments on an earlier draft and Thomas Carr for meticulous editing.

T. H. Carr (Ed.). *The Development of Reading Skills.* New Directions
for Child Development, no. 27. San Francisco: Jossey-Bass, March 1985.

Mental Models and Discourse Comprehension

Mental Models. Watching a movie based on a familiar novel often brings on the feeling that something is awry. The rooms are too large, the furniture too new, the protagonist too handsome. Such a feeling presumably grows out of the contrast between what actually unfolds on the screen and expectations built on earlier imaginings about the people, places, and events of the story. We assume that these imaginings reflect a fundamental part of discourse comprehension, which involves the construction of a mental model. Mental models are mental representations of particular states of affairs, such as events or places or someone's wishes. In discourse comprehension, listeners and readers try to construct mental models that embody the content of the text (Collins and others, 1980; Johnson-Laird, 1980, 1983).

For the listener or reader to construct a mental model, the sentences in a discourse should be coherent and describe a plausible set of ideas or sequence of events (Johnson-Laird, 1983). Coherence depends in part on coreference among the sentences of the text: For the comprehender to construct a single integrated mental model, every sentence must directly or indirectly refer to something mentioned in another sentence. Plausibility requires the discourse to be interpretable within a unified framework consistent with the comprehender's knowledge of time, space, causation, and human intention. It is possible to compose a passage that is coherent but not interpretable within a unified framework; for example:

> Robbie owned a bike. It was made in Great Britain. Great Britain is an island. On the island are several monolithic structures. These structures may have been early astronomical observatories. Modern observatories use telescopes.

However, coherence and plausibility are ordinarily associated in natural discourse.

This analysis yields a reasonably straightforward approach to the process of discourse comprehension. To understand a coherent, plausible discourse is to construct a mental model of the events, descriptions, or arguments that underlie it, integrating one's general knowledge and the information in the text into a unified representation.

Knowledge. Even the very young comprehender brings an enormous amount of real-world knowledge to the task of language understanding, knowledge that we assume is represented in the form of generic structures called *schemas* (Brewer and Nakamura, in press; Minsky, 1975; Rumelhart, 1980). To the degree that a segment of discourse makes contact with the comprehender's schema-based knowledge, the information can be used to construct a mental model that is much richer than the information explicit in the text. Even linguistically impoverished prose, such as *First bike ride — man — boy —*

push — wobble — peddle — fall — grin can be readily interpreted by most adults, using knowledge of first bike rides to construct a tentative model that goes far beyond the text. Schema-based knowledge thus powerfully influences the representation that is developed as spoken or written discourse is understood.

A classic demonstration of the influence of schema-based knowledge on comprehension supports the claim that adults' interpretation of text yields an integrated representation that includes more than the presented information. Bransford and others (1972) showed that subjects who heard such a sentence as *Two turtles rested on a floating log, and a fish swam beneath it* often thought they had heard the test sentence *Two turtles rested on a floating log, and a fish swam beneath them.* They apparently inferred that the fish swam beneath the turtles as well as the log, although this was not directly stated. When the original sentence was *Two turtles rested beside a floating log, and a fish swam beneath it,* subjects much less often claimed to have heard the test sentence (see also Garnham, 1981). These patterns of false recognition can be explained by the assumption that listeners constructed mental models of the state of affairs that the text was intended to convey.

Discourse Information. It is obvious that mental models are not completely inferential. The other major source of information used in constructing them is the explicit language of the discourse. This language details the setting, identifies characters, describes specific events, or lays out the ideas and arguments that the author wishes to make explicit. Some of the interactions between a developing model and the language of a text are illustrated in the following narrative about a first bike ride:

> One cloudy October day, Fred Bartlett took his son Robert out for his first bike ride. Robbie was very excited and said, "I sure am glad I got this Raleigh for my birthday." His father smiled and checked to see if the football field was clear. He picked Robbie up and put him on the new two-wheeler. His son was trying to be brave and had a very serious look on his face. Mr. Bartlett gave him a push, and the secretly terrified child began to peddle. He wobbled briefly and then went straight about fifty feet before he fell over. His father ran over and found a little boy lying on the grass with a big grin on his face.

Consider the differences between the mental models that a typical adult might produce for the previous minimal text and this extended narrative. Because little specific information is given in the minimal text, most of the model must be generated from schema-based knowledge, and seems likely to include the information that the bike is a bicycle (not a motorcycle), that the older person instructs the younger, that the older person is the father of the younger, and that the younger person falls off the bike. In these instances, the schema-driven inferences are confirmed by the language of the full text. However, a mental model for the minimal text might also place the ride on a sidewalk or street on

a warm sunny day. These inferences are not supported by the extended narrative. The information that the ride occurred on a football field on a cloudy October day, which should be represented in the mental model generated from the passage, comes from the text.

Certain linguistic features serve as cues for specific types of interactions between the information in the text and the developing mental model of the comprehender. In the preceding narrative, two individuals and a bike are mentioned frequently, but the expressions denoting them vary. The boy is referred to as *his son Robert, Robbie, I, him, his son, the secretly terrified child, he,* and *a little boy,* and the father is referred to as *Fred Bartlett, his father, he,* and *Mr. Bartlett.* The reader must correctly interpret each of these expressions, determining which person is intended. Part of the linguistic information can be used to figure out whether an expression denotes something that is already part of the mental model (given information) or something that is to be added (new information). Reference to given information is often marked by pronouns *(I, him, he)* or other anaphoric devices, such as definite noun phrases like *the secretly terrified child.* To understand the text adequately, the appropriate information must be located in the mental model and modified by adding the new material to the representation (Clark and Haviland, 1977). New information is more often conveyed in full noun phrases than in pronouns, and those noun phrases may be marked with an indefinite determiner (for example, *a push, a big grin*) (Halliday and Hasan, 1976). In the last sentence of the passage, *a* is used inappropriately to refer to information already in the reader's mental model (a little boy); such inappropriate marking seems to disrupt reading (Irwin and others, 1982) and the integration of information into a unified representation (deVilliers, 1974).

These are some of the basic features of mental models and their construction. We turn now to the issue of children's ability to create mental models to represent the information in spoken discourse.

Children's Understanding of Spoken Discourse

A number of experiments suggest that young children can construct mental models from spoken discourse. Their ability to integrate linguistic information with relevant knowledge is especially clear in a study by Brown and others (1977). In the second experiment of that study, second graders heard a narrative about a hunter of the fictitious Targa tribe. Although the story contained no information about weather, climate, or terrain, the children had heard a passage about the Targa a week before that described them as Eskimos living in a cold climate or as Indians living in a desert. In response to questions about weather and terrain, most of the subjects not only answered in accordance with the information acquired the week before but also said they were sure it was part of the story they had just heard. This suggests that they integrated the narrated content into a mental model incorpo-

rating prior knowledge. In other research children between the ages of four and six have been found to understand the intentions of characters and causal relations among events (Stein and Glenn, 1979) and to notice incongruities in stories violating schema-based expectations about events, such as the theft of a bicycle or losing money (Stein and Trabasso, in press; Wimmer, 1979), even though these implications were not spelled out in the stories that they heard.

Despite young children's ability to construct mental models from spoken discourse, there are apparent limitations on their performance. The second graders in the study by Brown and others (1977) seemed to develop less elaborate representations than those of older children who performed the same tasks. Omanson and others (1978) found that five-year-old children made many fewer inferences about the implicit content of stories than eight-year-olds did. Elementary school children in experiments by Markman (1977, 1979) regularly failed to detect omissions and inconsistencies in instructions and prose passages, leading Markman (1981) to suggest that they tended to treat the individual statements of texts as isolated units instead of constructing integrated representations. Other investigators have shown that children between the ages of five and seven often do not integrate the information in a passage well enough to recognize implied relationships accurately (Liben and Posnansky, 1977; Moeser, 1976; Paris and Upton, 1976; Small and Butterworth, 1981), even when the separate items needed to make the correct inferences are available in memory (Collins and others, 1978; Schmidt and others, 1979). As a result, a young child who has heard a short descriptive passage, such as

The bird is in the cage. The cage is under the table. The bird is yellow.

may not integrate the sentences into a mental model carrying the information that the bird is also under the table (Small and Butterworth, 1981).

Because these problems are most striking in preschool and young school-age children, they may be relevant to children's ability to understand text in the early stages of reading. However, the explanation for these problems is far from clear: There is no immediately obvious reason why children understand spoken discourse so well on some occasions and so poorly on others. We will discuss five possible sources of difficulty, each representing a different aspect of the construction of a mental model from spoken discourse, before we consider the further complications that written texts present.

Knowledge. Young children lack some of the general knowledge that older children and adults possess (Chi, 1978). The importance of such knowledge in language comprehension and memory has been demonstrated repeatedly. For example, Bransford and Johnson (1973) report a study in which sentences like *The notes were sour because the seam split* were found to be hard to recall—unless they were preceded by a word, such as *bagpipes,* that cued pertinent knowledge. In the experiment by Brown and others (1977), children who

had acquired relevant knowledge a week earlier remembered more of the story than children who had been given irrelevant information. Because of their inexperience and consequent lack of knowledge in many domains, younger children may construct relatively impoverished mental models, or fail to construct them at all.

Types of Mental Models. Brewer (1980) has argued that different types of mental representations underlie texts from various genres. He proposed that descriptive discourse is represented by visual-spatial structures, narrative by plan and event structures, and expository text by abstract propositions or thoughts. Some of these representations may be easier to construct than others. Along these lines, several researchers have suggested that narratives are easier to understand than expository texts (Bereiter and Scardamalia, 1982; Spiro and Taylor, in press). In the experiment by Markman (1979) cited earlier, elementary school children failed to notice inconsistencies in expository passages, although in other experiments much younger subjects were able to detect incongruities in narratives (Stein and Trabassso, in press; Wimmer, 1979). One possible explanation for this disparity is that it is harder to form a mental model for the abstract logical structures that underlie expository texts than it is for the actions and events portrayed in narratives.

Global Discourse Organization. The information in a particular type of discourse is often organized in a characteristic way. For example, in folktales from the oral tradition, information about the characters, time, and location of the story ("Once upon a time in a land far away, there was a princess...") typically precedes the recounting of the events (Propp, 1968). Nonfictional spoken narratives commonly begin with setting information ("Last Thursday, Robbie was riding his bike on the street...") (Chafe, 1980). Oral narrations of events regularly follow the chronological order in which the events occurred, and the elements of spoken descriptions tend to conform to the order in which things are encountered in a spatial layout (Clark and Clark, 1968; Levelt, 1981; Linde and Labov, 1975; Osgood, 1971).

Although many of these conventions appear to be very natural, alternative forms of organization are possible, and they are used. Certain of these alternatives have been found to disrupt younger children's language comprehension and memory. For example, Stein and Nezworski (cited by Baker and Stein, 1981) changed the order of mention of events in a narrative relative to the order of occurrence, marking the inversions in a way that indicated the deviation (for example, "Robbie broke his leg. It happened because he rode his bicycle into a parked car" instead of "Robbie rode his bicycle into a parked car. He broke his leg"). Although fifth graders recalled the information at least as well when it was conveyed in marked inversions as when it was normally ordered, first graders recalled some types of information less well from narratives in the inverted format. It seems that discourse forms whose organization departs from the conventional structure or discourse forms whose conventions are unknown to children may impede comprehension, either because of their cognitive complexity or because children lack appropriate discourse knowledge.

Using Discourse Cues. Children's difficulties with text integration may in some cases be traced to inefficient processing of anaphoric devices that mark repeated reference, such as pronouns. In an experiment by Tyler (1983), adults and five-, seven-, and ten-year-old children listened for mispronunciations of words in a spoken text. The mispronunciations were strategically located after pronouns or definite noun phrases that were coreferential with an expression in the preceding sentence, as in the following examples:

Mother saw the postman coming from a distance. *He* brought a leffer from Uncle Charles who lives in Canada.

Mother saw the postman coming from a distance. *The postman* brought a leffer from Uncle Charles, who lives in Canada.

The referent of the italicized expressions should have been part of the listener's current model, making *letter* (mispronounced *leffer*) contextually predictable. However, five-year-olds were slower to detect the mispronounced word following the pronoun than following the definite noun phrase, although adults and older children showed no differences between the two conditions. This suggests that the younger children had more difficulty accessing the referent of the pronoun from their representation of the content of the preceding sentence, which slowed their integration of the sentence into the developing mental model.

Information Integration. The final explanation that we will consider for disruptions in the formation of mental models is a general information-processing problem. Inferring relationships among the elements of a text demands that the relevant pieces of information (from the mental model, general knowledge, or immediate discourse) not only be stored in memory but also be actively in mind—held in working memory—at the time when the inference is to be made (Hayes-Roth and Thorndyke, 1979; Walker and Meyer, 1980). Children may be able to keep less information active in memory because of inefficient use of working memory capacity (Case and others, 1982), knowledge limitations (Chi, 1976), or diminished memory capacity (Pascual-Leone, 1970). They may also neglect to retrieve and represent information in working memory when it is needed for integrating new material. A large body of evidence shows that children before roughly the age of seven do not spontaneously employ memory storage and retrieval strategies commonly used by older children and adults. Although younger children are able to use such strategies when instructed to do so, and although they benefit when they use them, they do not invoke them without prompting (Brown and others, 1983).

When measures are taken to alleviate memory-related problems, children's ability to draw inferences also improves dramatically: Four-year-olds have been found to infer unseen relationships among objects (Bryant and Trabasso, 1971) and unstated relationships among things mentioned in sen-

tences (Harris and Bassett, 1975) nearly as well as adults. However, without some form of external support for the active maintenance of appropriate information in memory, young children's inferences about relationships among the elements of spoken discourse may be restricted.

Summary. We have suggested five aspects of the construction of mental models from discourse that represent possible problem areas in comprehension for preschool children — children who are about to begin learning to read. Thus far, however, we have focused on research concerning the understanding of spoken discourse. Because spoken and written language differ in substantial ways, the child confronted with a written text needs new solutions to some of the foregoing problems. In the next section, we consider the changes that occur in the transition from listening to reading.

Spoken Versus Written Discourse

Spoken and written discourse differ on a number of dimensions (Brewer, in press; Chafe, 1982; Rubin, 1980; Snow, 1983; Tannen, 1982). The dimensions that are most relevant for our purposes are interaction, contextualization, and transience.

Interaction refers to the mutual determination of form, content, direction, and pace of communication by the participants in an exchange. Encounters between people using spoken language typically include a speaker and an addressee who can respond to one another, make comments, and ask questions, and who do so under the constraint of contributing fairly rapidly or risking the loss of a turn at speaking. In written language, the writer receives no immediate feedback, but is solely responsible for shaping the discourse and unbothered by interruptions from the intended audience. Contextualization involves the sharing of spatial and temporal contexts. Speakers and listeners are often in the same place at the same time, but writers and readers are not: Written messages are usually produced and understood in different contexts. Finally, speech signals are transient: They are generally available to the listener only briefly. Written language is relatively permanent. As a result, it can be read a number of times, and the reader can refer back to previous text when necessary.

These and other, related dimensions create differences between spoken and written discourse that have implications for reading comprehension. We will discuss some of these differences in the context of the five facets of discourse comprehension introduced in the preceding section.

Knowledge. An oft noted advantage of the development of a writing system is that it allows the accumulated knowledge of a people to be passed from generation to generation in a form that is less subject to distortion and loss than oral transmission is. One obvious consequence of the accumulation of knowledge in print is that a wider range of topics and greater depth of coverage may be found in the books of an elementary school library than in day-

to-day encounters with spoken language. Written discourse thus draws on and adds to a more diverse knowledge base than spoken discourse typically does.

Some evidence that the possession of specialized knowledge can contribute to discourse comprehension comes from an experiment by Spilich and others (1979). They compared the ability of subjects who varied in their knowledge of baseball to recall and answer questions about an account of a portion of a baseball game. High-knowledge subjects recalled more and answered more questions correctly, and proportionately more of the information that they remembered pertained to major points from the passage. In general, people with more knowledge about a subject may be better at relating new information to old because information from a familiar domain can be maintained in active memory more efficiently than unfamiliar information can (Chase and Simon, 1973).

Types of Mental Models. Some types of discourse, including narrative, tend to occur in both spoken and written discourse. Other types of discourse, such as exposition, are more commonly written than spoken. Certain written texts may thus require the creation of mental models that are both different and more difficult to construct than the models used to represent most spoken discourse.

Whether it is the difficulty of constructing its underlying representation or some other factor, expository prose appears to slow down even skilled readers more than narrative does. Graesser and others (1980) found that college students read narrative passages faster than expository passages — on the order of 140 milliseconds per word faster — and that narrativity was by far the best predictor of variations in reading time in analyses that also examined effects of topic familiarity, number of words, syntactic complexity, number of propositions, and number of new referents introduced in the text. The significance of the problems created by expository prose can be appreciated by considering the amount of information that students are expected to learn by reading expository texts.

Global Discourse Organization. The information conveyed in a discourse of a particular type may be organized in various ways. For example, rather than opening with a setting as oral narratives do, modern written stories tend to open with an event (O'Faolain, 1951). Setting information is instead woven into the text. Such variations in global discourse organization may play a larger role in writing than they do in speaking. The press of time, limitations of memory, and the interruptions of interlocutors often constrain speakers' ability to organize a message. However, the author of a written text can organize and structure discourse over a longer period, even planning a 300-page narrative in which the reader receives information that forces a complete revision of the mental model on the last page. With expository text, a writer can organize a complex set of logical relations in text form and use headings and other structural marking devices to delineate them (Bereiter and Scardamalia, 1982; Chafe, 1982).

These and other differences between the usual circumstances and products of talking and writing may have increased the number of conventionalized global organizations in printed discourse. Brewer (in press) has claimed that written genres have a greater number of specialized text structures (newspaper articles, psychology journal articles, comic books, cookbooks, and so forth), each with its own conventions of content and form. Because different text organizations deal in different ways with the problem of presenting underlying cognitive structures in a sequential linguistic format, readers may benefit from a complementary inventory of comprehension strategies that are more varied than those used in listening. For example, because the pyramid style of newspaper writing summarizes important points before addressing the material in detail, readers who understand this organization can easily skim the material if they choose.

Using Discourse Cues. The absence of immediate conversational feedback and shared time and place requires written discourse to be more explicit than spoken. Chafe (1982) has provided evidence that writers pack more information into segments of text than speakers do. One of the important functions that this additional information serves is ensuring that readers correctly identify intended referents in their mental models. When speakers and hearers share the same context, simple expressions suffice to indicate the topic of an utterance. In written language, more cues are needed: A speaker in a conversation might nod his head and say *over there* to convey the same information as the decontextualized *The old man they had seen earlier walking his Saint Bernard came into view across the street.*

A related consequence of the contextualization of spoken language is that certain uses of pronouns and other referring expressions are more common in speech than they are in writing. The use of referring expressions to point out elements of the extralinguistic context is called *deixis,* while their use to indicate elements of a mental model that has been formed from a text is called *anaphora.* Someone watching a boy who has just hurled several objects at a wall might say to a companion, with no prelude, "What do you suppose he was doing?", where *he* is used deictically to indicate the boy. The same sentence in a written text with no introduction is cryptic. Instead, a referent is usually established before the pronoun is used, as in "I saw a boy hurl several objects at a wall. What do you suppose he was doing?". Here, *he* is used anaphorically to indicate something that the reader or addressee should have in mind as a result of understanding the prior discourse. Although deixis is possible in writing, it is much more frequent in speech.

Determining the referent of a deictic pronoun typically requires the identification of a salient element in the extralinguistic context or the current focus of attention. Understanding an anaphoric pronoun demands careful examination of the characteristics of the pronoun and its syntactic role in addition to an evaluation of the characteristics of candidate referents in the mental model. If readers attempt to understand anaphoric uses of pronouns in the

same way that listeners understand deictic uses of pronouns, perhaps by picking out the most salient element of their current mental model, they may be unsuccessful in determining the correct referents. There is some evidence that less-skilled readers approach anaphoric pronouns in this way. Frederiksen (1981) compared less-skilled and better high school readers' ability to recover the antecedents of pronouns, and found that the less-skilled readers relied more heavily on a salience strategy. This strategy involved falling back on the topic of the passage as the referent. As a result, less-skilled readers read sentences containing pronouns with nontopical antecedents more slowly, and they were less likely to identify the antecedent correctly than they were when the pronouns had topical antecedents. Such a pattern suggests that Frederiksen's less-skilled subjects may have dealt with pronouns in reading in a manner more appropriate to listening.

There is an additional distinction among the ways in which pronouns are used that has potential implications for understanding discourse cues in written language. This is the contrast between deep and surface anaphora (Hankamer and Sag, 1976; Webber, 1980). Certain types or instances of anaphora require a representation of the actual language of an earlier sentence to be recovered in order to understand the reference, while others, like those we have been considering, refer directly to nonlinguistic elements in the comprehender's mental model of the text. Anaphora of the former type, called *surface anaphora,* is less acceptable when sentences intervene between the anaphor and its antecedent. Compare these two examples of surface anaphora from Tanenhaus and others (in press):

> Somebody has to paint the garage. The paint is peeling and the wood is beginning to rot. Let's take a vote and see *who.*
>
> Somebody has to paint the garage. Let's take a vote and see *who.*

It is more difficult to interpret *who* as *who has to paint the garage* in the first example than it is in the second, where there is no intervening sentence. A plausible explanation is that the explicit linguistic representation of the initial sentence is no longer recoverable: After reading or hearing a sentence in discourse, readers and listeners have been shown to experience considerable difficulty in remembering the surface structure of prior sentences (Chang, 1980; Jarvella, 1971). However, with deep anaphora, interruptions are less disruptive, since the reference is to a component of the mental model:

> Somebody has to paint the garage. The paint is peeling and the wood is beginning to rot. Let's take a vote and see who has to *do it.*

If a reader is unable to remember the surface structure of a prior sentence, he or she can usually read it again. Listeners do not have this option. The transience of spoken language may thus lead speakers to use surface anaphora less

often than writers do, creating another type of discourse reference for readers to master.

Auditory and visual presentations of language have other subtle effects on discourse cues. Spoken English depends on intonation as a primary indicator of givenness and newness, with new information typically receiving higher stress than given information. Beyond such conventions as underlining for emphasis, written language possesses few means for indicating variations in intonation. Instead, skilled writers rely on syntax to mark distinctions between given and new information, placing new information later in sentences than the given information to which it relates (Smith, 1971). Bolinger (1957) has claimed that this organization capitalizes on readers' generation of implicit intonation contours in which the highest stress is located near the ends of clauses. In listening, intonation seems to influence adults' cross-sentence integration, while syntactic variations that may be used to distinguish given and new information have little effect (Bock and Mazzella, 1983). In contrast, structural variations do influence integration in reading (Yekovich and others, 1978; also compare experiments 1 and 2 with experiment 3 in Ehrlich and Johnson-Laird, 1982). These findings suggest that readers use syntax more heavily than listeners do for discourse cues, either for direct indicators of givenness or newness or for indirect cues mediated by implicit intonation.

Information Integration. Because it is easier to integrate material from separate sentences into a coherent mental model when the items of information to be related are simultaneously active in memory, conditions that increase the probability of concurrent activation should enhance integration. For example, Walker and Meyer (1980) found that adult readers integrated text information more often when the separate components occurred consecutively than when they were separated in the text.

However, only a subset of the information from a text will be readily accessible at any one time, because the amount of information from a discourse that can be activated simultaneously is limited. Kintsch and van Dijk (1978) hypothesize that these limitations are reflected in the number of propositions from a text that can be maintained in working memory. We assume that the comprehender must interpret these propositions in terms of a mental model and that the process requires some part of the model to be maintained in working memory. (Johnson-Laird, 1983, discusses the differences between a mental model approach and that of Kintsch and van Dijk.) There are indications that reading comprehension skill correlates with the ability to relate linguistic information to a mental model. In an experiment by Merrill and others (1981), less-skilled fifth-grade comprehenders appeared to have more difficulty relating information from sentences to a mental model than better comprehenders did. Nevertheless, the less-skilled comprehenders showed evidence of understanding the words in the sentences, as they would if they had developed only a superficial representation of the meaning (also see Oakhill, 1982).

Since spoken language is more often related to the context in which it is

understood than written language is, listeners' mental models are more likely than readers' to be supported by the extralinguistic context. The absence of external support in reading may increase the burden of maintaining currently important information in working memory. However, writing has an important advantage over speech in the provision of linguistic context: The text remains available. Thus, whenever the reader realizes that previous information is needed, he or she can look back to recover the content, rather than having to retrieve it from memory. Print can therefore take over part of the function of working memory in integration, allowing the reader to recover antecedent information by retracing through the text. In an eye movement study by Carpenter and Just (1977), adult readers performed such regression very precisely, looking directly back to the place in the text where a potential antecedent occurred. This indicates that the use of prior text as a support for memory in the integration of information may be a well-developed ability in skilled reading.

Implications for Learning to Read

We have examined several differences between written and spoken discourse which suggest that the ability to develop mental models from spoken language does not fully or adequately support the comprehension of written texts. In this section we will elaborate some potential implications of this suggestion for the acquisition of reading, focusing again on the roles of the comprehender's knowledge and the language of the text in the process of mental model construction. We assume in the following discussion that similarities between spoken and written discourse facilitate children's text comprehension, while differences create areas in which the beginning reader must acquire new knowledge and skills.

General Knowledge and Discourse Knowledge. We suggested earlier that comprehending different types of texts requires the construction of different types of mental models. We hypothesize that children learning to read bring to the task a background of general knowledge and familiarity with spoken discourse structures that prepares them to construct some kinds of mental models more readily than others.

Consider again the contrast between narrative and expository prose. The intuitive and empirically supported differences in the ease of understanding narratives and expositions may be due to the design of the human mind: Perhaps we are simply better equipped to deal with the kinds of information that narratives convey. Alternatively—or additionally—the knowledge of plans and events that underlies narratives, and the cognitive skill required in constructing mental models to represent them, may be better developed in most people than the knowledge and skills needed to construct mental models of expository prose.

Differences in the availability of the cognitive resources needed to con-

struct mental models for the comprehension of narratives and expositions may be particularly pronounced for young children. Children are likely to be acquainted with narratives and to know something about simple narrative structures because these structures are common in spoken discourse. Moreover, very young children possess implicit knowledge of causation and intention and their roles in real-world events (Gelman and Baillargeon, 1983; Hood and Bloom, 1979; Nelson and Gruendel, 1981), knowledge that is critical for the interpretation of narrative texts. The explicit teaching of simple narrative forms may thus be unnecessary, at least as an adjunct to reading instruction.

The situation for expository prose is different. The infrequency of exposition in spoken language makes such texts unfamiliar to inexperienced readers. The general knowledge of abstract argument structures needed to support the comprehension of expository discourse may be fragile in most young readers, and knowledge of appropriate global text structures nonexistent. Thus, there is little in the way of relevant prior knowledge to support reading comprehension.

Although instructional effort with respect to discourse comprehension may be better centered on expository prose, narratives serve other purposes in the reading curriculum. Stories are a class of narrative designed to entertain, and they are frequently structured to produce enjoyment: The classic mystery story is not written to maximize comprehension but to heighten suspense and curiosity about omitted events. (For an analysis of the structure of stories in terms of the affective states that they evoke in readers, see Brewer and Lichtenstein, 1981, 1982.) The motivational implications of this line of reasoning must be considered when working out instructional programs. It has often been noted (see Gibson and Levin, 1975) that, if a child is to read large amounts of text and become an independent reader, the material that the child receives should be interesting and entertaining, not just easily comprehended. (See Jose and Brewer, in press, for research on factors influencing story liking in young children.)

Discourse Cues and Local Integration Processes. The transfer from spoken to written discourse demands refinement and extension of the ability to integrate information from successive sentences in a text. However, memory deficits similar to those that limit preschoolers' and kindergartners' integration of spoken language also appear in novice readers. Johnson and Barrett (1981) asked third and fifth graders to answer questions that required drawing inferences from passages they had read. The third graders were more successful when both premises required for the inferences were in the same paragraph, instead of in different paragraphs. This finding held even when the children were able to recall both premises in response to other questions, indicating that the necessary information was available somewhere in memory. Fifth graders were less influenced by separation of the premises in the text. Johnson and Barrett (1981, p. 1221) suggest that older children strategically retrieve previous material, while younger children integrate items of information only

when the current one "happens to 'call up' the first from long-term memory or when the two are temporally close and, thus, jointly present in working memory." Alternatively, older children may be better at maintaining important information from previous text in working memory.

If children are more successful in inferring relationships between elements of text and information in the mental model when that information is in working memory, maintenance or reinstatement of important material is crucial in the integration of new information. Adults spend more time reading important than unimportant information in narratives (Cirilo and Foss, 1980; Mandler and Goodman, 1982), and important information is more accessible in memory (Fletcher, 1981). Selecting what is important in order to maintain it actively in memory requires a degree of prior knowledge relevant to the content or structure of the discourse. In types of texts that are less familiar to young readers, such as exposition, active maintenance of central information may be hampered by difficulty in recognizing what is important. Less-experienced readers may thus need help in learning to identify the main points of expository prose and in learning how to maintain them efficiently in memory (for example, through summarization strategies; Brown and Day, 1983).

Sometimes, however, the information needed to interpret and integrate information in text is not maintained and must be recovered from a less active state in memory. When adult readers encounter a reference to previously mentioned information, that information is commonly reinstated in working memory (Chang, 1980; Dell and others, 1983; Frederiksen, 1981; Lesgold and others, 1979; McKoon and Ratcliff, 1980). If necessary, the antecedent information may be inferred (Clark and Haviland, 1977), and in some cases, the reader looks back to previous material to recover it (Carpenter and Just, 1977). Reinstatement requires engaging in activities appropriate for the identification and retrieval of information in the mental model but not in working memory. Beginning readers may be less likely to engage in such activities because of the deficits in initiating strategic memory retrieval that are often seen in young children.

Another important component of reinstatement is the explicit or implicit understanding that more information is needed for adequate comprehension. Such understanding includes the ability to recognize that none of the currently accessible information matches the specifications of expressions referring to given information. Some of the difficulties that this may create for young readers can be appreciated by reconsidering the distinction between deictic and anaphoric uses of pronouns.

Deitic uses of pronouns predominate in the speech addressed to young children, where the topics of conversation center on the here-and-now rather than on events displaced in time or space. Karmiloff-Smith (1981) has argued that five- and six-year-old children's use of pronouns is fundamentally deictic, with pronouns taken as pointers to salient elements in the extralinguistic context, not as indicators of coreference with particular previously mentioned

entities, that is, not as anaphors. If the anaphoric function of pronouns is relatively unfamiliar to beginning readers—and Tyler's (1983) work suggests this is a reasonable assumption—they may fail to realize that a pronoun does not refer to any of the information that is readily accessible.

Evidence that lack of skill in processing anaphora can affect text integration in young readers has been reported by Garnham and others (1982). Their seven- and eight-year-old subjects fell into two groups matched for age, word recognition, and sight vocabulary but differing in comprehension ability. Each child read one of three versions of a passage that varied in plausibility and coherence. The plausible version described a normal sequence of events involving a young boy playing with a ball, while the two other versions contained an implausible sequence. These implausible versions differed in the degree to which pronouns in the passage could be linked to antecedents within the text. The coherent implausible version was written so that appropriate antecedents for the pronouns could be readily inferred, despite the absence of a normal event sequence, while the incoherent implausible version was written so that it was difficult to locate antecedents. On a subsequent test, the skilled comprehenders did not differ from the less-skilled comprehenders in recall of the basic ideas from the implausible incoherent passage, but they were significantly better on both coherent passages. The less-skilled comprehenders did no better on the coherent implausible version than they did on the incoherent implausible version, although their performance improved on the plausible passage.

Such findings strongly suggest that younger and less-skilled readers may not deal efficiently with pronominalization in text. Yet a major source of potential guidance in learning to understand anaphora appears to contribute very little to resolving the trouble: Basal reading materials and teaching manuals rarely offer instruction in handling anaphoric relations (Johnson and Barrett, 1981).

Some less-skilled comprehenders may experience enduring problems with the interpretation of anaphoric relationships and other components of the local, sentence-to-sentence integration process. Vipond (1980) found that variability in performance among less-skilled college readers who read and recalled technical passages could be attributed primarily to the difficulty of such local processes (see also Graesser and others, 1980). The ability to integrate information across consecutive sentences in written discourse thus appears to be correlated with reading success.

Conclusion

Our analysis of the problems of discourse comprehension faced by beginning readers has touched on three broad themes that bear a brief summary. These three themes are the general nature of text comprehension, the discourse comprehension ability of preschool children, and differences between spoken and written discourse.

With respect to the general nature of text comprehension, we argued

that the fundamental process is the construction of a mental model that captures the content of the text in a unified representation. Mental models are shaped in part by processes operating on the global structures and local language of texts to integrate new information appropriately. But, equally important, model construction draws on the comprehender's knowledge of such basic categories as human intention, causality, space, time, and logical relations, as well as of such prosaic matters as first bike rides.

With respect to early discourse comprehension, we suggested that, before children learn to read, they are capable of forming mental models from the texts that they hear. However, their ability is limited, perhaps by such factors as restricted general knowledge, inexperience in constructing certain types of mental models, unfamiliarity with various global text structures, difficulty in understanding anaphoric expressions, and deficits in the use of memory.

Finally, differences between written texts and the spoken discourse which children have mastered when they begin school have the potential to exacerbate their comprehension problems. Spoken discourse taps a narrower range of knowledge, it is structured in different ways, it uses different anaphoric devices, and it provides more contextual support for its interpretation than written texts do. The transfer of discourse competence to reading should be easiest for texts such as narratives that are common in both speech and writing, and that rest on knowledge that young children firmly possess. The major hurdle in the acquition of discourse comprehension skills may be expository prose. Since most of the knowledge that students are expected to acquire in school is conveyed in that format, facility in dealing with expository discourse represents a crucial step in the development of text understanding.

References

Baker, L., and Stein, N. "The Development of Prose Comprehension Skills." In C. M. Santa and B. L. Hayes (Eds.), *Children's Prose Comprehension: Theory and Practice*. Newark, Del.: International Reading Association, 1981.

Bereiter, C., and Scardamalia, M. "From Conversation to Composition: The Role of Instruction in a Developmental Process." In R. Glaser (Ed.), *Advances in Instructional Psychology*. Vol. 2. Hillsdale, N.J.: Erlbaum, 1982.

Bock, J. K., and Mazzella, J. R. "Intonational Marking of Given and New Information: Some Consequences for Comprehension." *Memory and Cognition*, 1983, *11*, 64–76.

Bolinger, D. M. "Maneuvering for Accent and Position." *College Composition and Communication*, 1957, *8*, 234–238.

Bransford, J. D., Barclay, J. R., and Franks, J. J. "Sentence Memory: A Constructive Versus Interpretive Approach." *Cognitive Psychology*, 1972, *3*, 193–209.

Bransford, J. D., and Johnson, M. K. "Consideration of Some Problems of Comprehension." In W. G. Chase (Ed.), *Visual Information Processing*. New York: Academic Press, 1973.

Brewer, W. F. "Literary Theory, Rhetoric, and Stylistics: Implications for Psychology." In R. J. Spiro, B. C. Bruce, and W. F. Brewer (Eds.), *Theoretical Issues in Reading Comprehension*. Hillsdale, N. J.: Erlbaum, 1980.

Brewer, W. F. "The Story Schema: Universal and Culture-Specific Properties." In D. Olsen, N. Torrance, and A. Hildyard (Eds.), *Literacy, Language and Learning.* Cambridge, England: Cambridge University Press, in press.

Brewer, W. F., and Lichtenstein, E. H. "Event Schemas, Story Schemas, and Story Grammars." In J. Long and A. Baddeley (Eds.), *Attention and Performance IX.* Hillsdale, N.J.: Erlbaum, 1981.

Brewer, W. F., and Lichtenstein, E. H. "Stories Are to Entertain: A Structural-Affect Theory of Stories." *Journal of Pragmatics,* 1982, *6,* 473–486.

Brewer, W. F., and Nakamura, G. V. "The Nature and Functions of Schemas." In R. S. Wyer and T. K. Srull (Eds.), *Handbook of Social Cognition.* Hillsdale, N.J.: Erlbaum, in press.

Brown, A. L., Bransford, J. D., Ferrara, R. A., and Campione, J. C. "Learning, Remembering, and Understanding." In J. H. Falvell and E. M. Markman (Eds.), *Handbook of Child Psychology.* Vol. 3: *Cognitive Development.* New York: Wiley, 1983.

Brown, A. L., and Day, J. D. "Macrorules for Summarizing Texts: The Development of Expertise." *Journal of Verbal Learning and Verbal Behavior,* 1983, *22,* 1–14.

Brown, A. L., Smiley, S. S., Day, J. D., Townsend, M. A. R., and Lawton, S. C. "Intrusion of a Thematic Idea in Children's Comprehension and Retention of Stories." *Child Development,* 1977, *48,* 1454–1466.

Bryant, P. E., and Trabasso, T. "Transitive Inferences and Memory in Young Children." *Nature,* 1971, *232,* 456–458.

Carpenter, P. A., and Just, M. A. "Reading Comprehension as Eyes See It." In M. A. Just and P. A. Carpenter (Eds.), *Cognitive Processes in Comprehension.* Hillsdale, N.J.: Erlbaum, 1977.

Case, R., Kurland, D. M., and Goldberg, J. "Operational Efficiency and the Growth of Short-Term Memory Span." *Journal of Experimental Child Psychology,* 1982, *33,* 386–404.

Chafe, W. L. "The Deployment of Consciousness in the Production of a Narrative." In W. L. Chafe (Ed.), *The Pear Stories: Cognitive, Cultural, and Linguistic Aspects of Narrative Production.* Norwood, N.J.: Ablex, 1980.

Chafe, W. L. "Integration and Involvement in Speaking, Writing, and Oral Literature." In D. Tannen (Ed.), *Spoken and Written Language.* Norwood, N.J.: Ablex, 1982.

Chang, F. R. "Active Memory Processes in Visual Sentence Comprehension: Clause Effects and Pronominal Reference." *Memory and Cognition,* 1980, *8,* 58–64.

Chase, W. G., and Simon, H. A. "Perception in Chess." *Cognitive Psychology,* 1973, *4,* 55–81.

Chi, M. T. H. "Short-Term Memory Limitations in Children: Capacity or Processing Deficits?" *Memory and Cognition,* 1976, *4,* 559–572.

Chi, M. T. H. "Knowledge Structures and Memory Development." In R. Siegler (Ed.), *Children's Thinking: What Develops?* Hillsdale, N.J.: Erlbaum, 1978.

Cirilo, R. K., and Foss, D. J. "Text Structure and Reading Time for Sentences." *Journal of Verbal Learning and Verbal Behavior,* 1980, *19,* 96–109.

Clark, H. H., and Clark, E. V. "Semantic Distinctions and Memory for Complex Sentences." *Quarterly Journal of Experimental Psychology,* 1968, *20,* 129–138.

Clark, H. H., and Haviland, S. E. "Comprehension and the Given-New Contract." In R. O. Freedle (Ed.), *Discourse Production and Comprehension.* Vol. 1. Norwood, N.J.: Ablex, 1977.

Collins, A., Brown, J. S., and Larkin, K. M. "Inference in Text Understanding." In R. J. Spiro, B. C. Bruce, and W. F. Brewer (Eds.), *Theoretical Issues in Reading Comprehension.* Hillsdale, N.J.: Erlbaum, 1980.

Collins, W. A., Wellman, H., Keniston, A. H., and Westby, S. D. "Age-Related Aspects of Comprehension and Inference from a Televised Dramatic Narrative." *Child Development,* 1978, *49,* 389–399.

Dell, G. S., McKoon, G., and Ratcliff, R. "The Activation of Antecedent Information During the Processing of Anaphoric Reference in Reading." *Journal of Verbal Learning and Verbal Behavior*, 1983, *22*, 121–132.

de Villiers, P. A. "Imagery and Theme in Recall of Connected Discourse." *Journal of Experimental Psychology*, 1974, *103*, 263–268.

Ehrlich, K., and Johnson-Laird, P. N. "Spatial Descriptions and Referential Continuity." *Journal of Verbal Learning and Verbal Behavior*, 1982, *21*, 296–306.

Fletcher, C. R. "Short-Term Memory Processes in Text Comprehension." *Journal of Verbal Learning and Verbal Behavior*, 1981, *20*, 564–574.

Frederiksen, J. R. *Understanding Anaphora: Rules Used by Readers in Assigning Pronominal Referents*. Technical Report No. 3. Cambridge, Mass.: Bolt Beranek and Newman, 1981.

Garnham, A. "Mental Models as Representations of Text." *Memory and Cognition*, 1981, *9*, 560–565.

Garnham, A., Oakhill, J., and Johnson-Laird, P. N. "Referential Continuity and the Coherence of Discourse." *Cognition*, 1982, *11*, 29–46.

Gelman, R., and Baillargeon, R. "A Review of Some Piagetian Concepts." In J. H. Flavell and E. M. Markman (Eds.), *Handbook of Child Psychology*. Vol. 3: *Cognitive Development*. New York: Wiley, 1983.

Gibson, E. J., and Levin, H. *The Psychology of Reading*. Cambridge, Mass.: M.I.T. Press, 1975.

Graesser, A. C., Hoffman, N. L., and Clark, L. F. "Structural Components of Reading Time." *Journal of Verbal Learning and Verbal Behavior*, 1980, *19*, 135–151.

Halliday, M., and Hasan, R. *Cohesion in English*. London: Longman, 1976.

Hankamer, J., and Sag, I. "Deep and Surface Anaphora." *Linguistic Inquiry*, 1976, *7*, 391–428.

Harris, P. L., and Bassett, E. "Transitive Inferences by 4-Year-Old Children?" *Developmental Psychology*, 1975, *11*, 875–876.

Hayes-Roth, B., and Thorndyke, P. W. "Integration of Knowledge from Text." *Journal of Verbal Learning and Verbal Behavior*, 1979, *18*, 91–108.

Hood, L., and Bloom, L. "What, When, and How About Why: A Longitudinal Study of Early Expressions of Causality." *Monographs of the Society for Research in Child Development*, 1979, *44* (6), (entire issue).

Irwin, D. E., Bock, J. K., and Stanovich, K. E. "Effects of Information Structure Cues on Visual Word Processing." *Journal of Verbal Learning and Verbal Behavior*, 1982, *21*, 307–326.

Jarvella, R. J. "Syntactic Processing of Connected Speech." *Journal of Verbal Learning and Verbal Behavior*, 1971, *10*, 409–416.

Johnson, D. D., and Barrett, T. C. "Prose Comprehension: A Descriptive Analysis of Instructional Practices." In C. M. Santa and B. L. Hayes (Eds.), *Children's Prose Comprehension: Theory and Practice*. Newark, Del.: International Reading Association, 1981.

Johnson-Laird, P. N. "Mental Models in Cognitive Science." *Cognitive Science*, 1980, *4*, 71–115.

Johnson-Laird, P. N. *Mental Models: Towards a Cognitive Science of Language, Inference, and Consciousness*. Cambridge, Mass.: Harvard University Press, 1983.

Jose, P. E., and Brewer, W. F. "The Development of Story Liking: Character Identification, Suspense, and Outcome Resolution." *Developmental Psychology*, in press.

Karmiloff-Smith, A. "The Grammatical Marking of Thematic Structure in the Development of Language Production." In W. Deutsch (Ed.), *The Child's Construction of Language*. London: Academic Press, 1981.

Kintsch, W., and van Dijk, T. A. "Toward a Model of Text Comprehension and Production." *Psychological Review*, 1978, *85*, 363–394.

Lesgold, A. M., Roth, S. F., and Curtis, M. E. "Foregrounding Effects in Discourse Comprehension." *Journal of Verbal Learning and Verbal Behavior*, 1979, *18*, 291–308.

Levelt, W. J. M. "The Speaker's Linearization Problem." *Philosophical Transactions of the Royal Society of London,* 1981, *B 295,* 305–314.

Liben, L. S., and Posnansky, C. J. "Inferences on Inference: The Effects of Age, Transitive Ability, Memory Load, and Lexical Factors." *Child Development,* 1977, *48,* 1490–1497.

Linde, C., and Labov, W. "Spatial Networks as a Site for the Study of Language and Thought." *Language,* 1975, *51,* 924–939.

McKoon, G., and Ratcliff, R. "The Comprehension Processes and Memory Structures Involved in Anaphoric Reference." *Journal of Verbal Learning and Verbal Behavior,* 1980, *19,* 668–682.

Mandler, J. M., and Goodman, M. S. "On the Psychological Validity of Story Structure." *Journal of Verbal Learning and Verbal Behavior,* 1982, *21,* 507–523.

Markman, E. M. "Realizing That You Don't Understand: A Preliminary Investigation." *Child Development,* 1977, *48,* 986–992.

Markman, E. M. "Realizing That You Don't Understand: Elementary School Children's Awareness of Inconsistencies." *Child Development,* 1979, *50,* 643–655.

Markman, E. M. "Comprehension Monitoring." In W. P. Dickson (Ed.), *Children's Oral Communication Skills.* New York: Academic Press, 1981.

Merrill, E. C., Sperber, R. D., and McCauley, C. "Differences in Semantic Encoding as a Function of Reading Comprehension Skill." *Memory and Cognition,* 1981, *9,* 618–624.

Minsky, M. "A Framework for Representing Knowledge." In P. H. Winston (Ed.), *The Psychology of Computer Vision.* New York: McGraw-Hill, 1975.

Moeser, S. D. "Inferences in Episodic Memory." *Journal of Verbal Learning and Verbal Behavior,* 1976, *15,* 193–212.

Nelson, K., and Gruendel, J. "Generalized Event Representations: Basic Building Blocks of Cognitive Development." In A. Brown and M. Lamb (Eds.), *Advances in Developmental Psychology.* Vol. 1. Hillsdale, N.J.: Erlbaum, 1981.

Oakhill, J. "Constructive Processes in Skilled and Less-Skilled Comprehenders' Memory for Sentences." *British Journal of Psychology,* 1982, *73,* 13–20.

O'Faolain, S. *The Short Story.* New York: Devin-Adair, 1951.

Omanson, R. C., Warren, W. H., and Trabasso, T. "Goals, Inferential Comprehension, and Recall of Stories by Children." *Discourse Processes,* 1978, *1,* 337–354.

Osgood, C. E. "Where Do Sentences Come from?" In D. D. Steinberg and L. A. Jakobovits (Eds.), *Semantics: An Interdisciplinary Reader in Philosophy, Linguistics and Psychology.* Cambridge, England: Cambridge University Press, 1971.

Paris, S. G., and Upton, L. R. "Children's Memory for Inferential Relationships in Prose." *Child Development,* 1976, *47,* 660–668.

Pascual-Leone, J. "A Mathematical Model for the Transition Rule in Piaget's Developmental Stages." *Acta Psychologica,* 1970, *32,* 301–345.

Propp, V. *Morphology of the Folktale.* Austin: University of Texas Press, 1968.

Rubin, A. "A Theoretical Taxonomy of the Differences Between Oral and Written Language." In R. J. Spiro, B. C. Bruce, and W. F. Brewer (Eds.), *Theoretical Issues in Reading Comprehension.* Hillsdale, N.J.: Erlbaum, 1980.

Rumelhart, D. E. "Schemata: The Building Blocks of Cognition." In R. J. Spiro, B. D. Bruce, and W. F. Brewer (Eds.), *Theoretical Issues in Reading Comprehension.* Hillsdale, N.J.: Erlbaum, 1980.

Schmidt, C. R., Paris, S. G., and Stober, S. "Inferential Distance and Children's Memory for Pictorial Sequences." *Developmental Psychology,* 1979, *15,* 395–405.

Small, M. Y., and Butterworth, J. "Semantic Integration and the Development of Memory for Logical Inferences." *Child Development,* 1981, *52,* 732–735.

Smith, C. "Sentences in Discourse." *Journal of Linguistics,* 1971, *7,* 213–235.

Snow, C. E. "Literacy and Language: Relationships During the Preschool Years." *Harvard Educational Review*, 1983, *53*, 165–189.

Spilich, G. J., Vesonder, G. T., Chiesi, H. L., and Voss, J. F. "Text Processing of Domain-Related Information for Individuals with High and Low Domain Knowledge." *Journal of Verbal Learning and Verbal Behavior*, 1979, *18*, 275–290.

Spiro, R. J., and Taylor, B. M. "On Investigating Children's Transition from Narrative to Expository Discourse: The Multidimensional Nature of Psychological Text Classification." In R. Tierney, P. Anders, and J. Mitchell (Eds.), *Understanding Reader's Understanding*. Hillsdale, N.J.: Erlbaum, in press.

Stein, N. L., and Glenn, C. G. "An Analysis of Story Comprehension in Elementary School Children." In R. Freedle (Ed.), *New Directions in Discourse Processing*. Norwood, N.J.: Ablex, 1979.

Stein, N. L., and Trabasso, T. "The Search After Meaning: Comprehension and Comprehension Monitoring." In F. Morrison, C. Lord, and D. Keating (Eds.), *Advances in Applied Developmental Psychology*. Vol. 2 New York: Academic Press, in press. demic Press, in press.

Tanenhaus, M. K., Carlson, G. N., and Seidenberg, M. S. "Do Listeners Compute Linguistic Representations?" In D. Dowty, L. Karttunen, and A. Zwicky (Eds.), *Natural Language Parsing: Psychological, Computational and Theoretical Perspectives*. Cambridge, England: Cambridge University Press, in press.

Tannen, D. (Ed.). *Spoken and Written Language*. Norwood, N.J.: Ablex, 1982.

Tyler, L. K. "The Development of Discourse Mapping Processes: The On-Line Interpretation of Anaphoric Expressions." *Cognition*, 1983, *13*, 309–341.

Vipond, D. "Micro- and Macroprocesses in Text Comprehension." *Journal of Verbal Learning and Verbal Behavior*, 1980, *19*, 276–296.

Walker, C. H., and Meyer, B. J. F. "Integrating Different Types of Information in Text." *Journal of Verbal Learning and Verbal Behavior*, 1980, *19*, 263–275.

Webber, B. L. "Syntax Beyond the Sentence: Anaphora." In R. J. Spiro, B. C. Bruce, and W. F. Brewer (Eds.), *Theoretical Issues in Reading Comprehension*. Hillsdale, N.J.: Erlbaum, 1980.

Wimmer, H. "Processing of Script Deviations by Young Children." *Discourse Processes*, 1979, *2*, 301–310.

Yekovich, F. R., Walker, C. H., and Blackman, H. S. "The Role of Presupposed and Focal Information in Integrating Sentences." *Journal of Verbal Learning and Verbal Behavior*, 1978, *17*, 265–277.

J. Kathryn Bock is associate professor of psychology at Michigan State University. This chapter was written while she was assistant professor of psychology at Cornell University and a visiting research fellow at the Max-Planck-Institut für Psycholinguistik.

William F. Brewer is professor of psychology at the University of Illinois at Urbana–Champaign.

Rarely do we appreciate the variety of grade 1 programs and the real possibility that different reading curricula have different effects on learning and the organization of cognitive abilities.

Impact of Classroom Activities on Beginning Reading Development

Mary Ann Evans

Each year some 4,000,000 North American children enter grade 1. While a few may already be reading, most are not. Nonetheless, six months later the majority will be able to read and print simple stories. Despite the pervasiveness and enormity of this cultural phenomenon, there is relatively little documentation of exactly what happens with first-grade classrooms and of the details of the instructional process by which the transformation from nonreader to reader occurs. This chapter is written to convey some of the diversity of grade 1 curricula, to explore the underlying question of whether curricula affect reading skill and the development and organization of cognitive and linguistic abilities that contribute to reading skill, and to address various reasons why this topic is worthy of consideration.

Debates over the best method of teaching reading — phonics, look-say, language experience, modified alphabet, and so forth — have plagued educational psychology for many years. The word *plagued* is used intentionally, because these debates and research efforts generally have not served the scientific and educational communities well for two main reasons. First, researchers and advocates have typically taken programs and would-be program differences at face value, assuming that lesson plans and descriptions of curriculum goals are implemented as written and never examining the composition and instructional processes of the programs as actually practiced (Bisell, 1971;

T. H. Carr (Ed.). *The Development of Reading Skills.* New Directions for Child Development, no. 27. San Francisco: Jossey-Bass, March 1985.

Goodlad and Anderson, 1963; Tewkesbury, 1967; Willows and others, 1980). Second, studies comparing specific instructional methods have often been focused on year-end achievement scores and viewed as a horse race with a winner and a loser. This approach has tended to generate defensiveness, anger, and calls of foul play from the loser and smug confidence from the winner that he or she has found "the answer." Such a context, in which one can easily lose face, has only served to sever educators from research efforts designed to understand education. If curricular components do influence learning outcomes, the need to study curricula and their effects coexists with a certain degree of anxiety over research results; this hinders both research and efforts to improve classroom curricula. The study of instructional methods can be less anxiety-inducing and ultimately more productive if we ask not what is the best (or fastest) way of teaching reading but whether different curricula contribute to different patterns of cognitive skills and if so, why. In this chapter, I describe this alternative approach and its implications for the understanding and instruction of normal and exceptional children.

Documenting Different Curricula

Comparing individual methods without examining the methods themselves is like analyzing the data from an experiment without knowing the conditions under which they were collected. Before questioning the comparability of what or how well children learn under varying instructional approaches, it is imperative to document the ways in which the approaches themselves vary.

The description presented in this chapter is based on the observation of twenty grade 1 and combined grades 1 and 2 classrooms. Half were reputed to follow an experimental curricular alternative to that traditionally offered. Each classroom was visited for four half days in November and December of the school year, and the activities of the children were systematically observed according to a number of categories of behavior. Using an interval sampling procedure, an observer in each classroom turned from child to child and recorded the activity of that child at that moment along a number of dimensions. The subject matter of the activity, the context in which it occurred, the verbal interaction accompanying the activity, and the materials used were noted. In addition, the observer judged the child to be actively, passively, or little involved in an activity or disruptive and whether the child's behavior was primarily directed by the teacher, the other children, or the child himself or herself. (Evans, 1979, describes the various observation categories in detail.) Over the course of the observations, approximately fifty samples of each child's behavior were taken. These samples were collapsed across children and sessions within each classroom to yield a profile of each classroom's curriculum.

The data derived from these observations make it possible both to describe the individual makeup of each classroom's curriculum and to examine whether classrooms reputed to be traditional or experimental in their methods

were indeed significantly different. Figure 1 shows how classrooms could be profiled and some ways in which the two groups of classrooms differed. It portrays the extent to which various skill and content areas were practiced within two learning contexts of four particular classrooms. Classrooms labeled A and B were supposedly traditional in their curricula. Classrooms labeled C and D were ones in which the reputedly alternative model of primary grade education was being implemented. The alternative model used self-directed play as a route to learning and a language experience approach as a route to reading.

The bars in Figure 1a represent 100 percent of the school day. They are bisected by a heavy black line; activities in which children were in a group led by the teacher are to the left of the line, and activities in which the children worked independently and played alone or with other children are to the right of the line. The extent to which children were engaged at different activities in these two contexts (that is, the percentage of total observations for each context in which these activities were observed) is displayed by the vertical bars, labeled *Mu* for music; *ST* for story telling, in which children listened to stories; *OLA* for oral language arts, in which children engaged in group discussion activities; *M* for mathematics; *reading; P* for printing, in which children either practiced printing per se or printed in the course of completing other work; *CA* for creative arts; *FM* for fine motor play, in which children manipulated puzzle pieces; *R* for role play, in which children engaged in fantasy play; *SW* for story writing, in which children dictated or printed stories; and *O* for other activities, such as sandbox play, management routines, and gross motor activities.

The bars in Figure 1b excerpt the reading portion of the school day shown in Figure 1a and detail the extent of various activities making up that general category. As in Figure 1a, activities to the left of the heavy black line occurred in a group led by the teacher, and activities to the right of the line occurred during independent work in which the teacher circulated throughout the classroom stopping to meet individually with selected children. The horizontal bars display the extent to which children engaged in four activities, labeled *WA* for word analysis activities, which emphasized letter-sound correspondences and orthographic patterns; *WP* for word practice activities, which emphasized the recognition of whole words on sight; *CM* for context and meaning activities, which emphasized comprehension of text and prediction of words from context; and *RT* for reading text either silently or orally.

Figure 1 shows that both the composition of the school day and the nature of reading activities differed substantially across classrooms. For example, children in classroom A spent 70 percent of their school day in group activities led by the teacher, while children in classroom D spent 67 percent of their day in independent work. The proportion of activities involving reading was greatest in classroom B (50 percent), and it comprised a large proportion of both teacher-led group and independent activities. While classroom A had about the same number of group reading activities, there were fewer indepen-

Figure 1. Four Classroom Content Profiles

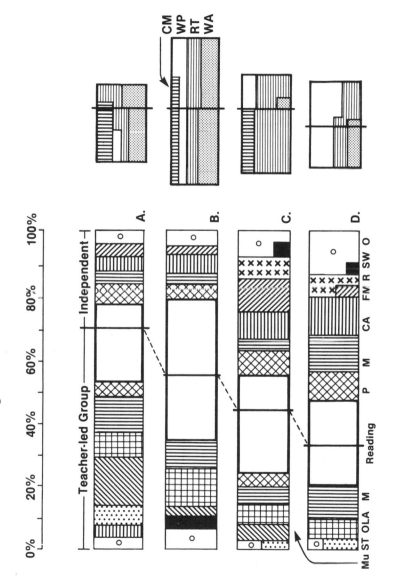

1a. Content/Skill Activities of the Whole Day

1b. Subareas of Reading Activity

dent reading activities; hence, the total classroom time devoted to reading (about 30 percent) resembled that of classroom D. The composition of the reading program also varied substantially between classrooms. Classrooms A and B presented a blend of all four reading components, with a heavy emphasis on word analysis activities. Classroom C emphasized the reading of text itself, and classroom D emphasized the reading of individual sight words; both classrooms placed relatively little emphasis on word analysis. Similar classroom profiles could be drawn for the nature of verbal interaction, student involvement in activities, materials used, and so forth. The point being illustrated here is that the way in which children spend their school day is very different from one classroom to another. Later in this chapter, I will argue that certain aspects of these differences are important in the development of reading skill.

Two Classroom Types

Despite the substantial variability among individual classrooms, statistical comparisons of the ten traditional classrooms with the ten alternative classrooms revealed a number of ways in which the two groups differed significantly. Perhaps the most fundamental difference was in the overall organization of the school day. Relatively few (an average 36 percent) of the activities in the alternative classrooms occurred when the children were in a group led by the teacher. Instead, in all these classrooms the children were engaged for at least half the school day in independent activities in which they played and worked on their own with only occasional directions from their teacher. They moved about freely, interacted with their peers, and met individually with their teacher to read stories that they had written. In contrast, children in the traditional classrooms spent an average 60 percent of the school day in large or small groups attending the teacher's lessons and the remainder of their time at their desks working on some assigned project. Interaction with their peers was limited to about 10 percent of their classroom activities.

Differences also emerged between the two groups in the nature and quality of language and reading activities. Although children in both sets of classrooms practiced recognizing words on sight, children in the alternative classrooms practiced their own personal bank of words from stories that they had dictated or printed themselves, not words from published readers. Similarly, the materials that they read were the stories that they had dictated or printed. Published readers were not to be used until a large number of words (recommended at 150) could be recognized on sight. In contrast, children in the traditional classrooms began with published readers and practiced decoding the words used in them. They engaged more often than children in alternative classrooms in activities that required sounding out words and noticing orthographic patterns, both in group and in independent work, and their independent activities more often required silent reading and printing. The two

groups did not differ in the emphasis on reading text for meaning, in the encouragement of oral language and thinking through group discussion, or in the extent of story writing. In light of the observed differences in reading activities, the two groups can be characterized as language-based, that is, as fostering reading through personalized text and language patterns unique to each individual child, and as component skill–based, that is, as fostering reading via common materials for all children, print-sound correspondence activities, and paper-and-pencil exercises. Despite the differences in the approach to reading instruction, the groups did not differ in the overall amount of time that students spent dealing with reading materials across a school day.

Curricular Effects

As the sample involved some 300 first graders in each of the two groups matched by classroom according to socioeconomic status and neighborhood, it can be assumed that a wide and random variation of individual abilities was equally represented in both groups of classrooms. Given that the nature of student activities within the two sets of classrooms was objectively demonstrated to be different, we can now explore whether the level of basic cognitive abilities and reading achievement differs as a result of the two curricula. More important, we can also ask whether the pattern of relationships between cognitive abilities and reading achievement differs, for, while both sets of classrooms aimed for grade 1 reading competence at the year's end, they did so via different routes. The language-based classrooms hoped to attain reading competence via strong oral language and integrative text skills. Their approach to reading instruction follows the top-down processing models of Smith (1978, 1979) and Goodman (1973a, 1973b, 1976) in which higher-order understanding of language and the wider world guides the reading of text in a psycholinguistic guessing game. Here, the printed stimuli are thought to provide relatively minor clues to the intended meaning of the passage, and single-word recognition is accomplished via configural information (Broadbent and Broadbent, 1977) and transgraphemic discourse-text relations (Smith, 1973). Thus, strong positive correlations might be expected between language skill and reading achievement in these classrooms. The skill-based classrooms strove to attain reading competence via the acquisition and deployment of lower-order word-processing skills allowing for the rapid encoding of graphemic stimuli and extraction of meaning conveyed by the printed text. The work of Gleitman and Rozin (1977), LaBerge and Samuels (1974), Perfetti and Lesgold (1976), and Stanovich (1980) can be cited as theoretical models for this instructional approach. Thus, strong positive correlations might be expected between reading achievement and performance on tasks requiring visual analysis or visual-motor and short-term memory skills in these classrooms.

To explore the impact of the two classroom curricula, a battery of tests was given at the end of the academic year. The range of potential outcome

measures that can be used to examine curricular effects is exceedingly diverse. Failure to choose measures that were equally fair to the curricula compared has been a major objection to past research that yielded significant differences in learning outcomes (see, for example, House and others, 1978). To circumvent such objections, a variety of tests felt to be equally relevant to both sets of classrooms was administered. Tests of printing, individual word recognition, and phonics were intentionally omitted, as it was felt that they might favor the skill-based classrooms. Similarly, assessment of the complexity of children's play and attitude to school was viewed as potentially more favorable to the language-based classrooms, which placed emphasis on self-directed play.

The battery that was finally chosen consisted of a blend of standardized tests, individually administered and informal tests, group pencil-and-paper tests, and tests requiring the manipulation of concrete materials. The tests can be categorized into tests of academic achievement, social skill, language development, and information processing. The last two sets of tests were especially important in determining whether both sets of classrooms were comparable in cognitive abilities generally correlated with reading skill.

Level of Skills. While the groups did differ in their year-end academic achievement, no differences were observed between the two groups on the other measures. Their social skill did not differ as assessed by the fluency (that is, the total speech output) with which they talked to an adult interviewer or by the level of their social perspective taking or decentration when required to describe a series of events from the viewpoint of a naive onlooker (Flavell and others, 1968). The maturity of their speech with an adult interviewer did not differ as assessed by the mean length of their utterances or by the complexity of their utterances. The latter was assessed with Lee and Canter's (1971) Developmental Syntax Scoring, which awards increasing points for correct use of increasingly complex morphological units. Their information-processing skills, as assessed by three different measures, did not differ. Group means were comparable on Raven's (1956) Coloured Progressive Matrices, a test of nonverbal problem solving requiring perceptual analysis that is highly correlated with general intelligence. Similarly, the two groups did not differ in their ability to draw from memory a series of increasingly complex geometric designs exposed for five seconds, a test requiring visual analysis, visual-motor integration, and short-term memory. Last, the groups were comparable on a test of Piagetian operational thinking (Kofsky, 1966), which asks subjects to group and classify colored objects.

Given the comparability of the language-based and skill-based classrooms on the measures that generally correlate positively with academic achievement, it is perhaps surprising that significant differences were observed in the level of reading skill achieved at the end of the school year. Average classroom scores were higher in the skill-based curriculum on the Stanford Reading Comprehension Test, a multiple-choice cloze test in which children read a series of short paragraphs; each paragraph is missing a content word, and

children are asked to select the missing words from printed choices. Similiarly, average classroom scores were also higher in the skill-based curriculum on an individually administered informal assessment in which children read a simple primer passage and then orally answered fact, vocabulary, and inference questions based on it. If a child answered more than 75 percent of these questions correctly, he or she proceeded to answer questions based on more difficult grade 1 and grade 2 passages. Many fewer children from the language-based classrooms achieved this level of success on the primer passage. While 68 percent of the children from the skill-based classrooms were able to proceed to the grade 1 passage, only 52 percent of the children from the language-based classrooms did so. Finally, significant differences were observed on the mathematics computation and concepts subtests of the Stanford Achievement Test, with average classroom scores being higher in the skill-based classrooms.

In summary, cognitive skills did not differ significantly between the two groups, but achievement levels did. The major difference lay in the more general attainment by children in the skill-based classrooms of basic reading competence sufficient for dealing with simple primer text. The larger number of students lacking basic reading skills in the language-based classrooms lowered the classroom means on the group-administered comprehension tests and individual reading of the primer passage. However, on high-level reading assessments from which the poorer readers were excluded, the classroom means of the two groups were comparable.

Integration of Skills. Some may view these results alone as indicating that the skill-based curriculum is superior in instruction of reading. Numerous studies have shown results similar to ours, in which teacher-directed instruction that emphasizes phonics is associated with higher reading achievement scores (for example, Becker, 1977; Bennett, 1976; Chall, 1967, 1979; Harris and Serwer, 1966; Weber, 1981; Wilder, 1977). Others may argue that the only thing that has been demonstrated thus far is that one approach to basic reading proficiency is more efficient than another and that the observed differences would disappear with time. However, a wide variety of studies indicates that maintenance and further development of new learning depend on existing skill and knowledge and on how well the new learning meshes with them (Bransford, 1979; Bransford and others, 1982; Brown, 1977; Brown and Deloache, 1978; Gagne, 1970). As such, one might expect the difference in the level of skill between the two curricula to be maintained. Moreover, the meshing of learning with existing skills suggests that the evaluation of curricula requires not only an examination of the level of achievement but also an examination of the pattern of intercorrelations between basic abilities and the instructed skill. Such examination would both further address the question of whether instructional approaches make a difference and demonstrate whether achievement levels appear to accord with students' abilities. While it would be ideal for learning conditions to eliminate individual differences by raising all students to a ceiling level of achievement, such learning conditions remain an

ideal in most classrooms. What one would hope to see, then, is a sensible pattern of relationships between basic abilities and the instructed skill (in this case, reading) indicating that students' level of mastery is in accordance with their cognitive ability.

To address the question of interdependence between cognitive measures, the mean classroom scores on the various measures were intercorrelated. Of the resulting sixty-six correlations, forty-three were at or above $+ .39$ (significant at the $p < .05$ level) in the skill-based classrooms in contrast to twenty-three in the language-based classrooms. In other words, means on the various measures in skill-based classrooms more often covaried, while the means in language-based classrooms were more often independent of one another. In addition, only one correlation was significantly negative in the skill-based classrooms, while twelve correlations were negative in the language-based classrooms. Hence, the educational experience under the teacher-directed skill-based approach was associated with the integration, mutual reinforcement, and interaction of cognitive skills (see also Guthrie, 1973).

In addition, strong positive relationships were observed in the skill-based classrooms when reading achievement was correlated with skill in reproducing geometric designs from memory and in solving the abstract design problems of the Raven's Coloured Progressive Matrices ($r = .82$ and $.52$, respectively). In the language-based classroom, nonsignificant positive correlations were obtained. Thus, the traditional approach seems to have provided learning conditions under which information-processing abilities were more likely to be reflected in reading progress. Similarly, mean length of utterance was positively correlated in the skill-based classrooms with scores on the Stanford Reading Test ($r = .48$) and with combined scores from the three passages of the informal reading inventory ($r = .61$). Unexpectedly, however, significant negative correlations ($-.41$ to $-.72$) were observed in the language-based classrooms between these two reading comprehension measures and the measures of syntactic complexity and mean length of utterance. Further, while performance on the simple primer passage was uncorrelated with language skill in the skill-based classrooms, it was negatively correlated with language skill in the language-based classrooms.

The Curriculum-Outcome Connection

Word-Processing Skills. The highly negative correlations in the language-based classrooms are disturbing, given the pedagogical base of these classrooms, which assumes that oral language skill is a basis for beginning reading. The inverse relationship between reading skill and language skill is not explained by the possibility that the language-based classrooms devoted time to the development of language skills at the expense of reading, as the extent of these two activities was not negatively correlated. Moreover, activities related to language arts did not correlate in any consistent way with measures of language skill in the language-based classrooms.

A more plausible interpretation of the correlational pattern is that the presumed importance of language skills in reading was pragmatically interpreted by the language-based teachers to mean that reading need not be as "systematically" taught to children whose language skills were good. Conversely, if children's language skills were poor, then more basic reading instruction was needed to compensate for missing language strength. Significant negative correlations ranging from − .38 to − .90 were observed in the language-oriented classrooms between the extent of word practice and word analysis activities in the fall and year-end language skills. Such negative correlations did not occur in the skill-based classrooms. As it is difficult to see any other causal relationship between the two, it may well be that word analysis activities were practiced differentially, depending on the language level of the particular class.

This brings us to a third and related interpretation, which ties the reading curriculum to the manner in which beginning readers deal with text. Several researchers (for example, Rozin and Gleitman, 1977; Stanovich, 1980) have argued that children must be able to recognize printed words efficiently in a context-free manner before spoken language and knowledge of discourse-text relations can facilitate their efforts to read. Only if one has the skills to extract the graphemic, phonological, and semantic information carried by print efficiently can one use prior sentence context and reader expectancies positively in the reading process. If this inference is correct, activities emphasizing print-specific skills would facilitate reading in the early stages of development, whereas activities emphasizing comprehension and prediction based on general knowledge and language skill would facilitate reading only when children had moved beyond dealing with very simple text.

This interpretation is supported by the contrasting pattern of correlations shown in Table 1 between fall activities and comprehension of the primer passage read by all children tested versus fall activities and comprehension of the grade 2 passage attempted only by the best readers (28 percent of the skill-based children and 18 percent of the language-based children). Word analysis and printing activities were positively correlated with achievement on the primer passage in both the skill-based and language-based classrooms. However, the relationship between achievement on the grade 2 passage and the same activities was generally not significant. Rather, classroom activities emphasizing comprehension and the use of predictive context were associated more with achievement among the more-advanced readers. Further, these activities were also associated with achievement on the primer passage but only in the skill-based classrooms.

This suggests that classrooms successful on the primer passage were successful because of the word-processing skills taught and that the use of expectancies generated from prior text work only when children have flexible resources for dealing with unfamiliar words. Research on individual differences in reading has revealed that poor readers more often have difficulties in

Table 1. Relationship of Reading Activities to
Reading Achievement by Curricula

	Skill-based		Language-based	
	Primer	Grade 2	Primer	Grade 2
Silent Reading				
Teacher-led	.69	.36	.20	.52
Independent	− .36	− .16	.04	.44
Sight-Word Practice				
Teacher-led	− .38	.13	.49	− .37
Independent	− .30	− .63	.06	− .46
Word Analysis Activities				
Teacher-led	.31	− .02	.31	.03
Independent	.41	− .20	—	—
Comprehension and Context Use				
Teacher-led	.35	.31	− .15	.28
Independent	—	—	—	—
Printing Activities				
Teacher-led	—	—	—	—
Independent	.44	.29	.34	.12

Note: If more than half of the classrooms in a group engaged in an activity less than 2 percent
of the time and the mean for that group was less than 4 percent, the activity was
considered to be too minimal for correlational analysis, and it is denoted here by − .

single-word identification (Guthrie and Tyler, 1976; Lesgold and others, 1981; Mitterer, 1982), and correlations between word recognition and reading comprehension ranging from .50 to .80 have been found (Biemiller, 1977–78; McCormick and Samuels, 1979; Perfetti and Hogaboam, 1975; Stanovich and others, 1981). Shankweiler and Liberman (1972) concluded that a major barrier to reading acquisition lies in dealing with words and their components and that poor reading comprehension is a consequence of reading words poorly, not the reverse. The more fully one has developed these print-specific encoding skills, the better the stimulus data that one supplies to the integrative comprehension process and the more accurate the understanding of text that one constructs from the data. Thus, in the teacher-directed classrooms, which emphasized print-specific skills and reading for meaning, reading achievement and language skills were positively related.

What might explain the negative relationship found between language skill and reading achievement in the language-based classrooms? Language skill interacts with any kind of data in the reading process, not just with complete and accurate data. The more powerful the language skills that are applied to erroneous data and the greater the preference for psycholinguistic guessing over word decoding, the greater the chance the reader will construct faulty interpretations that he or she will deem to be acceptable. Testing some of the children myself, I observed that many of the students in the language-based

classrooms, who could hardly read the primer text with any degree of accuracy, happily made up answers to the comprehension questions and requested to read the more difficult passages. Their strong interpretive skills, which had been fostered by a reading program in which they read stories that they themselves had written, generally encouraged them to overstep the bounds of their word processing skills. The negative relationship between language skill and word practice and analysis activities would exacerbate this problem by maximizing the possibility that children with the strongest language skill would have the least-practiced word recognition skills.

While constitutional factors may affect the development of skills contributing to reading in some cases (Pirozzolo and Hansch, 1982; Rourke, 1981), both recent research and the study reported here remind us that early instruction contributes to the development and deployment of subskills in reading, not only to year-end reading achievement. For example, Alegria and others (1982) observed that phonic segmentation skill was poor among first graders taught by the whole-word method and that it was uncorrelated to general reading performance. In contrast, children taught by a method emphasizing the alphabetic principle were better at phonemic segmentation, which correlated highly ($r = .65$) with their reading performance.

While word-processing skills may come easily for some children, for many others they are difficult to attain and depend on systematic and explicit reading instruction and corrective feedback from the instructional environment (Gleitman and Rozin, 1977; Stanovich, 1980). To the layman, it may seem obvious that reading skills depend on the reading skills taught, but this is a point that often seems forgotten in the chase for subcategories and diagnoses of learning-disabled children whose different patterns of performance are viewed as neuropsychological in origin. For example, Boder (1973) and Boder and Jarrico (1982) have distinguished between reading-disabled children who are "dysphonetic" or unable to apply phonic word analysis skills and children who are "dyseidetic" or have trouble processing the visual configurations of words despite adequately developed phonetic skills. The ratio of dysphonetic to dyseidetic readers is estimated at four to one. Given the present study and the research supporting the importance of word analysis skills, one cannot help but wonder how many dysphonetic poor readers are partially a product of the educational experiences that they have had. If reading could somehow be taught without looking at words, as it is sometimes taught without isolating the sound-symbols that comprise them, one might further wonder whether the number of dysphonetic and dyseidetic readers might be more comparable.

In contrast to the differential emphases on print-specific skills, the two curricula appeared comparable in their encouragement of reading for meaning. Unlike decoding skills, which develop largely as a result of instruction, the use of context and the search for meaning are a natural and powerful force in beginning readers. Numerous studies (for example, Biemiller, 1970; Cohen,

1974–75; Whaley and Kibby, 1981; Stanovich and others, in press b; Weber, 1970) have demonstrated that young children readily exploit contextual clues and that the majority of their reading errors are substitutions that allow for meaningful interpretation of the sentence up to and including the point of error. Thus, making sense of the printed page is a main principle even for beginners. But, sooner or later the interpretation must be based on what is actually printed, not on what is invented. Biemiller (1970) went on to show that, the sooner children move to a stage at which they attempt to take graphemic information into account and coordinate it with contextual cues, the more rapid their reading progress becomes. The present study suggests that the rate at which children enter this stage depends not only on their natural abilities but also on the learning conditions that they have experienced. Children in the language-based classrooms who mainly read self-generated, familiar, and highly predictable texts could rely successfully on their expectancies of what was there and be spared much of the need to develop highly print-specific skills. While recognition of the words in their word banks helped them to read their own stories, it would appear to have been relatively ineffective in dealing with the vocabulary of other materials. Hence, while it may be possible with practice to acquire enough stored pronunciations and meanings for particular printed words to enable one to deal with text on which one has been drilled (whether published or self-composed), this strategy breaks down when unfamiliar word configurations are encountered. Whether decoding skill involves letter-by-letter sound translation (Gough, 1972) analogical reasoning (Baron, 1979; Glushko, 1979) or rule-based print translation mechanisms (Baron and Strawson, 1976; Venezky, 1970), the beneficial use of discourse-text expectancies depends critically on these generalizable word-processing skills.

Teacher Direction and Feedback. In addition to emphasis on print-specific skills, a second curricular component that varied between classrooms was the relative extent of teacher-directed activities and independent work by the children. Previous research (Brophy and Evertson, 1976; Soar, 1973; Stallings and Kaskowitz, 1974) has revealed a positive relationship between achievement and teacher-led instruction with opportunities for practice and corrective feedback and negative correlations between achievement and self-directed independent or small-group work. Table 1 provides a means for partial assessment of the role of direct supervision in reading achievement in the two groups of classrooms that I studied. In both groups, teacher-led group silent reading was positively correlated with reading achievement. Independent silent reading, which occurred only in the most advanced language-based classrooms, was also positively related to reading scores in this group only. Otherwise, independent silent reading was uncorrelated or even negatively correlated with achievement. Similarly, independent sight-word practice was negatively correlated with reading achievement in both curricula.

While these data are limited, they accord with the aforementioned importance of teacher direction. During independent activities, teachers have

little control over critical factors, such as what and how words are practiced, whether texts read silently are read accurately and with comprehension, whether correct or incorrect responses are practiced, and at what pace the children proceed. Given the relatively inefficient learning strategies, mnemonic behaviors, and monitoring of comprehension in young children (Flavell and others, 1966; Flavell and Wellman, 1977; Markman, 1981; Ornstein and others, 1975), it would appear essential for teachers at the primary level to guide and correct children's reading so as to foster the objective extraction of meaning.

The one major exception to this generalization about the ineffectiveness of independent activities is the positive relationship observed between the extent of independent printing activities and reading achievement. Part of the significance may be due to the fact that higher reading skill leads children to print more stories during independent work. However, it may also be due to the role that printing has in bringing sound structure and phonetic analysis into conscious awareness (Rozin and Gleitman, 1977; Gleitman and Rozin, 1977). Phonemic awareness in turn correlates highly with reading achievement, and training in phonemic awareness has been shown to have a positive effect on reading achievement (Bradley and Bryant, 1983; Ehri, 1979; Johnson and Hook, 1978; and Chapter One in this volume).

Summary and Directions

Although many of the points made in this chapter are based on a contrast between language-based and skill-based programs, the extent to which programs foster generalizable word-processing skills and provide engineered and corrective supervision are dimensions applicable to any classroom. As Carr and Evans (1981) explain in detail, child-centered language-based curricula should, with some modifications, be able to foster beginning reading just as well as other approaches. What beginning readers in any classroom need are the resources to use knowledge, inferences, and print-specific skills flexibly and efficiently, not slavishly or inaccurately. The data from language-based classrooms suggest that requiring children to deal with text as they do with spoken discourse is a very difficult and clouded challenge if the children are not also given a firm grounding in the basic encoding skills by which printed text is recognized and related to existing knowledge. In light of the results presented here, it comes as no surprise that, while reading achievement is correlated with general intelligence at the grade 1 level, the contribution of intelligence to reading skill is greatly reduced if decoding speed is taken into account (Stanovich and others, in press a).

That the reading curricula described in this report were associated with different patterns of cognitive skill reinforces the view of Ysseldyke and Algozzine (1982, 1983) that we should diagnose instruction as well as the learner. In the past, reading programs have often been defined by the materials

used (for example, Chall, 1967; Bond and Dykstra, 1967) or the stated objectives (for example, Beck and others, 1979; Ruddell and Crewes, 1978) as though to ignore the people involved with them. The descriptive approach taken in this study represents an attempt to move beyond these limitations by documenting the children's activities. Clearly, much more remains to be done to detail the nature of each reading activity. For example, with respect to word practice activities, how many words are practiced and how? To what level of mastery? In coordination with what? (Omanson raises similar questions from a different perspective in Chapter Three of this volume.) While individual abilities and styles of learning will partly determine how any given child handles reading assignments, the nature and control of those assignments lies squarely with educators. If what happens in the classroom does not matter, we as researchers may be spared a huge task. But, if it does, one can only hope for more applied and collaborative reading research that will enable both academics and educators to appreciate and understand the complexity of instructional issues and to refrain from the confrontations and polarities of the past.

References

Alegria, J., Pignot, E., and Morais, J. "Phonetic Analysis of Speech and Memory Codes in Beginning Readers." *Memory and Cognition,* 1982, *10,* 451–456.

Baron, J. "Orthographic and Word-Specific Mechanisms in Children's Reading of Words." *Child Development,* 1979, *50,* 60–70.

Baron, J., and Strawson, C. "Use of Orthographic and Word-Specific Knowledge in Reading Words Aloud." *Journal of Experimental Psychology: Human Perception and Performance,* 1976, *3,* 386–393.

Beck, I., McKeown, M., McCaslin, E., and Burkes, A. *Instructional Dimensions That May Effect Reading Comprehension: Examples from Two Commercial Reading Programs.* Pittsburgh: Learning Research & Development Center, University of Pittsburgh, 1979.

Becker, W. C. "Teaching Reading and Language to the Disadvantaged—What Have We Learned from Field Research?" *Harvard Educational Review,* 1977, *47,* 518–543.

Bennett, S. N. *Teaching Styles and Pupil Progress.* London: Open Books, 1976.

Biemiller, A. J. "The Development and the Use of Graphic and Contextual Information as Children Learn to Read." *Reading Research Quarterly,* 1970, *6,* 75–96.

Biemiller, A. "Relationship Between Oral Reading Rates for Letters, Words, and Simple Text in the Development of Reading Achievement." *Reading Research Quarterly,* 1977–78, *13,* 223–253.

Bisell, J. S. *Implementation of Planned Variation in Head Start I. Review and Summary of the Stanford Research Institute Interim Report, First Year of Evaluation.* Washington, D.C.: U.S. Department of Health, Education, and Welfare, 1971.

Boder, E. "Developmental Dyslexia: A Diagnostic Approach Based on Three Atypical Reading-Spelling Patterns." *Developmental Medicine and Child Neurology,* 1973, *15,* 663–687.

Boder, E., and Jarrico, S. "Boder Reading-Spelling Pattern Test: A Diagnostic Screening Test for Developmental Dyslexia." New York: Grune & Stratton, 1982.

Bond, G. L., and Dykstra, R. "The Cooperative Research Program in First-Grade Reading Instruction." *Reading Research Quarterly,* 1967, *2.*

Bradley, L. and Bryant, P. E. "Categorizing Sounds and Learning to Read—A Causal Connection." *Nature,* 1983, *301,* 419–421.

Bransford, J. D. *Human Cognition.* Belmont, Calif.: Wadsworth, 1979.

Bransford, J. D., Stein, B., and Vye, N. "Helping Students Learn How to Learn from Written Texts." In M. H. Singer (Ed.), *Competent Reader, Disabled Reader: Research and Application.* Hillsdale, N.J.: Erlbaum, 1982.

Broadbent, D. E., and Broadbent, M. "General Shape and Local Detail in Word Perception." In S. Dornic (Ed.), *Attention and Performance VI.* Hillsdale, N.J.: Erlbaum, 1977.

Brophy, J. D., and Evertson, C. M. *Learning from Teaching.* Boston: Allyn & Bacon, 1976.

Brown, A. L. "Development, Schooling, and the Acquisition of Knowledge About Knowledge." In R. C. Anderson, R. J. Spiro, and W. E. Montague (Eds.), *Schooling and the Acquisition of Knowledge.* Hillsdale, N.J.: Erlbaum, 1977.

Brown, A. L., and Deloache, J. "Skills, Plans, and Self-Regulation." In R. S. Siegler (Ed.), *Children's Thinking: What Develops?* Hillsdale, N.J.: Erlbaum, 1978

Carr, T. H., and Evans, M. A. "Classroom Organization and Reading Ability: Are Motivation and Skill Antagonistic Goals?" In J. Edwards (Ed.), *The Social Psychology of Reading.* Silver Spring, Md.: Institute for Modern Languages, 1981.

Chall, J. S. *Learning to Read: The Great Debate.* New York: McGraw-Hill, 1967.

Chall, J. S. "The Great Debate: Ten Years Later with a Modest Proposal for Reading Stages." In P. A. Weaver and L. B. Resnick (Eds.), *The Theory and Practice of Early Reading: An Introduction.* Vol. 1. Hillsdale, N.J.: Erlbaum, 1979.

Cohen, A. S. "Oral Reading Errors of First-Grade Children Taught by a Code Emphasis Approach." *Reading Research Quarterly,* 1974-75, *10,* 615-650.

Ehri, L. "Linguistic Insight: Threshold of Reading Aquisition." In T. G. Waller and G. E. Mackinnon (Eds.), *Reading Research and Practice.* Vol 1. New York: Academic Press, 1979.

Evans, M. A. "A Comparative Study of Young Children's Classroom Activities and Learning Outcomes." *British Journal of Educational Psychology,* 1979, *49,* 15-26.

Flavell, J. H., Beach, D. H., and Chinsky, J. M. "Spontaneous Verbal Rehearsal in a Memory Task as a Function of Age." *Child Development,* 1966, *37,* 283-299.

Flavell, J H., Botkin, P. T., Fry, C. L., Wright, J. W., and Jarvis, P. E. *Development of Communication and Role-Taking Skills in Children.* New York: Wiley, 1968.

Flavell, J. H., and Wellman, H. M. "Metamemory." In R. V. Kail and J. W. Hagen (Eds.), *Perspectives on the Development of Memory and Cognition.* Hillsdale, N.J.: Erlbaum, 1977.

Gagne, R. *Conditions of Learning.* New York: Holt, Rinehart and Winston, 1970.

Gleitman, L., and Rozin, P. "The Structure and Acquisition of Reading I: Relations Between Orthographies and the Structure of Language." In A. S. Reber and D. Scarborough (Eds.), *Towards a Psychology of Reading.* Hillsdale, N.J.: Erlbaum, 1977.

Glushko, R. "The Organization and Activation of Orthographic Knowledge in Reading Aloud." *Journal of Experimental Psychology: Human Perception and Performance,* 1979, *5,* 674-691.

Goodlad, J. I., and Anderson, R. H. *The Nongraded Elementary School.* New York: Harcourt Brace & World, 1963.

Goodman, K. S. *Miscue Analysis: Application to Reading Instruction.* Detroit: Wayne State University Press, 1973a.

Goodman, K. S. "On the Psycholinguistic Method of Teaching Reading." In F. Smith (Ed.), *Psycholinguistics and Reading.* New York: Holt, Rinehart and Winston, 1973b.

Goodman, K. S. "Reading: A Psycholinguistic Guessing Game." In H. Singer and R. Ruddell (Eds.), *Theoretical Models and Processes of Reading.* (2nd ed.) Newark, Del.: International Reading Association, 1976.

Gough, P. B. "One Second of Reading." In J. F. Kavanagh and I. G. Mattingly (Eds.), *Language by Ear and by Eye.* Cambridge, Mass.: M.I.T. Press, 1974.

Guthrie, J. T. "Models of Reading and Reading Disability." *Journal of Educational Psychology*, 1973, *65*, 9-18.

Guthrie, J. T., and Tyler, S. J. "Psycholinguistic Processing in Reading and Listening Among Good and Poor Readers." *Journal of Reading Behavior*, 1976, *8*, 415-426.

Harris, A. J., and Serwer, B. L. "The CRAFT Project: Instructional Time in Reading Research." *Reading Research Quarterly*, 1966, *2*, 27-57.

House, E. R., Glass, G. V., McLean, L. D., and Walker, D. F. "No Simple Answers: Critique of the Follow Through Evaluation." *Harvard Educational Review*, 1978, *48*, 128-160.

Johnson, D. J., and Hook, P. E. "Reading Disabilities: Problems of Rule Acquisition and Linguistic Awareness." In H. R. Myklebust (Ed.), *Progress in Learning Disabilities*. New York: Grune & Stratton, 1978.

Kofsky, E. "A Scalogram Study of Classificatory Development." *Child Development*, 1966, *37*, 191-204.

LaBerge, D., and Samuels, S. J. "Toward a Theory of Automatic Information Processing in Reading." *Cognitive Psychology*, 1974, *6*, 293-323.

Lee, L. L., and Canter, S. H. "Developmental Syntax Scoring: A Clinical Procedure for Estimating Syntactic Development in Children's Spontaneous Speech." *Journal of Speech and Hearing Disorders*, 1971, *40*, 315-340.

Lesgold, A. M., Resnick, L. B., Roth, S. F., and Hammond, K. L. "Patterns of Learning to Read: A Longitudinal Study." Paper presented at the Society for Research in Child Development, Boston, April 1981.

McCormick, C., and Samuels, S. J. "Word Recognition by Second Graders: The Unit of Perception and Interrelationships Among Accuracy, Latency, and Comprehension." *Journal of Reading Behavior*, 1979, *11*, 107-118.

Markman, E. M. "Comprehension Monitoring." In W. P. Dickson (Ed.), *Children's Oral Communication Skills*. New York: Academic Press, 1981.

Mitterer, J. O. "There Are at Least Two Kinds of Poor Readers: Whole Word Poor Readers and Recoding Poor Readers." *Canadian Journal of Psychology*, 1982, *36*, 445-461.

Ornstein, P. A., Naus, M. J., and Liberty, C. "Rehearsal and Organization Processes in Children's Memory." *Child Development*, 1975, *46*, 818-830.

Perfetti, C. A., and Hogaboam, T. "Relationship Between Single-Word Decoding and Reading Comprehension Skill." *Journal of Educational Psychology*, 1975, *67*, 461-469.

Perfetti, C. A., and Lesgold, A. M. "Discourse Comprehension and Sources of Individual Differences." In M. Just and P. Carpenter (Eds.), *Cognitive Processes in Comprehension*. Hillsdale, N.J.: Erlbaum, 1977.

Pirozzolo, F. J., and Hansch, E. C. "The Neurobiology of Developmental Reading Disorders." In R. N. Malatesha and P. G. Aaron (Eds.), *Reading Disorders: Varieties and Treatments*. New York: Academic Press, 1982.

Raven, J. C. *Coloured Progressive Matrices*. London: Lewis, 1956.

Rourke, B. P. "Reading and Spelling Disabilities: A Developmental Neurological Perspective." In U. Kirk (Ed.), *Neuropsychology of Language, Reading, and Spelling*. New York: Academic Press, 1981.

Rozin, P., and Gleitman, L. R. "The Structure and Acquisition of Reading II: The Reading Process and the Acquisition of the Alphabetic Principle." In A. Reber and D. Scarborough (Eds.), *Toward a Psychology of Reading*. Hillsdale, N.J.: Erlbaum, 1977.

Ruddell, R., and Crewes, R. *Person to Person Teacher's Edition*. Boston: Allyn & Bacon, 1978.

Shankweiler, D., and Liberman, I. Y. "Misreading: A Search for Causes." In J. Kavanagh and I. G. Mattingly (Eds.), *Language by Ear and by Eye*. Cambridge, Mass.: M.I.T. Press, 1974.

94

Smith, F. *Psycholinguistics and Reading.* New York: Holt, Rinehart and Winston, 1973.

Smith, F. *Understanding Reading.* New York: Holt, Rinehart and Winston, 1978.

Smith, F. *Reading Without Nonsense.* New York: Teachers College Press, 1979.

Soar, R. S. *Follow Through Classroom Process Measurement and Pupil Growth. Final Report.* Gainesville: University of Florida, 1973.

Stallings, J. A., and Kaskowitz, D. H. *Follow Through Classroom Observation Evaluation.* Menlo Park, Calif.: Stanford Research Institute, 1974.

Stanovich, K. E. "Toward an Interactive-Compensatory Model of Individual Differences in Reading Fluency." *Reading Research Quarterly,* 1980, *16,* 32–71.

Stanovich, K. E., Cunningham, A. E., and Feeman, D. J. "Intelligence, Cognitive Skills, and Early Reading Progress." *Reading Research Quarterly,* in press a.

Stanovich, K. E., Cunningham, A., and Feeman, D. "The Relationship Between Early Reading Acquisition and Word Decoding with and Without Context: A Longitudinal Study of First-Grade Children." *Journal of Educational Psychology,* in press b.

Stanovich, K. E., Cunningham, A., and West, R. F. "A Longitudinal Study of the Development of Automatic Recognition Skills in First Graders." *Journal of Reading Behavior,* 1981, *13,* 57–74.

Tewkesbury, J. L. *Nongrading in the Elementary Schools.* Columbus, Ohio: Merrill, 1967.

Venezky, R. L. *The Structure of English Orthography.* The Hague: Mouton, 1970.

Weber, G. *Inner-city Children Can Be Taught to Read: Four Successful Schools.* Washington, D.C.: Council for Basic Education, 1981.

Weber, R. M. "First Graders' Use of Grammatical Context in Reading." In H. Levin and J. P. Williams (Eds.), *Basic Studies on Reading.* New York: Basic Books, 1970.

Whaley, J., and Kibby, M. "The Relative Importance of Reliance on Intraword Characteristics and Interword Constraints for Beginning Reading Achievement." *Journal of Educational Research,* 1981, *74,* 315–320.

Wilder, G. "Five Exemplary Reading Program." In J. T. Guthrie (Ed.), *Cognition, Curriculum, and Comprehension.* Newark, Del.: International Reading Association, 1977.

Willows, D. M., Borwick, D., and Hayvren, M. "The Content of School Readers." In T. G. Waller and G. E. MacKinnon (Eds.), *Reading Research: Advances in Theory and Practice.* Vol. 2. New York: Academic Press, 1979.

Ysseldyke, J. E., and Algozzine, B. *Critical Issues in Special and Remedial Education.* Boston: Houghton Mifflin, 1982.

Ysseldyke, J. E., and Algozzine, B. "Where to Begin in Diagnosing Reading Problems." *Topics in Learning and Learning Disabilities,* 1983, *2,* 60–69.

Mary Ann Evans is assistant professor of psychology at the University of Guelph. She specializes in social and cognitive development and learning disabilities, and has worked previously as both a research consultant for a large suburban school system and a consulting child psychologist.

A systems approach will help to gain a coherent understanding of the nature of reading.

Using Component Skills Analysis to Integrate Findings on Reading Development

Thomas H. Carr
Tracy L. Brown
Linda G. Vavrus

What have we learned from the preceding five chapters on reading development? It was claimed in the Editor's Notes to this volume that the recent history of reading research has focused too much on studies of individual reading-related skills and too little on studies of the system into which the skills are organized, too much on studies of single factors that correlate with individual differences and too little on studies of the overall pattern of influence to which the factors contribute. At first glance, one might conclude that the chapters collected here are more of the same. Each, with the possible exception of Chapter Five, describes research on a limited set of skills that comprise only a few of the many influences that could come to bear on reading progress. Of course, there is a twist to the chapters—they are all concerned with the interactions between two or more domains of knowledge or processing procedures. Thus, none of the chapters focuses on just one skill or dimension along which readers might vary, and this expansion of the field of view over that of the common tradition represents important progress.

T. H. Carr (Ed.). *The Development of Reading Skills.* New Directions
for Child Development, no. 27. San Francisco: Jossey-Bass, March 1985.

One also gets a strong feeling that at least some of the authors do not view the common tradition as the most valuable one and that they look to other approaches for their inspiration. Thus, Brown and Haynes argue vigorously in Chapter Two that researchers should identify and refine a set of conceptual tools, or model, to apply in the study of reading, and they propose something called *component skills analysis* as their framework of choice. In the commentary that follows, we will try, first, to summarize the contributions of the individual chapters in this volume, stressing the notion of interactions and interdependencies between domains of knowledge or processing. Then, we will expand on the discussion of component skills analysis begun by Brown and Haynes in order to expose a superordinate level of investigation that can help to organize the results of studies like the ones in this volume.

What Main Points Have Been Made?

In Chapter One, Treiman raises the issue of how a reading lexicon is established. She focuses on the development of the ability to conduct visual and phonological analysis of printed letter strings — an ability that allows beginning readers to relate printed strings to vocabulary knowledge originally gained through listening and speaking, not through reading and writing. Her specific concern is the interaction between knowledge of the phonological structure of spoken words and knowledge of the orthographic structure of written words. According to Treiman, knowledge of phonology constitutes an established base that figures critically in the child's success at understanding and mastering orthography. One might add to Treiman's impressive brief on this issue the possibility that, once readers have begun to master the writing system of their language, the newly gained knowledge of orthography feeds back and refines knowledge of phonology, creating a cyclic interaction between the two kinds of knowledge in which each facilitates further development of the other (see, for example, Carr and Evans, 1981a; Ehri, 1984; Henderson and Beers, 1980; Morais and others, 1979).

In Chapter Two, Brown and Haynes continue the discussion of how a reading lexicon is established, focusing on the conduct of visual and phonological analysis in a second language rather than in the first one. Their specific concern is the interaction between established knowledge and procedures for conducting visual and phonological analyses in one's native language and the nascent knowledge and procedures being developed to deal with the second language. By comparing visual and phonological processing skills of native speaker-readers of Spanish, Arabic, and Japanese who were studying English, Brown and Haynes have been able to show specific positive and negative transfer effects that seem to depend on the similarities and differences between the writing systems used in the native language and in English. They also raise the question of how visual and phonological analysis may relate to other components of reading, although they do not go into the matter in detail.

Omanson, too, is interested in the establishment of a reading lexicon, but in Chapter Three his focus is on semantic analysis and knowledge of word meanings, not on visual and phonological processing. Specifically, Omanson wonders how the presence in a text of words whose meanings are either unknown or just recently learned affects the content, organization, and retrievability of memory representations of the text. He therefore devotes his attention to interactions between the vocabulary knowledge that supports semantic analysis of words and the procedures of propositional analysis and integrative comprehension that are assumed to underlie the construction of text representations, relying for a starting place on a theory of comprehension developed by Kintsch and van Dijk (1978; see also Kintsch, 1974).

In Chapter Four, Bock and Brewer leave concerns for lexical processing behind. They are interested in children's understanding of coherence cues and higher-level schemas that govern the organization of information in a discourse. According to Bock and Brewer, children use these cues and schemas in conjunction with world knowledge to construct from the explicit content of the discourse a mental model of its more complete intended meaning, much of which is left implicit. Until a unified mental model is constructed that accommodates all the propositional content of the discourse in a sensible way, the task of comprehension is not complete. The major thesis developed by Bock and Brewer is that written language differs from spoken language in the types of coherence cues that must be understood, in the types of information that are conveyed and hence in the types of organizing schemas that are employed, and — perhaps increasingly as students depend more and more on expository prose for new learning — in the familiarity, completeness, and abstractness of the world knowledge being referenced. Thus, beginning readers, who are familiar with spoken language but whose exposure to written language has often been limited to relatively simple narrative, have much learning to do beyond the establishment of new perceptual mechanisms and vocabulary knowledge in order to become accomplished readers, learners, and enjoyers of text.

A persistent theme runs through these four chapters. Each proposes that the acquisition of some body of knowledge or the operation of some process that is necessary to reading depends for its success on the acquisition of some other body of knowledge or on the operation of some other process. Visual analysis depends on phonological analysis, visual and phonological analysis in one language depend on visual and phonological analysis in another language, propositional analysis depends on semantic analysis, integrative comprehension — which depends on propositional analysis — also depends on an understanding of coherence cues, discourse schemas, and rules for mapping explicit content onto world knowledge. The dependencies multiply from one chapter to the next, building a complicated web of connection among the various bodies of knowledge and processes.

When contemplating this web, one sees the need for an overarching organization. Bock and Brewer argue that children develop schemas that

represent constraints on the nature of events and on how pieces of information included in narratives about them should be related to one another. Similarly, reading researchers must develop schemas representing the constraints that we believe to exist on how bodies of knowledge or processes included in a theory of reading should be related to one another. Just as schemas for events help children to organize and interpret the contents of narratives that they read, remember, or ponder, a schema for the reading process would help us to organize and interpret the findings of studies like the ones presented in this volume. In turn, studies of the present kind, which focus not just on particular domains of knowledge and process but on relations between them, would help to develop and elaborate the schema by exposing and illuminating the interactions and dependencies that the schema must represent.

Our belief, then, is that a powerful and effective symbiosis can be achieved by combining studies of interactions and dependencies between knowledge-process domains with a well-conceived theory of the overall organization of the system comprised by the various domains. A division of labor can exist between investigators concentrating on one or the other kind of study. As long as investigators communicate actively and collaborate closely, such division of labor ought not to hinder the development of the kind of complete theory of reading that this symbiosis is capable of producing, and it may even facilitate theory development by allowing knowledge at the two levels of investigation to accumulate simultaneously.

The need for a system theory is underscored by Evans in Chapter Five. Concerned with the impact of instructional activities on initial progress in reading, Evans describes some striking differences in the correlational structure of reading skills and reading-related abilities that are associated with differences in the nature of the instructional activities in which beginning readers participate. Evans argues that reading researchers do not think enough about the possibility that different reading curricula have different effects on learning and the organization of cognitive abilities. One reason for this, we contend, is the absence of consensus on what constitutes a well-conceived theory of the organization of cognitive abilities. If we find it hard to think about cognitive organization, it is not surprising that we find it hard to think about how reading curricula might modify that organization.

An Approach to Building a System Theory: Component Skills Analysis

We will now elaborate the description of an approach to building a theory of cognitive organization that was provided by Brown and Haynes in Chapter Two. Component skills analysis attempts to understand reading as the product of a complex but decomposable information-processing system (Carr, 1981, 1982; Carroll, 1976; Frederiksen, 1980, 1981; Jackson and McClelland, 1979; Olson and others, 1984; Singer, 1982; Singer and Crouse, 1981). By *decomposable* we mean that the system is viewed as consisting of a finite number

of knowledge-process domains or component skills that are theoretically distinct and empirically separable from one another. The components interact to enable perception, comprehension, and memory of visually presented language. Nevertheless (according to the theory), they can be studied as relatively independent entities, and their interrelationships can be mapped.

Identifying the properties of the components as relatively independent entities is accomplished by applying the techniques of mental chronometry for isolating subsystems and exploring their operation (Carr, 1981; Carr, in press; Carr and others, 1981; Lachman and others, 1979; McClelland, 1979; Posner, 1978; Posner and McLeod, 1982; Chase, 1978; Sternberg, 1969). Mental chronometry measures the speed and accuracy with which people can make decisions about particular stimuli or configurations of stimuli under particular conditions. By examining changes in speed and accuracy as a function of the type of decision, the properties of the stimuli, and the nature of the conditions, it becomes possible to draw inferences about the mental operations that produce the decisions. Careful application of these techniques allows one to identify constellations of mental operations that function in a given task environment as coherent wholes, taking in input, working on input, and making output available to the rest of the system to be used as input by other independently functioning constellations of mental operations. By partitioning complex tasks into subtasks in accord with the specializations of its independently functioning units, the nervous system accomplishes complex tasks in efficient ways that are rather like the operation of highly modularized computer programs, especially if one thinks of the programs as running on partly distributed rather than completely centralized processors.

These relatively independent constellations of mental operations are the component skills. The further analytic step of mapping the interrelationships among components is accomplished by applying correlation-based techniques for identifying patterns in complex data sets. These techniques include simple correlation and partial correlation (Olson and others, 1984), multiple regression (Jackson and McClelland, 1979; Singer and Crouse, 1981), spatial mapping of correlation matrices (Carr and others, 1983), confirmatory factor analysis (Frederiksen, 1980, 1981; Joreskog, 1970), and profile analysis of individual differences (Nunnally, 1978; Vavrus, Brown, and Carr, 1983). Careful application of these techniques enables both convergent validation of the conclusions drawn from chronometric subsystem isolation (for example, Frederiksen, 1980) and identification of sources of individual differences in the efficiency of component skills or of the processing system as a whole (Carr, 1981, 1982; Carr and others, 1983; Jackson and McClelland, 1979; Olson and others, 1984; Singer, 1982; Singer and Crouse, 1981; Vavrus and others, 1983).

Such an abstract description needs concrete elaboration. What would a component skills analysis look like? How would it be carried out? We will sketch a quick picture here, but for a detailed understanding, one should consult the works just cited. A complete component skills analysis would contain

at least four kinds of information: first, structural information concerning the identities of the components and how they are organized, that is, what pathways of communication or information flow connect them; second, dynamic information concerning the system's operation, including how each component works, what knowledge base it depends on for success, what functional interactions or information exchanges take place between components, when these interactions or exchanges occur, and how the operation of the components and the occurrence of exchanges between them are controlled and coordinated to obtain smooth and effective performance of the system as a whole; third, developmental information concerning the way in which the system comes into existence, for example, the role of relatively stable general abilities, the role of maturational change, the role of existing skills, the role of instruction, and the role of practice; fourth, differential information concerning the parameters or characteristics of the system's operation that are important in determining its overall efficiency and hence individual differences in the skill as a whole. These factors might include the extent of particular types of knowledge, the efficiency of particular processes that make use of that knowledge, the attentional capacity needed for controlling and coordinating information flow from one process to another, and the supply of attentional capacity available to meet the need.

How Is the Analysis Carried Out? The standard approach to conducting a component skills analysis involves the construction of a battery of information-processing tasks that is then administered to a sample of readers from a population whose reading skill is to be modeled, such as beginning readers in the first grade (Chapter Five in this volume), second-language learners with particular first-language backgrounds (Chapter Two in this volume), normally progressing elementary school students (Singer and Crouse, 1981), normally progressing high school students (Frederiksen, 1980), or children and adolescents with varying degrees of reading difficulty (Olson and others, 1984).

The choice of tasks to be included in the battery is a serious matter on which the defensibility and ultimately the success or failure of the analysis depend. Each task chosen should tap a particular hypothetical component process of the reading system (or, as in applications such as Evans's, a more general information-processing ability that might underlie and contribute to the development of such component processes). Because it is impossible to construct a task that requires one and only one mental operation for its performance or even one and only one constellation of mental operations, it will generally be the case that no task is a pure measure of a single component skill. For example, one might like to get a measure of skill at converting from an internal representation of the visual form of a printed stimulus word (the so-called visual or graphemic code) to an internal representation of the phonology of the spoken version of the word (the so-called phonological code). To do this, one might ask people to pronounce orthographically regular but unfamiliar pseudowords shown on a projection screen or a computer display terminal and

measure the time it takes them to begin pronouncing each pseudoword after it appears on the screen (the pronunciation latency). One might conclude that people who take longer to begin pronouncing pseudowords are not as good at the hypothetical component skill of grapheme-to-phoneme translation as people who take less time. While such a conclusion might seem reasonable — it might even be reasonable — it must be remembered that grapheme-to-phoneme translation is not the only thing that the task requires. People must also focus their attention on the computer display, they must get visual input from the retina into the brain, they must form the visual code from which the phonological code is derived, they must translate the phonological code into an articulatory code that can drive an overt pronunciation, and they must execute the pronunciation. It is conceivable that, in addition to the particular skill of interest, which is supposed to be grapheme-to-phoneme translation, any or all these other processes could figure into the difference between people who are fast or slow at the task. (For a look at a number of other, more subtle, problems that could arise in this particular case, see Carr and Pollatsek, in press.) Therefore, one can only hope to find tasks whose performance reflects a particular component skill as strongly as possible and the influences of other processes as weakly as possible. If this criterion is met for all the hypothetical component skills, then comparisons among the tasks will allow one to determine the relative importance of their contributions to system operation.

Clearly, the important questions in such a situation are what component skills should be hypothesized to exist and what task should be chosen to represent each skill in the battery. To answer these questions, one needs a tentative model of the reading system from which to start and a task analysis that allows one to decide what component skills any given task is likely to emphasize most heavily. Note the apparent paradox here: Before one can start to construct a model of the reading system, one needs a model of the reading system. This paradox arises because of the iterative, bootstrapping character of such a research program. Each new round of investigation refines the results of the preceding round and, we may hope, corrects its mistakes. The works that we have cited devote much attention to these complicated questions, and space here is too limited to explore these issues in depth. We can, however, offer the example of a battery that we have used ourselves and discuss the kinds of results that it has produced.

An Example of Component Skills Analysis. Table 1 shows a component assessment battery that we used in our investigations of individual differences in reading efficiency among children and adolescents referred to a reading clinic for diagnosis of potential reading difficulty. The choice of skills to be assessed was guided by the tentative model of the reading system shown in Figure 1. Each labeled oval corresponds to a component skill — a constellation of mental operations plus the knowledge used by those operations. Each arrow corresponds to a pathway along which information can flow from one component skill to another; the arrowheads indicate the direction of flow. The solid

Table 1. Component Skills Assessment Battery

Skill Being Tapped	Test or Performance Measure
Visual code formation and evaluation	Same-different matching with differences based on cAsE (visual configuration)
Sight-word recognition	Pronunciation of familiar words graded for difficulty (Slosson Oral Reading Test)
Phonological translation	Pronunciation of unfamiliar pseudowords matched on structure with familiar words
Phonological awareness	Gates-McKillop Knowledge of Word Parts Test
Semantic vocabulary knowledge and predictive context use	Forced-choice cloze task modified from Stanford Achievement Test
Integrative processing and memory	Listening Comprehension Test of Durrell Reading-Listening Series
Working memory for item identities	Free-recall digit span
Working memory for item order	Serial-recall digit span
General pattern sensitivity	Raven's Coloured Progressive Matrices
Overall reading comprehension efficiency	Correct responses achieved per unit time on the Reading Comprehension Test of Durrell Reading-Listening Series

arrows are pathways whose existence seems to be fairly well established by the data now available. Dotted arrows correspond to pathways whose existence is not so well established by the data. This model is a slightly simplified best guess about what a schematic diagram of the reading system should look like. It is the result of several years' thinking and rethinking of the implications of the data that we know about (see Carr, 1981, 1982; Carr, in press; Carr and Pollatsek, in press; Carr and Evans, 1981a, 1981b). Even so, it is by no means a final product, and future expositions of the model may be changed in ways as yet unknown in order to accommodate new data. Indeed, the series of publications just cited displays such evolution.

The data generated by a test battery like that depicted in Table 1 are voluminous. As a first step toward extracting the relations between components that might exist in these data, we chose to conduct a simple, rather intuitive analysis based on the matrix of first-order correlations between all possible pairs of measures in the battery. The goal of the analysis was to transform the matrix into a spatial representation that would make it easy to see relationships between components that might be important in creating individual differences in the efficiency of the system's operation. Furthermore, we wanted to carry out this transformation in a straightforward way that made as few mathematical assumptions as possible, that was easy to understand, and that was not likely to miss relationships that might be important, even at the expense of identifying a few relationships that turned out later not to be important. That

Figure 1. A Tentative Model of the Reading System

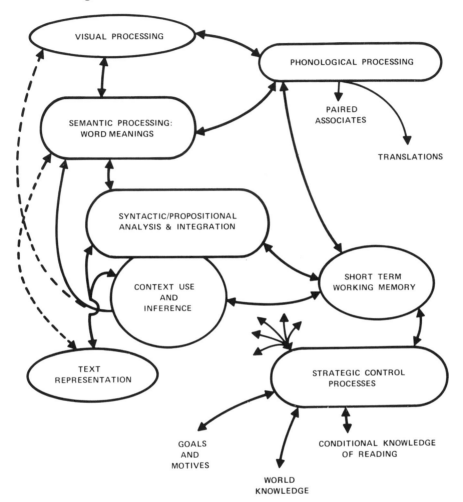

is, we wanted an exploratory picture of the data we had collected that would give a first glimpse of the structure that might underlie composite system performance and that would provide a rich source of hypotheses about the origins of the structure that more detailed experimentation could confirm or disconfirm at a later time.

The result of pursuing this goal was a nomothetic characterization of individual differences that we refer to as a *cognitive skills map* (Carr and others, 1983). In this map, the magnitudes of correlations are transformed into a kind of distance metric. First, each correlation is squared to obtain the proportion of simple variance shared by each pair of component skill measures. Then, the reciprocal of the squared correlation is calculated to produce a number ranging

between one and infinity; smaller numbers represent higher shared variances. Thus, the reciprocal of shared variance constitutes an individual differences distance metric in which shorter distances indicate stronger, closer relationships between component skills. The nature of the reciprocal transformation is to magnify small differences in shared variance, helping potential patterns to emerge that can be subjected to convergent validation in subsequent work.

Figure 2 shows the cognitive skills map constructed from data supplied by thirty-four reading clinic clients. They ranged in age from eight to fifteen years and in school grade level from second to eighth. Reading comprehension

Figure 2. Cognitive Skills Map of Correlations Among Individual Differences in Reading Skills

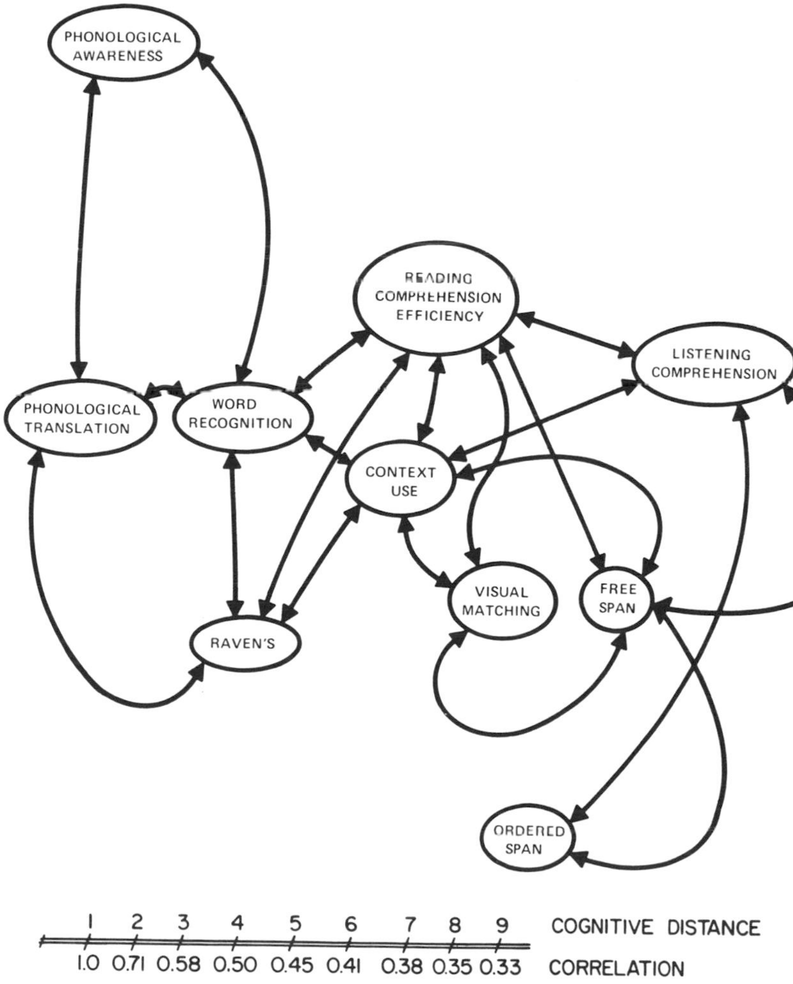

efficiency is the criterion measure of overall system performance. The individual component skill measures are arrayed around it in a way that depicts the cognitive distances among them as well as a two-dimensional drawing permits. The correlations identified by arrows between measures range from the + .86 represented by the distance of 1.35 between grapheme-to-phoneme-based phonological translation and word recognition to the + .36 represented by the distance of 7.73 between word recognition and phonological awareness. Correlations smaller than .35 were not statistically significant in our data base and are ignored in the cognitive skills map.

What Does It Mean? How should we interpret the pattern shown in the map? If one takes as a rough first approximation to the truth the claim that the reading system — at least early in its development — consists of a set of visual skills that must be mastered and integrated into a preexisting auditory language system, then one is led to a straightforward observation. The auditory tasks of listening comprehension, free memory span, and ordered memory span lie on the right side of the map, more closely related to reading comprehension efficiency and to each other than to the visual tasks. Of course, the generalization is not completely accurate: Listening comprehension is relatively close to the visually administered measure of context use as well as to reading comprehension efficiency, and free memory span is not too distant from context use and from visual matching.

Given that context use and visual matching are themselves closely associated, one begins to get an impression of partially overlapping groups of component skills, each group contributing both to individual differences in overall reading comprehension efficiency and to individual differences in neighboring groups. This impression is reinforced by the skills on the left side of the map, which consist of word recognition, phonological translation, and phonological awareness. This phonological word processing group makes contact, through word recognition, with reading comprehension efficiency and with context use, but it is unrelated to visual matching and the auditory tasks on the right side of the map. Sensibly enough, the Raven's measure of sensitivity to pattern correlates with the phonological word processing group and with context use in addition to reading comprehension efficiency, but it does not correlate with matching, the memory spans, or listening comprehension.

One might argue from these data that the efficiency of reading comprehension appears to depend on several clusters of component skills that are relatively independent of one another, though still positively correlated in absolute terms. These clusters include phonological word processing, context use, perceptual matching, and the integrative comprehension processes of semantic, syntactic, and propositional analysis. Such a conclusion is quite consistent with the orientations and the divisions of interest represented in the preceding chapters of this volume. Furthermore, detailed analyses reveal subsets of readers within the population that we have been studying who differ systematically in their relative proficiencies at these clusters of skills and who show corre-

spondingly systematic variations in their patterns of intercorrelation among them (Vavrus and others, 1983). This is consistent with the hypothesis that, because the skills are relatively independent of one another, they are capable of entering into more than one stable pattern of interskill influence. It remains to be determined whether these patterns constitute developmental stages that are related to one another longitudinally or parallel developmental options that represent alternative branches from some maturationally or experientially determined choice point. Much work must be done to verify these suggestions, but we are encouraged by the resemblances between our conclusions and those of other investigators who have taken different but in principle convergent approaches to component skills analysis (for example, Frederiksen, 1980, 1981; Graesser and others, 1980; Guthrie, 1973; Singer and Crouse, 1981). It appears, then, that consistent and coherent information about the reading system can be extracted from this family of approaches.

References

Carr, T. H. "Building Theories of Reading Ability: On the Relation Between Individual Differences in Cognitive Skills and Reading Comprehension." *Cognition,* 1981, *9,* 73–114.

Carr, T. H. "What's in a Model? Reading Theory and Reading Instruction." In M. H. Singer (Ed.), *Competent Reader, Disabled Reader: Research and Application.* Hillsdale, N.J.: Erlbaum, 1982.

Carr, T. H. "Perceiving Visual Language." In L. Kaufman, J. Thomas, and K. Boff (Eds.), *Handbook of Perception and Human Performance.* New York: Wiley, in press.

Carr, T. H., and Evans, M. A. "Classroom Organization and Reading Ability: Are Skill and Motivation Antagonistic Goals?" In J. R. Edwards (Ed.), *The Social Psychology of Reading.* Silver Spring, Md.: Institute of Modern Language, 1981a.

Carr, T. H., and Evans, M. A. "Influence of Learning Conditions on Patterns of Cognitive Skill in Young Children." Paper presented at the meeting of the Society for Research in Child Development, Boston, April 1981b.

Carr, T. H., and Pollatsek, A. "Recognizing Printed Words: A Look at Current Models." In D. Besner, T. G. Waller, and E. MacKinnon (Eds.), *Reading Research: Advances in Theory and Practice.* Vol. 5. New York: Academic Press, in press.

Carr, T. H., Pollatsek, A., and Posner, M. I. "What Does the Visual System Know About Words?" *Perception and Psychophysics,* 1981, *29,* 183–190.

Carr, T. H., Vavrus, L. G., and Brown, T. L. "Cognitive Skill Maps of Reading Ability." Paper presented at the meeting of the American Educational Research Association, Montreal, April 1983.

Carroll, J. B. "Psychometric Tests as Cognitive Tasks: A New 'Structure of Intellect.'" In L. B. Resnick (Ed.), *The Nature of Intelligence.* Hillsdale, N.J.: Erlbaum, 1976.

Chase, W. G. "Elementary Information Processes." In W. K. Estes (Ed.), *Handbook of Learning and Cognitive Processes.* Vol. 5. Hillsdale, N.J.: Erlbaum, 1978.

Ehri, L. C. "How Orthography Alters Spoken Language Competencies in Children Learning to Read and Spell." In J. Downing and R. Valtin (Eds.), *Language Awareness and Learning to Read.* New York: Springer-Verlag, 1984.

Frederiksen, J. R. "Component Skills in Reading: Measurement of Individual Differences Through Chronometric Analysis." In R. E. Snow, P.-A. Federico, and W. E. Montague (Eds.), *Aptitude, Learning, and Instruction.* Vol. 1: *Cognitive Process Analyses of Aptitude.* Hillsdale, N.J.: Erlbaum, 1980.

Frederiksen, J. R. "Sources of Process Interactions in Reading." In A. M. Lesgold and C. A. Perfetti (Eds.), *Interactive Processes in Reading.* Hillsdale, N.J.: Erlbaum, 1981.

Graesser, A. C., Hoffman, N., and Clark, L. F. "Structural Components of Reading Time." *Journal of Verbal Learning and Verbal Behavior*, 1980, *19*, 135–151.

Guthrie, J. T. "Models of Reading and Reading Disability." *Journal of Educational Psychology*, 1973, *65*, 9–18.

Henderson, L., and Beers, J. W. *Developmental and Cognitive Aspects of Learning to Spell: A Reflection of Word Knowledge.* Newark, Del.: International Reading Association, 1980.

Jackson, M. D., and McClelland, J. L. "Processing Determinants of Reading Speed." *Journal of Experimental Pscyhology: General*, 1979, *108*, 151–181.

Joreskog, K. G. "A General Method for Analysis of Covariance Structures." *Biometrika*, 1970, *57*, 239–251.

Kintsch, W. *The Representation of Meaning in Memory.* Hillsdale, N.J.: Erlbaum, 1974.

Kintsch, W., and van Dijk, T. "Toward a Model of Text Comprehension and Production." *Psychological Review*, 1978, *85*, 363–394.

Lachman, R., Lachman, J., and Butterfield, E. C. *Cognitive Psychology and Information Processing: An Introduction.* Hillsdale, N.J.: Erlbaum, 1979.

McClelland, J. L. "On the Time Relations of Mental Processes: An Examination of Systems of Processes in Cascade." *Psychological Review*, 1979, *86*, 287–307.

Morais, J., Cary, L., Alegria, J., and Bertelson, P. "Does Awareness of Speech as a Sequence of Phonemes Arise Spontaneously?" *Cognition*, 1979, *7*, 323–331.

Nunnally, J. C. *Psychometric Theory.* (2nd ed.) New York: McGraw-Hill, 1978.

Olson, R. K., Kleigl, R., Davidson, B. J., and Foltz, G. "Individual and Developmental Differences in Reading Disability." In T. G. Waller and E. MacKinnon (Eds.), *Reading Research: Advances in Theory and Practice.* Vol. 4. New York: Academic Press, 1984.

Posner, M. I. *Chronometric Explorations of Mind.* Hillsdale, N.J.: Erlbaum, 1978.

Posner, M. I., and McLeod, P. "Information-Processing Models: In Search of Elementary Operations." *Annual Review of Psychology*, 1982, *33*, 477–514.

Singer, M. H. *Competent Reader, Disabled Reader: Research and Application.* Hillsdale, N.J.: Erlbaum, 1982.

Singer, M. H., and Crouse, J. "The Relationship of Context-Use Skills to Reading: A Case for an Alternative Experimental Logic." *Child Development*, 1981, *52*, 1326–1329.

Sternberg, S. "The Discovery of Processing Stages: Extensions of Donders's Method." In W. E. Koster (Ed.), *Attention and Performance II.* Amsterdam: North-Holland, 1969.

Vavrus, L. G., Brown, T. L., and Carr, T. H. "Component Skill Profiles of Reading Ability: Variations, Trade-offs, and Compensations." Paper presented at the meeting of the Psychonomic Society, San Diego, Calif., November 1983.

Thomas H. Carr is associate professor of cognitive and developmental psychology at Michigan State University. His research focuses on the organization and development of skilled performances, such as reading and handwriting. He is also interested in the applications of basic knowledge to education and to the design of person-machine systems. He has just returned from a year as visiting scientist at I.B.M.'s Thomas J. Watson Research Center, where much of the preparation of this commentary was done.

Tracy L. Brown is completing postgraduate work in cognitive psychology at Michigan State University. His principal research interests include individual differences in reading ability and the roles of attention and automaticity in human performance.

Linda G. Vavrus is completing postgraduate work in education at Michigan State University. She is engaged in both basic and applied research on reading diagnosis and reading instruction at Michigan State's Institute for Research on Teaching.

The current phase in the history of reading research was founded on the belief that basic research and theory development would eventually lead to better reading instruction. This chapter is a progress report.

Bridging the Gap Between Theory and Practice in Reading

Dale M. Willows

The chapters in this volume represent a very broad spectrum of approaches to the study of reading, ranging from the very theoretical to the very practical. Close collaboration between theorists and the practically oriented has not been characteristic of research on reading. On the contrary, rather strict boundaries have been drawn between the theoretical and practical domains. In this commentary, I will consider the nature of the relation between theory and practice in reading research from a historical perspective: I will focus on some general factors that have hampered communications between theory and practice. Within this context, I will discuss the research reported in the first five chapters of this volume and suggest ways in which viewing that work from a broad perspective may lead to more productive relations between theory and practice in the future.

A Century of Research on Reading

There have been three discernible periods in the history of reading research. The first, which extended roughly from 1880 to 1920, coincided with the beginnings of experimental psychology. During this period, some prominent figures in experimental psychology (for example, Cattell, 1886; Dodge, 1900; Pillsbury, 1897) undertook research on letter and word recognition, eye

T. H. Carr (Ed.). *The Development of Reading Skills.* New Directions
for Child Development, no. 27. San Francisco: Jossey-Bass, March 1985.

movements, and legibility of print, among other topics. The focus of the research was on individual differences and visual perception rather than on reading per se, and the studies used normal adults as subjects. Although interest in the pedagogy of reading was growing (for example, Dewey, 1898; Hall, 1874; Huey, 1908), the early experimental psychologists did not attempt to derive any practical implications from their work. Indeed, Huey (1908) made no attempt in his classic work to determine the pedagogical implications of the research he summarized in the section on psychology. His recommendations concerning the teaching of reading seem to have been based on his own intuitions and on those of other educators. Thus, this early productive period in the history of research on reading was dominated by basic research without concern for practical applications.

During the next period in the history of reading research, which extended roughly from 1920 to 1960, experimental psychology, then dominated by behaviorism, abandoned the study of reading. There was hardly any basic research on reading, and no theories of the reading process were developed. The primary thrust of reading research during that period was practical, and the growing field of educational psychology produced an extensive literature on testing and on reading instruction. The testing movement resulted in numerous studies of reading diagnosis and assessment (for example, Gates, 1921), and it led to the development of standardized tests of reading. These in turn provided tools that teachers of reading could use to test the results of their efforts. As a consequence, a great many classroom studies of reading instruction were undertaken. These studies for the most part compared the effectiveness of one method of instruction in the classroom with the effectiveness of another. Their ultimate quest was to find the "best" method of reading instruction through strictly empirical means.

The most recent period in the history of reading research began about 1960 and continues into the present. This period has been characterized by a swing back to basic research on reading, but the goals are different: Basic research is now seen as a means to the end of improving reading instruction. By the late 1950s, as the influence of the behaviorist movement waned, there was a renewal of interest among experimental psychologists in the study of reading. Partially as a result of the publication of Jeanne Chall's (1967) *Learning to Read: The Great Debate* and of the results of Bond and Dykstra's (1966–1967) coordinated series of classroom studies, researchers embarking on studies of reading during this period were generally disenchanted with applied research as an effective tool for answering questions about how reading should be taught. Both of these major attempts to resolve the controversy about the "best" method of reading instruction demonstrated that the countless classroom studies had produced no clear-cut answers. What was clear from the findings was that a different approach was essential if reading research were ever to contribute toward the improvement of reading instruction.

The pioneers in the growing field of basic research on reading suggested what this approach might be. Their view was that an understanding of the

reading process is a prerequisite to the improvement of reading instruction. For example, Gibson (1965, p. 1072) wrote that "good pedagogy is based on a deep understanding of the discipline to be taught and the nature of the learning process involved," and Levin (1966, p. 140) suggested that "the prior question is *What is the process of reading?* rather than *What is the optimal teaching procedure?* Definitive answers to the second wait on the first." In a discussion of basic and applied research on reading, Carroll (1968, p. 274) strongly advocated what he termed "basic educational research" on the assumption that it would lead ultimately to better educational practice, arguing that "although results of many of the studies have no immediate applications, they promise to contribute towards a new theory of the reading process that will guide the development of practical materials and procedures for the teaching of reading."

Thus, when the movement toward basic research on reading began in the late 1950s and early 1960s, the prevailing view was that the development of better reading theories would eventually lead to the improvement of educational practice. Since the mid 1960s, when published results of basic studies on reading began to appear in the literature, the field has grown exponentially. Numerous researchers from a wide variety of disciplines (for example, child development, perception, verbal learning, neuropsychology, cognitive science, linguistics, educational psychology, artificial intelligence) have become active contributors to the literature of research on reading. Whereas fifteen to twenty years ago little other than practical advice for educators was being written about reading, today there are dozens of books and hundreds of articles in the field.

At this point, it seems reasonable to ask: Have the promises of the movement toward basic research on reading and the development of reading theories begun to be fulfilled? There are two subquestions. The first concerns the influence of the basic research movement on applied studies of reading. Such studies would seem to be an essential link between laboratory-based studies of isolated variables with selected populations and direct classroom applications. Thus, the first subquestion is, Have the increase in basic research on reading processes and the development of theories and models of reading resulted in more and better applied research on reading instruction? The second subquestion concerns direct applications of research findings to classroom practice. It can be stated as follows: Is reading instruction improving as a result of the findings of basic research on reading? I will address these two subquestions here within the context both of the last twenty years of research on reading and of the chapters in this volume.

Trends in Theory-Based Applied Research

In any science, it is relatively rare for theory-based research conducted with a high degree of experimental control to lead to immediate and direct applications. It is more usual that, as the theories and models in an area become increasingly refined and sophisticated, their practical implications

begin to be explored. This process of exploration involves assessing the potential usefulness of the theory under conditions that increasingly approximate the real-world domain of application. It is only after such field testing that major applications are warranted.

In the area of reading research, much the same sequence would be expected to be followed. Theories grounded in basic research on the reading processes would lead to laboratory-based educational research, which in turn would lead to field-based applied research. Only then would large-scale applications to reading methods and materials be justified. In an attempt to determine the extent to which research and theories on the basic processes involved in reading are contributing to theory-based applied research, two colleagues and I undertook a major review of the research literature that has emerged during the very productive current period in the history of reading research (Willows and others, 1983). Our goal was to examine trends in the reading research that has emerged since the field became basically process–oriented. We considered the research in terms of the types of questions being addressed and in terms of the types of research designs and methodologies being used.

The literature of research on reading is currently being published in thirty to forty different journals (Willows and others, 1983). These journals fall into three major categories: those concerned mainly with basic processes (for example, *Cognitive Psychology, Journal of Verbal Learning and Verbal Behavior, Journal of Experimental Psychology: Human Perception and Performance, Visible Language*), those that focus on basic educational, instructional, and developmental research (for example, *Child Development, Journal of Educational Psychology, Reading Research Quarterly, Journal of Reading Behavior*), and those that feature applied research and practical articles (for example, *Curriculum Inquiry, Elementary English, Journal of Reading, The Reading Teacher*).

On the basis of a preliminary analysis of the research in all three categories of journals, we selected *Reading Research Quarterly* and *Journal of Educational Psychology* as the most appropriate to review for trends in the relation between theory and practice in reading research. These educational journals are the two highest-status journals in which one would expect to find reading research that has been influenced by both theoretical and practical concerns.

Some of the data from our analysis have clear implications for the question, Have the increase in basic research on the reading processes and the development of theories and models of reading resulted in more and better applied research on reading instruction? Our study involved examining all reading-related studies published in *Reading Research Quarterly* and *Journal of Educational Psychology* in a fifteen-year period from 1967 to 1981 — a total of 267 studies in all — and classifying each study on its underlying goals and research methodologies. Our analysis revealed three fairly distinct types of research. These research types correspond quite closely to the categories represented by the three categories of journals mentioned earlier.

The three types are distinguishable in terms of research goals and

research methodologies. Basic process research on reading has as its primary goal the development of theories of the reading processes, and high internal validity (Campbell and Stanley, 1963) is an essential feature of its research design. The criterion of high internal validity dictates that the research methodology uses strict experimental controls, unambiguously quantifiable measures, and replicable procedures. Basic educational and instructional research is concerned with issues more closely related to learning and reading instruction, but, like all basic research, its methodology gives considerations of internal validity priority over those of external validity. In contrast, applied instructional research directly addresses questions of practical importance to classroom learning, and its research methodology is guided by considerations of external validity. The emphasis on external validity requires that the research setting and procedures closely approximate the classroom situations in the real world to which the results should generalize. Thus, like the real world, this research involves complexity that is difficult to define and measure.

In classifying the 267 articles on reading, we found that the vast majority could be placed in one of these three categories. Figure 1 shows the number of each type of article in the sample of literature that we examined. It is evident from Figure 1 that the number of basic studies and of basic educational studies of reading increased substantially, but the number of applied studies published in two journals remained essentially the same over the fifteen-year period. Thus, it appears that applied research is making few attempts to explore the implications of theories and models of the reading process for classroom reading instruction. At least, few results of such applied studies are being published in high-status educational research journals.

The Gap in the Theory-Practice Continuum

At the time when he was promoting basic educational research as the most promising direction for research on reading, Carroll (1968, p. 267) suggested that the goals of researchers reflect a "hierarchy of motives each imperceptibly merging into the next, as follows: Curiosity → Better understanding of natural phenomena → General, undefined utilitarian aims → Well-defined practical goals." A continuum of motives extending from the purely theoretical to the purely practical suggests that movement of information would occur from theory to practice and back again through research. However, our analysis of fifteen years of the reading research literature suggests that there is relatively little movement across a theory-practice continuum. In most instances, a particular line of research is pursued only by research of the same type, if it is pursued at all. In addition, there is a serious gap in the continuum. Although the theories and models emanating from basic research on the reading processes are having some influence on the questions addressed in basic educational research, the instructional theories and empirical findings emerging from basic educational research are not being followed up with applied research.

Figure 1. Trends in Reading Research Between 1967 and 1981

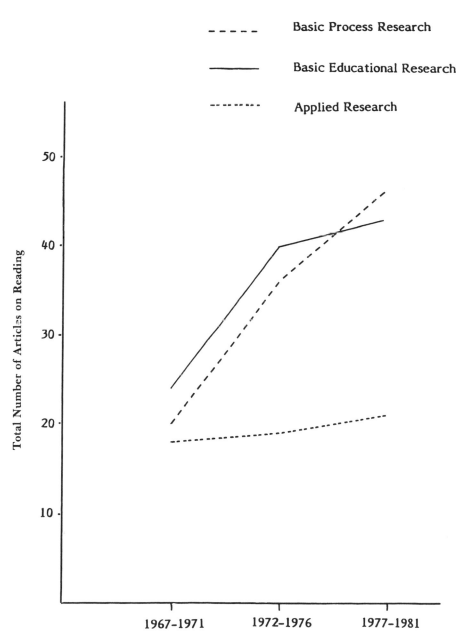

Years of Publication of the *Reading Research Quarterly*
and the *Journal of Educational Psychology*

Most often, reports of basic educational research conclude with suggested practical implications, but these speculations are hardly ever tested under more externally valid conditions. Moreover, the direction of information flow is predominantly one-way from theory toward practice. So, laboratory research frequently bypasses many of the issues that are most important in reading instruction (Kintsch, 1979). Thus, rather than a theory-practice continuum, the flow of information in reading research would seem to be more accurately described as discontinuous and unidirectional, as shown in Figure 2. Hence, there is very little movement from theory to practice and even less movement from practice to theory.

Bridging the Gap

Better communication between theory and practice in reading requires that there be much greater movement of information across the gap between them. Given the overwhelming dimensions of the current reading research literature, no one individual could possibly keep up to date with all aspects of the field. In order to bridge the gap, teams of researchers need to follow the implications of a particular line of research all the way from theory to practice. In order to cross the boundaries between the three research types, research teams must include members who are conversant with the literature in each of the three categories of journals. Exemplary teams of this type have existed for some time (for example, Resnick and Beck, 1976), but they have been the exception rather than the rule. More characteristic have been researchers who work in relative isolation within one of the three groupings; they are often naive concerning central issues in the literature beyond the boundaries of their own research domain.

Perhaps the single greatest weakness in the literature has been the very limited input near the applied end of the theory-practice dimension. Researchers conducting applied studies of reading have to sacrifice some internal validity in order to achieve an adequate degree of external validity. As a result—as the trends in Figure 1 show—such studies are rarely accepted for publication in high-status educational research journals. Thus, the researchers who have the experimental sophistication needed to design these studies shun such research. There are, however, occasional role models (for example, Calfee,

Figure 2. Information Flow Between Theory and Practice in Reading

1976) who venture across the boundary between basic educational research and applied research, undertaking studies that are both practical, in that they address educationally relevant issues in the classroom (thus maintaining a high degree of external validity), and good, in that they use the research designs, quantitative methods, and statistical analyses that typify basic research to the extent that the situation allows (thus also maintaining a relatively high degree of internal validity). More such gap crossing by basic researchers is needed if the aims of the current reading research movement are to be achieved.

Chains of Studies as the Foundation for a Bridge

If basic research and theory are ever to help us answer the question, How should reading be taught? a secure bridge of research extending from theory to practice must be constructed. The project is staggering, and without explicit planning it will never be completed: Reading is an extremely complex developmental process with many interacting subprocesses. The first stage in the construction of such a bridge can be conceptualized as the laying in place of a series of chains representing various reading subprocesses; each must be composed of sound links and firmly anchored at the ends. This will not be easy. Indeed, some psycholinguists view reading as such a complex language process that they consider any attempts to fragment reading into component subprocesses futile. However, a solid and secure bridge between theory and practice will ultimately require us to make complex interconnections between such chains, and ensuring that each chain is complete and secure on its own is fundamental to future construction. The chapters in this volume represent some of the major chains that will form the foundation for a bridge between theory and practice. At this point, there are varying numbers of links in each chain and many weak and missing ones, but construction is well underway.

Four chapters in this volume present the results of basic process research and basic educational research. Each focuses on a different set of reading subprocesses: Chapter One is concerned with the development of phonemic analysis and reading and spelling acquisition. Chapter Two examines the role of the relation between the visual and orthographic structure of languages and reading proficiency. Chapter Three considers the influence of semantic knowledge and comprehension of text. Chapter Four traces the development of young children's knowledge of discourse devices in the acquisition of reading skills. The fifth chapter presents the results of applied research. Its author contrasts the process and products of two appraoches to reading instruction. In the next five sections, I will consider the contribution that each chapter makes toward building a bridge between theory and practice.

Phonemic Analysis in Reading and Spelling. In Chapter One, Treiman reviews the literature and presents the results of some of her own research concerning the development of phonemic analysis. Her particular focus is on the analysis of onsets, consonant clusters that occur at the beginnings of spoken

syllables, and on the relation between the processing of onsets and children's reading and spelling performance.

The research goals and the types of experimental designs clearly reflect a basic research orientation, with no immediate concerns for application. This is evident both from the sources of the literature reviewed—it is almost exclusively from the basic process and basic educational research publications—and from the high internal validity (and relatively low external validity) of the research approaches employed. However, Treiman's chapter makes an important contribution to bridge building. Drawing from basic process research and theories (primarily based on studies of adult subjects), she establishes the importance of syllable onset as a significant unit of speech processing, intermediate between the syllable and the phoneme. She goes on to report a series of her own studies, in which she traces the development of children's processing of onsets and the extent to which difficulty in processing onsets is reflected in first and second graders' decoding of pseudowords and in the invented spellings of first graders just learning to write.

The chain that Treiman is constructing seems to be fairly well anchored at the theory end, and it has some good solid links well into the middle range between theory and practice. Where it is weak is at the practice end. For example, in her investigation of first and second graders' decoding of pseudowords, Treiman did not take into account the details of the school reading programs that the children had experienced. Current reading programs are quite variable in the rate and order of decoding instruction. Some do not teach initial blends until quite late in first grade. Thus, it could be that the differential error rates on CCV and CVC nonsense words among first graders simply reflect a differential emphasis in their reading programs. In order to avoid basing theory development on instructional artifacts, future studies should consider potentially relevant classroom factors.

A research team that included members experienced in approaches to so-called phonics instruction might well complete the chain of studies and bridge the gap. Thus, Treiman's chapter extends and integrates theory and research from two of the three major categories, and the particular line of inquiry that she has selected may have important implications for classroom practice in reading and spelling instruction.

Visual and Orthographic Processing and Reading. In Chapter Two, Brown and Haynes examine the influences of visual and orthographic processing on reading acquisition by comparing the reading performance of college students with different language backgrounds—Japanese, Arabic, and Spanish—who learned to read English as a second language. Their specific interest was in examining the patterns of facilitation and interference in the second-language reading performance that might be attributable to the degree of correspondence between the writing system of the first language and English.

It is evident from Brown and Haynes's chapter that the literature of research relevant to second-language teaching and learning is primarily of the

basic educational and applied types and that most of this L2 reading research suffers from two major shortcomings: the absence of a methodologically sound and coherent conceptual framework and the failure to distinguish between important literacy background variables. The special contribution of Brown and Haynes's own work is that it undertakes to address both weaknesses: It demonstrates that current component skills models of the reading process may provide an appropriate theoretical framework for L2 research, and it makes L2 reading comparisons between different language groups that vary in literacy background factors.

The line of research exemplified by Brown and Haynes's work is clearly of theoretical interest within a component skills view of the reading process, and there are obvious long-term practical implications for students learning to read English as a second language. Thus, on a theory-practice dimension, it is well worth constructing a chain of studies linking basic process research to applied research. However, it is also clear from their chapter that the chain of studies on which Brown and Haynes are working is just beginning and that it will require the forging of many new links if it is to extend from theory to practice. At this point, a number of links near the applied end and in the middle range are poorly connected, and there are no strong anchors at either end. Given that Brown is a theoretical psychologist and Haynes an instructor and researcher in English as a second language, their future team efforts are likely to contribute toward the completion of a sound and firmly anchored research chain that will eventually result in better second-language reading instruction.

Word Knowledge and Reading Comprehension. On the basis of theoretical models of comprehension processes, Omanson explores in Chapter Three different ways in which children's reading comprehension is affected by variations in word knowledge. He presents evidence from research with fourth graders that the children recalled 20 percent of stories containing recently taught words and only 11 percent of stories containing unfamiliar words and that propositions containing recently taught words were more likely to be recalled and propositions containing unfamiliar words were less likely to be recalled than propositions containing only familiar words. These findings are interpreted with respect to the ways in which word knowledge affects reading comprehension processes.

In terms both of the immediate research goals and of the research methodology, the work presented in Omanson's chapter is clearly anchored in theory. But, it is obvious that the chain of studies to which he is contributing also has significance for educational practices in the area of memory and comprehension of school texts. On the basis of the literature cited, there appear to be some good solid links near both the theoretical and practical ends, but there are some weak and missing links in the middle of the chain. For example, the research on which Omanson based his theoretical conclusions was conducted with fourth graders. Although he compared the performance of skilled and

less-skilled readers, there may be important age-related developmental differences within his sample that would render his theoretical position inadequate for younger or older children. In addition, even in the condition that involved recently taught words, the level of story learning was very low—20 percent. It may be that the high density of unfamiliar or recently taught words made the task very difficult for all the children. Had the passages contained only two or three unfamiliar words—a situation that probably more closely approximates what fourth graders would normally encounter in school—their recall patterns might have been quite different.

Since Omanson is already contributing to the efforts of a research team that includes members addressing both theoretical and practical questions in the areas of word knowledge and reading comprehension, the important research chain that he discusses promises to contribute to better reading comprehension instruction.

Discourse Knowledge and Reading Acquisition. In Chapter Four, Bock and Brewer focus on young children's abilities to comprehend spoken discourse and on the probable effects of differences between speech and writing on the transfer of discourse knowledge to reading comprehension of text.

In considering the task of comprehending and remembering discourse, Bock and Brewer emphasize the importance of real-world knowledge structures or schemas to which the reader or listener can, through language, relate the content of spoken or written discourse and form mental models that go beyond the information in the discourse itself. Bock and Brewer suggest five components of the comprehension process that may represent sources of difficulty to preschool and young school-age children in the construction of mental models, namely schema-based knowledge, the form and content of the mental model that must be constructed, the global organization of texts, knowledge of discourse cues for relations between the mental model and the text, and information processing. They review research evidence from the literature on children's comprehension of spoken discourse to suggest that these five areas may represent possible problems for young children about to begin learning to read. Then, they suggest that there are two critical components of the transfer from spoken to written discourse: learning to deal with unfamiliar text structures that convey unfamiliar kinds of information and developing the skills needed to integrate information from successive sentences in a text without the support of external, nonlinguistic context or the linguistic cues provided by spoken language.

Although the study of the factors involved in young children's discourse processing is of theoretical interest, much research is needed before the practical implications of this line of research for the early stages of reading acquisition will be known. From Bock and Brewer's chapter, it is clear that there are some strong research links near the theoretical end on a theory-practice dimension, fewer in the middle range, and hardly any at the applied end. Beyond the differences between spoken and written discourse, there are other

factors that may have a major influence on beginning readers' ability to process and remember textual information. For example, the attentional demands of visual word recognition may seriously limit young children's capacity to comprehend larger units of text (Samuels, 1976). Also, in the early stages of school reading instruction, the vast majority of texts are narrative. Thus, the difficulties with expository prose envisioned by Bock and Brewer will not arise until somewhat later, when textbook-based instruction becomes more common. Furthermore, these early stories have information-laden illustrations on virtually every page. Illustrations that provide background and contextual information may well influence discourse processing, both oral and written (Willows and others, 1981). Thus, there is a need to conduct basic educational research and applied research examining the role that discourse-processing factors play in young children's reading acquisition and reading comprehension with a variety of kinds of texts and illustrations. At this point, Bock and Brewer have just begun the construction of an interesting chain of studies that requires many more links before it can be extended into the practical domain.

Instructional Process and Reading Outcomes. In Chapter Five, Evans compares two approaches to beginning reading instruction. One is a child-centered approach in which the physical setting and classroom activities are designed to encourage self-motivated learning in an environment fostering individual exploration and peer interaction. The reading program for this group is language-based and promotes reading through personalized text and language patterns unique to each individual child. The other approach is teacher-directed, in that the teacher directly instructs the children and determines a large proportion of their activities. The reading program in these classes is skill-based, fostering reading via common materials for all children, print-sound correspondence activities, and paper-and-pencil exercises.

The research goals and the methodology of Evans's work place it clearly within the applied research domain. However, in contrast to the group-comparison classroom studies comparing individual methods that were common in the education literature prior to 1960, Evans's research is not concerned simply with outcome, the question of which method is best. Her comparison involves examining what is happening in the classroom and relating instructional process to reading outcomes. Such research characterizes a new breed of classroom study that is beginning to appear in the high-status educational research literature (for example, Calfee and Piontowski, 1981). What is distinctive about this type of classroom study is that the teaching methods are quantified rather than simply described. Quantification allows the researchers to use statistical procedures to relate what is happening in the classroom to measures of program success. This approach meshes very well with a component skills view of reading. The extent to which various component skills are promoted by the instructional approach taken in the classroom should predict the children's level of reading achievement. In a general way, the data reported by Evans support this expectation.

There are two ways in which Evans's work represents an important contribution to the movement of information from theory into practice. First, the research attempts to bridge the theory-practice gap by drawing from the basic reading research and basic educational research literature. Second, by using this literature as a basis for understanding outcomes in terms of the cognitive processes that may be involved, Evans helps to answer why one method of reading instruction is more effective than another.

Within the bridge-building analogy, Evans's research represents an anchor point at the applied end where most of the individual component skills chains of research must eventually come together. In view of the weak and missing links in each of the individual chains, it is not surprising that the results of Evans's research do not answer the question, How should reading be taught? definitively. Neither of the two teaching methods included in her comparison is theory-based, in the sense of having an empirically verifiable theoretical basis. Until many of the individual research chains investigating component skills subprocesses extend securely from theory to practice, it is unlikely that theoretically sound reading instruction will be developed.

In summary, the answer to the question, have the increase in basic research on the reading processes and the development of theories and models of reading resulted in more and better applied research on reading instruction? seems to be a very qualified yes. At least, the theories that are being developed as a result of basic process research are serving to guide basic educational researchers, such as Evans, in conducting internally valid, instructionally relevent studies. However, both the research trends since the beginning of the current period in the history of reading research and the patterns evident in the four basic research-oriented chapters in this volume suggest that theory-based applied research is still relatively rare. However, it is encouraging that high-caliber researchers, such as the authors of the chapters in this volume, have begun to cross the theory-practice barrier. We can hope that other researchers will follow their lead and test the implications of their theories under externally valid conditions to ensure that the last twenty years of reading research eventually benefit educational practices.

Trends in Reading Instruction

Debates about the "best" method of reading instruction raged long before researchers entered the fray to shed some scientific light on the subject. Systems of reading instruction were being developed and promoted as early as the sixteenth century (Mathews, 1966). From that time to the present, claims of success in developing the "best" in reading instruction have come from many quarters (for example, Fuller, 1974; Ledson, 1975). All these approaches have been based almost entirely on the logic, intuitions, and esthetic preferences of their originators, and they have usually been promoted on the basis of subjective and unsystematic observations of favorable results with a small and select group of children.

When applied research on reading came into prominence in the period between 1920 and 1960, the basis of the approaches to instruction changed little if at all. As in the past, programs and methods were devised largely on intuitive grounds with neither empirical data nor theoretical rationale to justify them (Williams, 1970). What did change was the type of evidence used to promote the approaches. No longer were testimonials alone considered adequate evidence of the effectiveness of a program. Control groups, representative samples, and statistically sound comparisons became important criteria in evaluating claims to success. However, even if one particular approach had emerged as substantially "better" in many such outcome studies, there would have been no way of determining what it was about the method that mattered. Three quarters of the program might have been totally ineffective, but the remaining 25 percent might have been very powerful. Nevertheless, research results from classroom studies have commonly been used by advocates and publishers of reading programs to support their claims to validity on scientific grounds.

The inadequacy of comparing individual methods in attempts to resolve the "Great Debate" (Chall, 1967) about the best method of teaching reading is amply demonstrated by Aukerman (1971). In that encyclopedic work, Aukerman describes about 100 different approaches to beginning reading and presents evidence from classroom studies that seems to demonstrate that almost all are better than some other method, usually traditional instruction. The absurdity, of course, is that each approach has many aspects and that any set of the approaches selected at random would differ on some dimensions and coincide on others. As Evans notes in Chapter Five, global comparisons that do not quantify the teaching methods or that do not even describe them in detail make no contribution to a cumulative body of evidence on which methods and materials are most effective in reading instruction. The hope of the movement toward basic research on reading was that it would lead to a more rational basis for developing programs.

Now that there have been more than twenty very productive years of basic research and theory development in reading, it must be asked whether the accumulated knowledge is filtering into classroom practice. That is, is reading instruction improving as a result of the findings of basic research on reading? From the findings of recent applied research examining the teachers' manuals and reader content of a number of current reading programs (Beck, 1981; Beck and Block, 1979; Beck and others, 1983; Durkin, 1981; Willows and others, 1981) it appears that in general it is not. Reading instruction today is based, as it always has been, more on intuitions and marketing considerations than on research. Despite the surprising degree of consensus among basic process researchers that reading can be best understood within a component skills model (Carr, 1981; Frederiksen, 1981; Stanovich, 1980) and among basic educational researchers that programs of reading instruction should consider reading acquisition from a developmental, subskills perspective (Calfee,

1977; Chall, 1983; Samuels, 1976), major publishers of current reading programs appear to be placing less rather than more emphasis on subskills than they have in the past.

The building of a research bridge between theory and practice does not guarantee that classroom instruction will benefit. It does seem likely, however, that if more research chains were extended across the gap into the applied domain, and if the results of these studies were published in applied research journals where educators would read them, there would be a much better chance that theoretical developments would have an impact on practice.

The translation of research results into improved instruction requires "an abiding appreciation of the complexities of curricular design and classroom practice" (Venezky, 1977, p. 344). Relatively few researchers well versed in the literature of basic research on reading have become actively involved in systematic efforts to develop better, theoretically sound reading programs. The coordinated efforts of researchers like Beck and her associates at the Learning Research and Development Center at the University of Pittsburgh (Beck, 1977) and Calfee and his associates at Stanford University (Calfee, 1983) promise to produce the type of theory-based field-tested reading programs anticipated by the pioneers of the basic research movement in reading when it began twenty to thirty years ago. Perhaps we need only be patient for another decade until these "best" methods of reading instruction come into general use.

References

Aukerman, R. C. *Approaches to Beginning Reading.* New York: Wiley, 1971.

Beck, I. L. "Comprehension During the Acquisition of Decoding Skills." In J. T. Guthrie (Ed.), *Cognition, Curriculum, and Comprehension.* Newark, Del.: International Reading Association, 1977.

Beck, I. L. "Reading Problems and Instructional Practices." T. G. Waller and G. E. MacKinnon (Eds.), *Reading Research: Advances in Theory and Practice.* Vol. 2. New York: Academic Press, 1979.

Beck, I. L., and Block, K. K. "An Analysis of Two Beginning Reading Programs: Some Facts and Some Opinions." In L. B. Resnick and P. A. Weaver (Eds.), *Theory and Practice of Early Reading.* Vol. 1. Hillsdale, N.J.: Erlbaum, 1979.

Beck, I. L., McKeown, M. G., and McCaslin, E. S. "Vocabulary Development: All Contexts Are Not Created Equal." *Elementary School Journal,* 1983, *83,* 177–181.

Bond, G. L., and Dykstra, R. "The Cooperative Research Program in First-Grade Reading Instruction." *Reading Research Quarterly,* 1967, *2.*

Calfee, R. C. "A Proposal for Practical (but Good) Research on Reading." *Research in the Teaching of English,* 1976, *10,* 41–50.

Calfee, R. C. "Assessment of Independent Reading Skills: Basic Research and Practical Applications." In A. S. Reber and D. L. Scarborough (Eds.), *Toward a Psychology of Reading.* Hillsdale, N.J.: Erlbaum, 1977.

Calfee, R. C. "Improving Student Literacy: A Theoretical Model." Paper presented as part of the symposium on improvement in student literacy at the annual meeting of the American Educational Research Association, Montreal, April 1983.

Calfee, R. C., and Piontowski, D. C. "The Reading Diary: Acquisition of Decoding." *Reading Research Quarterly,* 1981, *16,* 346–373.

Campbell, D. T., and Stanley, J. C. *Experimental and Quasi-experimental Designs for Research.* Chicago: Rand McNally, 1963.

Carr, T. H. "Building Theories of Reading Ability: On the Relation Between Individual Differences in Cognitive Skills and Reading Comprehension." *Cognition,* 1981, *9,* 73–114.

Carroll, J. B. "Basic and Applied Research in Education: Definitions, Distinctions, and Implications." *Harvard Educational Review,* 1968, *38,* 263–276.

Cattell, J. M. "The Time It Takes to See and Name Objects." *Mind,* 1886, *11,* 63–65.

Chall, J. S. *Learning to Read: The Great Debate.* New York: McGraw-Hill, 1967.

Chall, J. S. *Stages of Reading Development.* New York: McGraw-Hill, 1983.

Dewey, J. "The Primary Education Fetich." *Forum,* 1898, *25,* 315–328.

Dodge, R. "Visual Perception During Eye Movement." *Psychological Review,* 1900, *7,* 454–465.

Durkin, D. "Reading Comprehension Instruction in Five Basal Reader Series." *Reading Research Quarterly,* 1981, *16,* 515–544.

Frederiksen, J. R. "Sources of Process Interactions in Reading." In A. M. Lesgold and C. A. Perfetti (Eds.), *Interactive Processes in Reading.* Hillsdale, N.J.: Erlbaum, 1981.

Fuller, R. "Breaking down the IQ Wall: Severely Retarded People *Can* Learn to Read." *Psychology Today,* 1974, *8,* 96–102.

Gates, A. I. "An Experimental and Statistical Study of Reading and Reading Tests." *Journal of Educational Psychology,* 1921, *12,* 303–314; 378–391; 445–464.

Gibson, E. J. "Learning to Read." *Science,* 1965, *148,* 1066–1072.

Hall, G. S. *How to Teach Reading and What to Read in Schools.* Boston: Heath, 1874.

Huey, E. B. *The Psychology and Pedagogy of Reading.* New York: Macmillan, 1908.

Kintsch, W. "Concerning the Marriage of Research and Practice in Beginning Reading Instruction." In L. B. Resnick and P. A. Weaver (Eds.), *Theory and Practice of Early Reading.* Vol. 1. Hillsdale, N.J.: Erlbaum, 1979.

Ledson, S. *Teach Your Child to Read in Sixty Days.* Toronto: Richards-Readskill, 1975.

Levin, H. "Reading Research: What, Why, and for Whom?" *Elementary English,* 1966, *43,* 138–147.

Mathews, M. *Teaching to Read Historically Considered.* Chicago: University of Chicago Press, 1966.

Pillsbury, W. B. "The Reading of Words: A Study in Apperception." *American Journal of Psychology,* 1897, *8* (3), 315–393.

Resnick, L. B., and Beck, I. L. "Designing Instruction in Reading: Interaction of Theory and Practice." In J. T. Guthrie (Ed.), *Aspects of Reading Acquisition.* Baltimore, Md.: Johns Hopkins University Press, 1976.

Samuels, S. J. "Hierarchical Subskills in the Reading Acquisition Process." In J. T. Guthrie (Ed.), *Aspects of Reading Acquisition.* Baltimore, Md.: Johns Hopkins University Press, 1976.

Stanovich, K. E. "Toward an Interactive-Compensatory Model of Individual Differences in Reading Fluency." *Reading Research Quarterly,* 1980, *16,* 32–71.

Venezky, R. L. "Research on the Reading Process: A Historical Perspective." *American Psychologist,* 1977, *32,* 339–345.

Williams, J. P. "From Basic Research on Reading to Educational Practice." In H. Levin and J. P. Williams (Eds.), *Basic Studies on Reading.* New York: Basic Books, 1970.

Willows, D. M., Borwick, D., and Butkowsky, I. S. "From Theory to Practice in Reading Research: Toward the Development of Better Software." In M. Pressley and J. R. Levin, (Eds.), *Cognitive Strategy Research: Educational Applications.* New York: Springer-Verlag, 1983.

Willows, D. M., Borwick, D., and Hayvren, M. "The Content of School Readers." In G. E. MacKinnon and T. G. Waller (Eds.), *Reading Research: Advances in Theory and Practice.* Vol. 2. New York: Academic Press, 1981.

Dale M. Willows is associate professor of reading in the Department of Curriculum at the Ontario Institute for Studies in Education. Having divided her time during the last twelve years between the experimental psychology of reading and classroom and clinical work in reading education, she has a long-standing interest in bridging the gap between basic research on reading and instructional practices.

*What journals publish research on reading? What books provide
systematic introductions to the area?*

Resources on Reading

Thomas H. Carr

Because reading generates considerable interest in educational, developmental, and cognitive psychology, many journals publish research on the topic, and books on reading are being published at a great rate. However, a few journals and one series of books are especially useful. The major journal devoted specifically to reading research is *Reading Research Quarterly*. Another reading journal to monitor is the *Journal of Reading Behavior*. The *Journal of Educational Psychology* and *Cognition and Instruction* both publish a large number of articles on reading. Journals of developmental psychology that publish high-quality reading research include *Journal of Experimental Child Psychology* and *Child Development*. Finally, a number of journals devoted to cognitive psychology publish high-quality reading research. They include *Journal of Verbal Learning and Verbal Behavior; Journal of Experimental Psychology: Human Perception and Performance; Memory and Cognition; Journal of Experimental Psychology: Learning, Memory, and Cognition; Cognitive Psychology; Cognition;* and *Discourse Processes*. The series of books that those interested in reading research should keep track of is called *Reading Research: Advances in Theory and Practice*. Published by Academic Press, the series is now up to Volume 5. T. G. Waller and G. E. MacKinnon edited the first four volumes. Derek Besner joined Waller and MacKinnon in editing Volume 5.

In addition to these ongoing resources, several treatises can provide introductions to the area of reading that are more systematic than one is apt to encounter in journals or edited books. These include *The Reading Process:*

T. H. Carr (Ed.). *The Development of Reading Skills.* New Directions
for Child Development, no. 27. San Francisco: Jossey-Bass, March 1985.

Cognitive and Psycholinguistic Perpectives, by John Downing and Che Kan Leong (New York: Macmillan, 1982); *Orthography and Word Recognition in Reading,* by Leslie Henderson (London: Academic Press, 1982); *The Process of Reading: A Cognitive Analysis of Fluent Reading and Learning to Read,* by David C. Mitchell (Chichester, Englans: Wiley, 1982); *Competent Reader, Disabled Reader: Research and Application,* by Martin H. Singer (Hillsdale, N.J.: Erlbaum, 1982); and *The Psychology of Literacy,* by Silvia Scribner and Michael Cole (Cambridge, Mass.: Harvard University Press, 1981). Of course, no list of reference books would be complete without two classics, Edmund Burke Huey's *The Psychology and Pedagogy of Reading* (Cambridge, Mass.: M.I.T. Press, 1968; 1908) and *The Psychology of Reading,* by Eleanor Gibson and Harry Levin (Cambridge, Mass.: M.I.T. Press, 1975).

Thomas H. Carr is associate professor of cognitive and developmental psychology at Michigan State University.

Index

A

Alegria, J., 88, 91, 107
Algozzine, B., 90, 94
Anaphoric pronouns, as discourse cues, 64–66, 69–70
Anderson, J. R., 22, 23, 31, 51
Anderson, R. C., 22, 31, 44, 52
Anderson, R. H., 78, 92
Arabic students, and second-language literacy, 24–30
Attention and automaticity, 23–24
Aukerman, R. C., 122, 123

B

Baddeley, A. D., 22, 31
Baillargeon, R., 68, 73
Baker, L., 60, 71
Barclay, J. R., 71
Baron, J., 6, 11, 15, 17, 22, 31, 33, 89, 91
Barr, J., 24, 31
Barrett, T. C., 70, 73
Barron, R. W., 22, 31
Barton, D., 11, 15
Bassett, E., 62, 73
Beach, D. H., 92
Beck, I. L., 17, 39, 46, 49, 52, 91, 115, 122, 123, 124
Becker, C. A., 1, 3
Becker, W. C., 84, 91
Beers, J. W., 12, 16, 96, 107
Bell, L. C., 52
Bennett, S. N., 84, 91
Bereiter, C., 60, 63, 71
Bertelson, P., 107
Besner, D., 127
Biemiller, A. J., 2, 3, 87, 88, 89, 91
Bissell, J. S., 77, 91
Bissex, G. L., 12, 15
Blackman, H. S., 75
Blanchard, H., 55n
Bley-Vroman, R., 20, 31
Block, K. K., 122, 123
Bloom, L., 68, 73
Bock, J. K., 1, 2, 55–75, 97, 119–120

Boder, E., 88, 91
Bolinger, D. M., 66, 71
Bond, G. L., 91, 110, 123
Borwick, D., 94, 124, 125
Botkin, P. T., 92
Bowey, J. A., 5, 17
Bradley, L., 6, 16, 90, 91
Brady, M. E., 39, 52
Bransford, J. D., 57, 59, 71, 72, 84, 92
Bressman, B., 17
Brewer, W. F., 1, 2, 55–75, 97, 119–120
Broadbent, D. E., 23, 31, 82, 92
Broadbent, M., 82, 92
Brophy, J. D., 89, 92
Brown, A. L., 58, 59, 61, 69, 72, 84, 92
Brown, J. S., 72
Brown, T. L., 2, 3, 19–34, 95–108, 117–118
Bryan, W. L., 22, 31
Bryant, P. E., 6, 16, 61, 72, 90, 91
Burke, C. L., 20, 32
Burkes, A. M., 52, 91
Butkowsky, I. S., 124
Butterfield, E. C., 107
Butterworth, J., 59, 74

C

Calfee, R. C., 6, 16, 115–116, 120, 122, 123–124
Campbell, D. T., 113, 124
Campione, J. C., 72
Canter, S. H., 83, 93
Carlson, G. N., 75
Carnine, D. W., 52
Carpenter, P. A., 67, 69, 72
Carr, T. H., 1–4, 21, 22, 31, 33, 55n, 90, 92, 95–108, 122, 124, 127–128
Carrell, P. L., 20, 31
Carroll, J. B., 98, 106, 111, 113, 124
Carter, B., 16
Cary, L., 107
Case, R., 61, 72
Cattell, J. M., 109, 124
Chafe, W. L., 60, 62, 63, 64, 72
Chall, J. S., 84, 91, 92, 110, 122, 123, 124

Ordering Information

The paperback sourcebooks listed below are published quarterly and can be ordered either by subscription or single-copy.

Subscriptions cost $35.00 per year for institutions, agencies, and libraries. Individuals can subscribe at the special rate of $25.00 per year *if payment is by personal check.* (Note that the full rate of $35.00 applies if payment is by institutional check, even if the subscription is designated for an individual.) Standing orders are accepted. Subscriptions normally begin with the first of the four sourcebooks in the current publication year of the series. When ordering, please indicate if you prefer your subscription to begin with the first issue of the *coming* year.

Single copies are available at $8.95 when payment accompanies order, and *all single-copy orders under $25.00 must include payment.* (California, New Jersey, New York, and Washington, D.C., residents please include appropriate sales tax.) For billed orders, cost per copy is $8.95 plus postage and handling. (Prices subject to change without notice.)

Bulk orders (ten or more copies) of any individual sourcebook are available at the following discounted prices: 10–49 copies, $8.05 each; 50–100 copies, $7.15 each; over 100 copies, *inquire.* Sales tax and postage and handling charges apply as for single copy orders.

To ensure correct and prompt delivery, all orders must give either the *name of an individual* or an *official purchase order number.* Please submit your order as follows:

Subscriptions: specify series and year subscription is to begin.
Single Copies: specify sourcebook code (such as, CD8) and first two words of title.

Mail orders for United States and Possessions, Latin America, Canada, Japan, Australia, and New Zealand to:
      Jossey-Bass Inc., Publishers
      433 California Street
      San Francisco, California 94104

Mail orders for all other parts of the world to:
      Jossey-Bass Limited
      28 Banner Street
      London EC1Y 8QE

New Directions for Child Development Series
William Damon, *Editor-in-Chief*

CD1 *Social Cognition,* William Damon
CD2 *Moral Development,* William Damon
CD3 *Early Symbolization,* Howard Gardner, Dennie Wolf
CD4 *Social Interaction and Communication During Infancy,* Ina C. Uzgiris
CD5 *Intellectual Development Beyond Childhood,* Deanna Kuhn
CD6 *Fact, Fiction, and Fantasy in Childhood,* Ellen Winner, Howard Gardner

Thomas H. Carr (Ed.).
The Development of Reading Skills.
New Directions for Child Development, no. 27.
San Francisco: Jossey-Bass, 1985.

New Directions for Child Development Series
William Damon, *Editor-in-Chief*

New Directions for Child Development (publication number
USPS 494-090) is published quarterly by Jossey-Bass Inc., Publishers.
Second-class postage rates are paid at San Francisco, California,
and at additional mailing offices.

Correspondence:
Subscriptions, single-issue orders, change of address notices, undelivered
copies, and other correspondence should be sent to Subscriptions,
Jossey-Bass Inc., Publishers, 433 California Street, San Francisco
California 94104.

Editorial correspondence should be sent to the Editor-in-Chief,
William Damon, Department of Psychology, Clark University,
Worcester, Massachusetts 01610.

Library of Congress Catalogue Card Number LC 84-80838
International Standard Serial Number ISSN 0195-2269
International Standard Book Number ISBN 87589-794-0

Cover art by Willi Baum
Manufactured in the United States of America

The Development of Reading Skills

Thomas H. Carr, *Editor*

NEW DIRECTIONS FOR CHILD DEVELOPMENT

WILLIAM DAMON, *Editor-in-Chief*

Number 27, March 1985

Paperback sourcebooks in
The Jossey-Bass Social and Behavioral Sciences Series

Jossey-Bass Inc., Publishers
San Francisco • Washington • London

For
Doug, Nathaniel and Annaliese
the constant

Introduction

The Invitation-Shaped Life

INVITATIONS ARE POWERFUL. Like tides, they ebb and flow, shaping the contours of our existence. Some invitations we desperately want but never get—"Will you marry me?" or "Would you consider a promotion?" Other invitations we never want to receive but must honor all the same—"We are letting you go," "The test came back positive," or "Your baby has Down syndrome." Invitations pound away at the coastlines of the soul. They contain a transforming force that can carve out possible and impossible futures.

No one escapes the forming motion of invitations. All the kids in the neighborhood are invited over for a playdate down the street; your child gets the call, but the kid next door doesn't. The list for the traveling team is posted; both parent and child hold their breaths to see who made the list. A daughter doesn't get invited to prom. A father isn't invited to give his daughter away. An aging relative isn't invited to a holiday dinner because poor hearing and dementia make it less fun for everyone. Raw and sensitive places form inside us.

Invitations shape who we know, where we go, what we do and who we become. Invitations can challenge and remake us. They can erode and devastate. And they can also heal and restore us. Being wanted, welcomed, invited and included are some of the most mending experiences on the planet.

For many years I have watched invitations ripple across lives. An event organizer I know dipped into pain and depression when all the volunteers—except the organizer himself—were invited to a celebratory dinner. During graduate school, a man I knew invited every woman in the library on a date. I witnessed the devastation on his face when each woman he asked said no.

I have had my own experiences of being turned out of individual hearts, as well as out of groups where I had once been invited. Yet I also have had invitations into lives and opportunities wondrously beyond my ability to comprehend.

Whether we wait for sleepovers or lunch dates, birthday parties or job offers, deals or weddings, everyone waits. Some wait for the invitations; others wait for the RSVPs. The giving and receiving of invitations offers something essential to our sense of well-being. Invitations assure us that we are wanted, welcomed and included. *Not* being invited sends destructive messages into the most vulnerable part of our souls. At the deepest level, these messages are often lies: "You are not worth knowing," "You are unwanted," "You don't matter," or "No one cares about you." Like the fingers of a cancerous tumor, these lies can devour our life. They come straight from the father of lies who plants untruth, like a malignancy, to do its soul-destroying work.

The things we say yes to and the things we say no to determine the terrain of our future. My convoluted journey is posted with invitations, and my RSVPs account for the twists and turns. Sometimes, half in love with my own self-destruction, I see a sign inviting me to "Stop!"—and I blow right through it anyway. Life is happening somewhere other than where I am, and I fear missing out on it. I choose my way, which is usually a fast track to somewhere or other. Other times I determine to follow Jesus and then anguish about which invitations are his. Which invitations appeal because I want to "make a difference"? Which ones do I avoid because they seem insignificant or ordinary?

Invitations from people I admire or enjoy can divert me from invitations that might be wiser for my family and better for my soul. Invitations can get so snarled up with zeal, naïveté and the need to prove myself that I say yes to the wrong things. Still, there are moments of trustful knowing when I sense that my yes or no comes from God. Learning to listen and respond to God's invitations is the path to real freedom. Invitations from God bring healing and liberation from the gnawing lies of the enemy.

RSVP

Navigating invitations is no small matter. Jesus tells a story in Luke 14:16-23 that gets at how easily we miss the most important invitations of all. "A certain man was preparing a great banquet and invited many guests. At the time of the banquet he sent his servant to tell those who had been invited, 'Come, for everything is now ready.' But they all alike began to make excuses" (Lk 14:16-18).

One had just bought a field, another had just bought five yoke of oxen, and a third had just gotten married. They were all busy, with better things to do. So they refused the invitation. "Please excuse me," they said; "I cannot come."

How do you navigate the variety of invitations that come your way? Let's look at four types of invitations that you probably field on a regular basis.

Jesus' parable makes it clear that there are *business and career invitations.* Some people had real estate that demanded attention, and others had invested in oxen that needed tending so as to increase profitability margins. Our own workplaces are not so different. They invite us to more productivity, vision, initiative and profitability. Business invitations often come in the form of questions: "Do you have the right people in the right seats on the bus?" "What is your BHAG (Big, Hairy, Audacious Goal)?" "How can our goals for this year top last year's?" "What is your growth rate?" "What is your five-year plan? Your ten-year plan? Your strategic plan? Your business plan? Your self-improvement plan?" These questions are invitations to expect more and more and more. Their answers provide fuel to make things happen. Saying yes to invitations of the workplace may make you a business success, but saying yes also comes with consequences. We can get so busy, stressed and driven that we don't RSVP to God's invitations. Like the people in the parable, we say no because business comes first.

Jesus' parable also includes *family invitations*. One of those invited had just gotten married and used that as a reason to say no. Every family system comes with invitations. Invitations to spend holidays and take vacations with certain extended family members or friends that exclude other family members or friends. Invitations to parent in particular ways. Invitations to volunteer for this committee or that worthy cause. Invitations to be home more or less. Invitations to climb a social ladder, join a certain club, spend more or spend less, or downsize or upsize. Repercussions of invitations given or withheld reverberate over generations. Our individual responses to these invitations are not just private; they have a way of throwing off family equilibrium and setting individual priorities at cross purposes. Dad refuses the wedding invitation because he doesn't approve of the match. A sibling refuses the invitation to the family reunion unless there is an apology. A sister invites one sister to her room and tells the other to "stay out." And then there is the constant litany of "invitations" to "Shut up," "Speak up," "Get up," or "Fess up." Invitations are relentless and carry tremendous emotional freight.

Educational invitations, which offer opportunities for self-improvement and enrichment, are endless. In the past year I have taken continuing education courses at the local high school and

Loyola University. In the fall I will learn icon painting. My husband is learning Spanish online. At age forty-five, a good friend of ours with an information technology background took a second bachelor's degree.

Children, of course, are flooded with invitations to learn. When my children were at home, our mailbox was flooded with glossy catalogs and brochures inviting them to camps and extracurricular programs: this sports team, that theater experience, this cooking class, that music course. On and on the invitations go. Learn horseback riding. Take the SAT prep. Study a foreign language. Saying yes to these invitations supposedly gives your child a leading edge in the competitive world ahead of them.

Finally, there are *entertainment and social invitations.* In Jesus' parable, a certain man invites folks to a party. Our world is filled with invitations that divert and entertain. Invitations to be on the go, in the loop and having fun never stop. Indeed, our commitment to fun is so strong that Neil Postman described us as a people who are "amusing ourselves to death." Entertainment is a multimillion-dollar enterprise devoted to keeping us diverted. Actors, musicians and TV personalities invite us to see the new movie and get the latest CD. If it's a nice day, amusement parks, water parks, national parks and even the park across the street invite us to leave work behind and go in search of fun. We can play sports or watch sports. We can accept the trial invitation to the health club. We can go to a party or to the beach. We can climb a mountain or use the invitational coupon at the new restaurant down the street. If none of these things appeal, there is always Xbox, Wii, Facebook, Twitter and TV, with anything on demand at any time. If technology is not our thing, we have board games, yard games, theaters and museums that invite us to enjoy.

Our culture invites us to experience everything! If we fail to take advantage of it all, we think we are missing out. But honestly, the web of invitations we are called to navigate is massive and complicated. In an attempt to say yes to as much as possible, people burn the candle at both ends. I love the lines from Edna St. Vincent Millay's poem "First Fig": "My candle burns at both ends / It will not last the night; / But ah, my foes, and oh, my friends— / It gives a lovely light!"

INVITATION STATUS

In our culture, the more invitations that come our way, the more valuable we are considered to be. The more clubs or associations we belong to, the more status we have—especially if we had to be nominated and wait to be invited in. By saying yes to the invitations, we prove that we are important, wanted and—of course—busy. The truth, however, is that when we say yes to invitations that keep us compulsively busy, we may be exhibiting a lazy ambivalence that actually keeps us distracted from the invitations that matter most. Squeezing every margin to the max, we are left with less time and space to respond to the invitations from God. We want to enjoy life, but ironically our many yeses to invitations keep us stressed, drained and inattentive to the divine invitations that bring real freedom and belonging. So it is that we say, "I can't come. I'm really busy. Please excuse me," to the most important invitation we receive. We've chosen to say yes to things besides God.

Clearly not all invitations are created equal. Each of us trusts some invitations more than others. Some of us trust invitations of the marketplace as though they reflect God's own orchestration. They are the way we forge an identity and get ahead. Business invitations to productivity, success and numerical growth are so compelling that increasingly pastors and church leaders say yes to them more than to God's invitations to wait or remember. An editorial in *Christianity Today* put it like this: "It's no secret that too many evangelical leaders are captivated more by business culture than biblical culture, spending more time absorbed in strategies and effectiveness and relatively little time in prayer. No, it doesn't have to be an either-or situation, but let's face it, it often is." We should also note that while Jesus had the biggest work assignment in human history—he had been invited to "save the world"—he never spent weeks writing a vision statement with steps for strategically reaching the world with the gospel.

Educational invitations appeal because they offer knowledge, opportunity and—let's face it—power. Invitations to compete in sporting events are not just good exercise but become part of a child's résumé. These invitations can seem so sensible that the idea they may be missing other invitations escapes us all. The angst and family energy poured into the educational and athletic choices for children so easily distract from seemingly less high-stake invitations to be in a youth group, attend church, eat with the family or go on a missions trip. But children aren't the only ones distracted by entertainment and athletics. Adults, too, build their lives around summering on the Cape or devoting winter weekends to skiing. And sometimes snowbirds skip town, moving down to Florida and Arizona until the sun returns up north.

As the flood of invitations from organizations, business, charities, family entertainment, athletics, fitness and education pull us in their wake, we must grab a branch and take stock. Are we ignoring the invitations that matter most? If God were to ask us, "What did you do with the fifteen years of evenings, weekends and vacation that you had in life?" would we answer, "Well, I watched TV, worked out and sat on the beach"? Do we have any idea what God's invitations to us are? Do our yeses to invitations simply divert or stroke our ego? Or do they nurture and grow body, soul and spirit? Do they build connections within the body of Christ and bring health to our marriage and family? Do the invitations we accept make us more free or less? Which invitations are shaping your world?

What we do with the invitations we receive dramatically affects how we do church. Invitations can be wonderful things, but the health and growth of the soul and the church do not primarily reside in business, educational or entertainment invitations. The growth of the church and the soul resides in responding to the invitations of God.

God's invitations are meant to mend, shape, anchor and grow us into the character of Jesus. They call us into our true selves in Christ. They free us from the lie that says, "The more invitations the better." Invitations from the Holy One serve God's dream for the world. They don't call me to become what I produce, what others think of me or what I know. They invite me to be free. And freedom comes from being an intentional follower of Jesus—one who is a little Christ in this world.

GOD THE GREAT INVITER

With our track record for cavalierly ignoring God-given invitations, I am amazed that God continues to send out the invites. As the first and the great Inviter, God devotes himself to sending out invitations to come join his divine community. How easily we miss the magnitude and honor of this invitation. A self-sufficient, joyful Trinity reaches out with welcome: "Come and join us. Please RSVP."

God's invitations begin with inviting all that is into being and into relationship with him: "Let there be . . ." Let there be quarks and nebula. Let there be butterflies and squid. Let there be male and female. Let there be *you*! When God breathed the breath of life into you, you were given the gift of being. Beings are made to connect, to interact and to love. The gift of being is an invitation to be in relationship with the great Inviter.

God initiates relationship. God invited Abraham, the Hebrew people, Isaac, Jacob, Moses, Gideon, David, prophets, fishermen, tax collectors, outcasts, women, men, crowds, enemies, betrayers, liars and children to know him and be with him. It doesn't matter if you were on the paid staff of hell: God's invitation goes out to you again and again. Everyone is equally yet uniquely invited into God's world and God's heart. Not one tribe or people group is excluded. The great Inviter says, "Come to my dinner party. Come be with me and meet my guests."

God's divine invitations come to us in church, in Scripture, in music, in art, in nature, in moral failure, in disappointments, in joy, in the words of friends and even in the words of enemies. God is humble enough to use the flower in your garden or perhaps even this book to invite you deeper into his love and call on your life.

No matter how God's invitations get delivered, they let us know that we are wanted, loved, named and known. The divine community of God longs for us to RSVP. As we accept the divine invitations, an inner knowing of our belonging to God takes root. This root taps into the healing wisdom and love of God, and it braces us against the storm of deforming lies that we are unwanted and don't matter to anyone unless we produce. In our yeses to God, trust blossoms out as fruit and freedom.

Without the lived experience of risking (which is another word for trusting) God's invitations, our Christianity can devolve into dogma that rattles around in our heads. Some people spend years of their lives in church, believing all the right things but lacking an inner sense of being invited into God's own heart. The Bible is full of examples of religious people whose faith began with right answers or actions but who missed invitations of the Holy One.

In the Gospels we see how Jesus navigated invitations while responding to and extending God's invitations. Invitations come to him from everywhere:

- From religious people and political leaders, who invited Jesus to prove his credibility (Mt 12:38; 16:1; Lk 23:2-12)

- From family and friends, who invited him to dinner and to help others (Lk 8:19; 10:38; Jn 2:1-4)

- From the devil, who invited Jesus to prove who he was by doing
  something amazing and spectacular (Lk 4:1-13)

Yet Jesus understood how to listen to God's invitations first. So
when his popularity soared, he knew how to step away from the
invitation to ride the momentum (Mk 1:37; 4:36; 11:8-11). Jesus
doesn't let the crowd crown him king but leaves and goes to Beth-
any. When invited to curry favor with the powers that be or to
hang out with the movers and shakers, Jesus knew how to say no
(Lk 15:1-2; 19:5, 45; 20:8, 45-47). When Jesus hit the ball out of the
park with his healing and exorcisms, people invited him to stay
and maximize his success. But Jesus heard another invitation.
Jesus' RSVP to God kept him free enough to go somewhere else
(Mk 1:38; 3:7; 5:1).

I understand the pressure of invitations. I am particularly prone
to say yes to invitations that hook my ego. It's appalling, but I will
travel across the country to give a talk on, say, "spiritual formation." But I wouldn't walk across the street to hear a similar talk
coming out of someone else's mouth. That's because it's no longer
about me. Invitations that bring notoriety, money, travel and
amusement can shape my life more than invitations that come
straight from God.

RESPONDING TO GOD'S INVITATIONS

Jesus knew his spiritual journey depended on responsiveness to
God's invitations. Although his job was the most crucial in human
history, Jesus did not get compulsive, preoccupied or unable to
practice the presence of God or people. In the midst of interruptions and overwhelming need, Jesus learned how to discern between invitations. He learned discernment by first saying yes to
God's invitations to rest, wait, pray, forgive, remember and love.
Time with God was not a luxury that got squeezed out when business picked up. God's invitation to "save the world" didn't stop
Jesus from attending to his own soul in the process. Saying yes to

the invitation to be with God was the wellspring of his heart and the source of all his actions.

Jesus' initiative came out of God's invitations. Board rooms, best practices, target groups, groundswells and his own best calls did not determine his agenda. God's invitations directed his movements.

- When pressed to rush to a dying girl, Jesus stopped to talk to a woman who surreptitiously touched him in a crowd. He invited her to identify herself and her desire (Mk 5:25-34).

- When invited to meet everyone's felt needs, Jesus refused (Mk 1:37-38; 5:18-19).

- When invited to meet family expectations, Jesus refused (Mk 3:31-35).

- When invited to define family in a narrow way, Jesus refused and included all who do "the will of God" (Mk 3:35).

- When encouraged to send hungry people away, Jesus invited the disciples to feed them (Mk 6:37).

- Jesus invited companionship at high and low moments (Mt 26:36-38; Mk 9:2-8).

- When people outside the "target group" of Israel invited Jesus to help, Jesus didn't always say no (Mk 7:26-29; Lk 17:11-17).

- Jesus invited children, women, tax collectors and sinners to be with him (Mk 10:13-14; 2:15-17).

- Jesus invited a young successful seeker to sell all he had and follow (Mk 10:17-21).

- Jesus invited people to "not fear," to "have faith," to "follow me," to "withdraw," to "come apart and rest" and to lose their life to gain it (Mk 5:36; 11:22; 1:17; 3:7; 8:34).

Jesus' actions, in and of themselves, often make no sense unless we see them as responses to some hidden invitation—an invitation received from time spent alone with his Father. When Jesus was interrupted while "on task," and when people pressed him with needs, the expectations of others easily could have set the agenda. But Jesus categorically refused to get caught up in the invitations that brought grandiosity, compulsivity, anxiety and drivenness. Jesus slowed down and waited to hear God's invitations and initiatives. He thought nothing of climbing a mountain or traipsing out into the desert for time alone with his Father. In the midst of activity, this consistent rhythm deeply and finely tuned Jesus' receptiveness and responsiveness to divine invitations.

God invites me out of doing, driving and striving. I can RSVP to the invitation in various ways. I can say, "Yes, your invitation be done," or "Not now," or "Sometime"—or even "Not on your life!" Not so very long ago, during what I now call the "Year of the Great Ambush," God clearly sent me the invitation to love and forgive. But I had been so hurt and betrayed that this invitation felt like death. So I resisted, went with the flow and put on ten pounds. My ego wanted what it wanted. Saying yes to the great Inviter was painstaking, deliberate and exhausting. Then again, invitations to follow Jesus are not necessarily easy. Jesus was invited to take up his cross; I have no reason to expect I won't be invited to do the same.

On the other hand, God's invitations can at times be over-the-top sweet. "Of course I want to train church leaders in the Dominican Republic!" "I'd love to adopt a Compassion child!" "I am excited to teach an adult education course in my community!" Sometimes God's invitations exactly match our own desires, and we can say yes with enthusiasm.

Although my responses to God's invitations are not consistent, I am sure of one thing: God's invitations never dry up. If I fail to RSVP, God doesn't cross me off the "A-list." The invitations keep coming: inviting me to begin again, inviting me to prepare for life in the course of life, inviting me to prepare for ministry in the course of ministry. The invitations are not intended for later—someday when everything quiets down and things become sane. They're not intended for "any day now," after my kids go to college or after I move. The invitations are intended for *now*, even as I juggle too many balls and drown in too much email.

God is engaged and sending out invitations. Sometimes these invitations seem less compelling than anything on my to-do list. Why would I want to say yes to the invitation to rest when I'm already so far behind? Why follow when I could lead? Why accept invitations to weep or to admit that I am wrong or to wait? Saying yes would just slow me down, sabotage my agenda and maybe even deconstruct my ego. This book is about invitations like these: divine invitations we miss or ignore because we've said yes to going with the cultural flow. Only free people know how to say yes and no.

THE SHAPE OF THIS BOOK

My hope is that this book will help you attend to the often hidden, quiet voice of the great Inviter. By saying yes to God's invitations, may you find the freedom and the courage to be who you were created to be.

This book includes a variety of invitations that have shaped me as a Christ-follower. They are by no means all of God's invitations, but they are ones that our achievement- and entertainment-addicted society tends to ignore or avoid. I believe these invitations are crucial to a church that is often shaped more by business and social invitations than by God's invitations.

At the beginning of each chapter is a chart offering an overview of:

• The invitation.

- Key related Scripture.

- Roadblocks that we might face in saying yes to God.

- Awareness that leads us to participate with the Holy Spirit for change.

- Practices that give God room to work with us. Many of these disciplines are described in further detail in *Spiritual Disciplines Handbook: Practices That Transform Us* (Adele Ahlberg Calhoun, InterVarsity Press, 2005).

Each chapter also provides several reflection questions or exercises that can help you explore and open more fully to God's invitations. They are ways you can RSVP in the moment. They are ways to break lies, start new habits and cooperate with the Holy Spirit for transformation and renewal. "The Spirit and the bride say 'Come!' And let the one who hears say, 'Come!' Let the one who is thirsty come; and let the one who wishes take the free gift of the water of life" (Rev 22:17).

1

Invitation to Participate in Your Own Healing

We live a long time in order to become lovers.
God is like a good parent, refusing to do our homework for us.
We must learn through trial and error.
We have to do our homework ourselves, the homework
of suffering, desiring, winning and losing, hundreds of times.

RICHARD ROHR

Projects of personal transformation rarely if ever
succeed by accident, drift or imposition.

DALLAS WILLARD

MY HUSBAND, DOUG, IS AN athlete whose body is protesting. He has had numerous knee injuries and torn his Achilles tendon twice. Doctors have operated on him, put casts on him and sent him home, thereby putting the full recovery from his injuries back into his hands and those of a physical therapist. It's not enough to have the doctor do his or her part; Doug has had to participate in

RESPONDING TO GOD'S INVITATION TO PARTICIPATE
IN YOUR OWN HEALING

INVITATION	To cooperate with the Trinity in my growth, healing and emotional maturity.
SCRIPTURE	"When Jesus saw him lying there and learned that he had been in this condition for a long time, he asked him, 'Do you want to get well?'" (Jn 5:6).
ROADBLOCKS	—Blindness to what needs mending and healing in me —Unwillingness to do the hard work that rehabs my soul —The desire for a quick fix —Blaming of others for what is wrong with me —A victim mentality —Addictive behaviors
AWARENESS	—Notice where I am stuck in patterns of behavior that break relationships. —Ask others what needs changing in me. —Notice who I was ten years ago and how or if I have changed at all. —Notice where I am not free from fears or the need for approval.
PRACTICES	—Ask others for *healing prayer*, which can increase my awareness of God and his part in my healing. —Have a *relationship* with a spiritual director, accountability partner, counselor or spiritual friend, which can help me participate with God on my healing journey.

his own healing. He has had to lift weights, ride a stationary bike, exercise and eat right.

Doug often commented on the difference between receiving physical therapy and going to the health club. Everyone undergoing physical therapy knew they were broken. No one pretended they were fine. No one hid their weakness; it was obvious. They were in the same boat. And when someone made progress, the physical therapist would whoop out a cheer, and soon everyone in the room would be clapping for the progress. As people participated in their own healing, each step forward gave hope to others.

But Doug couldn't stay in the rehab clinic forever. One day he was deemed mobile enough to be given the boot. His continued healing was placed in his own hands. He would need to exercise, day after day and year after year, without a cheering therapist beside him. If he didn't, his protesting body would quickly revert back to its problematic state, and all that work would go down the drain.

Whether it is body, mind or soul, we all have to participate in our own healing. Doctors, counselors and pastors don't wave magic wands over us and cure us. They may save our lives, but then they throw the responsibility for health back on us. It's not much different with God: God saves our lives, and then many of us treat that salvation like magic. We are safe, we are good with God, we are going to heaven: that's that.

Where do you wish Jesus would use magic rather than involve you? How would participating in your own healing draw you deeper into Jesus and freedom?

But God's salvation is an ongoing invitation to participate in our own healing. This does not mean we earn our salvation; it simply means we taste the fruit of it through participation. *Salvation*, in the ancient Hebrew sense of the word, means "to heal and make whole." Unlike other parts of creation, we human beings, as image-bearers of God, have been given the unique task of participating with God as he heals, mends, and saves us and the world.

MY PART AND GOD'S PART

The invitation to participate in my own healing came to me just as it came to the man at the pool of Bethesda in John 5.

Soon another Feast came around and Jesus was back in Jerusalem. Near the Sheep Gate in Jerusalem there was a pool, in
Hebrew called Bethesda, with five alcoves. Hundreds of sick
people—blind, crippled, paralyzed—were in these alcoves.
One man had been an invalid there for thirty-eight years.
When Jesus saw him stretched out by the pool and knew
how long he had been there, he said, "Do you want to get
well?"

The sick man said, "Sir, when the water is stirred, I don't
have anybody to put me in the pool. By the time I get there,
somebody else is already in."

Jesus said, "Get up, take your bedroll, start walking." The
man was healed on the spot. He picked up his bedroll and
walked off. . . . A little later Jesus found him in the Temple
and said, "You look wonderful! You're well! Don't return to a
sinning life or something worse might happen." (Jn 5:1-9, 14
The Message)

The man Jesus spoke to that day had carved out a life in a community where sickness was the norm. The lives of these blind,
disabled, lame and paralyzed folk revolved around a pool that af-
forded healing, renewal and change. There was one major hitch,
however; when the water was stirred up, only the first one in was
healed.

Can you imagine what waiting at the pool was like? Did people
commiserate, hope or despair? Did they help one another or compete with one another? How long did they think, *Maybe next time*?
Or maybe they dreamed up strategies, such as, *What if I help him
get in and then he waits around and helps me in?* Or, *What if I lie
closer to the pool?* At some point, the "what ifs" probably got harder
and harder to bear: *What if no one helps me in? What if I never get
in? What if this is all there is?*

I wonder about the sick man Jesus met at the pool that day. Did his parents drop him there? Had they initially tried to beat the odds and get him into the water? Over thirty-eight years, had the quirky nature of the "cure" dulled the man's drive to participate in his own healing? Had life become a string of handouts and disappointed hopes? When did the man begin to define his sickness as "normal"? Did he have an identity apart from his physical condition? Or did he tell himself, *I am the paralyzed one who has been here longer than anyone else?*

When Jesus met the invalid, his tolerable (if unwanted) "normal" had been going on for nearly four decades. Jesus didn't beat around the bush. He fixed his eye on the sick man and asked a question that hinted at an invitation: "Do you want to get well?"

Where in your life are you longing for freedom and health? If Jesus said, "Do you want to get well?" how would you answer him?

The obvious answer would be "You bet!" But the man didn't respond with an unqualified yes. Instead, in his response we hear flagging hope, defensiveness and a series of rationales for his condition. "You think I can do what it takes to be healed? Don't think I haven't tried. I've tried, but somebody else is always ahead of me. They are the lucky ones. They get the break. I, on the other hand, remain unhelped, unchosen and unhealed, as you can clearly see."

Has disappointment ever closed you down to possibilities? Has it provided rationales for remaining in your "normal"? I may not be an invalid, but I can create a normal with a diabolical focus on what is missing at any moment in time. Life invitations can be all around me, new possibilities awaiting me, beauty and deeper love surrounding me, yet I will bemoan the fact that I can't get into a particular pool of blessing like someone else has. My awareness of future possibilities narrows and is obscured by what I don't have. So Jesus' question is as real to me as it was to the man at the pool that day long ago: "Do you want to get well?" Do you really *want* to let go of your diseased sense of "normal" and change?

I want to snap, "Well, Jesus, what do you think? Do you think I like being such a mess?"

I am struck by all the things Jesus *didn't* say or do in response to the litanies of pain and defensiveness he heard from people. Jesus didn't say to the man, "You sound like a victim to me; what are you afraid of?" He didn't say, "Well, you have been here for thirty-eight years; I've got to wonder." He didn't say, "Your healing is not someone else's responsibility, is it?" or even, "Is this pool the only choice you have?" Jesus responded to the sick man's litany with eight audacious words: "Get up! Pick up your mat and walk." Rather than pursuing therapeutic conversation or touching him with a healing hand, Jesus invited the man to act. He invited him to take responsibility for his wellness and do something he hadn't been able to do for thirty-eight years. Go figure.

Jesus' invitation called the invalid to reclaim the desire for wellness that initially brought him to the pool. Transformation and healing always begin in a place of desire. There needs to be some deep inner willingness to take a risk on Jesus and begin again and again.

Have you ever had a desire that dogged you with pain and disappointment—a desire that you just couldn't seem to get met? Living with an unfulfilled desire for a long time can shut us down to the possibilities of life. We figure out how to survive with a tolerable if unwanted "normal." Some make do and try to forget. Others agonize and define themselves by their unmet desire. "Hope deferred makes the heart sick," says Proverbs 13:12.

Jesus invited the man to take up his desire and walk. The man could have responded to the divine invitation to participate in his own healing, or he could have kept on rationalizing about why his life was such a disappointment. He could have held onto his identity as a sick man, or he could have risked the possibility of heal-ing, which Jesus offered.

STUCK IN PAIN

Responding to the invitation to wellness is not always a straight-forward path. We all know people who define their lives by their illnesses. If you know them for more than five minutes, you know about their pain and how it has distorted their lives. Re-member Miss Haversham in Charles Dickens's *Great Expecta-tions*? Her entire life was defined by the fact that she was jilted on her wedding day. People can become very attached to their pain and illness. It is possible to so erect a life around sickness and dysfunction that even religion and spirituality are used to keep one in the same stuck place. No wonder that the question "Do you want to get well?" is answered by what you do more than by what you say.

Jesus' invitation is not an easy one: "Get up." Stand up on atro-phied legs. "Pick up your mat." Challenge your limits and compe-tencies, and shoulder responsibility for your healing. The invita-tion made the man feel completely out of control. But by telling the paralyzed man to do something he couldn't do, Jesus was hon oring something deeper within this man than his sickness.

Something in Jesus' words spoke hope into the man's will. En-countering Jesus validated and catalyzed his desire to be well. So when Jesus said, "Get up," the man didn't say, "You have got to be kidding. I can't!" He took a risk. He pulled his legs in under him, pushed with those atrophied muscles and—wonder of wonders—they held him up!

At once the man was cured; he picked up his mat and walked. Jesus cured the man, but it wasn't a magical zap. The cure was an invitation that had to be both received and acted upon. Jesus didn't heal the man without his participation or his desire.

The invalid at the pool risked saying yes to Jesus' invitation, and a whole new world of possibility opened up before him. He walked from sickness to health and from outside the worshiping community to inside. From one normal to another normal. Yet that isn't the end of the story.

Later on that day, Jesus saw the man in the temple. He had not been allowed to enter the temple while he was sick. The man's elation must have been overwhelming. Jesus gave the man a warning, however: "See, you are well again. Stop sinning, or something worse may happen to you." Here Jesus was not just talking about avoiding the "biggie sins." He was saying, "Stop living as if life is static. Stop accepting your disease, and seek to be well from the inside-out."

The invitation to get up and walk was just the first in a series of invitations. Now the man was to "stop sinning." There is more to life than physical healing; there is character change and deep-down renovation of the heart. This man, like us, would have to keep the healing process of change alive inside him. He must do that by noticing his sin patterns and telling the truth about them so he doesn't get stuck in some other "normal" that is just as life-thwarting as sitting beside a pool.

It is not hard to get stuck. It's easy for me to settle into "this little life of mine." We settle into roles that shape our identity: I am a mom. I am successful. I am funny. We also settle into living with things we aren't proud of: I have a temper. I am impatient. I have a critical spirit.

Do you want to be well? If you do, you will need to repent of the things you are proud of, as well as of the things you are not proud of. Why? Because the things you are proud of are often filled with ego. Repentance and obedience are ways we cooperate with the Holy Spirit so that we can stop sinning. Repentance is how we get at the root of our true "disease": sin. Jesus made it very clear: a miraculous healing is only the beginning. And if the man refused the invitation to change on the inside, he could end up worse off than he was before.

Our lives may not look as desperate and diseased as those of the people surrounding the pool of Bethesda. But none of us are free of diseases and deep sin patterns. At our church we have a time during Communion when people can go forward for healing prayer. People struggling with physical ailments find it easy to go for prayer, while those of us struggling with crippling inner foibles and lives of "wholesome" desperation stay rooted to our seats and our "normal." But our "normal" might be

- broken by compulsions such as workaholism, alcoholism, shopping, Internet porn or videogame addictions
- defined by past pain and disappointments
- riddled with bitterness, criticism and gossip
- filled with confusion about how to be a consistent and kind parent

When our inner lives are broken, we may resist the invitation to admit that we too are invalids in need of healing.

THE JOURNEY TO WHOLENESS

The struggle for wholeness is not simply happening on a physical level. To RSVP to God's invitation to be well is to walk straight into the mystery and responsibility of desire. When a desire for change is awakened within us and shouldered in *Where are you being* the presence of God, we risk a new "nor- *invited to risk or trust* mal." Do we trust God with our desire? *God with a desire?* Are we willing to stop sinning? Are we willing to participate on the journey to healing and wholeness?

I could give a thousand examples of what this looks like, because I am such a great one for sinning and calling it normal. I am

part of a small cadre of women who, in jest, call ourselves the
"Original Critical Spirits." But it is not all jest. Each one of us has
had to address our addiction to critiquing and criticizing everything and everyone. We have had to participate in our own healing by repenting of our sin and then risking that Jesus could give
us grace to change. For me, that has meant not hanging out with
particular people who "enabled" my criticism addiction. It has
also meant refusing, for a period of time, to critique anything.
Anything! Stepping out and doing my part didn't feel normal or
easy. But shutting up was the only way I could hear God's other
quiet invitation—an invitation to awaken the healing presence of
Christ within me.

Participating in my own healing has meant responding to invitations that could potentially shape my soul and character.
Sometimes these invitations to health have been subtle, and
sometimes not. God has invited me on occasion to these things:
to give up interrupting, to *not* read books, to stop playing so
much online solitaire, to call my ailing parents every day and to
ask my husband every day for forty days, "What can I do for you
today?"

These invitations addressed a self-oriented, settled way of doing
my life. My ideas matter to me, so I interrupt a lot. I like to read to
the exclusion of other invitations. Online solitaire isn't a bad escape, but it's not necessarily a good one either. (And it begs the
questions: Why do I need to escape? What am I escaping from? Is
this the best way to live my life at this moment?) Calling my parents daily is a rhythm now, but it also means I call friends less.
Asking my husband what I could do for him addressed the many
ways I expect him to do for me. Taking him for granted was something I didn't want to do. So I attended to a discipline that helped
me serve and love him. A yes to one invitation is always a no to
another.

My responses to these God-given invitations shape my life and change the rhythms of my day. God doesn't wave a magic wand over me and say, "Abracadabra, Adele is more loving now." God works within my choices and desires as I respond to his invitations. I don't want to be a poor listener or a deadbeat daughter. I want to change. But if I go with the flow of my autopilot mode, nothing new happens. My relationships and soul remain the same: endangered and in need of triage. Jesus says, "Do you want to get well?" To reflect the life of Jesus means that I gather up my desire, stop loitering around a pool of excuses and offer up my diseased life to his healing cure.

COOPERATING WITH GOD UNDER THE CIRCUMSTANCES

Transformation and healing always begins with cooperating with God *where you are*—not where you think you should be as a mature disciple, but where you are now. Transformation for Jonah began in the belly of the whale. Transformation for Peter came out of denial. Transformation for Thomas began in doubt. Transformation for David was possible even after adultery.

These people embraced their present realities and shouldered the invitation of cooperating with the Holy Spirit in their transformation. "Get up. Take up your mat and walk." Respond to the invitation Jesus is giving you. Risk that Jesus will provide the grace to do what his invitations require you to do. Jesus sees you beside your pool. He knows that participating with God's healing plans can make you feel out of control. He knows that it sometimes feels like more than you can do.

Jesus knows because he, too, sat beside a pool—a brook in the Garden of Gethsemane. It was the season of Passover, and the brook of Kidron ran red with blood from the temple sacrifices. There Jesus struggled to accept God's invitation to pick up his cross and walk. God couldn't save the world without his yes. But that yes not only felt like death; it *was* death.

Learning to live freely and lightly may mean struggling to take up your mat so you can learn to walk. I am so glad that Jesus struggled to cooperate with God. I am not alone. Furthermore, Jesus has given me the Holy Spirit to help me in my own struggles and weakness. I am not left with self-help books or New Year's resolutions. Jesus has come along and given me grace to take up my bed and walk.

For love of us, Jesus became sin and died so that we wouldn't have to spend our lives beside a pool, competing for help and cures. We can take up our mats and walk tall and free. Jesus' death and resurrection brings hope of transformation (1 Pet 2:24). We can change. We will have to cooperate with God, just as Jesus did. We will have to die on our own midget crosses. We will have to put off the old and put on the new. The *new*! This is not some new program, tip or technique. It's not coercion or forced training. It's participating in your own healing. It's receiving each moment as a gift, as a new start. It's living as if life were not static but, rather, an unfolding reality. It's taking up the cross of your own transformation and receiving God's ongoing gift of salvation.

Will you RSVP to the invitation to honor the rigors and demands of following Jesus? Transformation isn't magic; it is rigorous. Remember the "What would Jesus do?" bracelets? It's not enough to ask, "What would Jesus do?" We need to ask, "What inside me needs to change so that God's motivations and desires are mine?" Becoming like Jesus means participating in your transformation in ways that change your inside heart as well as your outside behavior.

John Ortberg likens the transformative path of Christ to sailing. Sailors can't make the wind show up; the wind has a mind of its own. But that doesn't mean there is nothing for them to do. Sailors can choose to be alert and ready to catch the breeze or the gale. They can hoist and trim the sails so that when the wind comes, they move. They can cooperate with whatever little breath of wind comes their way. They can be ready so that when the gale comes along, they don't sink. They hear and feel the wind and take hold of the helm and move. Jesus said, "The wind blows wherever it pleases. You hear its sound, but you cannot tell where it comes from or where it is going. So it is with everyone born of the Spirit" (Jn 3:8).

THE WINDS OF CHANGE

Do you feel the wind of the Spirit blowing? Do you hear it? It is a wild, unpredictable force that disrupts our static living and sets us on a course of freedom and transformation. The changes that happen on our journeys are always about our response to the winds of invitation that blow into our lives. And all the invitations in this book change nothing unless we say, "Yes. Your will be done, on earth and in me." When we learn to participate—when we say yes to the healing that needs to happen in us—this yes flows out into our relationships and the world in which God has invited us to be light.

Jesus participated in God's healing of us. He knows our deep inner longings. He knows what operation needs to happen to set us free. And he knew that loving us to death was the way we could be healed. It was the way we would learn to take those little risks

There are so many things that need healing in us. Many things we can't bear to even look at now. Become still and read Jesus' words in John 16:12-13 slowly and out loud.

Ask Jesus if there are particular things he is trying to tell you that you are ignoring. Wait and listen.

Ask Jesus where he wants you to participate in your own healing.

Who are the "soul therapists" who could walk with you into your journey to health? Ask them to accompany you and cheer you on.

Tell Jesus that you are willing to cooperate with him so that you can live into freedom and wholeness.

of letting go with which each day presents us. It is where we would learn that love transforms and that love works. It dies. Love gives up self for the sake of others. And this sort of death always has power. It heals. And it can and will work in you as you say yes to the invitations of God.

2

Invitation to Follow

What Jesus wants from us is not admiration, but imitation.

RONALD ROLHEISER

RECENTLY I HAD TO FOLLOW another car to a destination. Sounds easy, right? The responsibility of getting where I needed to go rested on the shoulders of the leader; all I had to do was follow. But I found out that following is not for the faint of heart. The leader squeaked through yellow traffic lights; I got stuck on red. As I waited, more and more cars got between me and the lead car. I determined to catch up, so I shot through yellow (or red) lights and hoped that the lead car would wait somewhere up ahead. I caught up. Then dutifully trailing behind, I followed the leader as we headed out of town and onto open road. *Maybe this will be easier,* I thought. But no: the lead car went faster than I liked and took passing risks that made me cringe. Furthermore, when I wanted to stop for gas, the leader disagreed and said that we could make it to the gas station at the next exit.

My experience with following indicates that it can be even

FOLLOWING GOD'S INVITATION TO FOLLOW

INVITATION	To conform my life to Jesus' path of descent, service and sacrifice for the sake of others.
SCRIPTURE	"In your relationships with one another, have the same mindset as Christ Jesus: Who, being in very nature God, did not consider equality with God something to be used to his own advantage; rather, he made himself nothing by taking the very nature of a servant, being made in human likeness" (Phil 2:5-7).
ROADBLOCKS	—The need or compulsion to lead and be in charge —A belief in culture's or business' definition of leadership —An identity defined by leadership roles —Checking out when not in charge —Resistance to being one of "no reputation"
AWARENESS	—Notice where I withdraw support or where my interest flags when I am not in charge. —Notice how I interact with people I consider leaders and those I don't. —Notice how I respond to applause and how I respond to lack of it. —Notice what happens inside when I am unhappy with how someone else leads.
PRACTICES	—Put myself in a position to take direction, instruction or guidance from someone else. —Practice *secrecy* by keeping my accomplishments to myself. —Practice being a *lead servant*. Share my perks or give them away. Don't expect special treatment.

more difficult than leading. Following requires humility, risk, attention, awareness and guts. It means serving someone else's agenda and following her or his cues. Following requires that I let go of my own way and trail the leader. But everything in me resists trailing behind someone else, especially when I think I can make my own way or lead just as well. Following for any length of time tests both character and steadfastness.

Jesus' first invitation was to follow him (Mk 1:17). It was also the last invitation Jesus gave (Jn 21:22). From the beginning of his ministry to the end, Jesus focused on what it means to follow. He modeled following. He taught following. And he looked everywhere for followers. Following is a huge deal to Jesus, because following builds character, sands away the ego and shapes the heart.

Followers can't barge ahead or simply do the next thing that pops into their heads. They can't set cruise control or autopilot and zone out on what's happening. Followers must be alert, attentive and ready to turn on someone else's dime. Jesus' followers take up the challenge of turning where he turns, stopping when he stops, detouring where he detours, loving whom he loves and serving whom he serves. Followers risk doing things Jesus' way. In a world in which people want to do things their own way, following has fallen on hard times.

Leading is the action that gets air time and emphasis these days. Certainly, the church and the world need leaders, but our culture seems obsessed with leadership. We have leadership seminars, leadership headhunters, leadership networks and leadership books. Leaders make things happen; they are movers and shakers. Leadership comes with control, power, status, remuneration and attention. No wonder leadership sells. Given a choice between the perks and influence of leading and the discipline and humility of following, why on earth would anyone choose to follow? Who wants to be told, "Wow, you have great potential as a follower"? But is following only for those who don't have what it takes to be leaders?

JESUS' TEACHING ON LEADERSHIP

Jesus doesn't use the word *leader* at all, as far as I can tell. Once, when the disciples were arguing over which one of them was the greatest, Jesus said to them, "The kings of the Gentiles lord it over them; and those who exercise authority over them call themselves Benefactors. But you are not to be like that. Instead, the greatest among you should be like the youngest, and the one who rules like the one who serves. For who is greater, the one who is at the table or the one who serves? Is it not the one who is at the table? But I am among you as one who serves" (Lk 22:25-27). In John's Gospel, Jesus said, "Whoever serves me must follow me; and where I am, my servant also will be. My Father will honor the one who serves me" (Jn 12:26).

The embarrassing truth is that many of us like the power and control that come with taking the lead. We like leading because we get to tell people what to do. Quite often, we get served in the process. My family gave me a T-shirt that says it all: "It's good to be queen." I am ashamed of the way that this T-shirt's message fits me. Each time I wear it, I remember that Jesus never said, "It's good to be king." Jesus was among us as one who served (Lk 22:27).

Jesus didn't buy the pyramid structure of leading and following. He said that following and ruling (leading) are both about serving. Serving flattens the pyramid into a circle. Serving brings us down. I suspect Jesus' emphasis on service is what gave rise to the term *servant leadership*. Still, it is an irony that *servant* modifies *leader* rather than the other way round. Do we avoid the term *lead servant* because none of us really aspires to servanthood? Who warms to topics such as "How to Become Least and the Servant of All"? In my experience, it is easy to identify with Jesus' "servant leadership" style in a superficial way. We want to "serve," but we do it out of a superior heart—a heart that does not identify with the descending way of Jesus.

What does it feel like when you lead? What do you enjoy about it? Where does it hook your false self?

If we really intend to follow Jesus, we may need to rethink our take on leadership. Scripture includes some 1,400 references to people who serve, act as servants and offer service. Sometimes the word *servant* is simply used as a synonym for *slave*. But the word *servant* is used literally hundreds of times to describe the character of a follower who delights God.

- Abraham: the servant of God (Gen 18:3, 5; 19:2, 19)
- Abraham and Isaac and Israel: the servants of God (Ex 32:13; Deut 9:27; Num 32:25)
- Jacob: the servant of his brother, the servant of God (Gen 32:4, 10, 18; Is 44:1-2)
- Joseph: entered the service of Pharaoh (Gen 41:46)
- Moses: the servant of God (described this way over twenty-five times) (Ex 4:10; 5:15; Num 12:7; 34:5; 1 Kings 18:12; 2 Chron 1:3; Ps 105:26; Rev 15:3)
- Joshua: the servant of the Lord (Josh 24:29)
- Caleb: the servant of the Lord (Num 14:24)
- Samuel: servant of the Lord (1 Sam 3:9)
- David: servant of the Lord (described this way at least sixty times) (1 Sam 17:32, 34, 36; 2 Chron 6:42)
- Solomon: servant of God (1 Kings 1:19, 26)
- Job: servant of God (described this way five times) (Job 1:8; 2:3)
- Isaiah: servant of God (Is 20:3)
- The Messiah: the servant of God (Is 42:1; 43:10)
- The prophets: God's servants (Jer 7:25)
- Nebuchadnezzar: God's servant (Jer 25:9)
- Daniel: God's servant (Dan 10:17)

- All God's servants, both men and women: receive the Holy Spirit (Joel 2:29; Rev 19:5)

- Zechariah: servant of the Lord (Lk 2:29)

- Apostles: servants of the Most High God (Acts 4:29; 16:17)

- Paul: a servant of God and servant of others (Rom 1:1; 2 Cor 4:5; Phil 1:1)

- Timothy: a servant of God (Phil 1:1)

- Phoebe: the servant of the Lord, a great help to many people (Rom 16:1)

- Titus: a servant of God (Tit 1:1)

- James: a servant (Jas 1:1)

- Peter: servant of God and of the Lord (2 Pet 1:1)

- Jude: the servant of God (Jude 1)

- John: God's servant (Rev 1:1)

- Jesus: among us as one who serves (Lk 22:27)

Slaves and servants were nothing special in biblical times. Yet God singles out servants as the ones worthy of praise. God's servants are the biblical heroes. They are the men and women who, in the crunch of life, laid down their own plans, gave up their own agendas and let go of their own power. They disentangled their identity from their own version of success and became followers.

I have had many opportunities to work with teams of leaders. It can be a joy or a royal pain. It's a pain when the leaders haven't learned the lessons that following affords. Jesus' disciples had their own issues with following. They competed over who could be the greatest leader. We are not much different. Without a leadership role, some of us don't know how to function. We are bored, resistant and disengaged. We don't try to encourage someone else in their role up front but rather wait to give the critique, maintaining a constant internal dialogue of how it could be better if only we were in charge.

Some leaders can't imagine functioning in a context that doesn't use their tools: strategic planning, pithy mission statements and performance evaluations. It can be easier for them to trust objectives and goals than prayer and waiting. But when leaders know in the core of their being that they are also called to be followers, their work on teams can be amazing. No task is beneath them. Giving up power or status to help a less qualified person lead doesn't make them balk, and they serve without feeling diminished.

No wonder God puts such emphasis on followers. He knows we can want to lead for all the wrong reasons. We can want to follow for the wrong reasons too, of course. Still, God often chooses the reluctant person to accomplish his mission. Moses didn't want to lead. Deborah didn't want to lead alone. Gideon didn't want to fight. Jonah didn't want to be a missionary. Jeremiah didn't want to preach. And Jesus struggled to keep his face set toward Jerusalem and the cross. But when push came to shove, all these people followed.

Jesus' invitation to follow is an invitation to become like him: to literally "be there for him," and to be one of his lead servants in the world. Jesus' followers follow Jesus' example of humility and vulnerability. They risk his journey of descent—the journey that will be the making of us. Maturity, humility, patience, godliness— these are all fruit of following Jesus. These are the fruit of following Jesus down.

THE HUMBLE ALMIGHTY

Jesus laid aside divine power. Although he sustains the universe with his pinkie, he took the form of a human servant. Jesus left his place at the right hand of God. He saw our mess. He heard our cries. And he got off his throne and came down to us. God in person. God willing to descend, in the words of Henri Nouwen, "to the total dereliction of one condemned to death. It isn't easy really to feel and understand from the inside this descending way of Jesus. Every fiber of our being rebels against it. We don't mind paying attention to poor people from time to time, but descending to a state of poverty and becoming poor with the poor, that we don't want to do. And yet that is the way Jesus chose as the way to know God."

Jesus is not like some Greek god who occasionally left Mount Olympus to meddle in human affairs when he was angry or bored. In Jesus, God came down in the flesh—not as some exalted being, but as an earthbound human being dragging his limitations with him. Jesus was made "lower" (Heb 2:9).

What's it like for you to hang out with people you feel are a "little lower" than you are? When you associate with people beneath your supposed station, do you feel diminished? Are you concerned that others know that you are not like them, and that you can do better than the people you're with? Something in us so wants to move upward.

But Jesus came down. As Paul wrote in Philippians, Jesus emptied himself and became a servant, even to death. In the Garden of Gethsemane, Jesus asked God for a way out—a way that wouldn't be so wretched, ignominious and shaming. But when no divine intervention came, Jesus thought of us. He heard our cries and continued to follow God's agenda down to a cross.

What does it feel like when you are a follower? When do you enjoy this position? How does following affect your ego?

One of my memories as a teenager was hearing about the murder of Katherine Susan Genovese at Kew Gardens in New York City. Early in the morning on March 13, 1964, she was attacked by an assailant on her way home from work. Her screams woke her neighbors, who flipped on their lights and looked down from their windows.

Someone shouted to leave the girl alone, and the assailant retreated. Stabbed and near death, the girl called for help. But no one who saw her attacked came down to help. No one immediately called the police. Some minutes later, the assailant returned. He robbed Genovese of forty-nine dollars and stabbed her to death.

This failure on the part of observers to get involved became known as the Genovese Syndrome: people hear the cry for help, but rather than following through with responsible action, they imagine that someone else will take care of it. Ignoring the invitation to follow love into a vulnerable place of sacrifice or jeopardy, we figure that someone else will do it.

But Jesus heard our cries and responded. He came down and followed God's will into the maw of death. He did this so we can know that in God's eyes we are all equally valuable, loveable, important and worth dying for.

Following always involves a coming down, a humbling of oneself and a serving of others. Jonathan Edwards, the Puritan theologian, captured this condescension of God in his sermon "The Excellency of Christ." Edwards wrote:

> It is true that he [Christ] has awful majesty; he is the great God, and is infinitely high above you; but there is this to encourage and embolden the poor sinner, that Christ is a man as well as God; . . . and he is the most humble and lowly in heart of any creature in heaven or earth. . . . You need not hesitate one moment; but may run to him, and cast yourself upon him. . . . Whatever your circumstances are, you need not be afraid to come to such a Savior as this. . . . Be you never so poor, and mean, and ignorant a creature, there is no danger of being despised; for though he be so much greater than you, he is also immensely more humbled than you.

Let Jesus' words roll over you: "Come, follow me." Come and be "last and servant of all."

- "Anyone who wants to be first must be the very last, and the servant of all" (Mk 9:35).

- "The greatest among you will be your servant" (Mt 23:11).

- "The student is not above the teacher, nor a servant above his master" (Mt 10:24).

- "No one can serve two masters" (Lk 16:13).

I sometimes hear people talk about leaders as people who make things happen. But it takes followers to make Jesus' agenda happen. My friend Julie tells me that physicists define a *leader* as an extremely hot and highly conductive channel of plasma that plays a critical role in the electrical transfer of a spark from one electrode to another. The *leader*, in this sense, is actually the way a spark follows the path between electrodes. Following the path is how the spark can make an impact and not fizzle out before it has achieved its purpose. The leader doesn't get out front and require the spark to do what it wants; it becomes a channel, or a way, that can be followed to produce a dynamic end.

God's followers lead by walking in the way that travels down into paths of service. They listen to God's agenda for this world. The prophet Micah put it like this: "What does the LORD require of you? To act justly and to love mercy and to walk humbly with your God"

List your roles as leader and follower.

Who follows you?

Who do you follow?

Where do you participate as a member of a group rather than as a force to be reckoned with?

What do you see about yourself?

What does God see about you?

Take your list to God in prayer. What would it look like to be a lead servant in these roles?

(Mic 6:8). This is sometimes called "God's Great Requirement." It is a statement of God's will for those who want to follow.

FOLLOWING JESUS

Several years ago I read Jeffrey Sachs's book *The End of Poverty: Economic Possibilities for Our Time*. Sachs develops a plan that he believes will eliminate hunger and subsistence poverty in our lifetime. I love that this was God's idea first. God intends for his people to help those who are powerless to change their economic futures. And his plans for helping the poor are found throughout Scripture. In Deuteronomy 15, God said, "There need be no poor people among you. . . . Be openhanded and freely lend them whatever they need" (Deut 15:4, 8). God intended for wealthy people to find parcels of land and give seed for planting to the poor. Furthermore, those with fields were not to harvest everything. They were to allow grain to remain at the edges of the fields so others could come and glean enough to feed their families. Following God's agenda meant that the rich never charged the poor interest. They forgave loans. They didn't pass laws that favored the rich. They cared that the poor not be powerless or without advocates. In other words, their own lives became vulnerable to the poor.

Following Jesus means caring about more than me and my family. It means identifying with God's broken heart over poverty and his holy anger at injustices in our world. It means following his lead on who and what matters.

It is easy to find out specifically what God cares about today. Hundreds of websites provide a bird's-eye view of the world God loves (see, for example, www.globalissues.org/article/26/poverty-facts-and-stats). I carry a list of global facts in my wallet and keep another on my desk to help me remember to follow. When I open my wallet, my list reminds me to open my heart to everyone Jesus opened his heart to: poor people, marginalized people, politically (in)correct people, unemployed people, liberal people, fundamentalist people, sick people, homeless people and even enemy people. My list includes some of the following facts.

- Almost half the world lives on less than $2.50 a day. When a child needs a pair of shoes or a uniform to go to school, these economics don't work.

- The poorest 40 percent of the world's population accounts for 5 percent of global income. The richest 20 percent accounts for three-quarters of world income.

- According to UNICEF, 25,000 children die each day due to poverty.

- Twenty-eight percent of all children in developing countries are estimated to be underweight or stunted.

- Water problems affect half of humanity.

- Over one billion people in developing countries have inadequate access to water, and 2.6 billion people lack basic sanitation.

- For the 1.9 billion children from the developing world, there are 640 million without adequate shelter (1 in 3), 400 million with no access to safe water (1 in 5), and 270 million with no access to health services (1 in 7).

- Over two million children die each year because they are not immunized.

- Fifteen million children are orphaned due to HIV/AIDS.

- The Millennium Project reports 300-500 million cases of acute malaria worldwide on an annual basis. About 1.1-2.7 million people die from malaria every year—mostly children under five years of age.

- In the last twenty-four hours, 30,000 children died of preventable diseases. Often they died for lack of a twenty-cent pill that purifies water.

Sometimes I try to imagine that to God these are not just facts; they are people God knows and loves. And then I imagine Jesus saying, "Adele, follow me." I need reminders of what it means to stay the course of following. Following may begin with the "sinner's prayer," but it can't stop there. Following is meant to make my heart one with Jesus. It is meant to make Jesus' prayer for this world come true: "Our Father, who art in heaven, hallowed be your name. Your kingdom come. Your will be done, on earth as it is in heaven." Let the words grip you. "*Your* kingdom come" (not mine!). "Your will be done" (now, not later when I'm not so preoccupied). "Your will be done on earth" (by me), "as it is in heaven."

God cares that his kingdom of fairness and justice comes. He cares that I buy fair-trade commodities. He cares that profits reach those serving at the bottom of the production process. He cares that those who work in sweatshops in Mongolia, China and Nepal—those who make my cashmere sweater—get a livable wage.

My adult children, Nathaniel and Annaliese, are both vigilant in reminding me that if I have food in the refrigerator, more than one pair of shoes and a place to sleep, I am richer than 75 percent of this world. Years ago Nathaniel made me go to www.global richlist.com/ and type in my salary so I could see in graph form exactly how my income stacks up with the rest of the world. My kids see their budgets as moral documents about how they love their neighbor, and they prod me to do the same. "Mom, do you really need that?" "Are you too comfortable?" They follow the downward path of living simply and sacrificially.

God created a world with enough for everyone. There is enough land and water and even enough food. The problem is not supply. The problem is distribution. But there is a more basic problem still: a problem of caring and sharing. Distribution and lack of care are both matters of grave and loving concern for God. If you

want to make God smile, follow him into this world. Serve his
agenda, which always includes the poor, the oppressed, the orphans, the widows and those in need. As I make my life vulnerable
to the poor, my heart becomes one with Jesus.

MONEY, SEX AND POWER

Let me be very specific for a moment about how following looks
and how it affects our relationship to money, sex and power.

Money. Scripture makes it plain: there is no such thing as *my*
money. Every cent I have belongs to Jesus, and he trusts me to
invest it in more than my own humming, expanding economic
security. Vacations, weekends away, fine wine, fast cars, expensive
toys, designer clothes and exotic adventures may be wonderful
things. But when I can't stop craving more and more of these
things, nonmaterial values like love, generosity and availability
erode. My heart shrinks. I get addicted to spending on myself. The
notion of downsizing becomes anathema. Jesus said that every
day you choose to lay up treasure on earth or in heaven. Do you
really want to follow someone who says things like this? Treasure
on earth—that inexhaustible desire for more—or treasure in
heaven: which will it be?

I am so glad for people that show me how to follow Jesus and
his heart for others. They are not downsizing-averse. They also
demonstrate how money and possessions can bring pleasure to
God and sustenance to others. A college student at our church and
her boyfriend, for example, decided to spend no money on clothes
for a year. They stayed out of stores and bought only toiletries.
That way they could give more money to others. Another friend
makes it her goal to give others the same things she buys for herself and her family. It's how she has chosen to love her neighbor as
herself. She has covered other people's insurance costs, housekeeping costs, college tuitions, travel expenses, and on and on.
These people make me aware of how little I want to live on less.

They keep me engaged in the struggle to follow God rightly with my money. They help me distinguish between wants and needs. And in the current economic crisis, they have shown me that following the ups and downs of my diminishing retirement fund isn't nearly as important as staying the course and following Jesus.

Sex. Our world has 24/7 access to Internet porn, sexually explicit movies, ads, books and magazines. Kids have "friends with benefits" and think nothing of taking graphic cell phone photos that they send to friends (often called *sexting*). Our oversexualized culture turns people into objects that can be used for my pleasure, whether that is in thought, consensual sex or abusive relationships. This objectifying of people destroys our capacity for authentic intimacy while panning modesty as silly puritanism. So how does one follow Jesus' example of purity and intimacy in body relationships? I'll never forget how my college roommate's boyfriend said he didn't believe Jesus could help him face temptation because, in his words, "Jesus never had a chick." All I can say is that Jesus had healthy interactions with women in an era in which a category for mixed-gender friendships didn't even exist. Jesus wasn't an innocent or a prude. He was pure. And purity is quite different than prudery or even innocence. Prudery minimizes bodily joys and misses the fact that God is in the hormones and plumbing. Innocence is something that hasn't been tested, and when it is lost, it cannot be recovered. But purity comes out of testing, and it can be found anew, even after moral failures, if we will repent, make a U-turn and follow Jesus.

I don't think for a minute that this is easy. It can take real courage and humility to put guards on the computer—not just for your kids but for yourself. It is brave to talk to your spouse or a trusted friend about your struggle to follow Jesus in purity of body and mind. It is a strength, not a weakness, to go for sexual addiction counseling. It is wisdom, not legalism, to think twice about the movies you watch. It is respectful of yourself and others to dress modestly. I love that Paul wrote in Romans 12:1, "Offer your bodies as a living sacrifice, holy and pleasing to God—this is your true and proper worship." He didn't say, "Forget you have a body." He didn't say, "Just say no," as good as that advice might be. Paul said to say yes. He said to offer your body. Do something with it. Offer it with all its urges and failings back to the God who made it. This is your spiritual act of worship.

Don't you think that's breathtaking?

How do money, sex and power lead the agendas of your life?

Power. In the Gospels, Jesus displays tremendous concern about power. More than once he went head to head with those who used the power of religion, tradition and politics to manipulate or coerce. Control was the name of their game. It was how they kept the status quo, got what they wanted or proved they were right.

Control comes naturally to us. French philosopher Jean-Paul Sartre described the human condition as "En soi et pour soi": in myself and for myself. Every two-year-old knows that the word *no* brings power. Controlling the toy and winning the game matters. Adults simply take this to its logical conclusion. It was an adult, not a child, who said, "The one with the most toys wins." Using power and control to safeguard our conventional futures and our dominance is how adults secure our kingdoms. Every one of us has control issues. It may simply be taking sides at the elders meeting, or attempting to control when your family has dinner together, or resisting the corporate culture of which you are a part. All of us get hooked by power. I can't tell you how often I have sat at a dinner party and listened to a couple arguing about who has the details of an incident right. There is power in being right!

It's ironic, but those of us who "have" often feel like we never have enough. Not enough money, sex or power. Money, sex and power reveal our values. They reveal who I am following.

WHO AM I FOLLOWING?

Following Jesus takes us to the places Jesus went. As we follow, we begin to hear some of the things he said to his disciples as words directly aimed at us. "You give them something to eat." "You take up your cross and follow me." Following Jesus may land us in Gethsemane, awash in struggle. Following might find us lugging a cross that leads to death: death of our comforts and little luxuries and always more. The good news of the kingdom includes justice, peace, goodness, generosity and love for all peoples and nations. Do you really want to follow Jesus where he goes?

Accepting Jesus' invitation to follow is not just agreeing with a list of ethical principles and beefing up your willpower. It is about falling in love with Jesus. When we do that, we fall in love with people. When we do that, we serve and care about justice issues. Justice and concern for God's world aren't just themes for prophets or leaders. They are the heartbeat of followers. In God's economy, nobody is known for what they have; we are all known for what we have given away. We are known for how we have followed Jesus—down—to the point of giving our lives for others.

Practice detachment from being out front and in the lead. Follow the discipline of secrecy. Don't drop names or accomplishments or successes. Don't let people know how influential and powerful you are. Find out about others. Encourage them. Empower them. Listen to them. Follow hard after Jesus.

Following is where discipleship begins and ends. It is Jesus' first invitation and one of his last. My dream is not for the church or world to be filled with servant leaders. It is a much more modest and radical dream. May the world be filled with *followers*: real, true, crazy-in-love followers of Jesus.

May it be filled with followers whose sole purpose is Jesus' purpose. "I have come down . . . to do [follow] the will of him who sent me" (Jn 6:38).

A familiar catch phrase in leadership seminars is "Great leaders are made, not born." Dare I suggest a new phrase? "Great leaders are reborn in order to be made followers."

The Lord's joy is reserved for servants who follow. In the end, the words that matter most are these: "Well done, good and faithful servant. . . . Come and share your master's happiness!" (Mt 25:23).

3

Invitation to Practice the Presence of People

The greatest weakness of most humans is their hesitancy to tell others how much they love them while they're still alive.

O. A. BATTISTA

THE PRACTICE OF THE PRESENCE OF GOD is a lovely Christian classic written in the seventeenth century. It records the wisdom of a Carmelite lay brother named Lawrence, who spent much of his life working in a monastery kitchen. There, surrounded by pots and pans, Brother Lawrence discovered that circumstances don't determine God's proximity. It didn't matter whether Brother Lawrence was peeling potatoes, repairing sandals, or praying in the chapel or alone in his cell: anytime and everywhere, God was nearby. A plaque at a friend's home reads: "Bidden or unbidden, God is present." To apprehend God's nearness, all Brother Lawrence needed to do was learn to "practice the presence." By keeping his attention open to God in everything, he found God in everything.

In 1999, Mike Mason wrote a book called *Practicing the Presence*

FOLLOWING GOD'S INVITATION
TO PRACTICE THE PRESENCE OF PEOPLE

INVITATION	To see people as Jesus does—as the most important things in the world.
SCRIPTURE	"For to see your face is like seeing the face of God, now that you have received me favorably" (Gen 33:10). "Then [Jesus] turned toward the woman and said to Simon, 'Do you see this woman?'" (Lk 7:44).
ROADBLOCKS	—The placement of priority on tasks before people —Preoccupation with certain things so that I fail to notice those around me —Inability to handle interruptions gracefully —Self-centeredness
AWARENESS	—Notice when I put myself before others. —Notice whom I talk to and whom I don't talk to. —Notice my reactions to being interrupted. —Notice everything I can about my spouse, parents, kids, colleagues. Out of this noticing, what prayers come to mind?
PRACTICES	—Practice *courtesy*, which can give me eyes to see others. —*Intercession* for others and their needs, which can help me see the world more clearly.

of People. Mason's book invites us to learn to need and want people. It is a study in loving our neighbor and seeing others through God's undimmed eyes. Practicing the presence of people lets people know that they matter and have our undivided attention. Brother Lawrence and Mike Mason both remind me that holy invitations to love always take me out of self and into God. When we love someone, we can't take our eyes off them. We gaze and stare. We behold. Could it be that the continual reminder in Scripture to "behold" is God's way of reminding us to practice the presence? Someone amazing is at hand. Take a good look. Notice. Savor. Attend.

Still, saying yes to the invitation to love God or any other human being on a daily basis requires something far more than chemistry. Loving is not cursory, superficial, easy or conceptual. Love demands all of us: body, mind and soul. And things that happen in the totality of who we are take practice.

A friend of mine felt disoriented when she moved from St. Louis to Boston's North Shore. Neighbors didn't welcome her. Store clerks didn't talk to her. And drivers were downright rude to her. Not to be put off by curmudgeonly New Englanders, she decided to take a bouquet of flowers to a neighbor. She told me that the neighbor seemed embarrassed by the gift and worried that she might want something. A few days later, the neighbor knocked at the door with a cake. "I got the distinct impression that this cake was not about friendship," my friend says. "It was not an invitation to be in relationship. It was about not wanting to owe me anything—not wanting to be indebted. Not wanting to be known or loved."

I understood my friend's experience even more when I moved from New England to the Chicago heartland. I was used to the reticent Northeast, so when sales clerks talked to me, I wondered what they wanted. When drivers were polite and took turns, I criticized them for going so slow. Boston's way of life was still at work inside me. But when a new acquaintance invited a half-dozen of her friends to come and help me unpack boxes, iron tablecloths, polish silver and shelve books, I couldn't help but "behold." This woman saw me. She helped me move in, organized two weeks of meals and gave me her housekeeper for a month, saying, "No one should have to move into a house and clean it too." I was overwhelmed. Far from home, I was seen and invited into a new home.

Culture, family, experience, temperament and geography all seem to play a part in how we see who we see—and if we really see anyone at all. With relationships being one of the most vulnerable things on earth, it's no wonder some of us are risk-averse. Some families naturally include and extend invitations; others do not. Some temperaments get energy from people; others do not. God knows all the variables regarding personality and temperaments, and God still doesn't modify the invitation to love. Introverts and New Englanders are no exception! God wants each of us to find out what it is like to live as though people really matter. He wants us do this because, whether you live in Boston or Chicago or Timbuktu, love is the litmus test of the Christian faith. Jesus put it simply: "By this everyone will know that you are my disciples, if you love one another" (Jn 13:35).

BEING AS MUCH LIKE GOD AS POSSIBLE

Jesus' invitation to let people really matter summons us to be as much like God as we can possibly be. And if we say yes, it will grow our heart, which sometimes is very much like the Grinch's—ten sizes too small. Saying yes to being like God is how we grow a heart that loves billionaires, food-stamp recipients, nerds, Goths, rock stars, jocks, social climbers, workaholics, alcoholics, sex offenders, beauty queens, 911 operators, babysitters, CEOs, janitors, editors, winners, losers, stamp collectors, Democrats and Republicans. And that's only the beginning! There are over six billion people on this planet, and for them to know God's love, they are going to have to see it in someone very much like me. Yet I barely love my friends, let alone my enemies. Perhaps that's one reason God called our family to leave New England. The Midwest helped me become a nicer person. Still, it takes a lot more than *nice* to learn to love. It takes all of me: all my heart, soul, strength and mind. Furthermore it takes a whale of a lot of practice to love anything like God does.

I have not been a quick study in practicing the presence of people. I am a multitasker who likes to accomplish things. Really slowing down and seeing people doesn't come naturally to me. I saw this very clearly when I lived in Trinidad. To survive there, I had to learn to *lime*. *Liming* is how relationships happen in Trinidad. *Liming* is not an hour blocked out on my calendar for coffee with a friend; it is what you do whenever you see someone.

Because we had no phone, people often spontaneously popped by to lime. They rattled the gate and shouted, "Hello the house." No matter what I was doing, the custom dictated that I stop and invite them in for a sweet drink. Liming requires no agenda or purpose; hanging out is its own reason. My adjustment to liming wasn't easy. Store clerks and bank tellers limed with other clerks while I waited for service. Students and neighbors and friends and colleagues did the same.

Living in Trinidad showed me how much easier it is to turn love into rules and doctrine than it is to follow God into the thick of relationships. I ran smack into how hard it was to stop, lay down my agenda and really see people enough to enjoy liming with them. I was undone by how easily I dismissed and neglected people who interrupted rather than figuring out how to take them in—practice their presence— and give or receive some love. But slowly, over the years, liming worked away on me. I found out that there's always more than meets the eye with people and that time spent loving and seeing others is never wasted.

How do you feel about liming with people—that is, passing the time of day with others without an agenda, simply relaxing and being present with them even on short notice? How do you feel about people who interrupt and throw off your agenda?

A STUDY IN PRACTICING THE PRESENCE

The Gospels are filled with stories of how Jesus limed with people. People were never just strangers or interruptions that got in the way of all he needed to do. People weren't a nuisance; people were the reason Jesus came. He accumulated friends and attended parties. People traveled with him, ate with him, distracted him, quarreled with him and loved him. No one was invisible or beneath his attention. No one faded into the background. No one was written off as hopeless, disgusting, "none of my business" or "not my type." Jesus practiced the presence of beggars, women, soldiers, tax collectors, vagrants, religious folks, disenfranchised people, lepers, scholars and children. And I can't imagine Jesus liming with all these folks unless he actually liked people.

Jesus knew how to give people the gift of presence. It is a gift we all are looking for. Listen to children: "Look at me," "See what I did," "Are you watching me, Mommy?" Watch adults adeptly passing on their credentials so as not to be overlooked, taken for granted or left out: "I live on Beacon Hill"; "I went to Harvard"; "I'm just back from skiing in Aspen." At a deep level, people want to be seen. Everyone hopes for someone to see and invest some attention and time in them. Everyone wants someone to practice their presence. Yet how easy it is to not really see living, breathing human beings. I can be so caught up in my own agenda and thoughts that I am virtually blind. I look right through people I pass on the street. If someone yells my name, I might see and remember there is a world outside my own head. Then I might stop and lime with them, but often I am too preoccupied to stop and imagine that anyone else might be as real and important as I am. Seeing takes all of me, and it takes practice.

Before I moved from Boston to the Windy City, my friend Ginny introduced me to her Chicagoland friend Karen. I must confess that I didn't expect Karen to remember me. She had a lot going on in her life and was a relatively public figure. Yet before I had all the boxes unpacked in my new home, she called and invited me to an exhibit at the Art Institute. In the midst of decisions, organizational pressure and incredible responsibilities Karen remembered the friend of a friend. She made room in her life and her covenant group for me.

ON THE EDGE OF DEFEAT

Love can sound like a lovely, lofty ideal, but it sometimes boils down to remembering a face, a name or a conversation. This sort of seeing happens in our bodies. And this fact, of course, is humbling. We forget names. We forget the name of the person talking to us right now because when they introduced themselves, we were only paying half attention. Love is not a sweet, dithery feeling; it is a risky, humbling, time-consuming affair. When it is not humbling us with our self-centered blindness to others, it is guzzling our time like a race car guzzles gas. And since time is short, time is money, time is a-wastin' and time is up, it takes practice to take the time to *see* people. Make no mistake: loving ice cream, sunsets, fireworks and your ever-faithful golden retriever is a whole lot easier and less time-consuming than practicing the presence of another human being.

How easy is it for you to see goodness in people you dislike?

Eugene Peterson writes,

> Every day I put love on the line. There is nothing I am less good at than love. I am far better in competition than in love. . . . I am schooled and trained in acquisitive skills, in getting my own way. And yet I decide, every day, to set aside what I can do best and attempt what I do very clumsily—open myself to the frustrations and failures of loving, daring to believe that failing in love is better than succeeding in pride. All that is hazardous work. I live on the edge of defeat all the time.

Jesus knows this about me. He also knows that relationships can be demanding, messed up and a boatload of harm. Still he longs for me to take on the risks of really seeing and loving people even when it hurts my heart. Even when it is arduous. Even when, in the words of C. S. Lewis, love isn't a "safe investment. To love at all is to be vulnerable."

Practicing the presence of people isn't always safe or comfortable. We all have scars to prove it. Even Jesus does, because in Jesus, God became a vulnerable human being. He opened himself wide to us and invited us to be his friends. We betrayed him. Even now, Jesus has the nail scars in his hands and feet to prove that not even God is immune to the hurt of love. The Holy One has a place of vulnerability, and the place of vulnerability is you! God has a heartbreaking desire for our friendship. Frederick Buechner's lines from *Godric* say it all: "What's friendship, when all's done, but the giving and taking of wounds?"

> *Do you feel your relationship quota is full? What does God want to say to you about this?*

A broken heart is the irrefutable sign that people are never loved in general or in theory. People can only be loved in practice and in particular. They can only be loved by choice. To choose to love someone means your agenda and perhaps even your life may be forfeited.

Mike Mason recounts how his friend Daniel Adair once said,

Whenever I meet someone new, I take that person and fix him or her in my heart. To do this, I literally see that person as a star, and I reach up and set that star in my sky. Where once was a patch of empty dark, there now blazes the living light of a soul I know and love. To set all people above me in this way helps me both to remember and to cherish them. When I'm lying alone in my bed at night, I look up into my sky and see all those stars, all the stars of everyone I've ever known, and one by one I remember them by name. Isn't this exactly what the Lord does with His friends? He sees us and calls us by name and gives us a place in his heaven.

Jesus invites us to see people and fix them in our hearts. He invites us to look beyond the oddities, wounds and brokenness for the face of God. I love the story of Jacob and Esau, twins who had a major falling out. Jacob deceived his brother, and the estrangement ran so deep that Jacob ran for his life. Years passed. The wounds remained. Then one day, still wracked by fear of Esau's reprisals, Jacob tentatively headed back home. When Esau received Jacob and his family with love, Jacob said, "For to see your face is like seeing the face of God, now that you have received me favorably" (Gen 33:10).

SEEING MORE THAN MEETS THE EYE

Each of our faces reflects a facet of the image and beauty of our Father in heaven. Every face flashes with family recognition. Gaze a moment on someone's face, and you might catch a fresh glimpse of the Holy One, or catch a facet of the body of Christ that blinds you with its glory. Each one of us reveals something of the divine beauty that all others long to see.

Luke 7 is a remarkable chapter about how Jesus sees people for more than meets the eye. In Luke 7:9, Jesus saw a Roman centurion, who had more faith than any Jew he had met so far. Imagine seeing faith in an "enemy"! In Luke 7:13, Jesus saw more than just a funeral for someone he didn't know; he saw a woman and became present to her grief. What he saw got him involved: "his heart went out to her and he said, 'Don't cry'" (Lk 7:13). In Luke 7:24-26, Jesus asked the crowds three times: "What did you go out to see?" He wanted to know whether the people were open to seeing reality in a different way. By Luke 7:36, the theme of seeing others is hard to miss.

Luke 7 tells a story of just how much Jesus sees.

One of the Pharisees asked him over for a meal. He went to
the Pharisee's house and sat down at the dinner table. Just
then a woman of the village, the town harlot, having learned
that Jesus was a guest in the home of the Pharisee, came with
a bottle of very expensive perfume and stood at his feet,
weeping, raining tears on his feet. Letting down her hair, she
dried his feet, kissed them, and anointed them with the perfume. When the Pharisee who had invited him saw this he
said to himself, "If this man was the prophet I thought he
was, he would have known what kind of woman this is who
is falling all over him."

Jesus said to him, "Simon, I have something to tell you."

"Oh? Tell me."

"Two men were in debt to a banker. One owed five hundred silver pieces, the other fifty. Neither of them could pay
up, and so the banker canceled both debts. Which of the two
would be more grateful?"

Simon answered, "I suppose the one who was forgiven the
most."

"That's right," Jesus said. Then turning to the woman, but
speaking to Simon, he said, "Do you see this woman? I came
to your home; you provided no water for my feet, but she
rained tears on my feet and dried them with her hair. You gave
me no greeting, but from the time I arrived she hasn't quit
kissing my feet. You provided nothing for freshening up, but
she has soothed by feet with perfume. Impressive, isn't it? She
was forgiven many, many sins, and so she is very, very grateful. If the forgiveness is minimal, the gratitude is minimal."

Then he spoke to her: "I forgive your sins."

That set the dinner guests talking behind his back: "Who
does he think he is, forgiving sins!"

He ignored them and said to the woman, "Your faith has saved you. Go in peace." (Lk 7:36-50 *The Message*)

In a culture in which women and men didn't touch in public, the interaction bordered on bizarre. Horrified and disgusted men wonder, *Who let her in?*

Have you ever felt unwelcomed, invisible, uninvited or unwanted? No matter what baggage and messiness you carry, Jesus looks on you with love and undivided attention. He sees your goodness—that completely original facet of the divine image that you alone bear. And he can't take his eyes off you.

But let's get back to Simon and how he saw things. Simon saw two things, both of which he judged as *bad*. The woman was a disgraceful piece of work, in his opinion, and Jesus was a rabbinic imposter who couldn't recognize a prostitute when he saw one (v. 39). Simon didn't see the goodness in either one. Consequently, he missed seeing the glint of the image of God that flickered around him. As the woman continued her massage, tension and judgment escalated. But Jesus shifted the whole center of attention by saying to Simon, "I have something to tell you."

This might have been a good moment for Jesus to bring up a rule or offer some moral. Instead, he asked Simon a financial question. If a money lender cancels a small debt for one person and a huge debt for another, who will love him more: the big debtor or the small debtor? The answer seems so obvious. But the question pushed Simon to extrapolate beyond his stereotypes and snap judgments about the woman. He had to put both head and heart together to answer. In other words, it was not enough to think about the sorry state of being in debt; Simon had to feel what it might be like to be in debt and then have the debt canceled. Jesus' question offered Simon another lens through which to see this woman. Jesus put it to him like this: "Do you see this woman?"

Years ago I heard a news report on how long it takes to make a first impression. The report suggested that it takes three seconds for people to reach a first impression. Of course Simon saw the woman. But Jesus asked Simon to look again. He invited Simon to get past his first impression and to practice the woman's presence. There was more to her than met the eye. Jesus invited Simon to pay attention to the sad and untold story behind this woman's tears. If Simon would have looked hard and practiced her presence, he might have become aware of his own blindness. He might have begun to ask himself, *What made me miss her goodness? Why didn't I welcome her? Do I have any responsibility for what I see?*

Loving the Lord your God with all your heart and your neighbor as yourself is all about learning to see past the judgment of badness to the Creator's desire for this person. It may take time and a lot of looking, but it is how we practice the presence of people. We give them our attention and ask for clarity to see them as Jesus did. We ask to recognize their needs as quickly as we recognize our own. This doesn't mean we become outgoing and extroverted if we are not. It simply means that we begin to notice people and to really look at what their words and faces are telling us. By practicing their presence, we give them the gift of mattering!

Simon, no doubt, thought himself a good man—an upright Jew who worked hard to please God. He was outgoing and hospitable. He knew how to generously host a lunch for his friends and Jesus. But look again at Simon. His welcome of Jesus was anything but wholehearted. Simon invited him in and then held him at arm's length. He invited Jesus in and then actually neglected him by withholding himself, the kiss of welcome, the footwashing and the cleansing oil. Simon didn't see Jesus' goodness either. His neglect revealed the secrets and motives in his heart.

Irony runs thick here. Jesus asked, "Do you see this woman?" Do you see that she is the one who offers the kiss? She is the one who bathes the feet and anoints them with oil. She is the one who practices hospitality. She is the one who practices the presence of Jesus. Jesus didn't see scandal in the woman's actions. This embarrassing display of public affection by a "fallen woman" revealed God's own divine image and love. And Jesus saw it. He saw her pass on the cure of love in a context of neglect. Where Simon saw *bad*, Jesus saw *good*.

Simon was blind to the fact that if you want to please God, who is loving and forgiving, you have to have more than theology in your head. You need God's loving, forgiving heart as a lens to see by. You need to feel what it is like to have had a debt canceled.

THE CURE OF LOVE

God is not a concept we master. Relationships don't just happen in our head. God is a being who invites interaction. He gives us the gift of his presence, and we begin to see people the way he does. We notice how people are judged, oppressed and sidelined. We see the unfairness of life and want to pass on the protection and cure of love. Practicing the presence of people doesn't mean we sit around talking about how educators, governments, social workers and aid agencies should fix and nix these issues. We don't leave everything up to UNICEF or World Relief or the Red Cross. We see what's going on: we see the woman everyone else avoids, we wince in pain and we act.

In the midst of the recent financial crisis, I have spoken to people who are reeling in pain and anxiety. I can't solve their anxiety, but I can give them the gift of presence. I can listen for the untold story behind their fear. I can also look for the real story that comes cloaked in people's behavior. I can't see it all, but I can keep from going blind. I want to be committed to passing the cure of love along to one human being and then another and another.

This is, I believe, Jesus' vision of the church. Love your neighbor as yourself. Risk seeing them through Jesus' eyes. Risk treating others as you would treat yourself or your own kids and family. Risk being taken for a ride. Risk being used. Risk leaving your judgment of someone behind. Risk loving. Mike Mason puts it like this, "If love were a sport, people would be the goal posts." Pass on the cure of love. Start scoring goals. And it won't be long before you have the joy and scars to prove it.

Who has passed on the cure of love to you? What was it like?

A few years ago my elderly mother told me about finding herself short of cash in the checkout line at the grocery store. She reached for her credit card but couldn't find it. The more she searched for it, the more alarmed she became. She began to apologize and fret to the clerk, "I know it was here! I can't imagine where it is. Do you think I dropped it? Maybe it's at the bottom of my purse." As she poured the contents of her purse out on the conveyor belt, she imagined the frustration in the line behind her. That made her less focused and more distracted and anxious.

Suddenly my mother heard a voice behind her saying, "Would this help you?" A young woman was waving a twenty-dollar bill in her hand. My mom was overcome with gratitude and agreed to accept the money if she could return it. She went home, wrote a thank-you note, and sent back the money. Two days later she received this reply:

Throughout the next week, try to notice one new thing about the people with whom you work or live. What have you been blind to? How can catching a glimmer of God's image in another person change the way you pray for them?

Thank you so much for the wonderful note. You really made my day. . . . I'm glad I could help. We don't have any family in this state. We are South Dakotans. So I enjoy an interaction with friendly people. I try to treat everyone as if they are all my family. In God's eyes we are. I work in nuclear medicine. Feel free to look me up sometime if you are at the hospital. . . . I would like to buy you a cup of coffee. [We] miss our grandparents. God bless you and may he keep you safe. P.S. I want you to know I will never cash that check.

That day, one stranger practiced the presence of another stranger and passed on the cure of love. Practice the presence of God. Practice the presence of people. There may be nothing you are less good at. But practice is all it takes to become Christ's presence in this world.

4

Invitation to Rest

*There is a realm of time where the goal is not to have
but to be, not to own but to give, not to control but to
share, not to subdue but to be in accord.*

ABRAHAM HESCHEL

*We must have some room to breathe. We need freedom to
think and permission to heal. Our relationships are
being starved to death by velocity.
No one has the time to listen, let alone love. . . .
Is God now pro-exhaustion? Doesn't He lead people
beside the still waters anymore?*

RICHARD A. SWENSON

WHEN LABOR DAY COMES around every September, with its trib-
ute to the working man and woman, most of us get the day off. It's
our last rest stop before running the marathon of September, October, November and December. Ready or not, we let summer go.
The competitive juices start flowing. We put noses to the grind-
stone and take a crack at proving our identities and value all over

FOLLOWING GOD'S INVITATION TO REST

INVITATION	To set aside the compulsion to "do, do, do" and live into God's creational rhythms that nourish and restore the body, soul and relationships.
SCRIPTURE	"Therefore, since the promise of entering [God's] rest still stands, let us be careful that none of you be found to have fallen short of it" (Heb 4:1).
ROADBLOCKS	—A sixty-hour work week —The inability to relax even when time is available —An identity that is attached to work, accomplishments and achievements —The belief that resting is a waste of time —So ignoring the body's cues about rest that I live from a perpetual state of depletion —The belief that everything rides on my shoulders
AWARENESS	—Notice what my body is trying to tell me through headaches, irritability, upset stomach or other cues. —Notice where I am trying to do everything on my own steam or in my own power. —Notice where "good enough" could be good enough and stop there.
PRACTICES	—Observe *Sabbath*: take one day in seven to refrain from work and enjoy the gifts of God, family and friends. —Pray the *Liturgy of the Hours* as a way of enjoying little rests in the middle of my work day.

again. After all, raises, grades, bonuses and promotions don't go to slackers. They go to those hungry enough to hit the pavement, knuckle down and burn the candle at both ends.

Work is a huge emphasis for Americans. We get more kudos for being insanely busy, overextended and on the edge of exhaustive collapse than we ever get for taking a much-needed rest. I recently offered spiritual formation training to the staff of a well-known Christian organization. I found these ministry leaders depleted, anxious and unrested. Few to none of them took their full vacation time. They were aware of and self-reproachful about their workaholism, but they didn't know how it could be different. Somehow or other, overwork had become a badge of honor that reflected spiritual zeal.

Perhaps you have heard the phrase "There's no rest for the wicked" (which originates in Isaiah 48:22). But there is no rest for the good either. Christians reward overwork as much as anyone. And church leaders must struggle to model alternatives to the work addictions that ruin families, damage souls and sometimes kill us.

In our insanely busy world, with all the 24/7 pressure to drive and strive, weekends are no longer time to rest but time to catch up on more work! We work in the garden, wash the car, do the books, take the kids to soccer games and go shopping. Vacations aren't restful either. We make elaborate efforts to travel somewhere exotic— and then take laptops to stay connected to work so that we can earn our identity while we play. It's how we sustain the myth that we are indispensable. External rhythms of Sabbath, vacation and holidays are spaces vouchsafed to us for rest. But we are so unrestful at our cores that these rhythms guarantee nothing. We may simply use them to impress others (and ourselves) that we have been there and done that.

Take a memory inventory. What memories keep you enslaved to earning an identity? Were you rewarded for not being who you are? Did you feel unwanted? Unworthy? Like you didn't belong? Bring your memories to Jesus one by one. Spend part of your rest time allowing him to touch you.

The 1981 film *Chariots of Fire* is based on the true story of Eric Liddell and Harold Abrahams, two British sprinters who qualified for the 1924 Olympic Games. Abrahams determined to prove himself to a prejudiced, British old-boy network. His goal was to break a world record, thus validating his worth and proving his identity. Abrahams hoped that being a winner would gain him access to the halls of influence and power. In the movie, a fellow runner, Lord Andrew Lindsay, says, "Think what it [winning] means to a man like Harold. For Harold it's a matter of life and death." Just before his race, Abrahams confesses to a friend, "In one hour's time I'll be out there again . . . with ten lonely seconds to justify my whole existence." For Abrahams, there was no rest. Life was a race. It was self-justifying work. Everything boiled down to what he accomplished and what people thought of him.

Liddell, a devoted Christian, believed running was an experience of who he was in God. In the movie he tells his sister, "I believe that God made me for a purpose. . . . But he also made me fast, and when I run, I feel his pleasure." Liddell's core identity was rooted in God rather than running. He was not out to prove who he was. So when his qualifying heat was scheduled for Sunday (the day he observed Sabbath), Liddell felt free not to compete. Upbraided by the Prince of Wales and the British Olympic Committee, Liddell remarked that obeying God mattered more to him than a race. At the moment of impasse, Lord Lindsay, who had already won a silver medal, offered Liddell his place in the 400-meter race, which was not run on Sunday. Liddell won gold.

Liddell wasn't a slave to earning an identity, but neither was he in bondage to rules. A friend of mine knew Eric Liddell. During World War II, she was interred by the Japanese in a prisoner-of-war camp in China, where Liddell was also incarcerated. My friend told me that in that bleak and frightening place, Liddell organized sports and games for children whenever

How do you spend most of your time off?

the guards allowed it. And he did it on Sunday! Liddell knew who he was at the core of his being. He knew how to work, how to rest and how to break the rules. He knew that races and games in a POW camp could be of God—even on Sunday.

Few of us think twice about saying no to anything we want to do on the Sabbath. We are devotees of the Protestant work ethic, with its adages commending full-throttle living:

- "The early bird catches the worm."
- "No pain, no gain."
- "Early to bed, early to rise makes a man healthy, wealthy and wise."
- "A penny saved is a penny earned."
- "Time is money."
- "There's no such thing as a free lunch."
- "Work won't kill you."
- "Do your best."
- "Never give up."
- "The one with the most toys wins."

These bits of advice make us a productive nation. But they also make us a restless, driven and exhausted people. Ask us what we would do if we had one extra hour in our day, and the vast majority of us will say, "I'd sleep." Just because we choose our work doesn't mean we aren't slaves to it.

IF YOU AREN'T RESTING, YOU ARE A SLAVE TO SOMETHING

Slaves have no Sabbath, no rest, no time off, no six-day work week, no reprieve. Slaves exist to work. They can work themselves sick or work themselves to death, but stopping work is not an option. When there is no rest, bodies, as well as hearts and spirits, collapse. You may not feel like a "slave," per se. But if you compulsively work—

if you cannot stop, cannot take a vacation, cannot turn off the email—you aren't free. You are a slave with an income.

Work is a good thing. God gave Adam and Eve work to do. But God never intended for anyone to be a slave. He didn't intend for work to be the way people form identities or find favor with God. Work was to be an expression of who human beings already are. They are already loved and immeasurably important. Adam and Eve didn't need to be anxious about nonstop productivity. They had nothing to prove and nothing to hide, and they could simply be themselves, naked and unashamed. Each evening, Adam and Eve stopped work! They spent time with their Creator, reveling in the satisfying rhythms of work and rest. They reveled in the intimacy that grows when there is time for friendship. Yet eventually Adam and Eve made choices that make them unrestful and no longer free to be naked and unashamed. In fact, they became so uncomfortable in their own skin that they worked overtime—sewing fig-leaf aprons—to cover up their anxiety and hide who they were.

From that moment on, the never-ending work project of proving our worth takes over. Attempting to cover our restlessness and insecurity, we carefully sew together our fig leaves of education, success and productivity. In the process, it is easy to become slaves to work, forgetting that it is only free people who can rest. When God's people were slaves in Egypt, they were worked to death. God saw their misery—no vacation, no weekend, no Sabbath, no rest—and he came and set them free! And yet it wasn't long before these freed slaves wanted to go back to their slavery. At least it was familiar and didn't require time alone with God or doing something new and risky.

We aren't thinking of slavery when we ask others, "What do you do?" But the recent flood of job losses has made answering this question an exercise in vulnerability. It is hard to validate your existence without a job. Jobs define identities and bolster self-worth. No wonder people try to become indispensable at work. Being jobless makes us feel restless, fearful, overvigilant, compulsive and in need of fig leaves. An identity based on doing is always precarious and unrestful. And it is not what God intended.

I know this is true. But honestly, when I wanted a self and didn't know how to find one, work was the path I took. I said yes to everything and everyone that made me feel useful and productive. The yeses felt good and propped up my identity. Yes, I would serve on the seminary Wives' Board while my husband was at Gordon-Conwell. Yes, I would organize the craft fair. Yes, I could teach the class. Pushing my limits with yeses proved my worth and value. Saying yes meant I'd be included and not miss out! God knows I didn't want to miss out. Missing out meant loss, loss meant grief, and grieving wasn't anything I had time to do.

So I juggled more and more balls. I worked full time, led retreats across the country, took meals to sick friends, led small groups, hosted long-term guests and on and on. These were all good things, but the limits of my energy, time and talents caught up with me. I started dropping balls and disappointing others. The illusion that I could go everywhere, know everyone and do almost anything—the myth that there was no finiteness to my time and energy—caught up with me. I had confused having a self with being indispensable.

I knew I was a "human doing" out of control. Riddled with insecurity, I had said yes to too many things. Now unable to focus, I couldn't see what I enjoyed about my compulsive doing. I was so restless I wondered if I had attention deficit disorder. Exercise, rest, shared healthy meals, human touch and hearing God's voice all seemed like luxuries, not staples.

So I went on a "no spontaneous yeses" streak. Even the simplest request I answered with, "Let me get back to you." People didn't like it. They would say, "You're good at this. What do you mean you can't?" It was hard to let people down. Yet with each no, I reclaimed some space in my life—space I hoped would relieve my restlessness and compulsiveness.

But it didn't work. I said no to one kind of doing only to clean out closets, read books, work crossword puzzles, paint a room or organize photo albums. I thumbed through catalogs, overate, watched movies, fantasized about how to redecorate the house and shopped. I wasn't resting. I was simply letting other behaviors sap my time, money and energy, just like my work had done.

How do you like to spend your Sabbath?

I had no idea at the time that my "not work" behaviors were actually what are called "soft addictions." Not long ago I read that 91 percent of us have soft addictions. Soft addictions are behaviors we cannot stop. They are ways we overuse good things: food, caffeine, exercise, TV, the Internet, texting, Facebook, work and shopping. None of these things are bad in and of themselves. But when we can't get through a day or a week without a fix of buying something or playing video games, we have a soft addiction. If you want to know what your soft addictions are, notice how giving up some of the things you count on to cope affects you. What happens to the time that is freed up? People don't usually die from soft addictions. But my soft addictions never really helped me live freely and gracefully. I could snack with gusto, walk regularly with friends, drink my morning cup of "solace"—and remain grumpy and depleted.

JESUS' INVITATION TO REST

When I came upon Jesus' tantalizing invitation to live freely and lightly, I knew it was what I needed to say yes to. Here was a picture of the restful identity I sought: "Are you tired? Worn out?

Burned out on religion? Come to me. Get away with me and you'll recover your life. I'll show you how to take a real rest. Walk with me and work with me—watch how I do it. Learn the unforced rhythms of grace. I won't lay anything heavy or ill-fitting on you. Keep company with me and you'll learn to live freely and lightly" (Mt 11:28-30 *The Message*).

Jesus' job was huge. The interruptions, tests, criticism and needs never let up. He had to learn to pace himself when rest wasn't easy to come by. Mark writes that so many people were coming and going that Jesus and the disciples did not even have a chance to eat. This kind of schedule is familiar to most of us. Yet Jesus knew how to stop. He knew how to choose rest. He invited his coworkers, "Come with me by yourselves to a quiet place and get some rest" (Mk 6:31). Jesus knew when to say no to need so he could stay connected with God. Because he was deeply at rest in who he was, Jesus could resist the constant temptation to do something to prove who he was.

I longed to live by such "unforced rhythms of grace," but my only rhythm seemed to be *Presto*! I determined to watch how Jesus did it. The first thing I saw was that Jesus lived by the rhythms God set up in Genesis 1. Neither the Father nor the Son was defined by constant activity and perpetual motion. Neither worked 24/7. Their identities weren't propped up by what they produced.

GOD'S COSMIC RHYTHMS

I love the creative process and know all about being compulsive. But the Creator wasn't restless or compelled to keep at it day and night. God tackled the job of creating in chunks, leaving rhythmic space between evening and morning, between beginnings and endings. At the end of each day's work, we read, there was evening and morning: the first (or second, or third) day (Gen 1:5, 8, 13, 19, 23, 31). God imprinted the creational rhythms of work and rest on the cosmos because these rhythms already existed in him. God's way of existing was—and is—restful.

That does not mean God gets tired or sleepy. God rests in who he is and what he has done. He relishes work. But after six days of working, God rested from all his work. "Then God blessed the seventh day and made it holy, because on it he rested from all the work of creating that he had done" (Gen 2:3). The seventh day syncopated the created order with the rhythm of God's existence: work is not everything, and rest is not optional. The One who holds the universe together by the power of his pinkie has a restful identity that is not derived from work alone. God's unforced, rhythmic gifts honor both our talents and our vulnerabilities. They address the natural limits of bodies and minds.

A TRANSCENDENT ANCHOR IN THE MIDST OF DOING

Because rest is fundamental to God, it is fundamental to the well-being of all creation. Rest is a transcendent anchor in the midst of doing. God wants us to rest because he knows a society that encourages overwork is no different from a society that encourages lying, murder, stealing and promiscuity. Work reflects God's image, but it can also be so destructive to our life that God says, "Six days you shall labor and do all your work, but the seventh day is a Sabbath to the LORD your God. . . . In six days the Lord made the heavens and the earth, the sea, and all that is in them, but he rested on the seventh day" (Ex 20:9-11).

God invites and even commands us to trust him to manage the world for twenty-four hours each week without our labor. Sabbath is the day that reminds us who we are. We don't have to justify our existence by striving and driving. We aren't less of a contribution to the world because we honor our limits and produce less one day a week. We are God's well-loved creatures, created in his beautiful image, no matter what we do or don't do. We didn't earn this identity as the beloved; it was bestowed like a kiss from God before we ever left the womb. Keeping Sabbath is one way we enter into the restfulness of who we are in God.

REST: A PLACE THAT CAN BE MISSED

The book of Hebrews was written to a group of people who, in the difficulty and press of life, made rest and Sabbath negotiable rhythms. Under Nero, observing Sabbath could lose you your job and then your life. Disheartened and disaffected believers apparently felt it was enough to believe, pray and go to worship when they could sneak it in. In the face of these realities, the author to the Hebrews went overboard in exhorting Christ's followers to enter God's rest: "Therefore, since the promise of entering his rest still stands, let us be careful that none of you be found to have fallen short of it" (Heb 4:1). In Hebrews 4:1-11, the word *rest* occurs ten times in eleven verses. I suspect the writer of Hebrews emphasized rest because ignoring its practice makes us more vulnerable to the hardships of life. Sabbath rest is meant to fortify us for times of trouble and nourish us in times of depletion. The author of Hebrews didn't want his readers to be like the Israelites who saw God part the Red Sea and then failed to enter God's rest. He didn't want their hearts to go "astray" (Heb 3:10). He wanted them anchored to the rest of God.

It is not enough to know that God made the Sabbath. It is not even enough to believe in the Giver of rest. To have rest, we must not neglect it. We have to stop. Lay all that deadly doing down. Enter the unforced rhythms of grace. Repent of all the self-justifying and fig-leaf-making work—both good and bad—that keeps us depleted, exhausted, distant from God and others and running on empty.

Risk entering Jesus' rest so that you can learn what it means to live freely and lightly. The prophet Isaiah put it like this: "In repentance and rest is your salvation, in quietness and trust is your strength, but you would have none of it" (Is 30:15).

TO EXPERIENCE REST, WE MUST BE INTENTIONAL

Rest undoes the world's propensity to define people by what they produce. It also offers us the freedom to be "body people"—that is, people who know that they have bodies and resolve to take care of them. In the press of work, I can forget that I am a body person. I sit too long in one position. I don't get up and walk around. And then I beg my husband to massage my neck.

I suspect that the paucity of rest in our depleted lives has actually boosted the spa care industry. After all, when our shoulders get tight and our stomachs churn from overwork, we realize we aren't some sort of disembodied spirits. We have bodies with aches and pains. But we don't just *have* bodies; we *are* bodies. Bodies come with daily limits and daily needs. Bodies are not machines that need a tune-up every forty thousand miles. Bodies require daily attention and care. Bodies need to be heard and trusted. As we learn to notice what is going on in our bodies, we can begin to detect things like lethargy, pain, escape strategies, energy levels, caffeine dependency, addictions, signs of burnout, exhaustion levels and relationship anxieties. These messages are meant to be taken seriously.

Take a body inventory. What do your shoulders feel like? Your neck? Where do you hold tension in your body? What is needed to release this tension? Ask someone you trust to touch your body and pray for you.

I don't have to look far to see the evidence of my body's limits. The water bottle sitting beside me on the counter reminds me just how far I can go without a drink, a splash or a refill. Wherever I go, the water bottle goes too. I wash my hands from it. Drink from it. Splash the back of my neck when I am hot. And put it against my face when I have a hot flash. It's my own little spa in a bottle.

It's nothing like the old European spas where sick, ailing, broken, injured, exhausted and depressed people traveled to "take the waters." At those spas people slowed down, ate simply, drank tons of water, and bathed in mineral baths or hot springs. They sweated out toxins in saunas. They cleaned out pores with body wraps. And they waited for rest to cure them. Spas provided ways to cooperate with the body's healing process. It didn't happen fast, and you couldn't squeeze it in between appointments.

Few of us can manage this sort of spa experience anymore. It's a luxury for which we don't have time or money. We go full-tilt until our bodies break down, and then we look at our options. Can I fit in a massage? Do I need a physical therapist? Can I take a few days' sick leave? (This is the only "rest" some of us ever give our bodies.) Can I get away for the weekend?

These options can offer your body a cure and much-needed rest. But there is more to rest than a brief stint on a massage table or a weekend at the beach. If that were all we needed for health, God would not have instituted Sabbath or extended an invitation to rest.

The body-satisfying, soul-replenishing rest to which God calls me happens when: (1) *I pay attention to my physical limits* and the toll that work has taken on my soul. It means noticing how both body and soul become depleted, grimy, wounded, overextended, and in need of renewal and cleansing. Once my body has my attention, (2) *I can become intentional about creating space* for treatment, healing and renewal. Just as I make appointments to see friends and get my hair cut, I can make space for the life that comes from the rhythms of rest or Sabbath. Finally, with that space, (3) *God can reach out to me* with his healing hands. He can massage truth into my aching heart and throbbing body. In that space, God can touch lies with truth. As I submit to Jesus' touch, I lean into the goodness of my created being and let him detox my need to earn an identity. I recognize healing as I become more and more able to live freely and lightly.

A physical therapist knows where to massage to bring increased blood and lymph circulation so that tension and tightness lift. Jesus' touch is no less curing. His touch healed and restored men, women and children. His touch released tension, lifted burdens, and brought truth and restfulness to body and soul. Jesus knows just where to touch us to cleanse the toxins, disease and dirt from our lives. Jesus touched and still touches people with a love out of which we cannot fall. Within that love, there is rest and the freedom to be naked and unashamed.

REST AND SABBATH ARE WAYS WE LISTEN AND MEND

Rest and Sabbath aren't legalistic ways we earn God's favor. They are creational rhythms providing space for depleted people to be renewed and refreshed in love and work. Sabbath and rest create space for listening to two things: our bodies and Jesus.

1. Listen to our bodies by setting aside our to-do lists. It means noticing things like headaches, stiff necks, sweaty palms, upset stomachs, and likes and dislikes. Become aware of your soft addictions and the memories that play back in tapes you can't turn off. Bodies, not just minds, store memories that shape us.

2. Listen and watch Jesus. Jesus was often ridiculed for the freedoms he exercised on the Sabbath (Mk 2:23-26; Lk 13:10-14; Jn 5:10; 9:14). Rather than taking care of the Sabbath with little rules and rituals, Jesus made it clear that the "sabbath was made for humankind, and not humankind for the sabbath" (Mk 2:27 NRSV). The Sabbath takes care of us. Its practice offers us health and connection with God and the family of faith, rather than only our own tiny "God and me" notions. Sabbath keeps us from drifting away. It is evidence to us and the world that we are not slaves to our to-do lists. We are God's cherished treasures—treasures worth taking care of. Sabbath is a way we honor our limits and notice our need for restoration and re-creation. We can worship, play games, take naps, make love, enjoy good food, take hikes and read books.

If you work on Sunday, you can still set aside other days or times for rest. The world tries to convince us that there is no time for rest. But Sabbath rest can be entered anytime and anywhere. God's promised place of rest does exist. The author of Hebrews wrote, "There remains, then, a Sabbath-rest for the people of God; for anyone who enters God's rest also rests from their works, just as God did from his. Let us, therefore, make every effort to enter that rest" (Heb 4:9-11).

Ironically, entering into rest and Sabbath takes effort. One of the "laws of infernal dynamics" is "The energy required to move an object in the correct direction, or put it in the right place, will be more than you wish to expend but not so much as to make the task impossible." In other words, it is easier to just keep on keeping on than it is to stop. But without the God-given rhythms of rest and Sabbath, I doubt the church will ever be able to show anyone how to live "freely and lightly." We, like everyone else, will work, work, work to prop up our identities through overdoing. Then, sapped of energy and depleted in body and soul, we will take sick days for rest.

The antidote to 24/7 doing is as close as this evening. In Christ we can let go of self-justifying work and rest. Jesus has completed the Father's work of redemption. You are not a slave, but free. And right now Jesus sits at the right hand of God, praying for you to come to him and recover your life. Keep company with him and embrace the restful, at-ease-in-your-own-skin identity he

How can you begin to reclaim time in each day as a mini-Sabbath rest?

offers you. "My Presence will go with you, and I will give you rest" (Ex 33:14).

5

Invitation to Weep

The range of what we think and do is limited by what we
fail to notice: And because we fail to notice that we fail to notice—
there is little we can do to change until we notice how
failing to notice shapes our thoughts and deeds.

R. D. LAING

I am bold in saying this, but I believe that no one is ever changed,
either by doctrine, by hearing the Word, or by the preaching or teaching
of another, unless the affections are moved by these things. . . . In other
words, there is never any great achievement by the things of religion
without a heart deeply affected by those things.

JONATHAN EDWARDS

MY NEIGHBOR FROM PARIS and I valiantly struggle to carry on conversations. When Christine's English flounders and my high-school French fails me, we move to other topics. Recently, I tried to convey my distress over my mother's Alzheimer's disease. I chose small words for a huge grief and was not sure Christine was getting anything I said. But when her eyes filled up with tears,

FOLLOWING GOD'S INVITATION TO WEEP

INVITATION	To open myself to the naturalness of tears as Jesus did, learning to feel and weep over the things that move God's heart.
SCRIPTURE	"Jesus wept" (Jn 11:35). "The LORD regretted that he had made human beings on the earth, and his heart was deeply troubled" (Gen 6:6).
ROADBLOCKS	—The belief that tears are a sign of weakness that occurs in women and children —Fear of what others will think of me if I cry —Stuffing of grief and its emotions —Discomfort in the presence of those who weep —Living in my head; an underdeveloped emotional intelligence
AWARENESS	—Notice others' pain, not attempting to fix it but rather to feel it. —Notice where my heart is moved to compassion. —Notice what happens to me when I feel deeply hurt or grieved.
PRACTICES	—Practice *compassion*, a spiritual practice that leads to caring for others. Practice being with someone in pain. Hold their sorrow with the hands of God. —Let my compassion move me to *action*. How might I act on God's behalf?

something inside me relaxed into friendship, because I knew that we were both fluent in the universal language of tears. Her tears and two words—"Courage, Adele; courage"—were balm enough in a painful moment.

Taboos on crying are well-enforced in Western cultures. Boys are often ridiculed for tears and told, "Crying is for sissies," or "Big boys don't cry." Women are sometimes shamed with comments like "Don't be a crybaby," or "Tears are so manipulative." In some specific situations, of course, tears are accepted or at least tolerated. We give ourselves and others permission to weep at bodily injury or the death of a loved one. But if we let the tears linger too long, we find out how unacceptable they are. Tears are something to get over so we can get on with living. I was reminded of this recently when I told a friend that I was writing a chapter on the invitation to weep. "You have got to be kidding!" he snorted. "Who wants to cry?"

Avoiding tears is standard operating procedure for many. In *A League of Their Own*, Coach Dugan of the Rockford Peaches makes the statement, "There's no crying in baseball." Athletes, whether men or women, are supposed to be models of strength and determination. When they mess up, they suck it up and hang tough. No tears! But any Red Sox coach, player or fan will tell you that it's not true. We've all had to blow our noses, dry our puffy eyes, throw cold water on our faces and regain our composure. And Chicago Cubs fans have built a cult-like camaraderie upon the foundation of their tears since 1908 (the last time the Cubs won the World Series).

Can you weep and not move into self-condemnation?

Tears find their way into every venue of life, from the smallest private playing fields to the largest public arenas. Still, we don't want to be caught crying. And if we are caught crying—God forbid!—we feel so embarrassed, uncomfortable and conspicuous that we start apologizing: "I'm sorry. I'll be all right. Just give me a minute."

But maybe we should go ahead and have a good cry. The penchant to hold back tears can be onerous, unhelpful and ill-advised. When we tell someone to stop crying, we ask them to abort a basic, God-given, human response. Perhaps without knowing it, we communicate, *Your feelings are wrong. You are making me uncomfortable.*

Tears are natural. They are uniquely engineered by God in the human sympathetic nervous system. Emotional tears—not reflex tears that occur when you get something in your eye—have a specifically therapeutic chemical makeup. They include higher concentrations of proteins, manganese, prolactin and adrenocorticotropic hormone (ACTH), one of the best-known indicators of stress. They also release enkephalin, which is an endorphin and natural painkiller. How remarkable that God has hardwired us to weep when we come to the end of our resources! Tears wash away the buildup of toxic chemicals that accrue under stress. They are part of the process that can restore psychological and physiological balance. Tears ease the pain of broken bodies and broken hearts. As they wash down our faces, tears

- heal
- signal the end of our resources
- improve social support
- inhibit aggression
- elicit compassion
- minimize pain
- establish solidarity
- move people to action
- open the heart to God and others

William Frey, author of *Crying: The Mystery of Tears*, writes, "It is likely that crying survived the pressures of natural selection because it has some survival value." Indeed. This makes me wonder whether God originally designed tears as a way to express our need for cleansing from the consequences of sin as well. Traditional Eastern Orthodox theology asserts that tears cleanse, renew and make way for the kingdom. When sin and the brokenness of the world give rise to godly sorrow, our hearts soften toward God and birth compassion for others. Kimberley Christine Patton writes that, in Eastern Orthodox thought, "Rather than depleting the weeper and the well of human experience, tears generate the kingdom of God." The desert fathers believed that tears open a path to virtue, making us clean, empty vessels that God can fill with prayer and his presence. But it is not just the ancients who write of their experiences with godly sorrow. Richard Foster writes that he was vouchsafed the "grace" of tears, deep heart weeping, while he mourned the sins of God's people and thanked God for his love and mercy.

The curative relief of tears hit me hardest at a time when I couldn't weep. I was sick with grief and loss, but no matter how much I hurt, I couldn't seem to join those who "go out weeping" (Ps 126:6). I longed for tears to quench my parched heart and cleanse the toxins from my soul. I wanted the catharsis of tears, but for twelve months, no tears came. During that pain-riddled

What do you want to weep about but find that you can't? What do you want to say to God about that?

season, well-meaning friends tried to cheer me up. They reminded me that the fruit of the Spirit is joy. I knew it was true. But what was I to say when suffering was more of a companion than joy? I didn't think I mistrusted God. I wasn't unwilling to follow. I simply needed grieving room. Eventually the tears returned, but they were not for my own sorrows. They were for the sadness of a friend. What a relief it was to cry.

TEARS ARE BIBLICAL

The Bible doesn't teach us that life is only sweetness and light. And God does not tell the brokenhearted to edit their emotions, "buck up" or "hang tough." When we reach the end of our resources, God supplies a watery gift that can cleanse, release and heal. We know this because the pages of the Bible are wet with weeping. *Young's Concordance* cites some 690 references in Scripture that are associated with crying. And a search on the website bible.org (http://bible.org) pulls up 894 references to crying. People cry in slavery, defeat, despair and exile. People weep through loss, betrayal, death and sin. They shed tears in anger, doubt and confusion over the ways of God. Fathers and mothers weep. Children weep. Infertile women and virgins weep. Patriarchs, priests and prophets weep. Cities weep. Kings weep. Armies weep. The disciples weep. Mary weeps. The elders in Ephesus weep. Paul weeps. John weeps. Some weep for themselves, and some weep for the profound suffering of others. Some cry tears of repentance. Some weep for seeing the world as God sees it. When people feel forgotten by God, they cry out. When they fear that God won't come through on his promises, they weep. Weeping can open us to God even as it supplies evidence, should we need it, that Eden is no more.

- "Ah, God, listen to my prayer, my cry—open your ears. Don't be callous; just look at these tears of mine" (Ps 39:12 *The Message*).

- "I am worn out calling for help; my throat is parched. My eyes fail, looking for my God" (Ps 69:3).

- "I'm tired of all this—so tired. My bed has been floating forty days and nights on the flood of my tears. My mattress is soaked, soggy with tears" (Ps 6:6-8 *The Message*).

Authentic worshipers seek God in desperate realities: body-racking pain, exile, earthquakes, oppression, disease, poverty, heartbreak, betrayal and warfare. The Hebrew Psalter offered Israel—and now us—a way to lament broken realities, unmet expectations and doubt in the presence of our Creator. Dan Allender writes, "Lament cuts through insincerity, strips pretense, and reveals the raw nerve of trust that angrily approaches the throne of grace and then kneels in awed, robust wonder." In laments, ambivalence and sorrow are poured out under the gaze of God. We

cry out, with the father of a son brought to Jesus for healing: "Lord,
I believe; help my unbelief!" (Mk 9:24 NKJV). Often weeping becomes part of the storm crest of a search for God, answers and
relief. "I'm on a diet of tears—tears for breakfast, tears for supper,"
wrote the psalmist. "All day long people knock at my door, pester-
ing, 'Where is this God of yours?'" (Ps 42:3 *The Message*).

Time and again, when I have reached
the end of my rope, I have prayed these
words or reached for Jeremiah's uncen-
sored poems in Lamentations. Here the
raw nerve of my weeping finds solidarity
with other worshipers: "I am . . . familiar
with misery under the rod of his fury.
[God] has led and guided me into darkness, not light. . . . He has walled me in

> *Listen to the things
> that make you weep.
> What do you want
> to say to God about
> those things?*

so that I cannot escape; he has weighed me down with chains;
even when I shout for help, he shuts out my prayer. . . . I have been
deprived of peace, I have forgotten what happiness is and thought,
'My lasting hope in Yahweh is lost'" (Lam 3:1-2, 7-8, 17-18 NJB).

Sometimes I feel this grim. Jeremiah gives me a way to pray my
pain as well as risk on God. In the silent abyss of grief, as doubts
ebb and flow, Jeremiah opens for me a listening space where I can
risk trust. "This is what I shall keep in mind and so regain some
hope: Surely Yahweh's mercies are not over, his deeds of faithful
love not exhausted; every morning they are renewed; great is his
faithfulness! 'Yahweh is all I have,' I say to myself, 'and so I shall
put my hope in him.' . . . It is good to wait in silence for Yahweh to
save" (Lam 3:21-24, 26 NJB). This is the one hope Lamentations offers. So I "wait in silence" for Yahweh's faithfulness in saving.

God's sorrow for humankind runs like a thread through the redemption story. God is not immune to human suffering. Just six
chapters into the Bible—and before we see evidence of any human
tears—we find a grieving Creator: "God saw that human evil was

Can you weep over the places where you are stuck and the things that you are denying, rationalizing or blaming on others?

out of control. . . . God was sorry that he had made the human race in the first place; it broke his heart" (Gen 6:6 *The Message*). This is the Bible's first record of God's outward expression of emotion and vulnerability. The relationship El Shaddai had hoped to have with his human creatures lies within a hair's breadth of ruin. Human freedom had ushered in acres of pain, betrayal, deceit, murder, polygamy and other ills. And God responded with grief (Eph 4:30). This divine sorrow is not the result of a self-indulgent temper. God doesn't have tantrums, mood swings or fits of despair. God's grief is "clean," an aching with unchanging and steadfast love for those he loves the dearest.

I was struck by God's grief when I read about an incident that happened after September 11. In January 2003, Reverend Parker and her colleagues were working at the morgue in New York City's Bellevue Hospital, sorting through the exploded remains of September 11 victims. As they worked, each one independently and repeatedly reported hearing a droning noise that they couldn't explain. Each one interpreted this low, mournful sound as that of "God crying." When asked to explain why God might be weeping, Parker replied, "My sense was that those whom he loved the dearest had been ravaged and hated and destroyed by those whom he loved the dearest."

In Genesis 6, God grieves over the mess his most beloved have made. And in the mess he finds one man who is different: Noah, the ark builder, who rides the flood of God's tears for forty days and nights. Yes, it is poetic license to say that God rained tears, cleansing the earth and flooding out all that was causing him unspeakable pain and sorrow. But look what happened. After the mournful rain, God was free to re-create a joyful new beginning.

"The fountains of the deep and the windows of the heavens were closed, the rain from the heavens was restrained, and the waters receded" gradually (Gen 8:2-3 ESV). A new day begins with blessing and the promise that "as long as the earth endures," the Creator's mercy will never cease (Gen 8:22). Out of God's grief come joy and the promise that this cycle will continue for the duration of human history. Grief's open wound will be stanched, and the raw nerve of pain will not endure.

What limitations, inadequacies, imperfections, and poverty or thinness of soul make you weep? What do these limits and imperfections reveal?

"Weeping may stay for the night, but rejoicing comes in the morning" (Ps 30:5). After night, the dawn. After mourning, the morning.

GOD MOVES INTO THE NEIGHBORHOOD

God started over with Noah. But free human beings quickly accrue a peck of sins and sorrows. Again and again and again the Holy One, vulnerable to the grief and sorrows of his beloved tribe, reaches down to repair and restore. When reaching down doesn't solve human brokenness, God comes down himself, in human flesh. God moves into the neighborhood and walks in our shoes. God incarnate was in solidarity with human sin and misery. Jesus was wounded for our transgressions and crushed for our iniquities (Is 53:4-5).

The Apostles' Creed puts God's vulnerability succinctly. Christ "suffered under Pontius Pilate, was crucified, dead, and buried." Every time I say the creed, I want to put a period after the words "he suffered." Jesus suffered. Period. Linger here before moving on to the rest: "under Pontius Pilate he was crucified, dead, and buried." In Jesus, God stepped into our brokenness and bore our sufferings in flesh and bone. According to the author of Hebrews, he laments with loud cries and tears, which is not the usual picture we have of Jesus. But here it is: "During the days of Jesus' life on earth, he offered up prayers and petitions with fervent cries and tears to the one who could save him from death, and he was heard because of his reverent submission. Son though he was, he learned obedience from what he suffered and, once made perfect, he became the source of eternal salvation for all who obey him" (Heb 5:7-9).

Jesus related to God through tears, and he invites us to do the same. Even a cursory look at Jesus and his teaching reveals a God who is at home in the watery world of tears.

- Jesus taught that people who weep and mourn are "blessed" (Mt 5:4). They are on the right path, and it is well with them, for the God of all comfort has made the kingdom especially accessible through tears.

- Jesus wept over the loss and terror of war and oppression. He knew that under Vespasian and Titus, the Roman army would raze the temple and Jerusalem's streets would run with blood. So, "as he approached Jerusalem and saw the city, [Jesus] wept over it" (Lk 19:41).

- When Jesus came upon a funeral procession for a woman who had lost her son, he was moved to act. Intending to mend her heartache, "he said to her, 'Don't cry.' Then he went over and touched the coffin. . . . The dead son sat up and began talking" (Lk 7:14-15 *The Message*).

Another glimpse of Jesus' solidarity with us in our tears occurs when his friend Lazarus got sick. His sisters, Mary and Martha, sent word to Jesus to come quickly. But Jesus didn't. Instead, he came four days after Lazarus died. Mary and Martha met Jesus separately but with the identical laments: "If you had been here, my brother would not have died" (Jn 11:21, 32). *If you had:* three small words carry the weight of human expectation. Things could have been different. They had expected more.

Jesus offered Martha the comfort of a new understanding: "Your brother will rise again" (v. 23) he said, adding, "I am the resurrection and the life. The one who believes in me will live, even though they die; and whoever lives by believing in me will never die" (vv. 25-26). Then Jesus asked her whether she believed this. To receive the comfort Jesus offered, Martha had to let go of her expectations about what Jesus should have done. And Martha seems to have done this. She risked that in Jesus the seed of grief could flower into joy and hope and life— not just at the last day, but now.

What do the sorrows of God and the tears of Jesus and the grief of the Holy Spirit offer you?

But this isn't the end of the story. When Mary fell weeping at his feet, Jesus didn't respond with resurrection theology. "When Jesus saw her weeping, and the Jews who had come along with her also weeping, he was deeply moved in spirit and troubled. 'Where have you laid him?' he asked. 'Come and see, Lord,' they replied. Jesus wept. Then the Jews said, 'See how he loved him!'" (Jn 11:33-36).

The raw nerve of Mary's tears and lament elicited a different response. Jesus was troubled and moved to tears. The mourner's sorrows and unmet expectations had a visceral impact on him. Mary's anguish rolled out of Jesus' eyes and down his face. In the face of death, the Man of Sorrows grieved with others. But his tears were not helpless tears. Jesus' tears, like God's tears, were evidence that he would act. The last enemy, death, may snatch away, but the Man of Sorrows is also the resurrection and the life. When Jesus raised Lazarus from death to life, he demonstrated and foreshadowed the great and incomprehensible joy that awaits all who follow him.

Following doesn't erase all sorrow. Following requires a risk: the belief that not only are death and sorrow not the worst things that can happen, but they are something that Jesus bears with us. Even the bad things the devil would use to destroy us or those we love can work for our good, our growth and God's glory. We know this because it was true of Jesus' excruciating path to Calvary. Watch the sorrows mount up:

- Jesus told his disciples, "I have eagerly desired to eat this Passover with you before I suffer" (Lk 22:15).

- When Jesus told the disciples that one of them would betray him, they began to be sorrowful (Mk 14:19).

- Judas went to betray Jesus, and it was night (Jn 14:30).

- Jesus shared his agony with his disciples. "And being in anguish, [Jesus] prayed more earnestly, and his sweat was like drops of blood falling to the ground" (Lk 22:44). "'My soul is overwhelmed with sorrow to the point of death,' he said to them. 'Stay here and keep watch'" (Mk 14:34).

- Jesus invited his friends to pray with him, only to find them sleeping, "exhausted from sorrow" (Lk 22:45).

- "Very truly I tell you, you will weep and mourn while the world rejoices. . . . Now is your time of grief, but I will see you again and you will rejoice, and no one will take away your joy" (Jn 16:20, 22).

Jesus is the Man of Sorrows—God vulnerable to our sin and pain. But Jesus is also the resurrection and the life—God who conquers death to mend our broken lives. If you want to know the power of his resurrection, you will need to stand in solidarity with Jesus and this hurting world. That means accepting his invitation to vulnerability, weeping and redemptive love.

INCARNATING THE GOOD, CLEAN TEARS OF JESUS

How do we live the paradoxes of suffering and joy, weeping and laughter, death and life?

1. *Receive the invitation to lament.* Tell the Man of Sorrows and the God of all comfort your sad tale. You don't need to understand every *why*. You don't need perfect words. Pray Jeremiah's laments or psalms. And when words fail you, remember that God's own Spirit "does our praying in and for us, making prayer out of our wordless sighs, our aching groans. He knows us far better than we know ourselves . . . and keeps us present before God. That's why we can be so sure that every detail in our lives of love for God is worked into something good" (Rom 8:26-28 *The Message*). Let the tears come. The Holy One collects tears and puts them in his book and bottle (Ps 56:8).

2. *Receive the invitation to put your pain and any senseless suffering of the world into the wounds of Jesus.* Jesus went to the cross so our sin and pain wouldn't just stick to us. It has somewhere to go, somewhere it can be transformed rather than just transmitted. There are no tears and sorrow too deep for God to transform. Don't stuff your pain down; put your pain into the wounded hands and feet of Jesus. Watch the divine judo that turned an act of unjust violence into hope and life. Carlo Maria Martini prays, "Grant that we may know you and know ourselves, that we may know the sufferings of humankind and the troubles with which many hearts have to struggle, so that we may have an ever new and truer experience of you."

3. *Receive the invitation to let others into your pain just as Jesus did.* Don't go it alone. Don't let tears or pain isolate you from others. Odd as it may seem, personal trials and sorrows are rarely meant to be purely private matters. They are meant to make us vulnerable to God and others. Jesus said to his disciples, "You are those who have stood by me in my trials" (Lk 22:28). Jesus didn't hibernate in his grief. He risked the vulnerability that could lead to deeper friendship, love and trust. Jesus received comfort from his friends because he was humble enough to let them in on his trials. Love and mercy and comfort aren't things we control or

earn. They are healing gifts that come to us when we have precisely nothing to give. When we are at the end of resources—when tears flow—that's when the healing and integrating love of others can flow in.

4. *Accept the invitation to weep with those who weep (Rom 12:15)*. The heart is stretched through suffering and enlarged, and this agony and enlarging of the heart prepare us to enter the anguish of others. By walking through the valley of the shadow ourselves, we become tender toward the pain of others. The world needs people who are fluent in the language of tears. Let those who suffer know, "You don't need to pay me to listen," and "I will help and act to relieve your pain in any way that I can and that is good for you." I have paid therapists to help me "get over" my pain. But I often wonder if I did this because I could find no one really willing to be patient with my pain over the long haul. I believe that weeping with others can make us healthier and more able to see the world as God does. Jesus stood in solidarity with us. He shared our pain. Christine's tears for my mother's Alzheimer's disease incarnated Jesus' own tears. Listen to the pain of others with resurrection hope.

5. *Say yes to God's invitation to let the world's tears move you to compassion and action*. It is easy to simply feel guilty about all the problems we cannot fix. But God doesn't intend for you to fix everything. Where do God's tears and compassion come most naturally to you? MADD (Mothers Against Drunk Drivers) began because a bereft mom stood in solidarity with other grieving moms. Rachel, currently a student at Wellesley College, spent the summer after her first year of college in Uganda. She came home and formed a nonprofit organization that cares for street children. When my friend Paul retired, he began committing months every year to Habitat for Humanity. My son works in Liberia because he wants to help a country recovering from years of civil war. I don't know where you weep with Jesus, but go there. Stand in solidarity

with him and with those in need of mercy, justice or reconciliation. The kingdom is near those who mourn. Let the world move you to tears of action.

6. *Receive the invitation to grieve your sin, receive cleansing and be transformed.* The apostle Paul wrote, "Godly sorrow brings repentance that leads to salvation and leaves no regret" (2 Cor 7:10). Scripture teems with choices worth regretting. But God promises to take everything the devil would use to undermine and destroy us and turn it to our good, our growth and his glory. He did it on Calvary, and he can do it for you. There is nothing Jesus won't forgive. You can weep away your remorse and guilt in his arms. He will never let you go.

TEARS ARE NOT THE FINAL WORD ON ANYTHING

For millennia, God's pity for his creation has moved him to action. The Creator comes to mend, heal, rescue and cure. Never does he flag with compassion fatigue. Never does he remove himself from our pain. He sees us through: from death to life and from tears to joy. "And I heard a loud voice from the throne saying, 'Look! God's dwelling place is now among the people, and he will dwell with them. They will be his people, and God himself will be with them and be their God. "He will wipe every tear from their eyes. There will be no more death" or mourning or crying or pain, for the old order of things has passed away.' He who was seated on the throne said, 'I am making everything new!'" (Rev 21:3-5).

How can you enter into the sorrow of Jesus for this world and weep with him?

Every tear goes. Every sorrow gets redeemed. Out of darkness, light. Out of death, life. Let us hold the paradox of suffering and death alongside the goodness and love of God (2 Cor 4:10). Let us risk serving Jesus with humility and tears like Paul (Acts 20:19).

Let us taste the quandary and reality of how to be sorrowful yet always rejoicing (2 Cor 6:9-10). For the melt-in-your-mouth sweet truth is this: tears may endure for the night, but joy comes in the morning.

6

Invitation to Admit I Might Be Wrong

Don't be afraid to admit that you are less than perfect.
It is this fragile thread that binds us together.

BRIAN G. DYSON

My own experience is that for human beings certainty does not exist,
has never existed, will not—in our finite states—
ever exist and moreover should not.
It is not a gift God has chosen
to give His creatures, doubtlessly wisely.

DANIEL TAYLOR

MY FRIEND GARY DICAMILLO turns failing companies around. He likes to say, "I have thirty-five years of mistakes behind me that can benefit companies that are in trouble." (Of course, he is not short on successes either.) He tells me the hardest thing about his job is getting the top performers and upper-management folks to admit that they need help before it's too late. These people think

FOLLOWING GOD'S INVITATION TO ADMIT I MIGHT BE WRONG

INVITATION	To humbly accept that my knowing is incomplete and that I don't have everything right so I can be open to hearing more from Jesus.
SCRIPTURE	"A person may think their own ways are right, but the LORD weighs the heart" (Prov 21:2). "All a person's ways seem pure to them, but motives are weighed by the LORD" (Prov 16:2).
ROADBLOCKS	—The tying of my identity to being right —The need to win every argument and be the expert in every discussion —The assumption that my study, sources or training set me above critique —A compulsive need to prove others wrong —Not backing down even when I might be wrong
AWARENESS	—Notice where I am unable to let something go uncorrected. —Notice when I get into arguments over details that may or may not be important. —Notice how I listen to and treat those I think are wrong. —Notice why it matters to me to be right. —Notice what happens when I don't defend myself and my opinions. —Notice how many friendships I have with folks I don't agree with.
PRACTICES	—Seek *humility*, which acknowledges the limits of my knowing and allows space for others to be on the journey. —Seek *teachability*, which allows me to keep on growing and changing. Being teachable opens me to the ideas and opinions of others. It does not mean I don't have my own beliefs, but that they are open to being refined and changed.

of themselves as smart, successful, "can do" people. And they don't like being wrong. Misjudging a trajectory, mismanaging a turn-around or miscalculating a return: these things don't happen on their watch.

To be fair, this sort of overconfidence dominates every aspect of the corporate ladder. Rank-and-file employees also overestimate their skills, strategies and judgments while minimizing their mistakes and faults. According to Alix Spiegel, our "optimistic" and overconfident national character accounts for our lack of accurate self-assessment. We would rather bluff, spin and manage an image than be wrong. We would rather be self-deceived than teachable. No wonder Gary has a job on his hands; he is dealing with impending disasters brought about by people who don't want to be wrong.

How does my need to be right affect my relationship with others? When has my refusal to admit that I could be wrong sabotaged or broken fellowship?

But it is not just business folks who spin to look right; politicians do too. Remember President Clinton's famous words on January 26, 1998: "I want to say one thing to the American people. I want you to listen to me. I'm going to say this again. I did not have sexual relations with that woman, Miss Lewinsky. I never told anybody to lie, not a single time—never. These allegations are false." But six months later, he owned up. Former Illinois governor Rod Blagojevich has yet to admit any of the indictments brought against him might be right. In 2008, a Rasmussen poll ranked Blagojevich the "least popular governor" in the nation. Yet Blagojevich conveyed his own assessment to the press at the Democratic National Convention in August 2008: "I think I'm a great governor." It remains to be seen if anyone can convince him that he might be wrong about that.

Business people and politicians—perhaps they are just the tip of the iceberg. People of religious persuasion, along with their pastors, priests, rabbis and imams, can hate to be wrong too. Furthermore, since religions claim to have a corner on the market of truth, the stakes are higher when it comes to getting it right. No wonder looking holy takes precedence over admitting and righting wrongs. Saving face becomes more important than admitting sexual scandals and subsequently attempting to set things right.

Admitting wrongdoing doesn't come naturally. People erupt in road rage because someone else drives wrong. Conventions become riots because someone else has it wrong. Kids and parents argue, and neither party thinks they are wrong. Overconfident students complain about their grades but are unwilling to admit their work wasn't as good as they thought. Academic hubris keeps teachers and scholars from admitting someone else's position might have more merit than their own or someone else's research may invalidate their findings.

Believing our own press and opinions in the face of credible evidence to the contrary has a long-standing history. The Smithsonian contains a leather-bound book called the Jefferson Bible. Using a razor, the third president of the United States cut out and arranged selected verses from the Gospels in chronological order to create a single narrative. Jesus' ethical teachings were left in, but his miracles and any references to the supernatural were left out. Jefferson decided where he was right and where the Bible had it wrong.

Most people are biased in favor of their own rightness even when the data proves them wrong. As a friend of mine says, "Often in error but never in doubt." All this begs the question: why are we so congenitally unable to see where we are wrong?

Lane Wallace, in an article for the *Atlantic,* writes that "the easy answer, of course, is simply that people are irrational" and so closely identified with their opinions that they are their opinions. Wallace cites a study which indicates that people tend to fend off any evidence that their strongly held beliefs are wrong. Compelling arguments and trustworthy data change nothing. In fact, re-

searchers found that exposing people to contradictory information actually entrenched people in their existing beliefs. If you are
wanting to change someone's opinion, this is not encouraging
news. It makes me want to enroll us all in a twelve-step program
where we work on step ten forever: "Continue to make a personal
inventory and when I am wrong, promptly admit it."

WHAT IS RIGHT? WHO IS WRONG?

The inability to admit we're wrong has a long history. When Satan
offered Adam and Eve the forbidden fruit, they ditched God's view
of what's right and believed their own
view. They determined what was right
for themselves. God came asking,
"What is this you have done?" (Gen
3:13). Rather than promptly admitting
wrong, Adam dodged with, "I was
afraid . . . so I hid" (v. 10). Then Adam
pushed the blame off on Eve; she was
the wrongdoer, not him. Eve didn't
want to be wrong either, so she said,
in essence, "The devil made me do it"
(v. 13).

*How do I respond when
I am criticized or
challenged about my
views? Can I respect and
give dignity to people
with whom I disagree?
How do I harbor
contempt for those from
different ethnic, racial,
economic, educational,
political or religious
backgrounds?*

The predilection to not be wrong is
as old as dirt and is cataloged throughout the Bible.

- God asked Cain, "Where is your
  brother Abel?" Rather than admit
  to being a murderer, Cain made excuses (Gen 4:9).

- God told Abraham that his wife, Sarah, was going to have a
  child. Sarah laughed out loud. When God asked why she
  laughed, Sarah promptly denied her mirth (Gen 18:13).

- Jacob did his father-in-law, Laban, wrong, and when confronted, he didn't own up but instead dissembled (Gen 31:31).

- God told Moses, "I am sending you to Pharaoh to bring my people the Israelites out of Egypt" (Ex 3:10). Moses argued that he was not the right man for the job and that God must have had it wrong (Ex 4:13).

- Saul didn't follow God's battle instructions. When Samuel confronted him, Saul patently denied he was wrong: "I have carried out the LORD's instructions," he said (1 Sam 15:13). Samuel asked why Saul didn't obey the Lord, but Saul held on to his perspective that he did obey.

- David committed murder and adultery, and it took Nathan to get him to admit his mistake (2 Sam 12).

Much of the Old Testament story can be summed up in the words, "Everyone did as they saw fit" (Judg 21:25). Proverbial wisdom puts it like this: "All a person's ways seem pure to them, but motives are weighed by the LORD" (Prov 16:2).

We may look at the world with a jaundiced eye, but we see the rightness of our beliefs and judgments as inviolable. Jesus ran into this bias again and again. People wondered whether anything good could come out of Nazareth. Discounting Jesus' credibility because he came from the wrong side of the tracks, hadn't studied in the "right" seminary or interned with the "right" rabbi was how they propped up their own rightness. And curiosity about Jesus' teaching and miracles was by no means an endorsement of his views. Torah experts went out of their way to prove he was wrong. As self-appointed "heresy police," they continually devised tests to examine the "rightness" of Jesus' beliefs about adultery, Sabbath-keeping, resurrection of the body, Scripture, ritual purity, healing and other issues. Should Jews pay taxes? When was divorce legitimate? Should people obey Mosaic Law when it meant breaking Roman law? Was Jesus orthodox or not?

Jesus' answers often challenged his inquisitors to reexamine their certitudes. Sometimes his answers were questions. Sometimes his answers were stories that got behind the defenses, motivations and pat answers of his cross-examiners. Jesus said:

> That's why I tell stories: to create readiness, to nudge the people toward receptive insight. In their present state they can stare till doomsday and not see it, listen till they're blue in the face and not get it. I don't want Isaiah's forecast repeated all over again: "Your ears are open but you don't hear a thing. Your eyes are awake but you don't see a thing. The people are blockheads! They stick their fingers in their ears so they won't have to listen; They screw their eyes shut so they won't have to look, so they won't have to deal with me face-to-face and let me heal them." (Mt 13:13-15 *The Message*)

Jesus wanted his stories to open a door to relationship. He hoped people would lay aside their certitudes about who he was and follow him around and talk to him for a while. If they did, then perhaps relationships and stories would turn their unequivocal rightness into something better—such as humility or faith in the one who was Truth. Hanging out with Jesus could be a catalyst for change. Relationships could build trust, and people could discover that Jesus was more than a cool rabbi; he was Israel's Messiah.

Throughout the Gospels, Jesus conveys truth through story as well as his person. And his invitation for people to get to know him is nothing less than an invitation to rethink what they thought they knew about

- who the Messiah was (Mk 8:27-29)
- what pleases God (Mt 6:1, 5, 7, 16, 19-21, 24)
- who is holy and who is not (Mk 12:38-40; Mt 5:21-22, 27-28)
- who gets into heaven first (Mk 9:36; 10:13-14)
- what the law is really about (Mt 5:17-48; 12:6-8; 15:1-2)

- who is blessed in the kingdom of God (Mt 5:3-12)
- the nature of the kingdom of God (Mt 5; 13)
- what the Messiah will do (Mt 11:3-6; 16:21-13)
- who is greatest in the kingdom of God (Mt 18:1-5; 20:21-23)
- what people who reject him deserve (Lk 9:54)
- who Jesus considers his family to be (Mt 12:46; Mk 3:31)
- who are acceptable disciples (Mt 9:9)
- who has the greatest faith (Mt 15:28; Mk 9:35)
- what constitutes a legal divorce (Mt 19:1-11; Mk 10:1-12)
- what should happen in the temple (Mk 11:12-15)
- what interruptions are for (Mk 5:21-43)
- what makes something ritually clean or unclean (Mk 7:1-13)

Jesus engaged with people on all these topics. But people who were certain about their views couldn't set down their rightness long enough to get to know Jesus. At first they might have been curious or impressed with his rabbinic skills and reading of Torah (Lk 4:22). But when he started messing with the letter of the law or when he applied Isaiah's prophecy to himself, it sounded so wrong. His hometown folks got so outraged when Jesus took them to task that they drove him out of town and tried to push him off a cliff! They were not going to be lectured by "Joseph's son" (Lk 4:22). After all, they knew exactly where he came from and who he was.

INFORMATION COCOONS

Have you ever related to people whose sole purpose seems to be proving you wrong? It's exhausting and discouraging. Dialogue doesn't work, because your opinions won't change their minds. Relationship flounders because only one "right" view matters.

Jesus began his ministry with the good news of relationship. He invited people to interact with God's kingdom and with himself. Jesus established common ground and invited folks to "come and see." He didn't come into this world to criticize, critique and judge. As John writes, "For God did not send his Son into the world to condemn the world, but to save the world through him" (Jn 3:17). Pointing out where people were wrong wasn't the first thing on Jesus' agenda.

Where have I formed relationships with people who think differently than I do? What have these people taught me?

He didn't prejudge whom to eat with, whom to heal, whom to allow to touch him, what to do on the Sabbath and whom to include among his followers. Jesus engaged all sorts of folks. He knew that relationship could take people places that arguments could not. Of course, with time, people certain of their rightness avoided relationship with Jesus and set out to prove him wrong. Still, the very last thing Jesus intended to do was write them off as lost causes or give up on them. He was at times angry and sad, and he rued their hardness of heart. But then he went up to Calvary and died for the very people who rejected any view but their own.

In the movie *Gran Torino*, disgruntled and prejudiced Korean War vet Walt Kowalski backs into a relationship with Thao, an Asian teenager who tried to steal his prized 1972 Gran Torino. Kowalski has nothing good to say about what he calls "gooks," gangs or God. But when Thao confronts him with his prejudice, Kowalski belligerently snaps, "Enlighten me." This miniscule movement toward rethinking his self-evident conclusions opens a door to humility, relationship and being taught by someone else. Slowly Kowalski emerges from what *New York Times* columnist David Brooks would call his "information cocoon." Kowalski begins to see things from Thao's eyes and hear things through Thao's ears. He grudgingly realizes that his views and his prejudices (prejudgments) were wrong. Relationship and learning another's story bring sight and truth to both Kowalski and Thao.

When people live in information cocoons, Brooks writes, they discredit data and people that disagree with their conclusions. Walt Kowalski lived in an information cocoon that blinded him to Thao's story. But relationship created a way out of his cocoon into the Asian story on his block and in his city.

Jesus reached for relationship. He listened to people's stories. He helped, healed and taught with love and authority unlike anyone else. Still, those convinced of their unequivocal rightness didn't see or hear God in any of this. Locked in their information cocoons, they became unteachable and unreachable. Lobbing objections from the sidelines, they could not imagine being in error or mistaken about Scripture—even though they were (Mt 22:29). Judging Jesus as wrong, they remained blind and deaf to the Truth in human form.

HERE COMES THE JUDGE

Early on we get lessons in judging from parents, friends, culture and generational history. If we are judged harshly for wrongs we have done, we learn to measure out harsh judgments. If we are prejudged without reference to our stories and starting points, we go and do likewise. But this affinity to judge does us a great disservice. It not only saddles us with the heavy weight of critiquing, criticizing and judging everyone under the sun; it also makes us unteachable. Jesus doesn't want us to shoulder the burden of judging. He wants us to have open and teachable hearts.

So Jesus invites us,

> Do not judge, or you too will be judged. For in the same way you judge others, you will be judged, and with the measure you use, it will be measured to you. Why do you look at the speck of sawdust in your brother's eye and pay no attention to the plank in your own eye? How can you say to your brother,

"Let me take the speck out of your eye," when all the time there is a plank in your own eye? You hypocrite, first take the plank out of your own eye, and then you will see clearly to remove the speck from your brother's eye. (Mt 7:1-5)

Judging isn't our assignment as followers of Jesus. That's a very good thing, as we are so limited and partial in our understandings. Christian orthodoxy teaches that God alone has divine and perfect perspective on the whole of everything. Jesus' teaching invites us to admit where our vision is flawed as opposed to absolute. He invites us to be teachable, which requires humbly admitting that absolute truth is beyond our reckoning. We are finite beings with logs in our eyes. If God is humble enough to enjoy being revealed in fallible human creatures, then perhaps we can humbly embrace the freedom of not being know-it-alls.

This doesn't mean we can't know truth. It simply means we cannot be certain that our take on truth is absolute or that our judgments about others are absolutely right. Simon thought he saw the truth about the sinful woman who washed Jesus' feet. Jesus reminded him he hadn't really seen the woman at all (Lk 7:44). The prejudgers thought they saw the truth about the woman caught in adultery (Jn 8:12). The disciples and townspeople thought they knew the truth about the woman at the well (Jn 4:27). Jesus' disciples thought they were right about the people who were killed when the tower of Siloam fell (Lk 13:4). Jewish leaders thought they were right about Jesus' identity (Jn 10:33).

All these folks assumed they had it right. They lifted the heavy weight of critiquing and passing sentence on others—only to be told by Jesus that they had logs in their eyes. Certainty can blind people. It can limit what one sees. Certainty is God's purview. Faith is ours. Faith doesn't depend on certainty. Faith is needed where doubts exist and knowledge is partial. God wants faith. And on the last day it is faith that God commends, not certainty.

Following Jesus is, in Henri Nouwen's words, a movement from "false certainties to true uncertainties, from an easy support system to a risky surrender, and from the many 'safe' gods to the God whose love has no limits." The people who "got" the good news were the ones whose doubts or certitudes didn't preclude their getting to know something and someone new: Jesus. They were humble enough to be taught. They could imagine being wrong and having a log in their eye. John the Baptist voiced his confusion about who Jesus was and asked for clarification. The disciples puzzled over Jesus' stories and teaching and asked him what it all meant. Even Nicodemus, a teacher of the law, personally engaged Jesus with his questions.

AN INVITATION TO TEACHABILITY

A relationship with the One who is the Truth is an invitation to teachability. So many of Jesus' teachings begin with, "You have heard that it was said . . . But I tell you . . ." (Mt 5:33-34, for example). We must unlearn and relearn. Knowing Jesus takes the humility of a child. Children know they are small. They know they are too little to take care of themselves. So they trust others to help, guide and teach them.

Being in error and needing help, guidance and a teacher to set us straight are not things we outgrow. Sometimes it's not too hard to admit I'm wrong. For example, in school I learned that our solar system has nine planets. Recently I was informed that Pluto has been demoted from planet status. It's no skin off my nose to admit that I was wrong about Pluto being a planet. But sometimes it takes real courage and humility to remove the log in my own eye. Benjamin Franklin astutely observed, "How few there are who have courage enough to own their faults, or resolution enough to mend them."

I often hear couples debating who is right about what happened. Each one refuses to admit that she or he might be wrong about some detail: how far they walked, how long ago it was, who was there. One of them may be a stickler for accuracy, while the other is after the big picture and not too concerned about details. Or perhaps they just have a habit of trusting their own memories more than someone else's. Either scenario is an invitation to lay down the need to be right and to grow in humility and teachability. These are habits that God much admires.

The type of humility that admits you are wrong when you know you are wrong is confession. The humility that admits you might be wrong when you're pretty sure you're right is maturity. Without both types of humility, we become rigid and unteachable. Without both types of humility, relationships flounder and implode.

IT'S GOOD TO BE WRONG

I can't begin to tell you how many times my husband, Doug, has handed me the "right" tomato-cutting knife when I've been using a different one. This used to irritate me. I would refuse to take his knife, contending that as long as my knife worked, it wasn't the "wrong" knife. More recently I have seen that accepting the "right" knife is a practice in being teachable. It's a small thing, but I have to begin somewhere. If I can't be wrong about a knife, I won't be humble enough to swallow being wrong about something else. I don't want miss out on God and the new things he has for me. So I lay down my rightness and ask to have "ears to hear."

What does it mean to have faith in Jesus rather than certainty about absolute truth?

My brother, Michael Ahlberg, knows a woman who suffered chronic and debilitating back pain. No medical relief or cure could be found. One day her son-in-law phoned from another state and asked if she would like a dog, thinking perhaps the companionship would do her good. The woman reminded him that she could barely take care of herself; she absolutely didn't want the responsibility of a dog. The son-in-law said, "Just think about it." Later the same day he called and asked again: "Mom, do you want a dog?" She said, "Never. No way!" He suggested she pray about it. The next day the son-in-law called again, asking if she had changed her mind and wanted a dog. His mother-in-law had not changed her mind. The son-in-law replied, "Mom, it's too late. I'm halfway to your house with a dog."

So she reluctantly accepted the dog on a trial basis. At night the dog began to curl up and press its warm little body right at the painful spot in her back. In the morning, she felt relief from her pain and felt well enough to start a new day. The mother-in-law was not mortified to have been wrong; in fact, she was *thrilled* to have been wrong! She was delighted that her son-in-law had been right. It made a huge change in her life and well-being.

Have you ever judged someone only to discover they were far better than you imagined? Have you ever rued a job only to find out that it held more opportunity than you had originally judged? Over and over again I have been wrong. I was wrong about my mom's health condition. Wrong about what a friend did. Wrong about what I remembered. Wrong about which child was at fault. Wrong about a biblical interpretation. The cosmos is way beyond my wee brain. And God, blessed be he, is deeper than all my best thoughts. Being wrong is not nearly the worst thing that has happened to me.

Jesus' invitation to take the log out of our own eye opens a door for transformation and healing. Owning our own faults, blind spots and failures in the presence of a God who already knows us can be a freeing thing. God doesn't love us more when we are right than when we are wrong. God's love for us isn't dependent on right answers or perfect doctrine or never failing at anything. The good news is that I don't need to be afraid of being wrong. Jesus' death on the cross undoes the lies that tell me I am loveable only when I am right.

We all know people who believe in Jesus but have never been able to admit they are wrong on much of anything. Perhaps as a child they were shamed by a teacher or parent for having been wrong. Perhaps love was withdrawn when they did something wrong, so that now they fear that being wrong means loss of love. Listen: the good news isn't an ideology you get "right." The good news is Jesus: Truth incarnate. You can get things wrong and admit to wrong, and the Truth will still love you.

CONFESSION IS GOOD FOR THE SOUL

An old adage says, "Confession is good for the soul." Admitting that I am wrong, or even that I *might* be wrong, reminds me that I am limited. And limits don't make me a bad or inferior person. They make me a human being. Human beings make mistakes. Human beings fail and break relationship. Failing, in and of itself, is no sin. But anything that breaks relationship is sin. Sin separates and isolates. Brennan Manning writes, "Sin is the starting point of all social estrangement. Every sin . . . leaves its mark on the psychic structure of the human soul. Every unrepented sin has a sinisterly obscuring effect on true openness." Sin is how we destroy ourselves. It is its own penalty. It diminishes our ability to receive and closes us down to truth, to God and to others.

Confession opens us wide to Jesus and one another. Confessing wrongs is foundational to maintaining healthy, growing relationships with God and others. The humility that admits "I'm sorry" or "You are right" can bring peace, clear the conscience, reestablish intimacy and gain us hearing with others. Without confession, relationships wither. Without confession, we remain blind to truth.

Truth is not just a head thing; truth needs to shape our deepest gut-level response to God and the world around us. Truth addresses both our thoughts and our habitual patterns of behavior. Accessing and listening to truth on these levels can be difficult, because our prejudices and reactions are outside of our conscious

awareness. Yet day in and day out, our decisions and relationships
are shaped by these habitual reactions and subconscious postures.
These learned patterns of interaction may or may not have anything to do with truth and faith.

TAKE THE CURE

God, who is Truth, desires truth. The way to truth is not simply
study. That is important. But truth in the inner person comes
through confessing and repenting of our sins. Repentance means
you rethink your practices, you think about your thinking and
you reconsider your direction. James wrote, "Confess your sins
to each other and pray for each other so that you may be healed"
(Jas 5:16).

Confession heals and cures us. Confession humbles us and
teaches us that although we may be wrong and in error, we are
loved all the same. I am often amazed at how the words "I could
be wrong" can stop the escalation of conflict and make me rethink
my opinions and ways. More often than not, when I get the words
"I was wrong" out of my mouth, the love and forgiveness that create intimacy follows. And if I keep at it, I become practiced in
humility and teachable of heart.

Jesus had a hard time with folks whose legalistic notion of truth
kept them from learning anything new. Their scrupulousness
about the letter of the law meant they missed the spirit of the law.
They could look right while shutting out truth that they didn't
want to hear. But it wasn't just those who were committed to their
own certainties who found Jesus' truth hard to bear; Jesus told his
closest friends that he had truth to tell them that they couldn't yet
bear (Jn 16:12-13). To bear that truth required openness that they
didn't yet have. It also required the presence, comfort and conviction of the Holy Spirit—the Spirit who brings freedom and courage to bear new things.

The Holy Spirit leads us deeper into Jesus, who is the Truth, the

Life and the Way. The Holy Spirit convicts us of sin and softens our hearts, so that we confess our wrongs and repent. The eyes and ears to see and hear truth are directly linked to a heart that is humble and teachable. If I believe I am never wrong about people or in error about my judgments, I won't hear or bear truth even when it is shouted in my ears.

How am I at trusting the Holy Spirit to lead another into truth? How do I discern when to correct another and when to keep my thoughts to myself for the time being?

I am all for orthodoxy. But let the orthodoxy be held in the hands and hearts of humble, teachable followers of Jesus. My years in ministry have been etched with "worship wars," "heresy trials" and "gender battles." Congregations fight over buildings, preaching, paint colors, youth ministry, budgets, mission trips, mission support and philosophy of ministry. Wounds are inflicted. Hurts are received. People gang up on each other and give up on each other. When no one wants to look at the log in their own eye, church life is hard or even miserable.

From the beginning, the church has had internal battles. Paul pled with Euodia and Syntyche to "be of the same mind in the Lord" (Phil 4:2). These women had worked and struggled and given their all for the kingdom. Paul was clear about their contribution. But instead of knowing them for the extent of their legacy, we know these women for their unwillingness to come to agreement. Whatever problem actually existed between them fades in comparison to their refusal to humble themselves and make peace. Paul appealed to them, asking each woman to "iron out their differences and make up. God doesn't want his children holding grudges" (Phil 4:2 *The Message*). The differences Paul wanted ironed out were not moral or doctrinal problems. They were more likely the scrimmages we have all experienced in church life: conflict over worship styles or what book can be taught in Sunday school. Paul exhorted Euodia and Syntyche to repair this breakdown in the body of Christ. The seriousness of disunity requires action. If these two women would humble themselves before God and one another, they could participate in a holy thing: the mending of the body of Christ. By confessing whatever grudge or judgment or need to be right that they refused to let go of, they could pour balm into Jesus' own wounds and stanch the Holy Spirit's grief.

By confessing and repenting, we acknowledge that:

- The unity and health of the body of Christ are more important than our own "rightness."

- At any given time, our judgments are limited and finite.

- Our agenda may not be the same thing as God's will. And God's will is what matters.

Peace in the church doesn't happen automatically. It is a fruit of the Spirit in the lives of humble, teachable followers of Jesus. Peace comes when we loosen our attachments to our own "rightness," judgments and critiquing ways. Peace happens when we lay down the burden of judging and focus on "whatever is true, whatever is noble, whatever is right, whatever is pure, whatever is lovely, whatever is admirable . . . [whatever] is excellent or praiseworthy" (Phil 4:8).

From time to time I receive emails about the wrongness of someone's theology, along with directions to set them straight. Separating weeds from wheat is a formidable task and one Jesus warned against. I'm certainly no fan of heresy. Still, I know the church has coexisted with it for years. And because I'm fallible, I am sure that I am unintentionally and unknowingly heretical somewhere or other.

So when righting wrong theology, I think about red and white blood cells. Red blood cells transport oxygen and carbon dioxide to and from the lungs, fueling and purging our tissue to keep our bodies full of fresh, healthy air. The absence, excess or damage of these cells can cause disease and even death. Five types of white blood cells work to support the body's immune system and defend it against attacks from viruses, bacteria and other toxins.

To thrive, the body of Christ also needs both red and white blood cells that love Jesus. The red cells bring us oxygen from various cultures, worship styles and traditions to which we may or may not belong. They are a breath of fresh air fueling and opening the church wider to God, ridding us of the waste products of our limitations. Meanwhile, the white cells vigilantly keep watch, protecting us from the toxic effects of winging off into our own private truths without looking at the life of Jesus, the creeds of the church and the pages of Scripture. Living churches can't exist without the cooperative presence of both types of blood cells. Without white cells, we risk infection and heresy. Without red cells, we stop breathing.

In the human body, red and white blood cells work side by side to maintain health. In the body of Christ, sometimes these cells forget that they, too, need to function in tandem to maintain the spiritual well-being of the church. The white cells just want to set the red cells straight, and the red cells just want to keep pumping the body fresh with new dreams and visions. Both kinds of cells need to humbly ask for grace to appreciate what the other one brings. I don't want to oversimplify a complicated issue, but I do know that love covers a multitude of "wrongs." As I talk to both red and white cells, I look

What was it like to be wrong when you were a kid? How has your past affected your experience of "being wrong"? Offer your experiences of feeling badly or shamed to God. Listen to what he says to you about them.

for the fruit of the love of Jesus. I ask where they are submitting to others. Red cells aren't a law to themselves. White cells aren't above being wrong. The health of the body of Christ depends on both white and red cells learning from the Spirit of Christ in one another. No wonder the New Testament is filled with so many "one anothers." It's the way to unity.

Jesus himself accepted the invitation to admit the possibility of being wrong. Jesus wanted God to be wrong about Calvary. In the Garden of Gethsemane, Jesus struggled to admit that his Father was right and he was wrong about what needed to happen. And saying, "Father, your will be done" wasn't a theological act of absolute certainty. It was risking on relationship with his Father. It was trust that even if everything went wrong, God could make it absolutely right. Jesus' act of humility, teachability and faith brought us salvation. Our practice of humility, teachability and faith keeps us tethered to Christ's example here on this earth.

Confession opens us to truth. Invite the Spirit of Truth to be your teacher. Ask for courage to confess where you might be wrong, prejudiced or a source of wounding in the body of Christ. Let the gift of being limited and loved lead you more and more deeply into faith.

7

Invitation to Forgive

All the cards in the deck of revelation about God's mercy
and kindness are stacked in favor of the unthinkable.

GAYLE SOMERS

Forgiveness flounders because I exclude the enemy
from the community of humans and myself
from the community of sinners.

MIROSLAV VOLF

ON THE WAY TO COSTCO ONE day, I was dumbfounded by a billboard. One of Jesus' most radical invitations stood overlooking the highway—advertised like the local casino—for all to see. The background was all black, and on it one word was written in stark white letters: FORGIVENESS. No explanation. No caveats. Just God's deep, gut-level invitation to live a life of forgiveness.

What does one make of a sign like that? For the normal bruises, wounds, scars and disappointments of life, forgiveness may seem like the high road, a noble ideal, a Christian virtue. But when horrific things happen—rape, molestation, torture, abuse, wars, prej-

FOLLOWING GOD'S INVITATION TO FORGIVE

INVITATION	To live into Jesus Christ's forgiveness so I can let go of the hate, hurt and brokenness of the past and live into freedom.
SCRIPTURE	"Therefore, I tell you, her many sins have been for-given—as her great love has shown. But whoever has been forgiven little loves little" (Lk 7:47). "Bear with each other and forgive one another if any of you has a grievance against someone. Forgive as the Lord forgave you" (Col 3:13).
ROADBLOCKS	—Being stuck in hate and bitterness —Lack of belief that freedom is possible —Anger at God —Being stuck in self-righteousness —Fear of becoming a doormat —Confusion of forgiveness with reconciliation
AWARENESS	—Notice where hurt keeps me from being open and free with others. —Notice where I am holding onto grudges and ne-glecting the way of love. —Notice where I don't want to let go of feelings of revenge or hatred. —Notice who I avoid and neglect because they have hurt me. —Acknowledge my inability to forgive on my own and invite Jesus to forgive through me.
PRACTICES	—*Meditate on Jesus' death* on the cross for me, which can open me to the wonder of his forgiving love. It can create a desire in me to become like him in his forgiving. —Make *a life confession*, which opens me to all the ways God has loved and forgiven me. Confession takes me into painful places and then bathes those places with love and God's own forgetfulness.

udice and ethnic cleansing, all of which rip lives and even coun-tries to shreds—forgiveness can seem anything but virtuous.

Identities can coalesce around being the party who was wronged, and then being wronged becomes the most riveting thing in life. Nothing exorcises the pain. Vengeance, bitterness and hatred saturate the air the victim breathes, and thoughts about how to make the perpetrator suffer take hold like a leech to the skin. Retaliation and vengeance seem less odious than the message on the billboard. Forgiveness? It seems stupid and maybe even dangerous!

Still, vengeance is a poor solution to anything. Miroslav Volf writes graphically about what an unforgiving spirit can do.

> Revenge doesn't say, "An eye for an eye." It says, "You take my eye, and I'll blow out your brains." It doesn't say, "An insult for an insult." It says, "You cross me once, you cross me twice, and I'll destroy your character and your career." It doesn't say, "You organize an act of terror, and we'll punish you." It says, "You organize an act of terror, and we'll use the overwhelming military force of a superpower to recast the political landscape of the entire region from which you came." Revenge abandons the principle of "measure for measure" and, acting out of injured pride and untamed fear, gives itself to punitive excess. That's why revenge is morally wrong. In its zeal to punish, it overindulgently takes from the offender more than is due.

AN ALTERNATIVE TO REVENGE

God's alternative to revenge is not truce or standoff or cold war or isolationism. It's forgiveness. Furthermore, God himself is the pattern and standard of what forgiveness looks like. "Bear with each other and forgive one another if any of you has a grievance against someone. Forgive as the Lord forgave you" (Col 3:13). This is God's heart for forgiveness. And Jesus enfleshes that heart in profoundly telling ways.

So does this mean forgiveness lets a perpetrator off scot-free?

What do you think about forgiving convicts, pedophiles, rapists and terrorists?

And what if someone won't admit they've wronged you? Or what if they pretend to be contrite but actually don't care a fig that they hurt you? What about forgiving pedophiles, rapists and terrorists (or whoever else is on your short list of the unforgivable)? Wouldn't forgiving them be adding injustice to injustice?

WHEN IS ENOUGH, ENOUGH?

Jesus' teaching on forgiveness raises all sorts of questions. Peter is the disciple who eventually voiced his (and our) concerns. He wanted to know when "enough is enough." Peter was brave enough to ask, "Master, how many times do I forgive a brother or sister who hurts me? Seven?" (Mt 18:21 *The Message*).

How does Peter's suggestion of "seven times" sit with you? Does it seem enabling or what? And what of Jesus' comeback: "Seven! Hardly. Try seventy times seven" (Mt 18:22 *The Message*). Jesus' followers are to never stop forgiving. Even when it seems humanly impossible, Jesus invites his followers to forgive. To illustrate the invitation, he tells a story.

> The kingdom of God is like a king who decided to square accounts with his servants. As he got under way, one servant was brought before him who had run up a debt of a hundred thousand dollars. He couldn't pay up, so the king ordered the man, along with his wife, children, and goods, to be auctioned off at the slave market.
>
> The poor wretch threw himself at the king's feet and begged, "Give me a chance and I'll pay it all back." Touched by his plea, the king let him off, erasing the debt.
>
> The servant was no sooner out of the room when he came upon one of his fellow servants who owed him ten dollars.

He seized him by the throat and demanded, "Pay up. Now!"

The poor wretch threw himself down and begged, "Give me a chance and I'll pay it all back." But he wouldn't do it. He had him arrested and put in jail until the debt was paid. When the other servants saw this going on, they were outraged and brought a detailed report to the king.

The king summoned the man and said, "You evil servant! I forgave your entire debt when you begged me for mercy. Shouldn't you be compelled to be merciful to your fellow servant who asked for mercy?" The king was furious and put the screws to the man until he paid back his entire debt. And that's exactly what my Father in heaven is going to do to each one of you who doesn't forgive unconditionally anyone who asks for mercy. (Mt 18:23-35 *The Message*)

Jesus' parable sounds remarkably modern to me. Think of the recent scandals at Arthur Andersen, Enron, Merrill Lynch and others. Remember Yasuo Hamanaka, who lost the Sumitomo Corporation billions in copper trading? Or Nick Leeson of Barings Bank, whose unauthorized speculative trading on Singapore's International Monetary Exchange caused the collapse of the oldest investment bank in the United Kingdom? And all this pales in comparison to Bernard Madoff, who cost his investors over 22 billion dollars. Is your gut reaction to forgive these people? When is enough, enough?

W. H. Auden quipped, "Every crook will argue, 'I like committing crimes. God likes forgiving them. Really the world is admirably arranged.'" The trouble is that the world doesn't work like this at all.

In Jesus' story, the king settles his account by auctioning off the servant and his family. Mosaic Law permitted servitude as a means of debt payment (Lev 25:39-42; Ex 21:1-2). But when the sentence is pronounced, the servant grovels at the king's feet and begs,

"Give me a chance [time] and I'll pay it all back" (v. 29). If Madoff had begged the judge for time to pay back all those he bankrupted, would you have endorsed leniency or "doing time"?

Blessing those who rob me and doing good to my enemies is not part of my usual repertoire (Rom 12:9, 17-21). I quite like the idea of mercy for me, but I much prefer that you pay. When I am caught speeding, I want mercy. But if I see you speeding down the highway, I hope the police catch you and give you a big fat ticket that teaches you a lesson. Justice for you, mercy for me.

Would you show mercy if it meant that you, like the king in Jesus' parable, would lose millions of dollars? Why or why not?

I keep waiting for the servant in Jesus' story to say, "I'm so sorry. I know I can never right this wrong." But that never happens. Instead of an apology, the king hears a cock-and-bull story about paying it all back! Even if the servant were Loan Shark of the Year and blessed by Lady Luck in every poker game he played, it's lunacy to think that time would favor him with the millions he owed. Still, the king (read: God) knows that things can happen with time. Sometimes mercy and forgiveness soften the heart. So the king kisses his rights and everything owed him goodbye. He offers his servant a second chance, free and clear. No debt. No system of repayment. No parole. No charges pressed. No demands. No revenge. The servant gets a fresh start—a do-over.

Remember the crook Jean Valjean in *Les Misérables*? After stealing silver from the church altar, he is nabbed by the police and brought before the priest with loot in hand. Rather than pressing charges, the priest informs the police that he had given Jean Valjean the silver. Handing Jean Valjean the silver candlesticks from the altar, he says, "You forgot to take these." The priest didn't harden his heart toward Jean Valjean or make him out to be worse than he was. He saw a broken human being who was worth more than his silver. And rather than counting his wrong against him, he risked the silver for the transformation of the man.

When someone wrongs us, it is so easy to harden our heart, malign them and their deeds, demand the full measure of the law, and paint them as beyond the scope of redemption. But the king in Jesus' story refuses to do any of these things. He refuses to treat this servant as beyond redemption. So separating this thieving servant from his wrongs, the king offers mercy. That means the entire cost of the loss falls on and is born by the king. Miroslav Volf suggests that condemning the fault and sparing the wrong-doer is the heart of forgiveness. Forgiveness risks that a forgiven crook might just go and do as he had been done by. Forgiveness might transform him.

But being forgiven doesn't transform the servant in this story. He collars someone who owes him a few bucks and says, "Time's up. Pay back what you owe me!" When the man asks for time, the servant assaults him and slams him in prison.

It's appalling! But it's like me. The servant pleas for mercy for himself and doles out the full weight of the law for others. Law can be used in so many ways. It can be dished out full strength, used for one's own benefit and wielded to ruin others. Or it can be mitigated with mercy followed by plans for the restoration of the wrongdoer and for her or his repayment to the community.

Every day in the name of justice, courts pass sentences on wrongdoers, and we are glad they do. But are we even slightly aware that a world of unmitigated and retributive justice would do us all in? Relationships between countries and people survive because forgiveness and mercy are given and received. It's how we overcome evil with good. This doesn't make forgiveness a substitute for justice. Forgiveness doesn't overlook wrongful acts. It condemns them, and in so doing, draws attention to the penalty that has been waived.

The servant in Jesus' story uses the law mercilessly and for his own benefit. He hardens his heart toward those who owe him money and refuses to separate them from their debt. The king's mercy hasn't made a dent; it has been squandered and wasted on the servant. But it doesn't have to be squandered and wasted on us.

Forgiving from the heart is not a theory or cognitive act. It is not simply a high ideal or virtue. Forgiveness costs; it rends the heart and changes the way we relate to those who wrong us. The servant closes his heart to mercy. When the king is told how his servant has behaved, he adopts the servant's own standard of justice and plays by his rules. It's only fair. The king throws the servant into prison where he cannot cause more harm. Then Jesus adds, "This is how my heavenly Father will treat each of you unless you forgive your brother or sister from your heart" (Mt 18:35).

How are you praying for a heart that works forgiveness into your relationships?

A RISKY PRAYER

Whenever we pray the Lord's Prayer, we say, "And forgive us our debts as we also have forgiven our debtors" (Mt 6:12). It's a risky prayer and a radical invitation to live into God's heart for wrongdoers. In the true story *Dead Man Walking* by Helen Prejean, a Catholic nun supports a convicted murderer and rapist on death row. Neither the victim's family nor the church can accept the nun's care for the perpetrator: they think he's all bad. The nun doesn't ignore or minimize the perpetrator's wrongdoing. She places blame. She condemns the wrong. But she also gives the perpetrator a gift. Separating him from his wrongdoing, she refuses to make him out to be all bad. She refrains from adding one injustice to another. By doing so, she joins her heart to God's heart for sinners and risks that love can lead even a perpetrator to repentance and the forgiveness of God.

Sooner or later, we all come to the end of our own forgiveness.

We can't stop hating someone. We get obsessed by a grudge and pursue a private vendetta that passes evil along. We wrong an enemy by judging them to be worse than they are. Forgiveness is a suffering we are not willing to bear, a risk we are not willing to take. That's when we need to look not just at Jesus' parable but at the cross.

THE CROSS: A SIGN OF WHAT GOD DOES WITH WRONGDOING

God could have condemned our wrongs by punishing us and making us suffer. Instead he suffered an abusive public execution (flogging, thorns, blood, nails and suffocation) and sacrificed himself. On the cross, God detached our sin and brokenness from us and grafted it onto Jesus. Paul writes:

> Since we've compiled this long and sorry record as sinners and proved that we are utterly incapable of living the glorious lives God wills for us, God did it for us. Out of sheer generosity he put us in right standing with himself. A pure gift. He got us out of the mess we're in and restored us to where he always wanted us to be. And he did it by means of Jesus Christ. God sacrificed Jesus on the altar of the world to clear that world of sin. (Rom 3:23-25 *The Message*)

The punishing arm of justice fell on him instead of us so that we could be "free of charge." The cross is the place God judges sin *and* the place God identifies with sinners. Miroslav Volf puts it beautifully when he writes, "Christ is not a third party inserted between God and humanity to take care of human sin. He is the God who was wronged." God is the King and the Judge who condemns our wrongs, and he is also the Suffering Servant who bears the burden of our wrongdoing for us.

God doesn't forgive us to put us on parole or blacklist us or exact demands or control us. He forgives us to heal us and gives us a fresh start on life. Jesus' death on the cross reminds me not to squander God's forgiveness. Deep within me the Spirit of Jesus, the Forgiver, is alive. And if I will take up my cross and follow, Christ himself will forgive through me.

The cross that a person bears is not his or her mother-in-law or job or poor health. My cross is the point of my unlikeness to Jesus. It is the place where I have not lived into the forgiveness of the King and his dream for this world.

LIVING INTO FORGIVENESS

A number of years ago I visited a monastery in Avila, Spain, where St. Teresa had a vision of the child Jesus. In her vision, Teresa met Jesus on a staircase and he asked her, "Who are you?" She responded, "I am Teresa of Jesus. Who are you?" And Jesus said to her, "I am Jesus of Teresa."

When I came to the spot where the vision happened, I was astonished to see that the event had been dramatized with two life-sized statues of St. Teresa and Jesus that looked absolutely real! I stood speechless. And I wondered: what would have to die in me for Jesus to say, "I am Jesus of Adele"? What would it mean to be like him? What would it look like to take up my cross?

In the Garden of Gethsemane and on the cross, Jesus said several things that might help me discover what taking up my cross looks like. He said:

- "Not my will, but yours be done" (Lk 22:42). Jesus laid down his own agenda, and he asks me to let go of my need for power and control.

- "Father, forgive them, for they do not know what they are doing" (Lk 23:34). Jesus let go of his right to get even. He separated wrongdoers from their wrongdoing. Jesus asks me to release the wrongs done to me, as well as my desire for revenge.

- "Father, into your hands I commit my spirit" (Lk 23:46). Jesus didn't come down from the cross in a spectacle of vindication.

He committed his spirit to God's hand. Jesus asks me to trust my life into God's hands.

* "It is finished" (Jn 19:30). Jesus opened his arms to the pain of the cross and trusted his future to God. Jesus asks that I let the past be finished through the work of forgiveness.

Working forgiveness into my heart and relationships is always painful. When I find myself unable to separate another from their wrongs, I do a fairly uncharacteristic thing for a Protestant: I sleep with a crucifix. I want to remember that this is what forgiveness feels like. I need to see what it cost Jesus to set a wrongdoer like me free. Jesus' wide open arms welcome all of us. Time and again, looking at the cross has been my path to doing what I thought I could not do. The cross has reminded me that Jesus is alive in me to forgive.

What does it look like for you to not paint someone who has wronged you as all bad?

PARTICIPATING IN GOD'S FORGIVING

Miroslav Volf writes profoundly about participation in God's forgiveness:

> It's so crucial to see our forgiving not simply as our own act, but as participation in God's forgiving. Our forgiving is faulty; God's forgiving is faultless. Our forgiving is provisional; God's is final. We forgive tenuously and tentatively; God forgives unhesitantly and definitively. . . . The only way we dare forgive is by making our forgiving transparent to God's and always open to revision. After all, our forgiveness is only possible as an echo of God's.

Forgiveness is a priceless antidote to a world filled with wrongdoing and evil. And although we may do it imperfectly, its presence in this world is a light that can't be put out. Marietta Jaeger-Lane is such a light. In 1973, her seven-year-old daughter Susie was kidnapped, raped, murdered and dismembered. For over a year, the family knew nothing of what had happened. Struggling with feelings of rage, fear and loss, Marietta eventually decided to let the press know she wanted to talk to the person who had taken her daughter. On the anniversary of her daughter's abduction, she received a phone call from a young man who asked, "So what do you want to talk to me about?" Marietta asked him how he was feeling, suggesting that his actions must have placed a heavy burden on his soul. Her caring words disarmed him, and he broke down in tears on the phone.

When the perpetrator was caught and sentenced to death, Marietta asked that the sentence be commuted to life imprisonment without parole. Her actions brought an onslaught of interviews and even a Senate hearing. Outlining her views on forgiveness in an interview with Oprah Winfrey, Marietta made it clear that forgiving doesn't mean condoning a wrong or relieving a person of responsibility. Nor does justice mean bringing the full weight of the law to bear. As a follower of Jesus, Marietta wanted to work for restoration, not just punishment. She wanted to let go of her hate and forgive.

Speaking to Oprah she said,

> I'd reached a point where I really felt concern for this young man, who was a very, very sick young man. And I felt to kill anyone in my little girl's name would be to violate and profane the goodness and sweetness and beauty of who she was. . . . I would simply say that one of the things that helped me to move my heart from fury to forgiveness was to keep reminding myself, "It's hard work." . . . I reminded myself over and over and over again that however I felt about this man, that in God's eyes, he was just as precious as my little girl. That's the kind of God I believe in, a God who's crazy about

all of us and a God who doesn't want terrible things to happen to any of us.

Marietta didn't forgive immediately or all at once. But with grace and time, Jesus' words "Forgive us our sins as we forgive those who sin against us" were fleshed out in Marietta's life. She condemned a wrong, but she mixed mercy with justice and revealed the heart of God to the nation.

THE PROCESS OF FORGIVING

Responding to God's invitation to forgive is dependent upon cooperating with the Spirit's work within us. It is not magic. It is painful. And I have found that it always includes the following.

Naming wrongs. Pretending things are okay or denying the wrong never brings healing. Forgiveness requires honestly naming our experience. It also demands being open to the possibility of a larger story or interpretation different than our own. Without naming the truth of wrongs done, there can be no justice or reconciliation.

Letting go of grudges, blame and pain. When the wrongs done to us become our identity, we are enslaved to the past and not alive to the present. At the cross I let the past go into Jesus' own wounds. I join my pain to his.

Letting go of revenge. No one makes us vindictive; it's a choice, like any other. And it is a choice that won't heal or make us feel better. It will poison us from within.

Separating the wrongdoer from their wrong actions. This is difficult to do when we feel morally superior to the wrongdoers. No one can judge another accurately when pain and anger are in the way. When we internalize how God separated us from our sin and set us free, we can ask for the grace to forgive.

Not tying my forgiveness to another's admission of wrongdoing. Forgiveness doesn't depend on the wrongdoer's response; only restoration does. It is easier to forgive when someone owns up. But we can still do our work to forgive without their confession.

Discerning between forgiveness and setting myself up for perpetual abuse. If I know someone is dangerous and that I am vulnerable, I observe healthy boundaries. But I still do the work of forgiveness.

Forgiving a wrong done is a soul-healing process, just as healing a broken bone is a body-healing process. An operation to repair a mashed bone brings swelling around the incision and wound. That swelling has to go down before other treatments begin. Even after rounds of physical therapy, one may have a limp or a nasty scar as a reminder of what happened. So it is with forgiving. We may always bear scars, but the scars are not open wounds. They are wounds that have been forgiven. And they can make us look a lot like Jesus.

Spend some time with Jesus at the foot of the cross. Consider the wrongs you have done and how they have hurt others. How does Jesus look at these wrongs? How does he look at you? Open your heart to what Jesus has to say to you.

Jesus has scars in his hands and feet right now, in his resurrected body (Rev 5:6). And those scars are eternal and visible evidence of both the cost and love of forgiving. Jesus' scars remind us that the most unjust day in human history, Good Friday, has become the most healing day of all. On that day, the Divine Judge separated us from our wrongdoing. Receiving upon himself the judgment we deserved, he let us go free and clear into a fresh, new start. The invitation is to go and do likewise.

Imagine what would happen if Christ-followers took up his invitation to forgive. Imagine what it would be like to mix justice with mercy and forgiveness. Imagine the new beginnings, the restorations, the healing. It doesn't have to be something we only imagine. It can be real enough to remake our world.

8

Invitation to Wait

*When mechanical clocks began to spring up in town
squares across Europe, the line between keeping
time and keeping control blurred further.*

CARL HONORÉ

*We are more busy than bad, more distracted than nonspiritual
and more interested in the movie theatre, the sports stadium,
and the shopping mall and the fantasy life they produce in us
than we are in church. Pathological busyness, distraction and
restlessness are major blocks today within our spiritual lives.*

RONALD ROHLHEISER

WAITING IS ONE OF GOD'S immensely sweeping invitations. To
wait expectantly and with open hands requires a relinquishment
of control that gets at the roots of our motivations, fears and idola-
tries. It is where we learn that God isn't a genie and that happiness
is not a matter of God meeting our expectations. While we wait,
we can sense the naked vulnerability of trust. No matter how dis-

FOLLOWING GOD'S INVITATION TO WAIT

INVITATION	To let go of my need to control people and circumstances so I can trust that God is at hand and be present in the moment as it unfolds.
SCRIPTURE	"Yes, my soul, find rest in God; my hope comes from him" (Ps 62:5). "Be still before the LORD and wait patiently for him" (Ps 37:7).
ROADBLOCKS	—An inability to lay down my agenda and go with what is happening —An addiction to hurry —Cramming too many things into the time available —Unrealistic deadlines —The inability to take the long view —The inability to see the present as more than a crack between the past and the future
AWARENESS	—Notice when I get impatient and stay in the moment with God. —Become aware of expectations for the day. What happens when my expectations are not met? —Notice what I do when I am not in control.
PRACTICES	—*Practice the presence of God* in the moment, which can be a way of opening myself to God. This practice invites me to trust that God has every moment in his unhurried hands. —*Say a breath prayer*, which is a prayer of simple trust that opens me to God. I breathe in the adequacy of God and breathe out my impatience.

ciplined, organized and prayerful we get, we never outgrow God's invitation to wait. The learning curve is lifelong. You might think that with years of practice, we would get the hang of it. But many of us would rather get our teeth drilled than wait.

Years ago, when people communicated by snail mail, I was waiting for what can only be called a love letter. Every day I would go into the front hall to pick through the assortment of bills, cards, advertisements and letters the mail carrier brought. Did I mention that I did this every day? Day after day? As each day passed, it became harder to wait. My heart did flip flops. My stomach ached.

One day, as I flipped through the stack of mail, I hit a bonanza. I had seven letters from dear friends on various parts of the globe! But rather than being elated, I was increasingly disappointed as I saw each return address. Throwing the letters on the floor, I knew my expectation was turning the good moment that had been given to me—seven letters from friends who cared about me—into a bad moment. But I did it anyway.

Waiting unearths what is in our hearts. It exposes what happens when our expectations go unmet. When Doug was out of work for a year, when our house didn't sell for a year, when we moved to Chicago, leaving our sixteen-year-old son with a car and credit card so he could finish his junior year: each second seemed a lifetime of waiting. But the waiting did something. It exposed my doubts and expectations about what God would do. It exposed a control streak a mile wide as well as a begrudging heart. I rue all the good moments I morphed into bad ones as I clung to my demands of what God ought to do.

Describe the feelings you experience when you have to wait. What do these feelings reveal about the way you think life should work?

EVERYONE WAITS

Waiting is a central, unchangeable, universal fact of life. The homeless are waiting for somewhere to go. Refugees are waiting to return home. Tracts of humanity wait for lasting peace or rain or medical resources or disaster relief teams. Children wait for birthdays. The elderly wait for their savings to run out. Commuters wait in traffic. Wait. Wait. Wait some more.

What are you waiting for? Perhaps what you are waiting for appears in this list:

- A circle of friends
- A relationship or a life partner
- A career or a job
- A calling
- A healing, whether physical or emotional
- For children
- For a child to return to the Lord
- For your finances to turn around
- For a break
- To get back home
- To get away from home

Although we are all on intimate terms with waiting, there are many ways to wait. My friend Gayle Somers suggests that while technology has given us the easiest lives ever it has rendered us virtually in capable of waiting. She writes, "Some of us have impatient temperaments by nature and I imagine no matter which age we're born in, we would struggle with impatience. But all of us are affected by the expectation of speedy results in life. And this cripples us. Sometimes I've wondered about how long it took, in geological time, for the earth to be made into a habitation for man—millions of years! Is that a sign of something? Is that a lesson about God and time?"

We are certainly in need of lessons other than those our quick-fix technological age affords. Hurrying our meals, our reading, our relationships, our prayers, our bodies and our souls might seem efficient and productive, but it also fuels a dangerous addiction to speed. When our expectations for instant access, quick results, fast food, fast lines, fast lanes, express delivery, fast recoveries and quick divorces are thwarted, when we *do* actually have to wait, our entire system goes into an internal state of emergency. We worry, can't sleep and get angry. We cry, plead, pray, binge, obsess or exercise: anything to alleviate the frustration of waiting.

DO SOMETHING OR WAIT?

Many of us get so frustrated with waiting that we'd rather make a quick decision and pick up the pieces than hang around in limbo and wait for clarity to come. Doing something feels so much better than doing "nothing." But waiting is not doing "nothing." And waiting is often better than doing "something." When an autistic child reacts in a hysterical manner, the most important thing for the teacher to do is stand there, still and waiting. The teacher is not to do something; she or he is not to step in. It is best for the teacher simply to wait and watch for what is really going on. By contemplating the child, the teacher may become aware of what precipitated the crisis. Rushing in to fix things too quickly can distort the pattern and perspective in the moment. Doing something can actually blur a teacher's discernment. Clarity comes through patient waiting in the now.

Patience is a characteristic of God and a fruit of his Spirit. You would think we would want it as much as we want love, joy and peace, which are the better-known fruits of the Spirit. But I don't. I resist the particular conditions required to grow the fruit of patience. It's embarrassing to admit how often I beg God to "do something" so that I don't have to wait and let patience grow.

It is some comfort that my all-too-human plea for God to "do something" is found in the mouths of countless others in Scripture. "I am worn out calling for help; my throat is parched. My eyes fail, looking for my God," the psalmist wrote (Ps 69:3). "But as for me, I watch in hope for the LORD, I wait for God my Savior; my God will hear me," wrote Micah (Mic 7:7). And Paul wrote, "For the creation waits in eager expectation for the children of God to be revealed" (Rom 8:19).

The Holy One could vindicate his presence. He could answer us at once! We wouldn't have to wait. So why doesn't he? Why is patience such a big deal anyway?

GOD WAITS

Patience is an important attribute because God is a "waiter" too. Scripture is a catalog, of sorts, of ways that the Holy One waits for us. God waited four hundred years for the time to be right to lead Israel out of Egypt. God waited for

- Israel to grow in numbers and desperation

- the arrogance of Pharaoh to reach its height

- the sin of the Amorites to be full (Gen 15)

- Moses to be the kind of man who could lead Israel out of Egypt

- Israel to become his unique people

God "waited patiently in the days of Noah" (1 Pet 3:20). He waited for the fullness of time to send his Son. And God still waits for us to respond to his invitation to be transformed. He does not hurry us along with force, coercion or control. God bides his time, waiting for us with open hands. The entire Trinity waits expectantly, patiently and with hope for us! When we can't let go of our expectations, the Holy Three stay open-hearted in their waiting. When we can't trust, God takes a long view.

I sometimes wonder if the first thing that went wrong in the Garden of Eden was that Adam and Eve got impatient. They wanted more than the blissful moment at hand. They wanted more control and a future that made them "as God." So they resolved to "do something," rather than hold off the serpent. They decided to "do something," rather than wait for the cool of the day when they could talk to God about their desire for more. Adam and Eve didn't wait to see what trusting in God's goodness would hold for them. They reached out their hands in insurrection and grabbed the one and only thing in Eden God had reserved for himself alone. They resisted God's fruit of patience and acted. Overturning God's reality of what was good and bad, Adam and Eve let what they *didn't* have determine their reality. It didn't matter what God said; they decided that "forbidden fruit" was good. They decided for themselves in any given moment what was good and bad. By refusing to focus on what they had and wait on God, Adam and Eve lost the bliss of Eden.

Paradise is lost. The goodness of the moment gives way. Pain and sorrow, labor and anxiety, alienation and heartbreak are inserted into the fabric of the human story. This picture would be too bleak for words were it not for one tiny ray of light: God makes a promise of hope with the power to reverse the deluge of destruction that Adam and Eve called down on their own heads. "And I will put enmity between you and the woman, and between your offspring and hers; he will crush your head, and you will strike his heel" (Gen 3:15). Like a ring around the moon heralding some reversal in the weather, God shines hope over the long, tortured history of humankind with a promise. In the ground that has been cursed, Yahweh plants a seed of promise: a "Great Reversal" of all that happened in Eden. Through the woman and her offspring, God will turn the things the devil uses to hurt and destroy us for our good, our growth and God's glory.

It will take time. God will wait for the fullness of time, and all of us will have to wait as well. While we do, it may look like nothing is going on other than antiquated wishful thinking. But it's not a matter of *if* this woman and her offspring will come; it's simply a matter of *when*. God's promise has taken root and is growing in the darkness through the millennia. Its shoot is pushing toward the light. And the prophet Isaiah tells God's people not to give up hope but to wait: "A shoot will come up from the stump of Jesse; from his roots a Branch will bear fruit. The Spirit of the LORD will rest on him" (Is 11:1-2).

The offspring of the woman is still on the way. Wait for *when*.

IF OR *WHEN* WAITING

The difference between *if* and *when* waiting came home to me when my kids applied to college. Day after day, they waited to see *if* they would get into the colleges of their choice. They knew *when* the letters bearing their futures should arrive; they didn't stress about that. They stressed about *if* they would be accepted. The *ifs* begat doubts, anxiety, control and impetuosity: "Don't get the mail. I want to know first!" they'd say, or "I want to apply to another school," or "I'm not going to get in anywhere good."

I am familiar with their reactions. I often wait in airports and train stations around the world for someone to meet me *when* I arrive. I fix the *who* and *where* firmly in my mind and relax. Someone will be there. I just need to watch and wait. But when I am unsure *if* someone will show up, it's different. Then I worry about finding my way, staying in a safe part of town, finding an affordable hotel and navigating in a different language.

Waiting for God's promise is not an act of passive resignation. It is not a fatalistic *Que será será:* Whatever will be, will be. Waiting on God demands alertness to the present moment. It is an active stance of watchfulness—a waiting for *when*, not *if*, God will come through. Henri Nouwen suggests that active waiters "know that what they are waiting for is growing from the ground on which they are standing. . . . The seed has been planted, . . . something has begun." God is already taking what the devil would use to destroy us and turning it for our good and growth and his glory.

Waiting for God is rooted in the expectancy that he is actually coming through on his word—even when we can't see it.

EXPECTANCY, NOT EXPECTATION

Expectant waiting requires openness to something good happening beyond our expectations. Expectations are what get us into trouble while we wait. We expect God to do things a certain way: our way. We have expectations about timing: our timing. Expectations bind our happiness to one particular end. I get this job. My house sells now. Unmet expectations are resentments and disappointments waiting to happen. The difference between waiting for our *expectations* to happen and waiting *expectantly* for this moment to unfold is huge. Being present to what is· this is what matters. What is happening here and now is important. What goes on while I wait may become the foundation for some new undreamed-of and unexpected future.

Begin to notice if you are waiting with expectations or with expectancy. What is the difference in the moment?

The truth is that God doesn't come to us in our future. God comes now—while we wait. It's not up to you to make things happen or to make God show up. What you can do is say yes to God's invitation to stay alert while you wait. It may land you on holy ground. Abraham was waiting for a promise that was slower than molasses in coming, and while he waited, God showed up in three strange visitors who gave him perspective and hope to continue waiting. It's not a matter of *if* God will show up, but of *when*.

Henri Nouwen writes, "Impatient people are always expecting the real thing to happen somewhere else and therefore want to go elsewhere." Going "somewhere else" can be much easier than staying where we are and waiting. But it is in the waiting that things happen in our souls. In the waiting our character is formed.

Life doesn't happen after our every expectation is fulfilled; it happens as we wait expectantly, with open hands and with God. Any moment can be a revelatory place rather than an empty space. Sheryl Crow sings in "Soak up the Sun": "It's not having what you want, it's wanting what you've got." Waiting is an invitation to become filled and transformed with the revelation of God's own heart in the moment.

APPRENTICES IN WAITING

Scripture is full of people who are God's apprentices in waiting. Noah waited through years of building the ark for something that had never happened before: namely, rain (Gen 7–9). Then he waited forty more days in a dark, crowded space while the ark rose and fell on the flood. When the deluge stopped, Noah waited another 150 days to get off the boat. Have you ever been in a dark, tight spot and wondered if you would ever be let out of it? Noah waited there, in a place where the promise that one day he'd get out must have seemed both hollow and the only way forward. But he waited on God, who, in the end, painted Noah's sky with a rainbow.

God promised Abraham three things: I will make you into a great nation, I will bless you and make your name great, and I will bless every nation through you (Gen 12). None of this happened fast. Abraham waited and waited. Nothing. No land, no son and no résumé of nations he had blessed. It got harder and harder to wait. So Abraham said to God, "You have given me no children; so a servant in my household will be my heir" (Gen 15:3). Then God took Abraham outside and said, "'Look up at the sky and count the stars—if indeed you can count them.' Then he said to him, 'So shall your offspring be'" (Gen 15:5).

Did Abraham's breath catch as he stared into the black night and watched the stars blink in and out of visibility? Did his mind bend with expectations about how, in a year or two, the promised children and land would start to come? God's promised *when* was still a quarter-century away; who could have imagined?

Abraham and Sarah couldn't. Their patience collapsed as the *when* became less and less likely. They wondered *if* God really will come through. Waiting to see *if* their expectations would happen, they became restless and controlling. They made contingency plans to get the promise moving with Ishmael. But their plan wasn't the way God intended to fulfill his promise. He intended to do miracles that would ripple out from them and touch the whole world. Even you and me.

Abraham did eventually see the light of a single star shine in that sky. His son Isaac was the first of many constellations of people and nations to come. Was all of Abraham's waiting a waste of time? Or was it the place that clarified Abraham's soul—the place where he lived into the difference between expectations and waiting expectantly? When the heart is filled with expectations, waiting is calculated and close-minded. However, when the heart is expectant, waiting can be spontaneous and anticipatory of the future God desires for me even if it is different from the one I want. Often it is in the waiting that the heart's motivations become clear. As the time lengthens and what we want isn't forthcoming, we see how attached we are to our own expectations and time table. Our hands are open to get what we want from God. But our hearts are closed to what he wants to give. Waiting refines our hearts. And it was where Abraham learned to risk God's goodness. Waiting in trust shaped Abraham into the kind of man who could risk God's goodness even when God wanted him to sacrifice his only star, Isaac.

Waiting is God's crucible for transformation. Waiting is how God gets at the idols of our heart. Waiting addresses the things we need besides God to be content: money, comfort, expedience, success or control. Adam, Eve, Noah and Abraham are just the beginning of a line of people who learn who God is while they wait.

Hagar learned who God was while waiting for her teenage son to die. Joseph learned who God was in the ups and downs of Pharaoh's court. Jacob expected nothing good from God and learned otherwise.

And the waiting goes on and on. Israel waited four hundred years to get out of Egypt. Moses waited forty years in the wilderness of Midian. Then he waited and wandered with Israel forty more years en route to the Promised Land. During that time God's people had to wait forty days at the foot of Mt. Sinai as Moses climbed up to meet with God. As time dragged by, they began to wonder *if* Moses would come back. "As for this fellow Moses who brought us up out of Egypt, we don't know what has happened to him" (Ex 32:23). Doubting *if* Moses would return morphed into doubting God. Restless, fearful, impatient and impetuous, they built an idol they could see: a golden calf that wouldn't disappear on them.

David waited fourteen years as a fugitive to receive the kingdom he had been promised. Gideon, Elijah, Elisha, Jeremiah, Ezekiel, Habakkuk, Isaiah: the list of people who waited in the Old Testament for God's promise, presence and intervention is long. Prophets came and went, reminding Israel that it was not a matter of *if* God would show up. It's not a matter of *if* the woman and her offspring will come. It is still—and always will be—a matter of *when*. "For to us a child is born, to us a son is given, and the government will be on his shoulders. And he will be called Wonderful Counselor, Mighty God, Everlasting Father, Prince of Peace" (Is 9:6-7).

What good things have come to you while you waited for something you wanted to happen?

The centuries of waiting are what form Israel into a unique people—God's people, a people who can recognize who the woman and her son are when they come. Waiting is how God's people develop the conviction, humility and longing to know they need saving and that only God can save them. In spite of years of what could only have seemed like dashed expectations, a remnant remained expectant. They risked that one way or another, God's promise to Adam and Eve was still on the way. Waiting for *when*, not *if*, the consolation and hope of Israel would happen made all the difference in how they lived and experienced God.

THE WAITING SPACE BETWEEN DESIRE AND DEMAND

To wait is not to sublimate or repress desire. God tells us to voice our desires. But expressing what we long for is different from demanding that God or someone else give it to us. Between desire and demand there is a space—a transformative space of waiting. This space is a revelatory place where God surfaces our expectations and need to control. This space is a litmus test of what's in our hearts. Do we trust God's goodness over the long haul, admitting that we don't always know what is best for ourselves or others? Are we the kind of people who can relinquish our demands and say, "God, I want to get married or have children or find a job. But you don't have to do what I want. I will wait in trust that your will is best for me."

The space between desire and demand is a risky waiting place. It is the place where we go to wait with God and let go of control. The place between desire and demand can hold longings, disappointments, loss, unmet expectations, joys and deep gratitude. It is the place where we learn to attach ourselves fully to God's will rather than our own so that we can wait with open hands and with hope and trust. "My soul finds rest in God," David wrote in Psalm 62. "Truly he is my rock and my salvation; he is my fortress, I will never be shaken" (Ps 62:1-2). Repeating these words like a chorus, he reminded himself that waiting is not an empty moment but a moment in which a strong and comforting God dwells.

Scripture is full of people who wait in the space between desire and demand. Noah, Abraham, David, the prophets, Jesus: they don't resign themselves to fate. In whatever happens, they learn to wait "open-endedly." While they wait, they let go of expectations about how God's promises should work and open their hands to God's promise to be with them. God's promises are not some magic wand that prevents us from ever suffering or waiting. We take a risk on God's promise to get us through the waiting and the suffering.

What are you waiting for right now? What would it look like for you to enter the space between desire and demand and to hold what you want before God with open hands?

There are so many different waiting rooms in life. I have found that the time spent in these waiting rooms often reveals that *circumstances* are not the only thing that needs changing: I do too. While I wait for a job or a relationship or a healing, I come face to face with anxieties, expectations, demands, and my need to control and direct the Holy One. Waiting is that holy place where my heart can be converted, my character honed and hope focused. I long for my son to recover (yet again) from malaria and typhoid fever. I long for some miracle to happen before my aging parents use up every penny they have on my mom's nursing home. I long for some godly young man to see what an amazing woman my daughter is. As I long for these things, I need to step into the space between demand and desire and wait with God. In that graced and sometimes painful place, expectations can give way to expectancy and an open-ended waiting on God's goodness. God's goodness anchors my waiting. It's not a matter of *if* God's goodness will come through; it's only a matter of *when*.

Time spent in life's waiting rooms can seem either like a senseless waiting game or else like waiting in the wings for God's grace and presence to help me live a very difficult present. While I wait I may meet new friends, find new opportunities, discover hidden joys, and learn the solidarity that suffers long and still trusts.

My children had a hard time waiting for supper when they were young, so they would frequently come to the kitchen and ask for a cookie. I would offer them carrots or "ants on a log" (raisins on top of a celery stick slathered with peanut butter). Rather than seeing this as a good thing, they would say, "I don't want that." I would reply, "That's your choice. But I am offering you something good." They would often choose nothing and then complain about how hungry they were for the hour before dinner. Of course, it's not just children who turn the good that is given while they wait into no good. It's not just children who don't trust the *when* of a parent's (or God's) timing.

GOD'S PERFECT *WHEN*

The New Testament begins with waiting going on everywhere. Elizabeth is waiting for a baby. Zechariah is waiting to speak. Simeon is waiting to see the salvation of Israel. Anna is waiting on God's promise. Israel is waiting for God's promised prophet to come. And then after years of waiting, in one breathtaking moment, an angel comes to Mary and says, "Greetings, you who are highly favored!" (Lk 1:28). At long last, Eve's "God, you are not the boss of me" is reversed. Mary, the second Eve, responds to God's invitation with "I am the Lord's servant. . . . May your word to me be fulfilled" (Lk 1:38). And her yes brings God to us in person: Jesus. In that moment, human ears hear what the human soul has been longing to hear throughout the ages. God has kept his promise. The woman and her offspring, young and innocent and without a scrap of worldly power, are here. These are the ones who will defeat Satan and his forces. They are our guarantee that waiting is worth the while. God hasn't forgotten us. He is faithful. The Holy One comes through. As Paul writes in 2 Corinthians 1:20, "For no matter how many promises God has made they are 'Yes' in Christ. And so through him the 'Amen' is spoken by us to the glory of

God." In Jesus' death and resurrection, the doors to paradise swing open once again. Death becomes a door. Amen and amen.

Titus wrote,

> For the grace of God has appeared that offers salvation to all people. It teaches us to say "No" to ungodliness and worldly passions, and to live self-controlled, upright and godly lives in this present age, while we wait for the blessed hope—the appearing of the glory of our great God and Savior, Jesus Christ, who gave himself for us to redeem us from all wickedness and to purify for himself a people that are his very own, eager to do what is good. (Tit 2:11-14)

Like Israel before us, we are waiting for something magnificent and wonderful that has never happened before. We are waiting for an event the church calls the second coming of Christ. And while we wait, we are given time to get ready—time to say no to ungodliness and yes to godliness. We are given time to be transformed. It may look like nothing much is happening: "Though outwardly we are wasting away, yet inwardly we are being renewed day by day" (2 Cor 4:16). Our waiting has a purpose. Every moment of every day is meant to lead us out of the darkness of self and into the light of love. Waiting makes us look like Jesus. It can produce purification, character and the listening wisdom that brings discernment.

At the end of each day, remember the things you have waited for throughout the day. What did you wait for patiently? Where did you lose patience? Listen to what God wants to say to you about your waiting.

So speak to your heart. Say as the psalmist did, "Rest in God alone, my soul! He is the source of my hope" (Ps 62:5 NJB). If you are waiting, it doesn't mean you are doing something wrong. It doesn't mean that God hasn't heard you. It's not a waste of time. God is at work making you into a person with the character and integrity that you need in order to participate in his dream for this world. You are in a moment in which you are developing a discerning, expectant heart. You are in a place where you can contemplate evidence of the unseen hand of God and grow in trust. Between desire and demand, the Holy Spirit gets at us and gives us grace— grace to wait and to see *when* God answers our prayers, not *if*. We have the courage to persevere and hope; the woman and her child have come.

9

Invitation to Pray

*Several times during the day, but especially in the morning
and evening, ask yourself for a moment if you have
your soul in your hands or if some passion or fit of anxiety
has robbed you of it. . . . If you have gone astray,
quietly bring your soul back to the presence of God,
subjecting all your affections and desires
to the obedience and direction of His Divine Will.*

ST. FRANCIS DE SALES

Prayer is the raising of the mind and the heart to God.

BALTIMORE CATECHISM

*If you are covering these chapters each week in a group discussion,
you might want to allow two weeks to cover the material here.*

When I was a child, cartoons were on TV only on Saturday
mornings. My brother and I would get up early and wait for broadcasting to begin. We would watch the TV "snow" until the United

FOLLOWING GOD'S INVITATION TO PRAY

INVITATION	To live entirely with and in God—relating to him at all times and in all things.
SCRIPTURE	"Pray continually" (1 Thess 5:17).
ROADBLOCKS	—Busyness and hurry —Tiredness and depletion —Escape behaviors —The belief that everything depends on me and that God can't be trusted to come through —Spiritual dryness —Anger with God
AWARENESS	—Notice how I spend my time and what I do with or without margins. —Notice where I need God's help, guidance and presence. —Notice when and where I am most centered and one with God. Go to that place regularly. —Notice how I greet the day and end the day. —Notice the conversations God seems to want to have with me.
PRACTICES	—There are many ways we can pray. Explore the many ways I can be with God: *centering prayer, breath prayer, praying Scripture, healing prayer* and *meditation*.

States flag appeared on the screen. Then a beautiful, deep bass voice sang a rendition of Albert Hay Malotte's arrangement of the Lord's Prayer. Cartoons followed!

Times have changed, but I am continually delighted by where the Lord's Prayer or the "Our Father" (Lk 11:2-4; Mt 6:9-13) turns up. During this past week, I have prayed the prayer Jesus invited his disciples to say alone, with others at a funeral, at a graveside and with hearty Bostonians who came in a blizzard.

I have also prayed this prayer in countries all over the world. It doesn't matter if I can't speak the language; when people begin to say the Lord's Prayer, the mutuality and interrelatedness of Jesus' body become palpable to me. I am not with strangers, unknown and alone. I am organically connected to others who gather up their lives and concerns in the prayer Jesus taught. In that moment, historical and geographical divisions are irrelevant; the world becomes flat. Walls exist on earth, but they do not reach up to heaven. Jesus' prayer offers connection, reconciliation and equal access in a world fractured by competition and strife. It levels the playing field and calls me into the concerns of God's own heart.

Jesus' disciples called him Rabbi, which means "teacher." Yet it is intriguing that only once in the Gospels do the disciples specifically ask Jesus to "teach" them something. The disciples could have asked Jesus for lessons in how to preach, or strategize or set goals or reach more people—and perhaps they did. But the one recorded lesson they request is, "Lord, teach us to pray, just as John taught his disciples" (Lk 11:1).

Why do you suppose the disciples asked Jesus to teach them to do something they already knew how to do? Good Jews already prayed prayers like the *Shema* (a prayer from Deuteronomy that begins "Hear, O Israel: The LORD our God, the LORD is one" [Deut 6:4]) at particular times throughout the day. They routinely went to the temple to pray using David's Psalter for prayers in worship. Some of the seriously religious fasted and prayed a day or more every week. Others memorized vast sections of the Torah, praying God's Word back to him. God's people had a long tradition of prayer:

- Hannah poured out her desire before God with tears.
- Jacob wrestled with God.
- Miriam prayed with song and dance.
- Elijah heard God whisper to him.
- Job prayed in sackcloth and ashes.
- Jonah argued with God.

- Everyone from prophet to priest to peasant to king presented sacrifices and prayed.

Jews had prayer practices galore. So what was it the disciples saw in Jesus' life that catalyzed their desire to learn something more about prayer? How long did it take for them to recognize that prayer was not a luxury reserved for times when life slowed down? When did they realize that prayer was not some ritual addendum to Jesus' strategies and plans but a word that described a relationship? I don't know the disciples' particular "aha!" moment. But at some point, they recognized that Jesus' life and agenda flowed from a practice of relatedness and interconnectedness with God. Prayer was his wellspring.

The disciples handed Jesus a teachable moment when they asked, "Lord, teach us to pray" (Lk 11:1). How would you answer? A seventy-year-old man once told me that he had never prayed and that he thought he was too old to learn how. But he wanted to listen to me pray. Another man, this one in his twenties, asked me, "Do you know how to pray? I have been looking for someone who could teach me to pray." Queries like this challenge my thoughts and prayers and probe the essential mystery of our faith: how do we know and relate to a God who is invisible?

So Jesus' response to his disciples' appeal intrigues me. Jesus didn't give some long explanation or seminar on prayer. There was no call to be dutiful. No secret method for getting results out of God. No mnemonics like ACTS: Adoration, Confession, Thanksgiving and Supplication (although that is a great way to pray). Jesus didn't say, "Just be spontaneous; tell God what's on your mind." Instead, Jesus' response was terse and minimalist, containing some seventy words. "When you pray, say . . ." (v. 2).

Jesus taught his followers by inviting them to say particular words. We may mindlessly rattle off the words and forget that these words have the power to read our hearts as well as to guide us into the heart of God. But if we authentically pray the Lord's Prayer, it pulls us out of heady words and wishful fantasies into the marrow of reality. Praying this prayer can unmask our illusions, crack us wide open to God and leave nothing in our lives untouched.

So while there are many ways to pray, I believe Jesus' invitation to pray this prayer begs our attention, creativity, strength and practice. If we will let the kingdom come and his will be done, praying this prayer will unmake and remake us over and over again.

OUR FATHER WHO ART IN HEAVEN

In Greek, the first word of the Lord's Prayer is "Father." The English translation begins with the word "Our." Either way, this prayer invites a seismic shift in orientation: that is, I am not a solo voice, and prayer is not just about me and mine. I belong to others in a subversive, revolutionary way. I do not pray alone or at the expense of others and their needs. I collaborate in prayer. In this family prayer, my life is connected, mingled, shared, broken, implicated and mended.

Who are your "ours"?

What does it mean to you to receive Jesus' invitation to be uniquely one in the midst of others?

How might praying in solidarity with Jesus and others affect your choices and plans?

The *our* in the Lord's Prayer is nothing less than an invitation to place others in the center of my concerns and prayers. I am awed at the implications this has. During the Nazi occupation of France, ordinary, unarmed citizens of the village of Le Chambon saved the lives of many Jews by hiding them from their enemies. Years later, when pressed to explain their actions and why they risked their lives to protect strangers, they were genuinely puzzled. They had only done what

needed doing. The people of Le Chambon understood the meaning of the
word *our*. They didn't believe they
could win while others around them
were losing. They didn't live for *my*
safety, home and family, but for *our*
safety, homes and families. They knew

What is it like to belong?
To be connected to
others in God?

themselves to be part of the *our* of God's family.

Take time to let the Holy Spirit speak to you about the word *our*.

OUR *FATHER* WHO ART IN *HEAVEN*

The word *father* can carry a lot of baggage, and we can project that
baggage onto God. But projecting an earthly father's failings onto
God obscures the God Jesus addressed. The God Jesus invited us
to pray to is not abusive. Nor is he an unapproachable authority,
an impersonal, disinterested energy or a punitive Santa Claus who
gives coal and switches to the naughty and toys to those who don't
pout or cry.

When Jesus said to pray "Our Father," he let us know that God,
by gracious decree, has chosen to be our *Abba,* a Hebrew word for
"Papa." This is God as Jesus invited us to know him. God's father-
hood gains us accessibility. We don't have to follow particular protocols, time schedules or conditions. *Father* is a word of nurture,
proximity and love. We can climb into the arms of Jesus' own Father and address not some resplendent force but someone with a
loving countenance who sings over us, delights in us and holds us
in his heart (Zeph 3:17). We are known, and our every potential,
every sorrow and every dream is understood.

When we turn our gaze toward our Father, we are present to
the One whose heart holds us and whose life courses through our
veins. Prayer is not some magic talisman or some wheedling whine
that squeezes results from an arbitrary deity. Prayer is being present to our Father. "Simply address yourself to Him who is in

How does "father baggage" cloud your experience of God?

What does Jesus want to tell you about his Father?

What is it like to have Jesus' own Father as yours as well?

With a child's simplicity, direct your inner gaze toward our Father in heaven. Hold the gaze for a few moments.

Heaven, and your prayer will reach Him," writes Romano Guardini. "No matter where you are, your words will reach Him. . . . Whatever you may experience, whatever may occupy you, your voice can rise and it will reach God." We have access to God, for he has chosen to be our Father. But Jesus also stressed that his Father is in heaven—that is, transcendent and of another reality.

A number of years ago, Boston rehabbed its planetarium, and when it was completed, huge billboards read, "Come see our planetarium, you infinitesimally small speck in the universe." That is one perspective. The Lord's Prayer brings another. Our divine Abba in "the heavens" is not remote and preoccupied, and I am not merely some mediocre, unimportant "speck in the universe" who is alone, unloved and unseen. God himself hears us cry, "Heaven, help us." And from the unseen world of his kingdom and rule, our transcendent Abba comes to us with help. "Our Father" pulls the reality of heaven down to our own address.

Take time to let the Holy Spirit teach you to pray, "Our Father who is in heaven."

HALLOWED BE YOUR NAME

The Lord's Prayer begins with the knowing and being known that emerges within the mutuality and accountability of loving relationships. From this foundation we address God as "Father" and pray, "Hallowed be your name." In our culture, making a name for oneself drives ambition and competition. Being known and recognized brings value, status and identity. Being unknown and name-less hurts. So to get the love or respect we want, we drop names of important people we know. Perhaps the reflected light of that name will bring some recognition of our worth to others. We hope that then others will "hallow" our names a bit more.

When my children were young, I enjoyed watching them hal-low their daddy's name. They would shamelessly say things like "My daddy is stronger than your daddy. My dad is the best cook in the whole world." (They never said this about me!) Defending daddy's honor, and celebrating his name, gave my children a sense of worth. They belonged to somebody who was Someone. Because that someone loved them, they felt valuable and their identity was secure.

Donald Miller suggests in *Searching for God Knows What* that we are all hard wired to have someone else tell us who we are. This explains why we try to look smart and do things to make others value us. It also explains why we hurt so bad when they don't. Miller writes, "It feels like there is a penalty for not being respected by other people, it feels like you are going to die unless you get some kind of respect and ap-preciation."

What does it look like for you to hallow God's name into the world?

How is your life shaped by God's attention to you? What do you want to say to God about this?

What names for God connect you to the loving gaze of your Creator?

We were meant to see our value through the adoring gaze of the Fa-ther, who mirrors back to us our worth. We don't need someone higher up the social food chain to like us and validate our existence. God has cre-ated, named and chosen us. We be-long to and are loved by the highest authority in heaven and earth. We are on a first-name basis with the Holy One, whom Scripture names in so many wonderful ways. Just as we protect one another's names, so too we should guard and protect the holy names of God, for they surround and protect us. As my children jumped to defend their father's character and goodness, so I hallow the name of my Father in heaven. I sometimes wonder what would have happened in Eden if Eve had told the serpent, "You can't talk about God like that. I know what this good Creator is like." What if she had hallowed God's name and given it protection in her life and words?

God has loosed his name in the world. Romano Guardini suggests that it drifts through common speech like a ghost or exile in a strange land. But when God's name is at home in us, we become an outpost in the world that protects, defends and hallows our Father's name.

Before moving into the "requests" section of the Lord's Prayer, consider what it means that God's name is on the loose among us.

YOUR KINGDOM COME, YOUR WILL BE DONE, ON EARTH AS IT IS IN HEAVEN

From the prayer of mutual belonging and being known, we move to a series of pleas that reflect God's dream for this world. Jesus said to pray, "Your kingdom come, your will be done, on earth as it is in heaven" (Mt 6:10). God's kingdom comes when inequalities, inequities, oppression and hypocrisy are righted. Where God's holiness and majesty reign, the substance of the kingdom becomes visible. So let's be clear: the prayer is for *God's* kingdom to come, not mine! It is for *his* will to be done on earth by me.

Of course, this is precisely where my struggle with prayer occurs. I have my own agenda and personal goals. And I like the idea that God is my accomplice in these enterprises: someone who brings me perks and absolute clarity about what to do next. But that notion is all wrong. God is not my accomplice, and absolute clarity about my future is not what's most important. "Your kingdom come" reminds me that I am an enlistee in God's purposes and will. Justice, mercy and the love of heaven are meant to come to earth through me. When they do, my actions have validity in eternity.

God's ways, however, are always in danger of being overruled by my will. Unlike the rest of creation, I am uneager to follow God's timing and cues. I am willful, anxious and notorious when it comes to doing my own thing. More than once my friend Lovelace Howard has asked me as I barge headlong into yet another thing: "Have you prayed the 'Nevertheless Prayer'?" She wants to know whether I am really praying, "Your will be done in my children, in my unemployment, in my marriage, in my singleness, with my boss, in my finances, in this setback, in this loss. Your will in my hectic, frantic, noisy life. Yes, I want this and this and that, and I don't want this and this and that. *Nevertheless* . . . I relinquish my will and choose yours. Your agenda. Your plan. In me on earth as is in heaven."

God's name, kingdom and will are all vulnerable to our choices. Jesus could have overruled God's will in Gethsemane. But instead, as the blood and sweat poured down his face, he prayed, "Nevertheless not My will, but Yours, be done" (Lk 22:42 NKJV). God is sovereign and works in all things—but he wants us for partners. It's just that his kingdom coming can feel a lot more like dying than holy elation. It asks me to make different choices about how I interpret success, failure and being in control. It asks me to place my control streak, woes, health issues and relational issues in the context of his will. It's not enough simply to be in

How are you bringing God's reign to your relationships and community?

How is God's kingdom shaping your choices and plans?

Where is God inviting your will to become more "willing"?

the world for God. We are to be *in* God for the world: living incarnations of his will and purpose on earth. And the Lord's Prayer invites me to consider, "Am I willing to receive what you give, release what you take and lack what you withhold? Am I willing to die a little death to my will so this fallen world will look more like heaven?"

The kingdom costs! It costs me. But "nevertheless" by "nevertheless," it quietly takes root—not just in the future but here and now. Every time the long arm of the Lord bends toward justice, the rewards of heaven come to earth. Every time the proud are overthrown, the humble raised up and the hungry fed, the kingdom of heaven breaks in. God's reign and holiness are near.

How does "your kingdom come, your will be done, on earth as it is in heaven" invite you to conversion?

GIVE US THIS DAY OUR DAILY BREAD

All we actually have is *now*. This moment is the only moment we can live. But the future stands in the wings, pressing for attention and whispering that we are vulnerable and at risk. So we set up nest eggs, long-term care insurance and retirement funds. We invest hours in long-term planning and future security, hoping that our foresight won't leave us destitute at the end. This is not necessarily a bad thing. But when the future distracts from living fully in the present with others, we have strayed from the moment and from God.

When I join Jesus in praying for daily bread, I am struck by three things. First, I am praying for daily needs, not future ones. Second, I am asking for my needs in the company of others and their needs. And third, I am remembering that Jesus is the true bread of life.

Jesus' future and security were so completely attached to God's will and kingdom coming right now through him that he wasn't anxious about what he didn't have for tomorrow. I am good at projecting worries, fantasies and "what ifs" onto tomorrow. But I can't seem to get the hang of projecting into the future the only sure thing about tomorrow: God's presence. Perhaps that is because the presence of God can only be experienced now, in the ebb and flow of daily needs.

How does the request for daily bread call for a conversion in your life?

The invitation to pray for our daily needs assures us that these requests are not selfish or shallow. But I am to remember that, as I pour my heart out to God, there are others. And for others to have their daily needs met today may mean becoming less attached to my needs tomorrow. The prayer "Give us this day our daily bread" becomes nothing short of an invitation to share our bread with others, while we trust that beyond daily bread stands the Bread-Giver and the Bread of Life. Daily bread is

What future anxieties are more real to you than God with you today?

Where do your prayers implicate you in others' daily needs?

What keeps you from being in the moment with God?

What needs or desires are present within you right now?

naturally and eternally connected to Jesus. The Lord's Prayer and the Eucharist both remind us that our sustenance and forgiveness are linked. We pray for bread: food for the body. Then we pray for forgiveness: healing for the soul. These things belong together. They remind us even millennia later that bread and forgiveness are forever the gifts of God to us.

FORGIVE US OUR DEBTS AS WE FORGIVE OUR DEBTORS

I have this idea that Jesus-followers should live in a state of harmony that the world doesn't experience. Yet Jesus taught his followers to pray "Forgive us our debts" because we need this prayer every bit as much as anyone else. Jesus' disciples weren't all that unselfish and community-oriented themselves. They arrogantly competed over who would be first in the kingdom, right up to the end. They ignored women, didn't care about hungry crowds and were willing to judge others with fire. Still, Jesus didn't turn them in for a better lot. He loved them to the end, forgiving again and again.

How does the prayer "Forgive us our debts as we forgive our debtors" invite conversion in your life?

What does it mean to offer Christ's forgiveness to another?

Spend some time telling Jesus the absolute truth about who you have become. Ask for his forgiveness.

What corners of your heart need to be scoured and freed by forgiving or being forgiven?

Forgiveness is God's remedy for broken relationships. It is how I scour out the meanness and rebellion in the corners of my soul. It is where I tell the absolute truth about who I've become. I am the kind of person who passes judgment, holds grudges, gossips and causes others pain and sorrow. I have no moral high ground. I am one of the beloved wrongdoers who need to be forgiven. Thank God he doesn't hold on to his hurt, wash his holy, immaculate hands of me and leave me to my own devices. He forgives and invites you and me to live into his "kingdom coming" by sharing his forgiveness with others. The prayer to be forgiven as we forgive has traction only when we remember how much we have been forgiven, and when we see that we want to be one with Jesus, whose love never fails.

LEAD US NOT INTO TEMPTATION

Since the world is filled with temptation, testing and trial, this phrase is best understood in the context of these realities. We are not given a reprieve on these things because we follow Jesus. Jesus himself had to face testing, temptation and trial. The presence of these things in life does not mean God is against me. They indicate that the kingdom of God can yet come in another place in my life. More trust can take root in my soul. "Lead us not into temptation and the time of testing and trial" is a request to not fall when the evil one attacks.

In matters of temptation, I am seldom ambushed. I walk into temptation on my own two feet. I stay up too late and then am impatient and irritable the next day. I feel misunderstood and turn a critical, cold shoulder. I am bored and go looking for something to eat.

The devil doesn't make me impatient, critical or gluttonous; I do! I settle into the well-worn ruts that temptation has carved in the landscape of my soul and take the path of least resistance. Oscar Wilde puts it neatly: "I can resist anything but temptation." So this prayer reminds me I have some things to unlearn.

Sometimes in matters of testing and trial, I am cold-cocked and taken by surprise. I didn't expect the accident, the argument, the slander, the meanness. I wasn't prepared for cancer, job loss, or the competition for ministry power and control. But it is these very places where obedience and trust become lived realities rather than theological constructs. These are the places where faith is born.

Trials and temptations can lead us into deeper places with

How does "Lead us not into temptation and the time of testing and trial" call you to conversion?

What are your habitual temptations? How could you seek grace and help in these areas?

Where has God shown up in your trials and hour of need? What do you want to say to him about this?

What deeper places might God be leading you to in areas of temptation and trial?

God—places we would not go on our own. A quotation from Léon Bloy says it well: "There are places in the heart that do not yet exist; suffering has to enter in for them to come to be."

BUT DELIVER US FROM EVIL

Jesus completed his prayer by offering up what is evil in the world to God. With these words we enter the fray of war, brutality, oppression and greed. The struggle between good and evil is certainly out there, but it is also in me. My human condition is a mirror of the battle between goodness and evil I see out there in the world. The battle is as close as the illusions that cloud my vision and the lies I believe. These illusions include: *I am better than they are. I don't need help. I have earned everything I ever got.* These lies include: *I am a failure. I am dirty. I am a mistake. God doesn't care. The one with the most toys wins. Bigger is better. I deserve it. They deserve it. We are the good guys.*

The evil one is a deceiver who distorts reality. If he can't tempt you to feel helpless, victimized, angry and afraid, he will tempt you to feel safe, self-satisfied and deserving. From these stances, hell is unleashed in our world. So we pray, "Deliver us from evil." Don't let evil leak out into this world through me.

I cannot say these words without remembering that Jesus was *not* delivered from evil. He went into the maw of sin and died. But in doing this, Jesus actually conquered evil and delivered us from the evil one. Jesus' victory gives us confidence to pray for a break in the chain reaction that arises from evil. And just as Jesus prayed for our deliverance from the lying destruction of the evil one, so we can pray for deliverance from the escalation of hatred, vengeance, negligence and selfishness among us. Truth and love undo the deceiver's lies in others and in us. And deliverance from evil includes working for God's kingdom of truth, justice and love. In the evil of this world, we pray that God's will will be done on earth as it is in heaven—in me and by me.

Stop and let the words "Deliver us from evil" work in your heart.

We end the Lord's Prayer with the doxology, "For yours is the kingdom, the power and the glory now and forever." These words are not found in Matthew or Luke. They come from the *Didache*, an ancient catechism from the early second century. This threefold blessing once again orients us to true reality. Who of us wants to live fruitless, useless, selfish lives reduced to our agenda and glory? God's glory and power have been loosed in this world. And we are enlistees, along with myriads of fellow pilgrims who want to see God's kingdom come as they make their way through God's power and live for his glory.

Where do you see evil at work in your life and community?

Begin to pray for deliverance. Ask God how you can participate in his kingdom coming.

Early believers prayed the "Our Father" three times a day, thus aligning their lives with God's will and kingdom. Are we prepared to let these familiar words shape our hearts into prayer and read our lives? Are we ready to know and love others as we are known and loved? My prayer is that God's will will be done in and through you! For that's how the kingdom in all its power and glory comes.

10

Invitation to Remember

One of the tragedies of our life is that we keep forgetting
who we are and waste a lot of time and energy
to prove what doesn't need to be proved.

HENRI NOUWEN

When we remember the past, it is not only the past;
it breaks into the present and gains a new lease on life.

MIROSLAV VOLF

HAVING MEMORIES IS A BIT like having bones. Bones determine the structure of our body; memories determine the structure of our souls. Over time, both bone and memories grow. Suffer trauma, and bones can break or memories can skew. The mending for either may mean a painful resetting. Yet who thinks much about bones or memories until they either hurt or you need them to get around?

This reality hit me when a friend told me about her daily visits to her husband, who had early-onset Alzheimer's disease. He had

FOLLOWING GOD'S INVITATION TO REMEMBER

INVITATION	To become aware of how my story fits into God's redemption story and how it is meant to set others free.
SCRIPTURE	"Remember that you were slaves in Egypt and the LORD your God redeemed you" (Deut 15:15). "On my bed I remember you; I think of you through the watches of the night" (Ps 63:6). "This is my body given for you; do this in remembrance of me" (Lk 22:19).
ROADBLOCKS	—Bitterness over past events —Inappropriate neglect of my past —Not doing the hard work that makes me an integrated person with a history that informs who I am but doesn't control who I become —Not looking for the presence or purposes of God in every event
AWARENESS	—Notice who you are when you visit your parents or siblings. What story are you telling yourself when you are at home? —When someone asks you to tell your story, notice what you tell and what you leave out. Talk to God about these things. —Notice how family history has shaped your story in good ways and deforming ways.
PRACTICES	—Practice *remembering* your life in decades. Who was God to you during that time? How did the events of that decade affect you and your choices? Where did you see God's hand at work?

forgotten their life together. He couldn't remember his daughters or their past. But day after day, my friend would go and visit, repeating the story of who she was and of their life together. One day as she looked up into her husband's eyes, she said, "You don't know who I am, do you?" He answered, "I don't know your name, but I know you belong to me." Somewhere deep down, a corporeal

How do you tend to remember events? How do you focus on the good things that have happened to you? How do you focus on the sad or bad things that have happened to you?

memory held. What a bittersweet reminder that "remembering when" is the bedrock of our connection to others.

"Remember when we got stuck in the blizzard?" "Remember when Dad couldn't find work for a year?" "Remember how the experience of the Great Depression turned a whole generation into savers?" How we remember is an absolutely critical part of our well-being. Memories shape who we trust and who we don't. Memories govern our choices, give us our bearings and form our futures. Without our memories, we forget who we are.

AN INVITATION FROM GOD

The word *remember* occurs nearly 450 times in the Old and New Testaments. The invitation to keep memory alive often comes straight from God.

- "Remember well what the LORD your God did to Pharaoh and to all Egypt" (Deut 7:18).

- "Remember how the LORD your God led you all the way in the wilderness these forty years" (Deut 8:2).

- "Remember that you were slaves in Egypt and the LORD your God redeemed you" (Deut 15:15).

- "Remember the days of old; consider the generations long past" (Deut 32:7).

- "I remember the days of long ago; I meditate on all your works and consider what your hands have done" (Ps 143:5).

- "This is my body given for you; do this in remembrance of me" (Lk 22:19).

I FORGET!

I suspect that God's invitation to remember is directly tied to how difficult it is to remember. Yes, we forget things, but we also have a hard time remembering things accurately. We can embellish sweet memories or worsen bad memories. We can remember in ways that make us look better than others. Sometimes trauma and emotionally vivid events shape our memories around lies: *You're stupid. No one will like you. You don't matter.* Dr. Louise Faber writes, "For many of us, our deepest memories are mental snapshots taken during times of high emotional impact or involvement." The more negative and aversive the "snapshots," the longer and more detailed (though not necessarily more accurate) the memories are. Memory is a powerful yet unreliable and ambiguous thing.

When God invites people to remember, he gives them ways of remembering that are true—ways that bring a future and a hope. God's ways of remembering include experiences of pain and hardship. But the remembering doesn't get stuck there, in the past, in bitterness or in the "good old days before everything went to pot." God's invitation to remember puts our individual stories into the context of a sacred narrative that "re-members" us in God's true history.

ENTERING THE SACRED STORY

Pope Benedict suggests that the Holy Spirit uses memory to make the sacred story alive to us. Remembering becomes a "pneumatic event": an act that enlivens our trust in God in the moment as well as healing passage into the future.

For generations, the Hebrew people have responded to God's invitation to remember by viewing their lives through the lens of the exodus story. Christians remember their lives through the events of Jesus' death and resurrection—the Passion story. Both sacred stories give people a way of placing their convoluted journeys in a larger context of meaning, direction and purpose. They rehearse what it looks like to trust God through thick and thin. These stories provide a rubric that can "re-member" experiences and offer new interpretations of memories to both Jewish and Christian communities. Sacred narratives are anchors in the storms of life. Whether you are a Jew reciting the *Shema Yisrael*, or a Christian repeating the Apostles' Creed, you are tethering yourself to the memory of who you really are. You aren't drifting alone in some vast, unknown sea. Your boat is sailing on the currents of God's sacred story.

Not long ago a friend described watching her granddaughter play with the Christmas crèche. Holding each figurine carefully, the little girl supplied the dialogue to her story: "Joseph, I am cold." "Mary, here is a blanket." "Keep baby Jesus warm." On and on it went. The two-thousand-year-old sacred story bent forward from its past and became this child's story. The story was not dogma. As the child remembered the story, it shaped her self-consciousness and self-awareness. The memory of the first Christmas bound her to others, to a heritage, to an identity and to the God of hope and glory.

When we forget our sacred story, amnesia about who God is sets in. God is no longer crazy about us. We are no longer the apple of his eye. The Holy One is not with us and in us to rescue, heal, restore and save. We are on our own. Amnesia about God and his story means that our identity and the meaning of our muddle of experiences sit squarely on us and our unreliable memories. This is a vulnerable and precarious place to be, because how we remember determines so much of who we are and who we become.

REMEMBERING WHAT REALLY HAPPENED

We all know that memory doesn't have to develop into love of God and love of neighbor. But it can. When my daughter, Annaliese, was eight years old, she went with us on a mission trip to the Dominican Republic. Every day she played with children who had no dolls, books, board games or shoes that fit. These children had none of the things she took for granted. Twenty minutes after we arrived home, Annaliese brought me her favorite pink backpack stuffed with her Cabbage Patch doll and a host of other toys. In her most authoritative voice, she said, "Please, send these to the children in the D.R.!" Memory had drawn Annaliese into God and his story.

After his people spent four hundred traumatic years in Egypt, God went to a great deal of trouble to remind them to remember the slavery, plagues, sacrificed lamb, harrowing nighttime escape and Pharaoh's chase to the Red Sea. How these events were remembered mattered. After all, memories can

- transmit pain and hatred from one generation to the next

- coalesce around an identity of slavery rather than freedom

- plant lies about who God is

So God invited Israel to annually remember in a way that didn't wound them again every time they recalled their past. The Holy One drew Israel into a whole series of festivals and feasts that recalled his presence with them (Deut 6:23). The celebrations reminded them of how their experiences could generate solidarity with their own servants (Deut 15:12-15). Rejoicing over their deliverance from slavery is motivation to care for the widows, orphans, strangers and the oppressed, as well as to show thanks to God (Deut 16:1-3, 12).

I love that one of the first things God had Moses and Miriam do when Israel's bitter past was over was to teach the people a song! When their enemies were shattered and washed away, they were given tunes to help them remember. I marvel at how memories associated with music have staying power. Whenever I hear "We Shall Overcome," I am back in the civil rights movement. When I hear "Where Have All the Flowers Gone?" I am back in the Vietnam War years.

Moses taught Israel to sing of how the angel of death passed right over them. He taught them melodies that reminded them that their fathers' God was no myth. God had come through and delivered them. He was not limited to the past, limited by the power of Egypt or even limited by their wavering belief. The Lord was their God. The song resounds with the personal pronouns: "I will sing to the LORD, for he is highly exalted. Both horse and driver he has hurled into the sea. The LORD is my strength and my defense; he has become my salvation. He is my God, and I will praise him, my father's God, and I will exalt him" (Ex 15:1-2).

The Exodus song reminds Israel of several things.

Its identity. Israel is loved by a God who doesn't forget his own. "For the LORD's portion is his people. . . . In a desert land he found him, in a barren and howling waste. He shielded him and cared for him; he guarded him as the apple of his eye, like an eagle that stirs up its nest and hovers over its young, that spreads its wings to catch them and carries them aloft" (Deut 32:9-11).

Why Israel is here. Israel's exodus story is meant to bless and serve others. "For the LORD your God is God of gods and Lord of lords, the great God, mighty and awesome, who shows no partiality and accepts no bribes. He defends the cause of the fatherless and the widow, and loves the foreigner residing among you, giving them food and clothing. And you are to love those who are foreigners, for you yourselves were foreigners in Egypt" (Deut 10:17-19).

Because Israel knows what it's like to be tortured, oppressed and set free by God, it is uniquely qualified to stand in solidarity with God and the oppressed: widows, aliens, orphans, victims, the impoverished and the enslaved. Israel's past teaches it how to bless others. "All peoples on earth will be blessed through you" (Gen 12:3).

Who God is. "The LORD himself goes before you and will be

with you; he will never leave you nor forsake you. Do not be afraid; do not be discouraged" (Deut 31:8). God is the God who not only goes into slavery with Israel; he is the God who sets Israel free.

God told the people of Israel to never forget their story: "When your children ask you, 'What does this ceremony mean to you?' then tell them . . ." (Ex 12:26-27). God warned them to "be careful that you do not forget the LORD, who brought you out of Egypt, out of the land of slavery" (Deut 6:12). And again: "Do what is right and good in the LORD's sight, so that it may go well with you" (Deut 6:18). Over the millennia, each Passover feast jogged Israel's memory so she would never forget her slavery. For God's miraculous vindication and rescue means nothing if Israel forgets her story. Sacred remembering is always about what we do with pain and hope. Richard Rohr puts it simply: "Pain that isn't transformed is transmitted." In one way or another, our futures all rest on the shoulders of how we remember our past.

Passover remembers how the Hebrew people's exodus story began in slavery and included the sacrificed lamb, the blood on the door lintels, a communion meal and rescue from the jaws of death. It remembers pain transformed. Centuries later, it is this very meal that Jesus made into a remembering about himself. "And [Jesus] took bread, gave thanks and broke it, and gave it to them, saying, 'This is my body given for you; do this in remembrance of me'" (Lk 22:19). When we hear these words, we remember our sacred story—it's the Passion story that gets rehearsed every time we receive the Eucharist or Holy Communion. This is the story that reminds us of how our pain, sin, suffering and death all get turned into joy, forgiveness and freedom through Jesus.

GETTING OUR STORY STRAIGHT

It took time for Jesus' disciples to figure out how the body and

blood of Jesus Christ were the linchpins of their story (Zech 9:9;
Jn 12:14-15). It took time because they wanted to be part of a story
in which the Messiah kicked his enemies' butts in the end—just
like at the Red Sea. They looked for a prophet like Moses to rescue
them (Acts 3:22). But Jesus ended up dead on a cross. No wonder
the disciples had to relearn their sacred story; their expectations
were blinding them to the real story.

But a thief hanging on a cross beside Jesus actually "got" the
story. Admitting the sorry mess of his own story, he said, "We are
punished justly, for we are getting what our deeds deserve. But
this man [Jesus] has done nothing wrong." Then he asked Jesus to
remember him and put him in his own sacred story: "Jesus, remember me when you come into your kingdom" (Lk 23:41-42).
Remember me. Give my story a different ending. And Jesus did
just that, saying, "Today you will be with me in paradise" (Lk
23:43).

Jesus' death on the cross opens up alternative interpretations of
the past as well as new possible futures. When Jesus reaches out
with love and forgiveness from the cross to embrace our pasts and
our futures, everything belongs. Everything finds its place in his
redemption story. Joys find their origin in God's goodness, and
wrongs receive judgment. Enemies are forgiven, and thieves find
their way to paradise. Jesus carries scars to prove it.

CARRYING SCARS

Jesus' scars are physical traces of memories—evidence of wrongs
done. But Jesus' scars aren't just the scars of a victim crucified by
the power of Rome. They are scars that reveal how divine love can
undo the powers of darkness, descend into hell, trump death and
set the world to rights. Jesus' scars are reminders that God has
entered hell and is prepared to be with us in our own private hells
of hurt—even as he draws us out of them toward healing and new
beginnings.

When someone hurts or snubs me, when they break my heart apart, it is so easy to remember what I don't like about them. I can carry the scar of my hurt around like a badge. But I can also remember that I once liked many of these people a lot. They had good qualities I admired and loved. But something went wrong. Often it went wrong inside me because I wasn't needed or valued in the way I wanted to be. Or perhaps we didn't see eye to eye on something.

So the question comes: how am I going to frame my story? Which memories will I choose to focus on? Will I let my pain "metastasize into the territory of the future" like a cancer, as Miroslav Volf so vividly describes? Will I recall the best or the worst about others? How will I fit my scars and love together?

How has the way you remembered something shifted over time and with grace?

The poet Edna St. Vincent Millay wrote about the choices we make to remember in "Souvenir." I quote the last two verses:

I remember three or four
Things you said in spite,
And an ugly coat you wore,
Plaided black and white.

Just a rainy day or two
And a bitter word.
Why do I remember you
As a singing bird?

The Passion story reminds me of how God remembers all of me—the good, the bad and the ugly. Yet God never wavers in his love. He remembers me as the apple of his eye, or perhaps like "a singing bird." The Bible tells me that Jesus' own love is alive inside me. His vision of others is available to me if only I will open my heart to the love revealed on the cross and allow it to shape my memories and my story.

YOUR EXODUS STORY

Has God ever showed up and helped you move from bondage to freedom, from pain to health, from sorrow to joy, from hatred to love? That's your exodus story. It is a story that remembers how, in small or large ways, you have been unjustly criticized, used and abused. It is a story filled with simple pleasures and adventures, as well as wounds and cries for God to vindicate. Your exodus story cost you scars, and it can cost to tell it.

Spend some time writing out your exodus story.

Where have you moved from bondage to freedom?

How have you moved from anger or fear or anxiety into trust and the fruit of the Spirit?

My own exodus story seems miniscule when played out on the backdrop of world atrocities. But I know for a fact that, as miniscule as my story is, there is enough there to turn my heart to stone and my life into a pit depending on how I remember. I do not resonate with the adages "Get over it" and "Let bygones be bygones." So sometimes I frame my losses through the poems and storylines of others that give voice to my experiences. Emily Dickinson is a favorite. And when I am sick of pat answers to life, I read her.

> They say that "Time assuages"—
> Time never did assuage—
> An actually suffering strengthens
> As Sinews do, with age—
>
> Time is a Test of Trouble—
> But not a Remedy—

If such it prove, it prove too
There was no Malady—

This poem provides solidarity in my trouble but no real hope of remedy. So I remember that, in order to frame and give meaning to my memories, I need more than commiseration or advice or willpower or even a new concept of God. I need a miracle like unto Israel's crossing of the Red Sea. I need a Savior who stands in solidarity with me and helps me remember that my story is also about healing, growth and freedom. My distorted memories are not the last word about me or reality.

I don't have to get stuck in my pain or hatred or sadness about the wrongs done to me. Memories twisted into self-defeating thoughts—*No one really loves me; every friend I have will abandon me*— don't have to be my future.

I can enter the Passion story and find that everything has been suffered, embraced, forgiven and set right in the presence and arms of Jesus. In his arms of love, I let the "re-membering" process begin. At various times in my life I have tried to recall all my joyful hours before God with gratitude. I have filled vases with beads, each bead representing one memory of God's goodness in my life. I have kept "Books of Remembrance," in which I record the consolations and joys that have come my way. At other times I have held sad memories before God and tried to listen to what he might want to say to me about them. Over and over again, light comes into my darkness, sometimes in a blinding flash and sometimes faintly and at the end of a tunnel.

Recently I decided to clear out a huge old trunk of letters and memorabilia from my past. All afternoon I sat on the floor, surrounded by memories of good times and bad times. I reread letters. I combed through small gifts. All the while, deep inside, I could feel something shifting. I tend to remember my life through the lens of what's missing. But when the tears came that afternoon, all I could say was, "Thank you, God. I have been loved so much. I have been loved so much. God, thank you." Nothing was missing from my life. Over and around it all was the love of God. That day a new chapter was added to my exodus story—a chapter about the girl who could remember her life with or without love.

An exodus story is always meant to set others free. How might your exodus story set someone else free? Ask God to help you discern who might benefit from your story.

When I feel so rotten that no good things have the upper hand, I remember the exodus story. Israel's story. Jesus' Passion story. My story. And countless other stories I have heard. Wounds don't have to go unhealed forever. Wrongs don't have to go on unrighted forever. And enemies can become reconciled in the arms of Christ. I remember my little life is a microcosm of a great and glorious story.

REMEMBERING WHO WE ARE

The Eucharist is Jesus' invitation to remember. I hold the communion bread and rehearse my exodus story. The hymn "Amazing Grace" puts it plainly: "I once was lost, but now am found; was blind, but now I see." Jesus Christ died so I could be free from slavery to memories that lead to death: *You don't matter. No one cares what you think. You will never have friends like other people.* Thank God. Jesus suffered to give me a new future and a constant hope. And if his death can be remembered as a door to life, then my life (and its little deaths) can be remembered that way too.

I want to join the throng of those who sing Moses' song—the song that remembers and anticipates the joyful consummation of God's story. I sing of reconciliation. I sing of justice. I sing of release from guilt and retribution. I sing the song of my true identity and yours as well. It is the music that harmonizes the pain and ecstasy of being alive.

In the beginning of the Bible, Moses helped the people of Israel remember the pain and joy of their lives in the exodus song. And in the end, when human history is wrapped up like a scroll and the new heaven and earth come down from God, we will still be singing the song of Moses. It is the song the faithful have always sung, the song that puts wrongs to right. It is the song that remembers God's victory over evil. It is the exodus song of the God who died to set us free.

Start keeping a "Book of Remembrances." List the places and ways you have experienced God's goodness in your life.

> I saw what looked like a sea of glass glowing with fire and, standing beside the sea, those who had been victorious over the beast. . . . They held harps given them by God and sang the song of God's servant Moses and of the Lamb: "Great and marvelous are your deeds, Lord God Almighty. Just and true are your ways, King of the nations. . . . For you alone are holy. All nations will come and worship before you, for your righteous acts have been revealed." (Rev 15:2-4)

Memories can be redeemed and offered up for the healing of the world. By the grace and goodness of God, may your scars and your exodus story prove it.

11

Invitation to the Most Excellent Way

*The invitation of love is not a proposal for
self-improvement or any other kind of achievement.
Love is beyond success and failure, doing well or
doing poorly. . . . Love is a gift.*

GERALD MAY

*We should always remember that love is the highest
gift of God. All of our revelations and gifts are little
things compared to love. . . . Settle in your heart that
from this moment on you will aim at nothing more
than that love described in 1 Corinthians 13.
You can go no higher than this.*

JOHN WESLEY

THESE DAYS, EXCELLENCE rules! People, as well as organizations, willingly fork it over for excellence. Bring on the excellent food, excellent decor, excellent cars, excellent vacations, excellent productivity, excellent people skills, excellent education and excel-

FOLLOWING GOD'S INVITATION TO THE MOST EXCELLENT WAY

INVITATION	To embrace the ego-sanding way of Jesus, who loves his neighbor as himself.
SCRIPTURE	"By this everyone will know that you are my disciples, if you love one another" (Jn 13:35). "And yet I will show you the most excellent way" (1 Cor 12:31).
ROADBLOCKS	—Placing my needs and wants first —The use of people to get what I want and need —Giving up on people who disappoint me or don't live up to my expectations —Confusing excellence with the most excellent way
AWARENESS	—Notice where I do things to get rather than give, and to be seen rather than serve. —Notice where excellence matters more to me than the most excellent way. —Notice who I have a hard time loving. What is in the way? What in me has to die to love as God does? —Consider asking your family, colleagues or friends, "What is your experience of interacting with me?" Or "How have I been loving or kind to you?" —Notice whom I neglect.
PRACTICES	—*Put others first,* which means all sorts of little deaths to self. —*Study how Jesus loved others.* Then go and do likewise.

lent profitability. And beware: average, ordinary, adequate and acceptable can leave you behind and make you expendable.

Excellence is a fine thing. It can even be a godlike thing. But if you have ever lived with or worked for someone whose only standard is excellence, you have encountered a merciless idol. Worship excellence, and she will have all of you, draining every single minute and breath you have. Forget being "good enough"; you have got to hit a home run every time. Yet if you are out of favor with the powerbrokers of excellence, even your home run may not matter.

It intrigues me that, in a culture obsessed with excellence, Christ-followers pay so little attention to Paul's assessment of the "most excellent way" in 1 Corinthians 13.

> And yet I will show you the most excellent way.
>
> If I speak in the tongues of men or of angels, but do not have love, I am only a resounding gong or a clanging cymbal. If I have the gift of prophecy and can fathom all mysteries and all knowledge, and if I have a faith that can move mountains, but do not have love, I am nothing. If I give all I possess to the poor and give over my body to hardship that I may boast, but do not have love, I gain nothing.
>
> Love is patient, love is kind. It does not envy, it does not boast, it is not proud. It does not dishonor others, it is not self-seeking, it is not easily angered, it keeps no record of wrongs. Love does not delight in evil but rejoices with the truth. It always protects, always trusts, always hopes, always perseveres.
>
> Love never fails. . . .
>
> And now these three remain: faith, hope and love. But the greatest of these is love. (1 Cor 12:31; 13:1-8, 13)

This chapter seems to get the most press at weddings. Yet I'm fairly sure Paul never intended his thoughts on the subject to simply be a nuptial poem. Paul, a.k.a. Saul of Tarsus, was no sentimentalist. He was a doer: fearless, ambitious and orthodox. He had a track record of getting things done legally, officially and expediently—even pogroms and persecutions. But when Saul met Jesus, his legal career, his single-minded vehemence, his family aspirations and his brilliance took a 180-degree turn. No longer the most excellent golden boy of the Jewish establishment, Paul got branded a heretic. Hardship, ostracism and heated religious debate ensued. Paul had to navigate planting churches and training leaders within the context of persecution and opposition. Within this context, Paul wrote about what is most excellent. And it isn't excellence that is most excellent! It is something far harder to come by. It is love.

Paul could have stuck with his career in Pharisaic law and become antiquity's most famous Hebrew scholar—possibly greater even than Gamaliel, whose writings one can still read. But Paul chose instead to give up an excellent legal career and enroll in the school of love.

Paul's short treatise on love is radical. Here is a heavyweight theologian, making a case for excellence not being limited to the gifted, talented, powerful or successful. It's not about the best of the best, or success or landing on top. It doesn't depend on strategy, vision, goals, ambition, budgets and bottom lines. The most excellent way is available to everyone; any Tom, Dick or Mary can take this road. What is most excellent can flower in children, in the illiterate, in the naive and in the average. Measurable success, productivity and accomplishments are not the most important things about us. What counts is letting the seed of God's own love grow in us. Paul is astringently clear: the most important and excellent things in the universe don't happen through sheer grit, ability or determination. They don't even happen through faith or hope. They happen through love: the path that never finds its end. God's most excellent way is a continuous, circular thread that runs throughout redemption history and that connects human souls with the heart of God and with each other for eternity. To express and receive this kind of love as perfectly as the God who defines it—well, that kind of love surpasses all else.

God's first concern is not a gold standard of excellent preaching, music, worship, facilities, hospitality, youth programs, giving, service or doctrinal purity. Don't get me wrong: these things matter. But excellence in these matters is far less important than doing these things with love. God is looking for people who are sincere lovers—people who can take the heat and love under pressure. These people are the real deal.

COUNTERFEITS OF LOVE

When I first bought pottery in Europe, I heard that if you turn the pottery over, you can sometimes find the word *sincere* on the back. It means that the pottery has no hidden flaws or cracks. It is not a counterfeit but the real thing. It is sincere. Love, like all genuine articles, has its counterfeits. And Paul begins with four ways we can fake love: through eloquence, knowledge, religion and giving.

Eloquence. "If I speak in the tongues of men or of angels, but do not have love, I am only a resounding gong or a clanging cymbal" (v. 1). I am not an excellent speaker, but I do know the shadow side of being a wordsmith. I can be more attached to words than to people. And the very words I use to inspire, woo, enlighten, direct and encourage can be all about me—every syllable of them. My ego, my turn of phrase, my impact. My sermons don't necessarily serve love or God either. They can prop up my false self and serve my ego. Eloquence that serves me is like static on a radio: it mars the message. It may sound great, but it's a counterfeit to love: all talk and no walk. I hope God is sticking his fingers in his ears.

You don't have to be a speaker to get obsessed with eloquence. You can get high on excellent preaching, scintillating lectures, articulate conversation or apt words. Critiquing people's facility with words can become a habit we can't curb. Directions, orations, political speeches, plain speech, garbled or untaught voices, crazy prophetic messages: everything gets sifted for its "eloquence quotient." When we have critical spirits like this, is it any wonder we seldom hear God speak to us? We are worshiping excellence and not the Creator, who gave us speech and ears to hear so we could know and follow the most excellent way.

Knowledge. "If I have the gift of prophecy and can fathom all mysteries and all knowledge . . . but do not have love, I am nothing" (v. 2). Knowing matters. What you believe and understand matters. But education, academics and understanding can all be self-protective counterfeits to the messy excellence of love. Remember Adam and Eve? They thought they were jettisoning their ignorance and powerlessness when they chose knowledge. But they were actually choosing information (and the power and control they hoped it would give them) over God. Their choice did give them knowledge—more knowledge than they knew how to handle, in fact. They learned how to hurt but not heal, how to hide and not reveal, how to rationalize rather than tell the truth, how to take life but not give it, how to know and not love.

When and how do you use "elaborate talk" as a substitute for doing the loving thing?

How does critiquing what others say keep you from hearing what they are saying?

Knowledge beguiles us. The more knowledge we have, the easier it is to think we know what is right and what others ought to do. When I first graduated from seminary, heresy bells were constantly going off in my head. I thought I knew what people had wrong, and I was equipped to set them straight. But this didn't mean I was any good at loving.

As I have hoofed along the most excellent way, I've found out how important it is to know what I *don't* know. After all, knowing God or anything else is not just a matter for the "little grey cells"; it is a matter for the heart. Knowledge alone will never give me God's eyesight or point of view. Knowledge alone can't give the benefit of the doubt or make a peace treaty. Seeing diamonds in the rough or refining gold out of base metals requires the supernatural alchemy of love. Without love in our hearts, we will have a hard time finding God or good intentions in human messiness.

Faith. "And if I have a faith that can move mountains, but do not have love, I am nothing" (v. 2). Miracle-working faith is im-

How do you let information and knowledge protect you from the messiness of love and relationship?

pressive. I'd love to have it, because it would certainly be preferable to my doubts. But Paul writes that even faith can be a counterfeit for love. It can be zeal and temerity and showmanship. That's why people become skeptical about road-show miracle workers. Much as I would like the gift of mountain-moving faith, I wonder if I'd be a safe place for that sort of gift to park. It might go to my head, and I might go on the road too. It could so easily become all about me.

Jesus' faith wasn't about him. It was about God. It was so much about God that when no miraculous eleventh-hour deliverance came in Gethsemane, Jesus still risked everything for love of God. Laying down your life, agenda and stuff is how you find out who you love and what you trust. This is what Paul advocates: "The only thing that counts is faith expressing itself through love" (Gal 5:6).

Altruism. "If I give all I possess to the poor and give over my body to hardship that I may boast, but do not have love, I gain

When has having the right notion of faith been easier than loving someone?

nothing" (v. 3). People give time and money to political, religious and personal causes all the time. They endow chairs in their names and give fundraising dinners for their favorite candidates, charities or missions. These are good things. But giving can also be a very ma-

nipulative business. You can give away everything you own, piece by piece, for selfish reasons: your legacy, your influence or the connections your contributions can buy.

I know this for a fact. A number of years ago, a friend of mine put her winter clothes in garbage bags and stored them in the garden shed. Her husband saw the bags and mistakenly threw them in the trash. When winter came, she was bereft. I had virtually no money at the time, but I gave to her what seemed to be then the "massive" amount of fifty dollars. Another friend came along and gave her four times as much as I had. And you know what? I felt bad that the larger giver got more credit and thanks than I did. So much for not having the gift be about me!

How has your giving been about you?

Each martyr, suicide bomber or Buddhist monk in flames has his or her own reasons for dying. These reasons don't have to include love; even spite will work. It's a sobering thing to realize you can do excellent things—such as sacrifice, serve and even die for others—and have it not count as love.

THE LITMUS TESTS OF LOVE

God doesn't fake love us. His love is real. Litmus tests that reveal and prove God's love for us are strewn through the pages of Scripture. The mixed bag of human freedom and the vagaries of history are riddled with God's love, which is not just talk or sentimentality. God is absolutely committed to our good and growth and his glory. God also knows that the good and beautiful life he has for us is found along the most excellent way of love. But the path of love can be shockingly difficult at times. It will test the sincerity of our following and the depths of our heart. The good news is that we have Jesus to guide us down this path. The very tests that proved his love can prove ours too. With Jesus' help, we can become the real deal. So let's look at Paul's open-book litmus tests for love.

Can you wait? "Love is patient" (v. 4). God knows how to sustain a deep, urgent desire for communion with rebellious human beings over a long period of time. God doesn't rush, hurry, push, demand, force or look at the clock. Immediate gratification and instant results aren't part of his love repertoire. We can be slow on the uptake. Still, Jesus doesn't hurry, push or control. He waited for his sometimes thick-headed disciples to understand. He trusted God's work within them when they all ran away. And he sustained his desire for friendship with them to the end. He went the distance on the most excellent way of love.

And we can too. When I was a self-centered high school student, my Sunday school teachers, Jack and Judy, took on the thankless task of loving me. They taught me skiing and sewing and took me camping. I rewarded them by soaking all the labels off their canned food and offering them WLTs (fried worm, lettuce and tomato sandwiches). But they didn't give up on me! They patiently continued to pour time, money and love into my pesky, needy heart. They trusted God in my life and gave me space and time to grow up from student into friend.

When are you kind? "Love is kind" (v. 4). I am in California as I write this, and my friend Lisha White just surprised me with a Vanilla Misto from Starbucks. She had four little people to get off to school this morning, but she still thought to stop and pick up a special coffee for me, her guest. Busy people can get going so fast that they have no time to see anything except what is on their own plate. Thank God he didn't content himself with his own plate of running the universe. He didn't limit himself to being civil and covering his bases. God went out of his way and in kindness saw me, an infinitesimal speck, as real and important.

The kindness of others has often been evidence to me that I matter to God. Somehow God opens someone's eyes to me. They notice I exist and pour some of God's loving kindness into my life. My first book was written primarily through the kindness of a friend who paid for my housekeeping. She had no idea that, for years, my excuse for not writing had been that I had to clean my house!

Kindness softens hard hearts, disarms the defended, mends the hurting, values the unnoticed, strengthens the weak and brings in God's kingdom. In a hard world, kindness shines with the face of God.

Are you fixating on what you don't have? "[Love] does not envy" (v. 4). Comparing what you have with what another person has focuses your attention on what's missing. Envy fixates on what it wants and doesn't have. Love rejoices in what another has and doesn't devolve into rivalry or discontent. Envy believes the better you have, the more you matter. Envy can't appreciate a house, a piece of beach or a success that it doesn't own. It can't read *Architectural Digest* without feeling deprived. It can't rejoice in another's wedding, another's promotion, another's baby or another's happiness if it happens to someone else. Envy isn't just about houses and cars and beauty, of course; you can be jealous of someone's wit, conversational skills or good fortune. You can mistakenly believe that, if it were all yours, the black hole of your heart would stop aching.

My inside understanding of the misery that envy bestows is considerable. And the only way I know to break its stranglehold is to practice gratitude—not just for what is mine, but for what is *yours*. God, thank you for Karen's generosity. Thank you for Lynda's hospitality. Thank you for Brad and Barbara's home. Thank you for Jack's curiosity and Mark's good heart. Thank you for Louise's compassion. Thank you for Amy's candor and Gayle's faithfulness. Thank you. Although these belong to others, my cup runs over.

Can you let your good deeds, accomplishments and achievements go unspoken? "[Love] does not boast, it is not proud" (v. 4). Résumés, awards, bonuses, exotic vacations, kids' athletic or academic successes: these are all conversational currency today. Of course, we are sophisticated in publicizing how capable, experienced, wonderful and giving we are. We don't want to look like we are social climbers with staggering insecurities. We don't want to seem proud. Truth is, love is a humble creature. When the omnipotent God came to earth, he came as a helpless baby and not with a string of bragging rights. Jesus wasn't out to impress but to love.

Recently I agreed to meet with a man seeking spiritual direction. As we began to talk, I realized that this man was a very big deal in the world of football. If I hadn't asked a certain question about his past, I would have remained oblivious to his fame. My guest didn't need to impress, because he had been impressed and shaped by God.

Do you run around doing and saying whatever pops into your head? "Love is not rude" (v. 5 NCV). Rudeness may mean no burping, farting or other excessively human behavior. But rudeness goes beyond physical inappropriateness to discourteous or cheap shots that disrespect people. Stinging comments, smart-aleck remarks, sarcastic and cynical jabs injure the goodness of a moment. The collateral damage of rudeness is huge. Rudeness is just a big, fat way of saying "I don't care about you." What have we come to when one child is excluded from an all-class party or a hostess is stood up at the eleventh hour because a better option turned up? Is this the "meaning" of America? It is mean to do only what feels good to you without regard for another's efforts and sensibilities. It is rude. And it is not the least bit like God.

God is courteous. He constantly says, "You first." Watch Jesus put others before himself. Watch as he undoes people's rudeness. When Bartimaeus is essentially told to shut up, Jesus says, "Call him." When children are belittled, Jesus blesses them. When a sinful woman gets shunned by Simon and his buddies, Jesus praises her for loving much. Jesus never belittles, patronizes or bullies. He comes to encourage, equip and nurture our lives. And by putting us first, he pours blessing on the heads of those who curse him.

Can you give someone else your accolades and limelight? "[Love] is not self-seeking" (v. 5). God is great, but he lets others shine. The Creator gives others significant spots in his redemption story. In fact, his story can turn on what they do and don't do. Sharing his glory is something God loves to do.

Several years ago, my good friend Mary Lederleitner was a doctoral candidate when she attended an academic conference in her field. She had the good fortune of speaking with the keynote speaker on several occasions. The speaker inquired about Mary's dissertation and was intrigued by her research. Over lunch one day, he asked if she would take his place as presenter on the following morning. Mary did not yet have any known credibility in her field, yet because he felt Mary had something important to say, this expert was willing to defer to her in a public forum where he had been paid to speak. This authority was secure enough to enable him to scrap his outline and handouts and spread the glory around. He didn't take advantage of her material and say, "Can I quote you?" He forgot himself and crossed over to Mary with goodness and generosity. Self-forgetfulness is the bliss of love's most excellent way.

Do you snap at others, yell at the kids, keep a record of slights or serve your red-hot anger up cold? "[Love] is not easily angered, it keeps no record of wrongs" (v. 5). Love can get angry, but it isn't a temperamental, hair-trigger habit. Love doesn't have tantrums and blow up like a two-year-old does. Personal grudges and lists of who is "naughty or nice" don't root in a loving heart. For love always reaches out to cover sin and restore relationship. This doesn't mean love ignores evil and never gets angry. After all, God himself takes a purposeful stance against evil—a stance that can be described as anger. But God's anger never poisons his desire to forgive, restore, love and redeem.

In my own experience, anger has often risen out of sadness or hurt that I must bring to God for mending. God tends the anger and pain within us so we can forgive and let go of the anger. God longs for my freedom. And letting go of anger is part of the excellent way to a free and loving heart.

Do you regularly rationalize, deny and blame others for your faults and the faults of this world? "Love does not delight in evil but rejoices with the truth" (v. 6). Delighting in evil sounds so twisted. But evil isn't just out there on the other side of the tracks or the other side of the ocean. Evil is inside us; it's as near as our need to look good rather than be good. Evil badmouths, discredits, abuses and demeans. Yet haven't we all experienced the diabolical bond that comes through shared criticism or loathing of another? Love doesn't delight in evil. It revels in the astringent nature of honesty and truth. Without truth, there is no repenting. Without love, there is no forgiving. The most excellent way of love delights in the truth, even when it puts us in an unfavorable light. For by that light we can begin repenting and forgiving. By that light we stay humble, dependent and aware that we need a Savior.

Which of the tests of love are most difficult for you?

Do you easily give up on people? "[Love] always protects, always trusts, always hopes, always perseveres. Love never fails" (vv. 7-8). God's love is so different from mine. God never gives up on me. God never loses sight of the true Adele he created me to be. Even when I turn on him and settle into my control-freak ways, God perseveres infinitely in loving and wooing me. God is willing to risk lack of significance, betrayal, rejection, exclusion, lies and death to love me to the end. This is not conceptual love. It is love in blood, sweat and tears. And it is the genuine article—not a counterfeit.

SAYING YES TO THE DIVINE INVITATIONS
The tests of love are ways we keep our feet traveling on the most excellent way. They are ways we knuckle down and grow into the

image of Jesus. Certainly we are better at many things than we are at loving. But we only get better at loving through practice. Life is our "open-book" test on love. Day in and day out as we plan, work, produce, commute and relate, we make life-altering choices to either love or neglect others. We can lay down our lives or make them all about us. We can wait or demand instant gratification. We can forgive or hold on to anger. True, we can never achieve perfect love. But failing at love is not the worst thing that can happen to us. Excluding difficult people so I can live as I want is far worse. Putting defenses around the heart so it won't be dashed to pieces is far worse. Not taking the most excellent way of love is worse.

C. S. Lewis wrote,

> If you want to make sure of keeping [your heart] intact, you must give your heart to no one, not even to an animal. Wrap it carefully round with hobbies and little luxuries; avoid all entanglements; lock it up safe in the casket or coffin of your selfishness. But in that casket—safe, dark, motionless, airless—it will change. It will not be broken; it will become unbreakable, impenetrable, irredeemable. . . . The only place outside Heaven where you can be perfectly safe from all the dangers and perturbations of love is hell. I believe that the most lawless and inordinate lovers are less contrary to God's will than a self-invited and self-protective lovelessness.

Love is the most excellent way because it serves more than excellence. Love serves and brings in God's peaceable kingdom. Love restores and heals the world. Love works. Love works on me. Love works on you.

A number of years ago, my husband and I were at a difficult place in our marriage. Nothing bad had happened between us, but I simply felt like my love had dried up and I couldn't take a deep breath any more. I knew I could make Doug happy; it was just that making him happy made me miserable. One day, on our way home from work, I had a small epiphany. It occurred to me that Doug might feel the same way I did. I asked him if he felt like making me happy made him miserable. "Yes," he admitted. I asked him what we should do. And he said, "Choose to love, of course."

We both chose love that day, and over the next months we each applied ourselves to the open-book test of love. It meant many little deaths to self. It meant letting go of my plans and agendas. But this walk down the most excellent way was graced by God. It shaped us both in love, and it healed our marriage over and over again.

Following Jesus leads us into the same tests of love he faced. Every day will bring choices to choose glory, fame, fortune and success—or love. Jesus chose the time-consuming, energy-guzzling, betrayal-strewn journey of love. He risked that things done for love are worth doing. And he chose your life over his.

One day, the most articulate faith will be fact. One day, the most glorious hope will be a present reality. Only the most excellent thing will remain: love. It is the one thing you can take with you from this life to the next. It is the lasting evidence that there is more to you than meets the eye—that there was and is and always will be the love of God.

Say yes to God's invitation to love. It will be the making of you and the blessing of this world. Let Paul's words roll over you again. And offer yourself up to God for the sake of his kingdom.

> Love never gives up. Love cares more for others than for self. Love doesn't want what it doesn't have. Love doesn't strut, Doesn't have a swelled head, Doesn't force itself on others, Isn't always "me first," Doesn't fly off the handle, Doesn't keep score of the sins of others, Doesn't revel when others grovel, Takes pleasure in the flowering of truth, Puts up with anything, Trusts God always, Always looks for the best, Never looks back, But keeps going to the end. Love never dies. . . . Trust steadily in God, hope unswervingly, love ex-

travagantly. And the best of the three is love. (1 Cor 13:3-8, 13 *The Message*)

Thank God that divine invitations never stop coming our way! But we will have to RSVP. We will need to trust that God's invitations matter more than anything else we can do and anywhere else we can go. The invitations can be hard ones, but the truth is that they invite you into freedom and your true self in Christ. My prayer is that you will say, "Yes, I can make it, God. You can count on me. I'll be there. I'll show up. Through your grace and the support of the body of Christ, I will lay down my addiction to lead and learn to follow. I will stop my constant doing and take a rest. I will begin fessing up when I'm wrong. I'll join my heart to yours and let you forgive through me. I am signing up for the most excellent way."

Prayerfully review the qualities of a loving person. Which qualities of love have shaped your life?

Where do you attempt to be really excellent? What would it look like to put this effort into loving?

Go with God.

Gratitudes

THIS BOOK WOULD NEVER have been written if my editor, Cindy Bunch, hadn't emailed me and asked, "Are you writing anything?" I emailed back, a little sheepishly, "Yes. Maybe." She wrote back, "Where are the attachments?" I replied, "I don't have a proposal." She whipped back: "Where are the attachments?" So it began. I didn't always feel like thanking Cindy for the hours in front of my computer, but now that I'm done, I say with all my heart, "Thank you, Cindy."

Four guardian angels have also prodded me along in my writing. Between them, they read all the chapters and provided wisdom, questions, clarity and much, much love. Emily Jones, Cindy Widmer, Shirley Morlock and Julie Baier: you have been selfless with your time and a gift throughout this project. Thank you.

My husband, Doug, has patiently borne my absences, my preoccupation with writing and my grumpiness about how badly it was going. He deserves stars in his crown. I intend to give him any crown I might ever get as well. My daughter, Annaliese, has spent numerous hours on the phone telling me, "Momsy, you can do this." Her attentiveness, even while her own plate was full of graduate studies, has comforted me greatly. She is an amazing treasure. Her brother, Nathaniel, and his fiancée, Elie, have cheered me on from Liberia. It is good to have such bracing support from across the sea. My mother and father, Phil and Coralee Ahlberg, would love to have the eyes to read this book. And although they can't, they both prayed for me to finish it. Thank you, dear hearts.

I am so grateful for the friends who daily prayed for me and offered understanding about my limits while I wrote. Lovelace Howard, Mickey Hargrave, Barbara Shingleton, Rama Ziengehals, Janet Anderson, Susan Skillen, and Andy and Rebecca Wasynczuck all pulled me away from my computer and kept me sane. My Chicago friends—Lynda and Mark Davies, Ruth and Jim Nyquist, Karen Bere, Dottie and Henry Bronson, Tracey Bianchi and the Sisson family—cheered me on. The Round Robin Sisters and Beth Domig help me make my way. Remembering you all is a great tonic and a healing part of my story.

Years ago Ruth Haley Barton invited me to be part of what would become the Transforming Center. This invitation, like so many others, continues to shape my journey. I am grateful for Ruth's presence in my life and for the invitations from God that the Transforming Center offers to others.

The flock at Redeemer Community Church has also given me time and encouragement to write, speak and use my gifts in the wider community. For this I am unspeakably grateful. For the women who walked and talked with me throughout the last year—you know who you are. Thank you. You have given me the gift of receiving me as I am. This book, in so many ways, belongs to you. Thank you.

Adele Calhoun
aaacalhoun@gmail.com

Notes

Introduction: The Invitation-Shaped Life

pages 14-15 "It's no secret that too many evangelical leaders": Editorial, "Mega-Mirror: Megachurches are not the answer or the problem," *Christianity Today*, August 6, 2009 <www.christianity today.com/ct/2009/august /24.20.html>.

Chapter 1: Invitation to Participate in Your Own Healing

page 34 John Ortberg likens transformation to sailing: John Ortberg, *The Life You've Always Wanted: Spiritual Disciplines for Ordinary People* (Grand Rapids: Zondervan, 2002), pp. 47-48.

Chapter 2: Invitation to Follow

page 44 "to the total dereliction": Henri Nouwen, *Jesus: A Gospel* (Maryknoll, N.Y.: Orbis Books, 2001), p. 7.

page 44 One of my memories: For more information about Katherine Genovese, see <http://en.wikipedia.org/wiki/Kitty_Genovese>. I remember hearing Tim Keller use this illustration in a sermon.

page 45 "It is true that he [Christ]": Jonathan Edwards, *Selected Writings of Jonathan Edwards*, ed. Harold P. Simsonson (New York: Frederick Ungar Publishing, 1970), p. 119.

Chapter 3: Invitation to Practice the Presence of People

page 55 "bidden or unbidden": Carl Jung is attributed with popularizing this statement.

page 60 Then I might stop and lime with them: Mike Mason's *Practicing the Presence of People: How We Learn to Love* (Colorado Springs: WaterBrook Press, 1999), and *The Mystery of Marriage* (Colorado Springs: Multnomah, 2005) have both played a significant part in my understanding of what it means to love others. In *The Mystery of Marriage*, Mason writes beautifully about what it means to grant another the same value and regard we hold for ourselves. See especially pp. 36-39 of *The Mystery of Marriage*.

page 61   "Every day I put love on the line": Eugene Peterson, *A Long Obedience in the Same Direction: Discipleship in an Instant Society* (Downers Grove, Ill.: InterVarsity Press, 2000), pp. 76-77.

page 62   Even when, in the words of C. S. Lewis: C. S. Lewis, *The Four Loves* (New York: Harcourt, Brace, Jovanovich, 1960), p. 169.

page 62   Frederick Buechner's lines from *Godric*: Frederick Buechner, *Godric* (San Francisco: Harper & Row, 1980), p. 7.

pages 62-63 Mike Mason recounts how his friend: Mason, *Practicing the Presence of People*, p. 238.

page 68   "If love were a sport": Ibid., p. 236.

Chapter 4: Invitation to Rest

page 71   The 1981 film *Chariots of Fire* is based on the true story: Tim Keller has used the movie *Chariots of Fire* to express the difference between God's self-giving work and our self-justifying work. See Timothy Keller, *Counterfeit Gods* (New York: Dutton, 2009), p. 73.

page 77   Not long ago I read that 91 percent: Julie Deardorff, "Soft Addictions," *The Chicago Tribune*, March 18, 2007 <http://articles.chicagotribune.com/2007-03-18/features/0703150210_1_overspending-issue-gadgets-and-sugar-soft-addictions>. This article includes a list of the top ten soft addictions. It highlights how treatment centers are opening up to treat such addicts. The Priory Clinic in London, for example, treats texting addicts.

Chapter 5: Invitation to Weep

page 88   Tears wash away the buildup of toxic chemicals: Jane Brody, "Personal Health," *New York Times*, February 22, 1984 <www.nytimes.com/1984/02/22/garden/personal-health-002144.html?pagewanted=all>.

page 88   "It is likely that crying survived": William Frey, *Crying: The Mystery of Tears* (Minneapolis: Winston Press, 1985).

page 89   "Rather than depleting the weeper": Kimberley Christine Patton, "'Howl, Weep and Moan, and Bring It Back to God': Holy Tears in Eastern Christianity," in *Holy Tears: Weeping in the Religious Imagination*, ed. Kimberley Christine Patton and John Stratton Hawley (Princeton, N.J.: Princeton University Press, 2005), p. 257.

page 89   Richard Foster writes that he was vouchsafed: Richard Foster, *Longing for God* (Downers Grove, Ill.: InterVarsity Press, 2009), p. 173.

page 89   *Young's Concordance* cites: *Young's Analytical Concordance to the Bible* (Grand Rapids: Eerdmans, 1979).

page 90   "Lament cuts through insincerity": Dan Allender, "The Hidden Hope of Lament," *Mars Hill Review* 1 (1994): 25-38.

page 91   Just six chapters into the Bible: It is intriguing that it seems to have taken humans longer to be moved to tears of grief than it took God. The Bible's first record of human tears is in Genesis 23:2, when Abraham wept for the death of Sarah. Yet once these human tears start, there seems to be no stopping them.

page 92   "My sense was that those whom he loved the dearest": Quoted in Patton and Hawley, "Introduction," *Holy Tears*, p. 21.

page 97   "Grant that we may know you": Carlo Maria Martina, *Perseverance in Trials: Reflections on Job* (Collegeville, Minn.: Liturgical Press, 2002), p. 52.

Chapter 6: Invitation to Admit I Might Be Wrong

page 103   According to Alix Spiegel: Alix Spiegel, "Americans Flunk Self-Assessment," *All Things Considered,* October 6, 2007 <www.npr.org/templates/story/story.php?storyId=15073430>.

page 103   "These allegations are false": A transcript of President Clinton's January 26, 1998, speech is available at <http://millercenter.org/scripps/archive/speeches/detail/3930>. On August 17, 1998, Clinton admitted before a grand jury that he had had an "improper physical relationship" with Lewinsky. That evening on national television, he admitted his relationship with Lewinsky was "not appropriate."

page 103   In 2008, a Rasmussen poll ranked Blagojevich: Alyssa Fetini, "Rod Blagojevich: Two-Minute Bio," *Time,* December 10, 2008 <www.time.com/time/nation/article/0,8599,1865474,00.html?iid=sphere-inline-sidebar#ixzz0nAESscEK>.

page 103   "I think I'm a great governor": Ibid.

page 104   Overconfident students complain about their grades: Research in education confirms that a student's assessment of their performance only moderately agrees with that of their teachers.

page 104   The Smithsonian contains a leather-bound book: See <http://en.wiki pedia.org/wiki/Jefferson_Bible>.

page 104   "The easy answer, of course": Lane Wallace, "All Evidence to the Contrary," *The Atlantic,* September 25, 2009.

page 106   As self-appointed "heresy police": See, for example, Mt 16:1;
19:3; 22:29-35; Lk 5:29-32; 6:2, 6-11; Mk 8.11; 10:2; 12:15; 14:60;
Jn 8:6.

page 109   Slowly Kowalski emerges: David Brooks, "Getting Obama
Right," *New York Times,* March 11, 2010 <www.nytimes.com
/2010/03/ 12/opinion/12brooks.html>.

page 112   Following Jesus is, in Henri Nouwen's words: Henri Nouwen,
The Only Necessary Thing: Living a Prayerful Life (New York:
Crossroad, 1999), p. 34.

page 115   "Sin is the starting point": Brennan Manning, *The Wisdom of
Tenderness: What Happens When God's Fierce Mercy Transforms
Our Lives* (New York: HarperOne, 2004), p. 118.

Chapter 7: Invitation to Forgive

page 121   The background was all black, and on it one word: In small print
on the billboard was a website address, www.Forgiveness
istheway.org. The site, begun by a woman whose young daughter
was paralyzed by a stray bullet in 2003, is maintained by a nonprofit educational services program devoted to reconciliation and
tells stories of people who have made the journey to forgiveness.

page 123   "Revenge doesn't say, 'An eye for an eye'": Miroslav Volf, *Free of
Charge: Giving and Forgiving in a Culture Stripped of Grace*
(Grand Rapids: Zondervan, 2005), p. 159.

page 123   This is God's heart for forgiveness: Other references to God's
forgiving character include Ephesians 4:32; Romans 12:19-20;
Matthew 5:44-45; Matthew 6:14-15; John 20:23.

page 124   Jesus' followers are to never stop forgiving: Furthermore, Jesus
makes it unmistakably clear: when grievances and hurts occur,
the first and second and third course of action is always to go
find the other person and work it out (Mt 18:15-17).

page 124   "As he got under way, one servant was brought before him": The
amount of the debt is a "hundred thousand dollars" in *The Message,* or "ten thousand talents" in other versions. One talent
was equivalent to fifteen years' wages for a laborer; ten thousand talents would be more money than the average man in
that era could earn in 150,000 years—about two or three billion dollars.

page 125 "Every crook will argue": W. H. Auden, "For the Time Being: A Christmas Oratorio," *W. H. Auden: Collected Poems*, ed. Edward Mendelson (New York: Modern Library, 2007), p. 394.

page 127 Miroslav Volf suggests that condemning the fault: Volf, *Free of Charge*, p. 141. Volf's *Free of Charge* is a compelling treatment of forgiveness. His steps of forgiveness have deeply affected my writing.

page 129 The cross is the place God judges sin: Jesus, the only innocent and perfect human being there ever was, identified so completely with us that on the cross he became sin (the antithesis of who he was). "God made [Jesus] who had no sin to be sin for us, so that in him we might become the righteousness of God" (2 Cor 5:21).

page 129 "Christ is not a third party": Volf, *Free of Charge*, p. 145.

page 131 "It's so crucial to see our forgiving": Ibid., p. 220.

pages 131-32 Marietta Jaeger-Lane is such a light: This story taken from *Not in Our Name: Murder Victims Families Speak Out Against the Death Penalty*, a publication of Murder Victims Families for Reconciliation; see <www.mvfr.org>. See also <www.journey ofhope.org/ pages/marietta_jaeger-lane.htm>.

page 132 "I'd reached a point where I really felt concern": Quoted in Karen Mains, *Comforting One Another* (Nashville: Thomas Nelson, 1997), p. 164.

page 133 "Forgive us our sins": Mt 6:12, English Language Liturgical Consultation, 1988.

page 133 separating the wrongdoer from their wrong actions: Miroslav Volf develops this step of forgiveness in a beautiful way in *Free of Charge*, pp. 129-41.

Chapter 8: Invitation to Wait

page 142 "what they are waiting for": Henri Nouwen, *Seeds of Hope*, ed. Robert Durback (New York: Bantam Books, 1989), p. 103.

page 143 Expectancy, Not Expectation: William P. Young provides a description of how expectancy and expectations are worked out in *The Shack* (Newbury Park, Calif.: Windblown Media, 2007), p. 206.

page 143 "Impatient people are always expecting the real thing": Nouwen, *Seeds of Hope*, p. 103.

Chapter 9: Invitation to Pray

page 155   No mnemonics like ACTS: The Bible as a whole lacks steps, charts, bullet points and comparative evaluations. Scripture is not a book of formulas and strategies for prayer or much of anything.

pages 157-58 "Simply address yourself to Him": Romano Guardini, *The Lord's Prayer* (Manchester, N.H.: Sophia Institute Press, 1958), p. 14.

page 159   "It feels like there is a penalty": Donald Miller, *Searching for God Knows What* (Nashville: Thomas Nelson, 2004), p. 107.

page 160   Romano Guardini suggests: Guardini, *The Lord's Prayer*, p. 34.

page 165   "I can resist anything but temptation": Oscar Wilde, *Lady Windermere's Fan* (1892), act 1.

page 167   They come from the *Didache*: Didache 8.1-3. The *Didache,* also called *The Teaching of the Twelve Apostles,* is perhaps the earliest known manual for Christian training apart from the New Testament. It instructs believers to pray the Lord's Prayer three times a day.

Chapter 10: Invitation to Remember

page 170   The invitation to keep memory alive: Other references to remembering "the God who brought you out of Egypt" include Ex 3:12; 6:7; 20:2; 29:46; 32:1; 32:4, 8, 11, 23; Lev 11:45; 19:36; 22:33; 25:38; 25:55; 26:13; 26:45; Num 15.41, Deut 5:6; 8:14; 13.5, 10; 20:1; Josh 24:17; Judg 2:12; 6:8; 1 Kings 9:9; 12:28, 2 Kings 17:7; 2 Chron 7:22; Neh 9:18; Ps 81:10; and Dan 9:15.

page 171   "For many of us, our deepest memories": Louise Faber, "New Understanding of How We Remember Traumatic Events," *Science Daily,* October 29, 2008 <www.sciencedaily.com/releases/2008/10/081028103111.htmiencedaily.com>.

page 171   The more negative and aversive the "snapshots": See "We Remember Bad Times Better Than Good," *Science Daily,* August 28, 2007 <www.sciencedaily.com/releases/2007/08/070828110711.htm>. This article summarizes a piece by Boston College psychologist Elizabeth Kensinger in *Directions in Psychological Science.*

page 171   Memory is a powerful yet unreliable and ambiguous thing: Miroslav Volf, *The End of Memory: Remembering Rightly in a Violent World* (Grand Rapids: Eerdmans, 2006), p. 39. His work is brilliant. I am in Volf's debt for many of the thoughts regarding this invitation.

page 171   Pope Benedict suggests that the Holy Spirit: Joseph Ratzinger, *Jesus of Nazareth* (San Francisco: Ignatius Press, 2008), p. 234.

page 173 So God invited Israel to annually remember: God jogs his people's memories through a liturgical calendar—a way of remembering God's involvement in their lives. Jesus observed this way of remembering as well; he celebrated Feast of the Jews (Jn 5:1), Passover (Jn 6:4), Feast of Tabernacles (Jn 7:38), Feast of Dedication (Jn 10:22) and Passover (Jn 12:1).

page 173 memories associated with music have staying power: See "Familiar Songs Act As Strong Memory Cues, K-State Researcher Finds," *Science Daily.* May 28, 2005 <www.sciencedaily.com/releases/2005/05/ 050528001217.htm>.

page 175 "Pain that isn't transformed is transmitted": Richard Rohr, *True Self, False Self,* read by Richard Rohr (Cincinnati, Ohio: St. Anthony Messenger Press, 2010). Audio book, 5 hrs.

page 176 They looked for a prophet like Moses: Jesus is the second Moses. "The LORD your God will raise up for you a prophet like me [Moses] from among you. You must listen to him" (Deut 18:15).

page 176 No wonder the disciples had to relearn: After Jesus' death, we see how it took time for the disciples to remember rightly. See John 2:17, 22 and 12:16 for example.

page 176 Joys find their origin in God's goodness: Miroslav Volf suggests that Jesus is not a "third party" that stands between us and God, receiving the wrath and judgment of God. Jesus' death is not God abusing the Son. Jesus is God himself satisfying both the law's demand and the victims' cry that wrongs be remembered and judged. See Volf, *The End of Memory,* p. 117.

page 177 "metastasize into the territory of the future": Ibid., p. 81. Volf suggests that remembering only what is bad about a person is "untruthful" remembering. It doesn't serve justice but "adds fuel to the fire" of misunderstanding. "To remember truthfully . . . is to render justice both to the victim and to the perpetrator and therefore to take a step toward reconciliation" (p. 56).

page 177 "I remember three or four": Edna St. Vincent Millay, "Souvenir," *Poems Selected for Young People by Edna St. Vincent Millay* (New York: Harper and Brothers, 1929), p. 52.

page 178 "They say that 'Time assuages'": Emily Dickinson, Number 283, *Final Harvest: Poems* (Boston: Little Brown, 1961), p. 174.

Chapter 11: Invitation to the Most Excellent Way
page 195 "If you want to make sure of keeping": C. S. Lewis, *The Four Loves* (New York: Harcourt, Brace, Jovanovich, 1960), p. 169.

TRANSF⟨⟩RMINGRESOURCES™
A Ministry of the Transforming Center®

Resources to Help You Experience Spiritual Transformation

Strengthening the Soul of Your Leadership
ISBN 978-0-8308-3513-3

Longing for More
ISBN 978-0-8308-3506-5

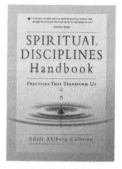

Spiritual Disciplines Handbook
ISBN 978-0-8308-3330-6

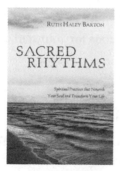

Sacred Rhythms
ISBN 978-0-8308-3333-7

Sacred Rhythms DVD
video download and participant's guide
available from www.Zondervan.com

Invitation to Solitude and Silence
ISBN 978-0-8308-3545-4

Invitation to Solitude and Silence Audio Book
available from www.oasisaudio.com

www.thetransformingcenter.org

TRANSF⬤RMING CENTER®
Strengthening the Soul of Your Leadership

The Transforming Center exists to strengthen the souls of pastors, Christian leaders, and the congregations and organizations they serve. Don't just learn about spiritual transformation—experience it in your own life!

Visit the Transforming Center online to learn more about:

- *Transforming Community*®, our two-year experience of spiritual formation for leaders. Certificate in Spiritual Transformation awarded upon completion.
- Regional and National Pastors' retreats
- Onsite teaching and spiritual guidance for your staff and elders
- Teaching and transformational experiences for your congregation
- Published resources—print and electronic

Join thousands of pastors and Christian leaders...
subscribe today to our free eReflections, spiritual guidance via email.

to subscribe, visit:
www.TheTransformingCenter.org
Transforming Center | 1600 Somerset Lane | Wheaton, IL 60189 | 630-588-8133